Lecture Notes in Computer Science   8748

Commenced Publication in 1973
Founding and Former Series Editors:
Gerhard Goos, Juris Hartmanis, and Jan van Leeuwen

Yamine Ait Ameur   Ladjel Bellatreche
George A. Papadopoulos (Eds.)

Model and Data Engineering

4th International Conference, MEDI 2014
Larnaca, Cyprus, September 24-26, 2014
Proceedings

 Springer

Volume Editors

Yamine Ait Ameur
IRIT-ENSEEIHT
2 rue Charles, Camichel, BP 7122
31071 Toulouse Cedex 7, France
E-mail: yamine@n7.fr

Ladjel Bellatreche
LIAS/ISAE-ENSMA
1 avenue Clément Ader, BP 40109
86961 Futuroscope Chasseneuil Cedex, France
E-mail: bellatreche@ensma.fr

George A. Papadopoulos
University of Cyprus
Department of Computer Science
1 University Avenue, Aglantzia, 2109 Nicosia, Cyprus
E-mail: george@cs.ucy.ac.cy

ISSN 0302-9743   e-ISSN 1611-3349
ISBN 978-3-319-11586-3   e-ISBN 978-3-319-11587-0
DOI 10.1007/978-3-319-11587-0
Springer Cham Heidelberg New York Dordrecht London

Library of Congress Control Number: 2014948575

LNCS Sublibrary: SL 2 – Programming and Software Engineering

© Springer International Publishing Switzerland 2014

Typesetting: Camera-ready by author, data conversion by Scientific Publishing Services, Chennai, India

Printed on acid-free paper

Springer is part of Springer Science+Business Media (www.springer.com)

Preface

In 2014, the 4th event of the international conference on Model Engineering and Data Engineering (MEDI 2014) took place in Larnaca, Cyprus during September 24th to September 26th. The main objective of the conference is to bridge the gap between model engineering and data engineering and allow researchers to discuss the recent trends in model and data engineering. It follows the success of the Obidos (Portugal, 2011), Poitiers (France, 2012) and Armantea (Italy, 2013) events.

For this event of MEDI 2014, two internationally recognized researchers were invited to give a talk. Dominique MERY from the University of Lorraine, France, gave a talk entitled "Playing with State-Based Models for Designing Better Algorithms" centered towards formal modeling and Mukesh Mohania from IBM research in Bengalore, India, with a talk entitled "Some Issues in Modeling User Behavior Data in Systems of Engagement" reporting the progress achieved within user data modeling. We would like to thank the two invited speakers for their contributions to the success of MEDI 2014. In addition to the two invited talks, Alfredo Cuzzocrea kindly accepted to animate a panel adressing big data mining and knowledge discovery.

MEDI 2014 received 64 submissions covering both model and data engineering activities. These papers range on a wide spectrum covering fundamental contributions, applications, and tool developments and improvements. Each paper was reviewed by at least three reviewers and the Programme Committee accepted 16 long papers and 12 short papers leading to an attractive scientific programme.

MEDI 2014 would not have succeeded without the deep investment and involvement of the Program Committee members and the external reviewers who contributed to review (more than 187 reviews) and select the best contributions. This event would not exist if authors and contributors did not submit their proposals. We address our thanks to every person, reviewer, author, Programme Committee members and Organization Committee members involved in the success of MEDI 2014.

The EasyChair system was set up for the management of MEDI 2014 supporting submission, review, and volume preparation processes. It proved to be a powerful framework.

Finally, MEDI 2014 received the support of several sponsors, among them CNRS, ENSEEIHT Toulouse, IRIT, INP Toulouse, ISAE-ENSMA, LIAS and University of Cyprus. Many thanks for their support.

September 2014   Yamine Ait Ameur
                                                      Ladjel Bellatreche
                                                  George A. Papadopoulos

Organization

Program Committee

El Hassan Abdelwahed	University Cadi Ayyad Marrakech, Morocco
Alberto Abello	Universitat Politècnica de Catalunya, Spain
Achilleas Achilleos	University of Cyprus, Cyprus
Yamine Ait Ameur	IRIT/INPT-ENSEEIHT, France
Otmane Ait Mohamed	Concordia University, Canada
Idir Ait Sadoune	E3S - SUPELEC, France
Abdelmalek Amine	GeCoDe Laboratory, Tahar Moulay University of Saida, Algeria
Franck Barbier	LIUPPA, France
Kamel Barkaoui	Cedric-Cnam, France
Ladjel Bellatreche	LIAS/ENSMA, France
Sadok Ben Yahia	Faculty of Sciences of Tunis, Tunisia
Djamal Benslimane	Lyon 1 University, France
Rafael Berlanga	Universitat Jaume I, Spain
Jorge Bernardino	ISEC - Polytechnic Institute of Coimbra, Portugal
Matthew Bolton	University of Illinois at Chicago, USA
Alexander Borusan	TU Berlin/Fraunhofer FOKUS, Germany
Thouraya Bouabana Tebibel	ESI, Algeria
Frédéric Boulanger	Supélec, France
Omar Boussaid	ERIC Laboratory, France
Stephane Bressan	National University of Singapore, Singapore
Francesco Buccafurri	DIIES - Università Mediterranea di Reggio Calabria, Italy
Damianos Chatziantoniou	Athens University of Economics and Business, Greece
Mandy Chessell	IBM, UK
Alain Crolotte	Teradata Corporation, USA
Xavier Crégut	IRIT/INPT, Université de Toulouse, France
Alfredo Cuzzocrea	ICAR-CNR and University of Calabria, Italy
Florian Daniel	University of Trento, Italy
Roberto De Virgilio	Università degli Studi Roma Tre, Italy
David Deharbe	Universidade Federal do Rio Grande do Norte - Departamento de Informatica e Matematica Aplicada, Brazil
Rémi Delmas	ONERA, France
Philippe Dhaussy	ENSTA-Bretagne, France
Khalil Drira	LAAS-CNRS, France

Mostafa Ezziyyani	University Abdelmalk Esaadi, UAE
Jamel Feki	Université de Sfax, Tunisia
Pedro Furtado	University Coimbra/CISUC, Portugal
Matteo Golfarelli	DISI - University of Bologna, Italy
Brahim Hamid	IRIT- University of Toulouse, France
Mike Hinchey	Lero-the Irish Software Engineering Research Centre, Ireland
Patrick Hung	University of Ontario Institute of Technology, Canada
Akram Idani	Laboratoire d'Informatique de Grenoble, France
Stephane Jean	LISI/ENSMA and University of Poitiers, France
Regine Laleau	Paris Est Creteil University, France
Nhan Le Thanh	University of Nice, France
Yves Ledru	Laboratoire d'Informatique de Grenoble - Université Joseph Fourier, France
Carson K. Leung	University of Manitoba, Canada
Zhiming Liu	Universiy of Birmingham, UK
Sofian Maabout	LaBRI. University of Bordeaux, France
Tiziana Margaria	University Potsdam, Germany
Aïcha Mokhtari	USTHB, Algeria
Kazumi Nakamatsu	University of Hyogo, Japan
Marc Pantel	IRIT/INPT, Université de Toulouse, France
George A. Papadopoulos	University of Cyprus, Cyprus
Oscar Pastor Lopez	Valencia, Spain
Elvinia Riccobene	DTI - University of Milan, Italy
Oscar Romero	Universitat Poltiècnica de Catalunya, BarcelonaTech, Spain
Dimitris Sacharidis	Institute for the Management of Information Systems - Athena R.C., Greece
Houari Sahraoui	DIRO, Université De Montréal, Canada
Patrizia Scandurra	DIIMM - University of Bergamo, Italy
Klaus-Dieter Schewe	Software Competence Center Hagenberg, Austria
Timos Sellis	Royal Melbourne Institute of Technology, Australia
Quan Z. Sheng	The University of Adelaide, Australia
Il-Yeol Song	Drexel University, USA
Zahir Tari	RMIT University, Australia
Manolis Terrovitis	Institute for the Management of Information Systems-RC Athena, Greece
A Min Tjoa	Institute of Software Technology and Interactive Systems, Vienna University of Technology, Austria

Panos Vassiliadis	University of Ioannina, Greece
Boris Vrdoljak	FER-University of Zagreb, Croatia
Edgar Weippl	Vienna University of Technology, Austria
Virginie Wiels	ONERA/DTIM, France
Guandong Xu	University of Technology Sydney, Australia
Bin Zhou	University of Maryland at Baltimore County, USA

Additional Reviewers

Abdennadher, Imen	Jiang, Fan
Alexandrov, Alexander	Kamoun, Akram
Anisetti, Marco	Kessentini, Wael
Baki, Islem	Khaghani Far, Iman
Ben Othmane, Amel	Khouri, Selma
Bennama, Miloud	Le Roux, Luka
Bikakis, Nikos	Li, Xin
Boden, Christoph	Manousis, Petros
Chardin, Brice	Ouhammou, Yassine
Crolotte, Alain	Percebois, Christian
Fu, Bin	Simos, Dimitris
Gassara, Amal	Tahamtan, Amirreza
Gkountouna, Olga	Teodorov, Ciprian
Haned, Faiza	Theocharidis, Konstantinos
Herrero, Víctor	Tranquillini, Stefano
Hobel, Heidi	Varga, Jovan
Hu, Liang	Yao, Lina
Huber, Markus	Zhang, Wei Emma
Ibrahim, Noha	Zhu, Yongjun

Table of Contents

Playing with State-Based Models
for Designing Better Algorithms

Dominique Méry

Université de Lorraine, LORIA, BP 239, 54506 Vandœuvre-lès-Nancy, France
Dominique.Mery@loria.fr

Abstract. Distributed algorithms are present in our daily life and we
depend on the correct functioning of complex distributed computing systems as, for instance, communication protocols for establishing sessions
between a smartphone and a bank account or synchronisation and management of shared resources among competing processes. Generally, the
design and the implementation of distributed algorithms are still error
prone and it is mainly due to the relationship between the theory of
distributed computing and practical techniques for designing and verifying the correctness of reliable distributed systems. Formal proofs of
distributed algorithms are long, hard and tedious and the gap between
the real algorithm and its formal proof is very important. In this talk, we
consider the *correct-by-construction* approach based on the refinement of
state-based models, which are progressively transformed, in order to obtain a state-based model that is translated into a distributed algorithm.

The stepwise development of algorithms has been first initiated in the
seminal works of Dijkstra [15], Back [7] or Morgan [23]. Next, UNITY [14]
has proposed a rich framework for designing distributed algorithms combining a simple temporal logic for expressing required properties and a
simple language for expressing actions modifying state variables under
fairness assumption. TLA/TLA$^+$ [18] proposes a general modelling language based on a temporal ogic of actions combined with a set-theoretical
modelling language for data and is extended by a specific algorithmic
language namely PlusCAL, which is translated into TLA$^+$ and which is
closer to the classical way to express a distributed algorithm. Finally,
Event-B [2,12] is a modelling language which can describe state-based
models and required safety properties. The main objective is to provide
a technique for incremental and proof-based development of reactive systems. It integrates set-theoretical notations and a first-order predicate
calculus, models called machines; it includes the concept of refinement
expressing the simulation of machine by another one. An Event-B machine models a reactive system i.e. a system driven by its environment
and reacting to its stimuli. An important property of these machines is
that its events preserve the invariant properties defining a set of reachable states. The Event-B method has been developed from the classical
B method [1] and it offers a general framework for developing the *correct-
by-construction* systems by using an incremental approach for designing
the models by refinement. Refinement [7,15] is a relationship relating
two models such that one model is refining or simulating the other one.
When an abstract model is refined by a concrete model, it means that

Y. Ait Ameur et al. (Eds.): MEDI 2014, LNCS 8748, pp. 1–3, 2014.

the concrete model simulates the abstract model and that any safety property of the abstract model is also a safety property of the concrete model. In particular, the concrete model preserves the invariant properties of the abstract model. Event-B aims to express models of systems characterized by its invariant and by a list of safety properties. However, we can consider liveness properties as in UNITY [14] or TLA$^+$ [18,17] but in a restricted way.

In our talk, we will summarize results related to proof-based patterns in Event-B (see for instance http://rimel.loria.fr) and ongoing works on translations of Event-B models into (distributed) algorithms. Proof-based patterns help for using refinement and for developing models from a very abstract one. The strategy for refining is a very crucial activity, when using Event-B, and the problem is to choose the abstract models that will be refined into *implementable* state-based models (see http://eb2all.loria.fr). We focus on the design of dustributed algorithms. For instance, the leader election protocol [3] is the kick-off case study which has led to questions on the use of Event-B for developing correct distributed algorithms: introduction of time constraints [13], probabilistic Event-B [16]. Moreover, the local computation model [25] (see http://visidia.labri.fr) has been integrated to the refinement-based approach. More recently, our joint work [21] leads to a general plugin for producing sequential algorithms from Event-B models and implement the call-as-event paradigm [19]. More recently, we extend the call-as-event paradigm by the service-as-event paradigm [22,6,4,5] and we take into account the design of distributed algorithms. Finally, we will compare the classical method [24] for verifying distributed programs and the refinement-based method that we have used in many case studies [11]. These results are used for lectures in school of cmputing engineering and master programmes and we will give some feedbacks from these experiences. Case studies [9,8,20] play a fundamental role for helping us to discover new strategies, namely proof-based patterns, for developing distributed algorithms.

References

1. Abrial, J.-R.: The B book - Assigning Programs to Meanings. Cambridge University Press (1996)
2. Abrial, J.-R.: Modeling in Event-B: System and Software Engineering. Cambridge University Press (2010)
3. Abrial, J.-R., Cansell, D., Méry, D.: A Mechanically Proved and Incremental Development of IEEE 1394 Tree Identify Protocol. Formal Aspects of Computing 14(3), 215–227 (2003), Article dans revue scientifique avec comité de lecture
4. Andriamiarina, M.B., Méry, D., Singh, N.K.: Integrating Proved State-Based Models for Constructing Correct Distributed Algorithms. In: Johnsen, E.B., Petre, L. (eds.) IFM 2013. LNCS, vol. 7940, pp. 268–284. Springer, Heidelberg (2013)
5. Andriamiarina, M.B., Méry, D., Singh, N.K.: Analysis of Self-⋆ and P2P Systems Using Refinement. In: Ait Ameur, Y., Schewe, K.-D. (eds.) ABZ 2014. LNCS, vol. 8477, pp. 117–123. Springer, Heidelberg (2014)

6. Andriamiarina, M.B., Méry, D., Singh, N.K.: Revisiting Snapshot Algorithms by Refinement-based Techniques (Extended Version). Computer Science and Information Systems (2014)
7. Back, R.: On correct refinement of programs. Journal of Computer and System Sciences 23(1), 49–68 (1979)
8. Benaïssa, N., Cansell, D., Méry, D.: Integration of security policy into system modeling. In: Julliand, J., Kouchnarenko, O. (eds.) B 2007. LNCS, vol. 4355, pp. 232–247. Springer, Heidelberg (2006)
9. Benaissa, N., Méry, D.: Cryptographic protocols analysis in Event-B. In: Pnueli, A., Virbitskaite, I., Voronkov, A. (eds.) PSI 2009. LNCS, vol. 5947, pp. 282–293. Springer, Heidelberg (2010)
10. Bjørner, D., Henson, M.C. (eds.): Logics of Specification Languages. EATCS Textbook in Computer Science. Springer (2007)
11. Cansell, D., Méry, D.: Formal and incremental construction of distributed algorithms: On the distributed reference counting algorithm. Theor. Comput. Sci. 364(3), 318–337 (2006)
12. Cansell, D., Méry, D.: The Event-B Modelling Method: Concepts and Case Studies, pp. 33–140. Springer (2007), See [10]
13. Cansell, D., Méry, D., Rehm, J.: Time Constraint Patterns for Event B Development. In: Julliand, J., Kouchnarenko, O. (eds.) B 2007. LNCS, vol. 4355, pp. 140–154. Springer, Heidelberg (2006)
14. Chandy, K.M., Misra, J.: Parallel Program Design A Foundation. Addison-Wesley Publishing Company (1988) ISBN 0-201-05866-9
15. Dijkstra, E.W.: A Discipline of Programming. Prentice-Hall (1976)
16. Hallerstede, S., Hoang, T.S.: Qualitative probabilistic modelling in event-b. In: Davies, J., Gibbons, J. (eds.) IFM 2007. LNCS, vol. 4591, pp. 293–312. Springer, Heidelberg (2007)
17. Lamport, L.: A temporal logic of actions. Transactions on Programming Languages and Systems 16(3), 872–923 (1994)
18. Lamport, L.: Specifying Systems: The TLA^{+}+ Language and Tools for Hardware and Software Engineers. Addison-Wesley (2002)
19. Méry, D.: Refinement-Based Guidelines for Algorithmic Systems. International Journal of Software and Informatics 3(2-3), 197–239 (2009)
20. Méry, D., Poppleton, M.: Formal Modelling and Verification of Population Protocols. In: Johnsen, E.B., Petre, L. (eds.) IFM 2013. LNCS, vol. 7940, pp. 208–222. Springer, Heidelberg (2013)
21. Méry, D., Rosemary, M.: Transforming EVENT B Models into Verified C# Implementations. In: Lisitsa, A., Nemytykh, A. (eds.) VPT 2013 - First International Workshop on Verification and Program Transformation, Saint Petersburg, Russie, Fédération De. EPIC, vol. 16, pp. 57–73 (2013)
22. Méry, D., Singh, N.K.: Analysis of DSR Protocol in Event-B. In: Défago, X., Petit, F., Villain, V. (eds.) SSS 2011. LNCS, vol. 6976, pp. 401–415. Springer, Heidelberg (2011)
23. Morgan, C.: Programming from Specifications. Prentice Hall International Series in Computer Science. Prentice Hall (1990)
24. Owicki, S., Gries, D.: An axiomatic proof technique for parallel programs i. Acta Informatica 6, 319–340 (1976)
25. Tounsi, M., Mosbah, M., Méry, D.: Proving Distributed Algorithms by Combining Refinement and Local Computations. Electronic Communications of the EASST 35 (November 2011) ISSN 1863–2122

Big Data Mining or Turning Data Mining into Predictive Analytics from Large-Scale 3Vs Data: The Future Challenge for Knowledge Discovery

Alfredo Cuzzocrea

ICAR-CNR and University of Calabria, I-87036 Cosenza, Italy
cuzzocrea@si.deis.unical.it

Abstract. *Mining Big Data* is among one of the most attracting research contexts of recent years. Essentially, mining Big Data puts emphasis on how classical *Data Mining algorithms* can be extended in order to deal with novel features of Big Data, such as *volume*, *variety* and *velocity*. This novel challenge opens the door to a widespread number of challenging research problems that will generate both academic and industrial spin-offs in future years. Following this main trend, in this paper we provide a brief discussion on most relevant open problems and future directions on the fundamental issue of mining Big Data.

1 Introduction

In recent years, the problem of *Mining Big Data* (e.g., [15,24]) is gaining momentum due to both a relevant push from the academic and industrial worlds. Indeed, mining Big Data is firstly relevant because there are a number of big companies, such as Facebook, Twitter and so forth, that produce massive, Big Data and hence need advanced Data Mining approaches for mining such data, as a first-class source of knowledge that can be further exploited within the same companies to improve their own business processes (e.g., [19]).

The first, critical result which inspired our research is recognizing that classical Data Mining algorithms are not suitable to cope with Big Data, due to both methodological and performance issues. As a consequence, there is an emerging need for devising innovative models, algorithms and techniques capable of mining Big Data while dealing with their inherent properties, such as *volume*, *variety* and *velocity* [23]. Inspired by these motivations, this paper provides a brief discussion on most relevant open problems and future directions on the fundamental issue of mining Big Data.

2 Open Problems

Currently, a wide family of open research problems in the are of Mining Big Data exists. These open problems are inspired by both methodological and practical issues, with particular regards to algorithm design and performance aspects. Here, we discuss some of them.

The first problem to be investigated in the Mining Big Data area is just represented by the issue of *understanding Big Data* (e.g., [29]), as an initial step of any arbitrary mining

Y. Ait Ameur et al. (Eds.): MEDI 2014, LNCS 8748, pp. 4–8, 2014.

technique over Big Data. Indeed, in real-life application scenarios, scientists and annalists first need to understand Big Data repertories, so that being capable of capturing and modeling their intrinsics features such as *heterogeneity* (e.g., [30]), *high-dimensionality* (e.g., [12]), *uncertainty* (e.g., [28]), *vagueness* (e.g., [9]) and so forth. This problem has been recently investigated, and several proposals appeared in literature.

Another relevant issue is represented by the problem of dealing with the *streaming nature* of Big Data. Indeed, a very high percentage of actual Big Data repositories are generated by streaming data sources. To give some examples, it suffices to think of Twitter data, or sensor network data, and so forth. In all these application scenarios, data are collected in a *streaming form*, hence it is natural to imagine novel methods for *effectively and efficiently acquiring Big Data streams* despite their well-known 3*V* nature. Here, algorithms and techniques need to deal with some well-understood properties of Big Data streams (e.g., [3]), such as *massive volumes, multi-rate arrivals, hybrid behaviors*, and so forth.

Big Graph Mining (e.g., [21]) is another critical research challenge in the Mining Big Data research area. This essentially because graph data arise in a number of real-life applications, ranging from *social networks* (e.g., [22]) to *biomedical systems* (e.g., [26]), and so forth. In this specialized research context, one of the most relevant issue to be faced-off is represented by *devising effective and efficient algorithms that scale well on large Big Graph instances* (e.g., [25]). Similarly to the previous research aspect, *mining Big Web Data* (e.g., [20]) is playing a leading role in the community, due to the fact that Big Web Data are very relevant in the actual Web and expose a very wide family of critical applications, such as *Web advertisement* and *Web recommendation*.

Privacy-Preserving Big Data Mining is another important problem that deserves significant attention. Basically, this problem refers to the issue of *mining Big Data while preserving the privacy of data sources that input the target (Big) Data Mining task*. This problem has attracted a great deal of attention from the research community, with a variegate class of proposals (e.g., [31]), and, in particular, it has been addressed via both *exact and probabilistic approaches*.

3   Future Research Directions

Mining Big Data is an emerging research area, hence a plethora of possible future research directions arise. Among these, we recognize some important ones, and we provide a brief description in the following.

Massive (Big) Data. Dealing with massive Big Data repositories, and hence achieving *scalable data processing solutions*, is very relevant for Big Data Mining algorithms. Indeed, this requires to investigate innovative indexing data structures as well as innovative data replication and summarization methods.

Heterogenous and Distributed (Big) Data. Big Data Mining algorithms are likely to execute over Big Data repositories that are *strongly heterogenous in nature, and even distributed*. This calls for innovative paradigms and solutions for adapting classical Data Mining algorithms to these novel requirements.

OLAP over Big Data. Due to the intrinsic nature of Big Data (e.g., [12,2,8,13]) and their typical application scenarios (e.g., [18,6]), it is natural to adopt *Data Warehousing and OLAP methodologies* [17] with the goal of collecting, extracting, transforming, loading, warehousing and OLAPing such kinds of data sets, by adding significant add-ons supporting analytics over Big Data (e.g., [1,12,18,10]), an emerging topic in Database and Data Warehousing research. Data Warehousing and OLAP are classical scientific fields which have been addressed since several decades by the Database and Data Warehousing research community. Symmetrically, the fundamental problem of computing OLAP data cubes has been contextualized in a wide family of data types. Unfortunately, despite the clear convergence, state-of-the-art solutions are not capable to deal with computing OLAP data cubes over Big Data, mainly due to two intrinsic factors of Big Data repositories: (*i*) *size*, which becomes really explosive in such data sets; (*ii*) *complexity* (of multidimensional data models), which can be very high in such data sets (e.g., cardinality mappings, irregular hierarchies, dimensional attributes etc.).

Analytics over Big Data. Big Data repositories are a surprising source of knowledge to be mined (e.g., [1,12,18,10]). Unfortunately, classical *algorithmic-oriented solutions* turn to be poorly effective to such goal, while, by the contrary, analytics over Big Data, which argue to support the knowledge discovery process over Big Data via *functional-oriented solutions* (still incorporating algorithmic-oriented ones as basic steps) seems to be the most promising road to be followed in this context.

Big Data Visualization and Understanding. Not only effectively and efficiently mining Big Data is a strong requirement for next-generation research in this area, but also *visualizing and understanding mining results* over Big Data repositories (e.g., [11]) will play a critical role for future efforts. Indeed, the special nature of Big Data makes classical data visualization and exploration tools unsuitable to cope with the characteristics of such data (e.g., multi-variate nature, (very) high dimensionality, incompleteness and uncertainty, and so forth).

Big Data Applications. We firmly believe that, in the particular context of mining Big Data, *applications over Big Data* will play a critical role for the success of Big Data research. This because they are likely to suggest several research innovations dictated by the same *usage* of mining Big Data in real-life scenarios, which will surely uncover challenging research aspects still unexplored. Examples of successful Big Data applications which make use of Data Mining techniques are: *biomedical tools over Big Data* (e.g., [5,27]), *e-science and e-life Big Data applications* (e.g., [4,14]), *intelligent tools for exploring Big Data repositories* (e.g., [7,16]).

4   Conclusions

Inspired by recent, emerging trends in Big Data research, in this paper we have provided a brief discussion on most relevant open problems and future directions in the Mining Big Data research area. Our work has puts emphasis on some important research aspects to be considered in current and future efforts in the area, while still opening the door to meaningful extensions of classical Data Mining approaches as to make them suitable to deal with the innovative characteristics of Big Data. Also, one non-secondary aspect to be considered is represented by developing novel Big Data Mining applications in different domains (e.g., Web advertisement, social networks, biomedical tools, and so forth), which surely will inspire novel and exciting research challenges.

References

1. Abouzeid, A., Bajda-Pawlikowski, K., Abadi, D.J., Rasin, A., Silberschatz, A.: Hadoopdb: An architectural hybrid of mapreduce and dbms technologies for analytical workloads. PVLDB 2(1), 922–933 (2009)
2. Agrawal, D., Das, S., El Abbadi, A.: Big data and cloud computing: current state and future opportunities. In: EDBT, pp. 530–533 (2011)
3. Amatriain, X.: Mining large streams of user data for personalized recommendations. SIGKDD Explorations 14(2), 37–48 (2012)
4. Cheah, Y.-W., Canon, S.R., Plale, B., Ramakrishnan, L.: Milieu: Lightweight and configurable big data provenance for science. In: BigData Congress, pp. 46–53 (2013)
5. Chen, X., Chen, H., Zhang, N., Chen, J., Wu, Z.: Owl reasoning over big biomedical data. In: BigData Conference, pp. 29–36 (2013)
6. Chen, Y., Alspaugh, S., Katz, R.H.: Interactive analytical processing in big data systems: A cross-industry study of mapreduce workloads. PVLDB 5(12), 1802–1813 (2012)
7. Cheng, D., Schretlen, P., Kronenfeld, N., Bozowsky, N., Wright, W.: Tile based visual analytics for twitter big data exploratory analysis. In: BigData Conference, pp. 2–4 (2013)
8. Cohen, J., Dolan, B., Dunlap, M., Hellerstein, J.M., Welton, C.: Mad skills: New analysis practices for big data. PVLDB 2(2), 1481–1492 (2009)
9. Cuzzocrea, A.: Retrieving accurate estimates to OLAP queries over uncertain and imprecise multidimensional data streams. In: Bayard Cushing, J., French, J., Bowers, S. (eds.) SSDBM 2011. LNCS, vol. 6809, pp. 575–576. Springer, Heidelberg (2011)
10. Cuzzocrea, A.: Analytics over big data: Exploring the convergence of datawarehousing, olap and data-intensive cloud infrastructures. In: COMPSAC, pp. 481–483 (2013)
11. Cuzzocrea, A., Saccá, D., Serafino, P.: A hierarchy-driven compression technique for advanced OLAP visualization of multidimensional data cubes. In: Tjoa, A.M., Trujillo, J. (eds.) DaWaK 2006. LNCS, vol. 4081, pp. 106–119. Springer, Heidelberg (2006)
12. Cuzzocrea, A., Song, I.-Y., Davis, K.C.: Analytics over large-scale multidimensional data: the big data revolution! In: DOLAP 2011, pp. 101–104 (2011)
13. Dean, J., Ghemawat, S.: Mapreduce: simplified data processing on large clusters. Commun. ACM 51(1), 107–113 (2008)
14. Erdman, A.G., Keefe, D.F., Schiestl, R.: Grand challenge: Applying regulatory science and big data to improve medical device innovation. IEEE Trans. Biomed. Engineering 60(3), 700–706 (2013)
15. Fan, W., Bifet, A.: Mining big data: current status, and forecast to the future. SIGKDD Explorations 14(2), 1–5 (2012)
16. Ferreira, N., Poco, J., Vo, H.T., Freire, J., Silva, C.T.: Visual exploration of big spatio-temporal urban data: A study of new york city taxi trips. IEEE Trans. Vis. Comput. Graph. 19(12), 2149–2158 (2013)
17. Gray, J., Chaudhuri, S., Bosworth, A., Layman, A., Reichart, D., Venkatrao, M., Pellow, F., Pirahesh, H.: Data cube: A relational aggregation operator generalizing group-by, cross-tab, and sub totals. Data Min. Knowl. Discov. 1(1), 29–53 (1997)
18. Herodotou, H., Lim, H., Luo, G., Borisov, N., Dong, L., Cetin, F.B., Babu, S.: Starfish: A self-tuning system for big data analytics. In: CIDR, pp. 261–272 (2011)
19. Kambatla, K., Kollias, G., Kumar, V., Grama, A.: Trends in big data analytics. J. Parallel Distrib. Comput. 74(7), 2561–2573 (2014)

20. Kang, U., Akoglu, L., Chau, D.H.: Big graph mining for the web and social media: algorithms, anomaly detection, and applications. In: WSDM, pp. 677–678 (2014)
21. Kang, U., Faloutsos, C.: Big graph mining: algorithms and discoveries. SIGKDD Explorations 14(2), 29–36 (2012)
22. Kum, H.-C., Krishnamurthy, A., Machanavajjhala, A., Ahalt, S.C.: Social genome: Putting big data to work for population informatics. IEEE Computer 47(1), 56–63 (2014)
23. Laney, D.: 3D data management: Controlling data volume, velocity, and variety. Technical report, META Group (February 2001)
24. Lin, J., Ryaboy, D.V.: Scaling big data mining infrastructure: the twitter experience. SIGKDD Explorations 14(2), 6–19 (2012)
25. Lin, Z., Chau, D.H.P., Kang, U.: Leveraging memory mapping for fast and scalable graph computation on a pc. In: BigData Conference, pp. 95–98 (2013)
26. O'Driscoll, A., Daugelaite, J., Sleator, R.D.: 'big data', hadoop and cloud computing in genomics. Journal of Biomedical Informatics 46(5), 774–781 (2013)
27. Paoletti, M., Camiciottoli, G., Meoni, E., Bigazzi, F., Cestelli, L., Pistolesi, M., Marchesi, C.: Explorative data analysis techniques and unsupervised clustering methods to support clinical assessment of chronic obstructive pulmonary disease (copd) phenotypes. Journal of Biomedical Informatics 42(6), 1013–1021 (2009)
28. Pei, J.: Some new progress in analyzing and mining uncertain and probabilistic data for big data analytics. In: Ciucci, D., Inuiguchi, M., Yao, Y., Ślęzak, D., Wang, G. (eds.) RSFDGrC 2013. LNCS, vol. 8170, pp. 38–45. Springer, Heidelberg (2013)
29. Power, D.J.: Using 'big data' for analytics and decision support. Journal of Decision Systems 23(2), 222–228 (2014)
30. Sun, Y., Han, J.: Mining heterogeneous information networks: a structural analysis approach. SIGKDD Explorations 14(2), 20–28 (2012)
31. Zhang, X., Liu, C., Nepal, S., Yang, C., Dou, W., Chen, J.: Sac-frapp: a scalable and cost-effective framework for privacy preservation over big data on cloud. Concurrency and Computation: Practice and Experience 25(18), 2561–2576 (2013)

Some Issues in Modeling User Behavior Data in Systems of Engagement

Prasenjit Dey[1], Mukesh Mohania[1], and Komminist Weldemariam[2]

[1] IBM Research, Bangalore/New Delhi, India
{prasenjit.dey,mkmukesh}@in.ibm.com
[2] IBM Research, Nairobi, Kenya
k.weldemariam@ke.ibm.com

Abstract. The proliferation of mobile devices has changed the way digital information is consumed and its efficacy measured. These personal mobile devices know a lot about the user behavior from the sensors and activities performed by the user. This data can be used to provide a lot of personalized information to the user, and a measure of effectiveness of the information to the information providers. However, there are lot of challenges in modeling and storing such data from these systems of engagement so that there is a right balance of the redundancy in the data stored, and the usefulness of the data for analysis. In this paper we present an architecture and issues of modeling such user behavior data from different activities a user does on the mobile device while consuming some information. The user behavior data is modeled as NOSQL JSON documents and sent to a cloud backend where some simple MapReduce analytics can be done to understand different aspects of user preferences and information effectiveness.

1 Introduction

Enterprises are fully realizing the value of data that they store it in Customer Relationship Management (CRM) systems, transactional systems, operational data store and data warehouse systems. Such systems are designed as 'System of Records' (SORs) and are used to derive the business insights by analyzing the data which is at rest in SORs. However, in last few years there is a paradigm shift in building the next generation enterprise management systems from the traditional "Systems of Records" to the "Systems of Engagement" (SOE) due to several factors, for example, new ways to interact with the systems through mobile devices, storing contextual information, disseminating data as a service on cloud [1]. Thus, the powerful combination of mobile or tablet devices as the frontend for sensing user behavior and cloud as backend for analysis across different application domains has led to the design of new architectures.

In this short paper, we firstly describe the characteristics of the end-user interaction and cognitive data and map them to Big Data characteristics [2]. We further outline how to model such data collected across different mobile applications and then how to analyze this vast data to derive various insights in context of system of engagement. We also outline some issues that are associated in building such systems that enable

Y. Ait Ameur et al. (Eds.): MEDI 2014, LNCS 8748, pp. 9–12, 2014.

collecting and modeling such fast moving data for efficient analysis. In our system, we store the user interaction data as JSON objects in IBM Cloudant and process it using MapReduce functions for data analysis [3].

2   High Level Architecture for User Behavior Data Collection

We now briefly describe below the system architecture (see Figure 1). We chose IBM Cloudant, as a NOSQL data store for storing user interaction and user behavior data (as JSON objects). Among other advantages, Cloudant also provides developers of large-scale and fast-growing web and mobile applications with a globally distributed database-as-a-service (DBaaS) for loading, storing, analyzing, and distributing operational application data [4, 5]. We process MapReduce functions to perform some analytics on the JSON objects. These functions can be exposed in Cloudant as RESTful service endpoints. Any application can call these endpoints and get a response which can be used, e.g., to create dashboards of these analytics in the application. One of the interesting research problems is -- What granularity of data can be collected and aggregated at mobile device level so that we can get useful insights as well as manage user privacy concerns?

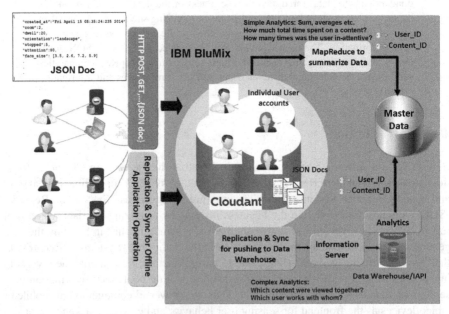

Fig. 1. System Architecture for User Behavior Data Collection

3   User Behavior Data Characteristics and Issues in Modeling Such Data

The user behavior data displays all the typical 4V characteristics of Big Data. We discuss below these 4Vs and outline various issues in modeling such data.

Volume: When users consume some information on a mobile device, the sensors on the mobile device collect a lot of data. The activity of the users on the application also presents a lot of data which may not be as high in volume as the sensor data but still quite high. The sampling rates for sensors such as accelerometer, camera, microphone, temperature etc. are very high and hence high volume of data is generated.

The key research question here is to understand what data to process at the client and what to send to the cloud? What level of detail of the data should we model? This will provide us with an understanding of what volume of data we need to store in the backend and what we can discard at the client. This falls in a new kinds of distributed storage and analysis mechanisms such as in Cloudant which is a distributed NOSQL JSON store. The large volume of the data requires MapReduce kind of distributed storage and analysis framework to get insights [5].

Velocity: All the activity events whether from sensors or the application in the mobile device have high velocity. This has impact on storing the data. Some crucial decisions need to be made such as what samples can be dropped without affecting the overall value of the data? How can the cloud storage backend handle such rapid spurts of data? We need to devise buffering mechanisms at the device to make sure the cloud backend is able to handle the flow of data. Moreover, when backend network connectivity is an issue for the mobile devices, the buffering mechanism should be robust enough to buffer this data and sync-up with the cloud when the network becomes available. Cloudant which is a distributed-data-base-as-a-service allows for such robust buffering and synchronization of this high velocity data.

Variety: The variety of data in user behavior is very high. This aspect of the behavior data is the key to our decision to go for a NOSQL data store. We model each session of interaction of a user as a JSON document. However, as new devices with new sensors emerge, and new applications are required, the events that are captured will keep on changing and evolving. The types of data vary a lot in their parameterization. For example, the camera data may contain bounding box coordinates, or microphone may have dB level number, or the Play/Pause event may have just Yes/No. A traditional relational data base schema would have been too constraining to model a-priori what could be the possible events. The flexibility of NOSQL document store allows for defining new events in future and still be able to analyze the new as well as the old data for various events. However, some interesting research questions are about how detailed the model should be for each event key and how to capture the temporal events? Another issue is how to model the unstructured data in relational world? Should the entities be extracted and store them in relational schemas or they should be stored in a native form? The key here is the flexibility of capturing and modeling the data and rapidly analyzing them to provide insights.

Veracity: The data from sensors are inherently unreliable. Sometime some of the sensors may not be of the same quality in all the devices or may not be present at all. Still more, the user who has control over what data is collected may not allow some data collection at all. The data model that we create should be able to handle such aspects. The NOSQL JSON document stores can create documents that have only those events in them and not the ones that are absent. This is a big advantage, since in relational database this would have resulted in sparsely populated columns whenever some sensor data is corrupt or not available. In this behavior-data world, complete quality of all the data cannot be ascertained but the efficient storing, analysis, and modeling of the majority of the data is of importance.

4   Conclusions

Enterprise management has been witnessing a paradigm shift from the traditional "Systems of Records" towards the "System of Engagement". A good example of such paradigm shift is that: the education industry is witnessing rapid adoption of digital learning content in personal devices such as tablets. This opens the door for anytime, anywhere learning by allowing (i) interactive learning and tutoring platforms that enable learners to take curriculum-centered content and assessments on their mobile/tablet devices; (ii) stimulate and personalize the learning, teaching and tutoring experience within (classroom) and outside (remote) modes. However, one of the key issues in building such system is how to collect and model the user behavior and interaction data (characterized as 'data in motion'). This paper has briefly discussed the architecture for collecting the user cognitive and behavior data and has mapped the characteristics of such data to 4Vs (Volume, Variety, Velocity, and Veracity) of Big Data. We have also outlined the several issues in modeling such data. In our system implementation, we have used Cloudant backend that allows for flexible modeling and analysis of data and highly scalable MapReduce functions that can be exposed as simple analytics services for other client applications can make such analysis re-usable and available for other users.

References

1. http://www.bersin.com/blog/post/Systems-of-Engagement-vs-Systems-of-Record—About-HR-software2c-design-and-Workday.aspx
2. http://inside-bigdata.com/2013/09/12/beyond-volume-variety-velocity-issue-big-data-veracity/
3. http://www.cloudant.com
4. http://support.mobileapptracking.com/entries/23675247-Android-SDK-v3-2-4-Quick-Start
5. https://developers.google.com/analytics/devguides/collection/android/v4/#tracking-methods

Automated Failure Analysis in Model Checking Based on Data Mining*

Ning Ge[1], Marc Pantel[2], and Xavier Crégut[2]

[1] LAAS-CNRS, France
Ning.Ge@laas.fr
[2] University of Toulouse, IRIT-INPT, France
{Marc.Pantel,Xavier.Cregut}@enseeiht.fr

Abstract. This paper presents an automated failure analysis approach based on data mining. It aims to ease and accelerate the debugging work in formal verification based on model checking if a safety property is not satisfied. Inspired by the `Kullback-Leibler Divergence` theory and the `TF-IDF` (Term Frequency - Inverse Document Frequency) measure, we propose a suspiciousness factor to rank potentially faulty transitions on the error traces in time Petri net models. This approach is illustrated using a best case execution time property case study, and then further assessed for its efficiency and effectiveness on an automated deadlock property test bed.

Keywords: Model checking, Failure analysis, Data mining, Time Petri net.

1   Introduction

Generating counterexamples in case a logic formula is violated is a key service provided by model checkers. Counterexamples are expected to display some unwanted but possible behaviors of the system and to help the user(s) in correcting the faulty design. Counterexamples often stand for error traces, which represent sequences of states and transitions and are therefore usually lengthy and difficult to understand. It is usually an exhausting work to understand the origin of failure and to extract useful debugging information using counterexamples. The origin of failure might be anywhere along these traces, thus requiring a lengthy analysis by designers. Based on the above understanding, we conclude that feeding back counterexamples in model checking provides limited help in understanding the origin of errors and in improving the model design. Our ultimate goal is to provide the designer with the suspicious ranked faulty elements by analyzing the error traces in the model checking results. The fact is, although model checking has been developed as a mature and heavily used formal verification technique, the automated failure analysis relying on model checking results is still mostly an open challenge.

---

* This work was funded by the French ministries of Industry and Research and the Midi-Pyrénées regional authorities through the FUI P and openETCS projects.

Y. Ait Ameur et al. (Eds.): MEDI 2014, LNCS 8748, pp. 13–28, 2014.
© Springer International Publishing Switzerland 2014

Failure analysis in model checking is difficult due to the use of abstractions. At the time of writing, the conflict between model precision and verification cost is a key issue in model checking. The abstraction is a must for model checking to reduce the size of state space. It eliminates property-irrelevant semantics and may also combine property-relevant semantics. But this semantics may help failure analysis.

According to the survey from [1], existing automated fault localization techniques in model checking usually produce a set of suspicious statements without any particular ranking. [2] proposed to analyze fault localization using one single counterexample that violated the expected properties in a particular case. Whenever a counterexample was found, the approach compared the error trace derived from the counterexample to all the correct traces that conformed to the requirement. On the observed error and correct traces, the transitions that led to the deviation from correct traces are marked as suspicious transitions. [3] proposed to rely on multiple counterexamples. It defined the concepts of positive trace and negative trace. The negative traces start from initial states and ended with error states. The transitions in positive traces are not prefix to any negative traces. It distinguished the transitions that existed in all positive traces; the transitions that appeared in all negative traces; the transitions that existed in one of positive traces but not in any negative traces; and the transitions that appeared in one of negative traces, but not in any positive traces. The algorithm then used the above marked transitions to identify the origin of failure. [4] proposed to define a distance between the error trace and the successful traces. The distance was then used to find the closest successful trace to the counterexample. The causes of error were then derived from the comparison results between the closest successful trace and the counterexample.

In this paper, we will improve the effectiveness of failure analysis in model checking by providing a suspiciousness factor, when a safety property is not satisfied. The safety property asserts that nothing bad happens [5]. Examples of safety properties include mutual exclusion, deadlock freedom, partial correctness, and first-come-first-serve [6]. They can be satisfied when no reachable error states (erroneous behavior) or deadlock states (no outgoing transitions) exist in the reachability graph. Otherwise, some unwanted states are detected, called violation states. Inspired by the Kullback-Leibler Divergence theory and the TF-IDF (Term Frequency - Inverse Document Frequency) measure in data mining, the suspiciousness factor is proposed to rank the suspicious faulty transitions. We construct error traces in the reachability graph using all the violation states. The suspiciousness factor is defined as the fault contribution of each transition on all the error traces. It is computed using the entropy and differential entropy of transition. We apply this approach to Time Petri net (TPN) model relying on observers to provide all the faulty execution traces and the violation states in the reachability graph preserving markings. This verification approach was studied in our previous work [7]. The proposed failure analysis method is illustrated using a TPN case study where the BCET (Best Case Execution Time) property is verified, and then further assessed for its efficiency and effectiveness on an automated test bed where the deadlock property is verified.

This paper is organized as follows: Section 2 gives some preliminaries; Section 3 introduces the core idea of the proposed approach; Section 4 details the proposed automated failure analysis approach using a BCET case study; Experimental results derived from a set of test cases are presented in Section 5 to assess the effectiveness and efficiency; Section 6 summarizes the contributions of this work.

2   Preliminaries

2.1   Time Petri Net

Time Petri nets [8] extend Petri nets with timing constraints on the firing of transitions. Time Petri nets are widely used to capture the temporal behavior of concurrent real-time system in a formal way. Our work relies on TINA (TIme petri Net Analyzer)[1] as the verification toolset.

Definition 1 (Time Petri Net). *A Time Petri Net (TPN) $\mathcal{T}$ is a tuple $\langle P, T, {}^{\bullet}(.), (.)^{\bullet}, M_0, (\alpha, \beta) \rangle$, where:*

- *$P = \{p_1, p_2, ..., p_m\}$ is a finite set of places;*
- *$T = \{t_1, t_2, ..., t_n\}$ is a finite set of transitions;*
- *${}^{\bullet}(.) \in (\mathbb{N}^P)^T$ is the backward incidence mapping;*
- *$(.)^{\bullet} \in (\mathbb{N}^P)^T$ is the forward incidence mapping;*
- *$M_0 \in \mathbb{N}^P$ is the initial marking;*
- *$\alpha \in (\mathbb{Q}_{\geq 0})^T$ and $\beta \in (\mathbb{Q}_{\geq 0} \cup \infty)^T$ are respectively the earliest and latest firing time constraints for transitions.*

Following the definition of enabledness in [9], a transition t_i is enabled in a marking M iff $M \geq {}^{\bullet}(t_i)$ and $\alpha(t_i) \leq v_i \leq \beta(t_i)$ (v_i is the elapsed time since t_i was last enabled). There exists a global synchronized clock in the whole TPN, and $\alpha(t_i)$ and $\beta(t_i)$ correspond to the local clock of t_i. The local clock of each transition is reset to zero once the transition becomes enabled. The predicate $\uparrow Enabled(t_k, M, t_i)$ is satisfied if t_k is enabled by the firing of transition t_i from marking M, and false otherwise.

$$\uparrow Enabled(t_k, M, t_i) = (M - {}^{\bullet}(t_i) + (t_i)^{\bullet} \geq {}^{\bullet}(t_k)) \wedge ((M - {}^{\bullet}(t_i) < {}^{\bullet}(t_k)) \vee (t_k = t_i)) \quad (1)$$

We use an example (see Ex. 1) to explain the syntax and semantics of time Petri nets.

Example 1 (TPN Example). The example in Fig. 1 models the concurrent execution of a process. The whole net shares a common synchronized clock. P_{init} is the place holding the initial token. When the *fork* transition is fired, concurrent $task_1$ and $task_2$ start at the same time within respective execution time [11,15]

---

[1] http://projects.laas.fr/tina/

and [19,27] associated to the transitions. Each transition uses a local clock which starts once the transition becomes enabled. When the control flow reaches the *join* place, the system will exit or restart the whole execution according to the running time.

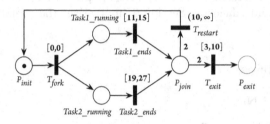

Fig. 1. Time Petri Net Example

2.2 Kullback-Leibler Divergence Applied to Textual Documents

The Kullback-Leibler Divergence (KL-Divergence) is also called information divergence, information gain, or relative entropy [10]. It is a fundamental equation of information theory that qualifies the proximity of two probability distributions. Many statistical procedures for inference use KL-Divergence information either directly or indirectly. It is also the theory basis of the TF-IDF measure.

Definition 2 (KL-Divergence). *The KL-Divergence is a measure in statistics that quantifies how close a probability distribution $P = \{p_i\}$ is to a model (or candidate) distribution $Q = \{q_i\}$. The KL-divergence of Q from P over a discrete random variable is defined as*

$$D_{KL}(P \parallel Q) = \sum_i P(i) \ln \frac{P(i)}{Q(i)} \tag{2}$$

Note: In the definition above, $0 \ln \frac{0}{0} = 0$, $0 \ln \frac{0}{q} = 0$, and $p \ln \frac{p}{0} = \infty$.

Many successful applications are based on Kullback-Leibler Divergence. We give an example about the text classification problem [11]. A textual document d is a discrete distribution of $|d|$ random variables, where $|d|$ is the number of terms in the document. Let d_1 and d_2 be two documents whose similarity we want to compute. This is done using $D_{KL}(d_1 \parallel d_2)$ and $D_{KL}(d_2 \parallel d_1)$.

2.3 Term Frequency – Inverse Document Frequency

Another major application of KL-Divergence is the TF-IDF (Term Frequency - Inverse Document Frequency) algorithm [12]. TF-IDF is a numerical statistic which reflects how important a term is for a given document in a corpus (collection) of documents. It is often used as a weighting factor in information retrieval and text data mining. Variations of the TF-IDF weighting scheme are often used by search engines as a central tool in scoring and ranking a document's relevance to a given user query. TF-IDF is the product of two statistics, TF and IDF. Suppose we have a collection of English textual documents and aim to determine which documents are most relevant to the query "the model checking". We might start by eliminating documents that do not contain the three words "the", "model", and "checking", but this still leaves many documents. To further distinguish them, we might count the number of times each term occurs in each document and sum them all together; the number of times a term occurs in a document is called TF. It stands for the frequency of a term in a document, and it reflects how important a term is in this document. However, because the term "the" is so common, this might incorrectly emphasize documents which happen to use the word "the" more frequently, without giving enough weight to the more meaningful terms "model" and "checking". The term "the" is not a good keyword to distinguish relevant and non-relevant documents and terms, unlike the less common words "model" and "checking". Hence IDF factor is incorporated which diminishes the weight of terms that occur very frequently in the document set and increases the weight of terms that occur rarely.

3   Core Idea

In the TF-IDF algorithm, each term in the documents will contribute to the keyword semantics. Some terms are considered as significant if they are more relevant to the keyword semantics. This is similar to the fault contribution caused by a given transition in an error trace in model checking. Fig. 2 compares the similarity between semantic contribution of terms in documents and fault contribution of transitions in error traces. Some terms in documents have closer semantic relation to the keywords, the occurrence of these terms provide more semantic contributions to the occurrence of keywords. Similarly, the fault propagation depends on the topology of error traces, the occurrence of some transitions will provide more fault contributions to the occurrence of violation states.

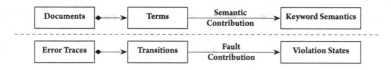

Fig. 2. Comparison to TF-IDF

The semantic contribution of a term in documents is measured by TF-IDF, where TF is the contribution of a term in single document, and IDF is the contribution of a term in a collection of documents. The fault contribution to the violation states caused by a transition on error traces can also be evaluated by a similar measure defined as Fault Contribution.

Definition 3 (Fault Contribution). *Fault Contribution (C_F) is a suspiciousness factor to evaluate a transition's suspicion level. It is used to rank the suspiciousness of transitions.*

4   Ranking Suspicious Faulty Transitions

Inspired by the TF-IDF algorithm, we propose a probabilistic failure analysis approach based on data mining. The relevance weight $C_F(t)$ is computed to assess the fault contribution of each transition t in error traces.

4.1   BCET Property Case Study

Before presenting the failure analysis algorithm, a BCET case study (see Ex. 2) is provided to help illustration.

Example 2 (Failure Analysis Example). Fig. 3 is a TPN model with 10 transitions $\{t_0, t_1, ..., t_9\}$. It has two main execution paths (respectively through t_1 and t_2), both have a loop with a bound of 2. The expected time property is: system's BCET is bounded within a given time T, i.e. BCET > T. We aim to automatically identify the potentially faulty transitions, and to rank them according to their fault contributions to the violation states. We first analyze the case when $T = 10$, then give the analysis results for $5 \leq T \leq 50$.

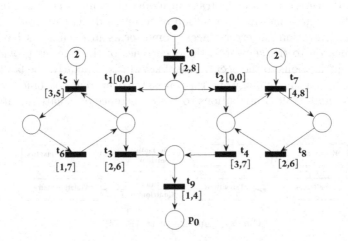

Fig. 3. Failure Analysis Case Study

4.2   Reachability Graph and Violation States

Reachability graphs are used to solve reachability problems in model checking. They contain all the states in the execution of a system and all the transitions between these states. In the TINA toolset, depending on the selected options, tina builds reachability graphs of different abstractions, expressed as Kripke transition systems (ktz). When a safety property is not satisfied, violation states can be found in the reachability graph.

According to the observer-based model checking approach for TPN presented in our work [7], we use the state class graph preserving markings as the reachability graph and turn the quantitative problem into a reachability problem. A TPN state can be seen as a pair (M, D), in which M is a marking, and D is a set of vectors called the firing domain. The reachability assertions are used to check the marking existence, such as $(M_P = 1)$ or $(M_P = 0)$, where M_P is the marking in the observation place P. Once the given reachability assertion is violated, the set of violation states in the reachability graph is built.

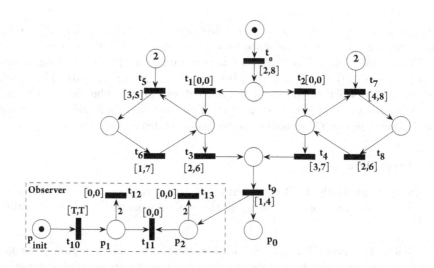

Fig. 4. Failure Analysis Case Study with BCET Observer

A BCET observer structure in Fig. 4 (in dotted line box) is thus associated with the end transition of the whole system t_9. The observer is linked from t_9. This connection ensures that the observer works in a read-only manner, thus cannot impact system's original behavior. We observe the tokens in places P_1 and P_2. The place P_{init} ensures that the observer structure starts at the same time with the observed system.

To explain how to check BCET property, we provide an erroneous scenario in Fig. 5. When the running time is less than T, t_{10} is not yet enabled, the place P_1

is empty. Meanwhile, if t_9 is already fired, P_2 has a token. In this scenario, the execution time of the system is less than T, then the BCET must be less than T. Therefore, the property BCET $> T$ is not satisfied. This property can be formally expressed by the formula $\neg(\neg p_1 \wedge p2)$. Then the assertion $N(\neg(\neg p_1 \wedge p2)) = N_A$ is used to check this property, where $N(\neg(\neg p_1 \wedge p2))$ is the number of states satisfying $\neg(\neg p_1 \wedge p2)$, N_A is the total number of states in system execution.

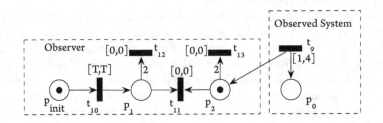

Fig. 5. Failure Scenario

When $T = 10$, we generate the reachability graph (Fig. 6) for TPN model with associated observer. The state number in this reachability graph (N_A) is 39. All the states are labeled with a number from 0 to 38. The checking result for $N(\neg(\neg p_1 \wedge p2)) = N_A$ is *False*, because $N(\neg(\neg p_1 \wedge p2))$ is 37. Therefore, there exist two violation states in the reachability graph. The violation states are those satisfying the formula $\neg p_1 \wedge p2$. They are directly found by the muse model checker in the TINA toolset, i.e. violation states are s_{11} and s_{23}.

4.3   Error Traces

We aim to compute the fault contribution of each transition in the error traces. The error traces are constructed using the violation states in the reachability graph.

Definition 4 (Error Trace). *For all the states $\{s_i\}$ on each path from the initial state s_0 to a violation state s_v in the reachability graph, all the outgoing transitions of s_i are gathered in a sequence called error trace π.*

We consider not only the transitions on the path that leads from s_0 to s_v but also the direct outgoing transitions of all the states in the execution traces that lead to correct states. Indeed, in TPN, the transitions outgoing from the same place can mutually influence each other. A correct transition can impact the firing of a faulty transition if they are both outgoings from the same place. The correct transition will diminish the C_F of the faulty transition.

Example 3 (Error Trace Example). In Fig. 7, s_0 is the initial state, and s_v is a violation state. In the execution trace from s_0 to s_v, there exist four states $\{s_0, s_1, s_2, s_3\}$ (apart from s_v). The states s_5, s_6, s_7, s_8, s_9 do not lead to the

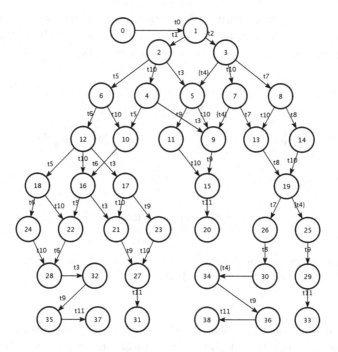

Fig. 6. Reachability Graph of Case Study (T=10)

violation state s_v. They are in the correct traces. When the system is in state s_2, it is possible to transit to s_7 or to s_3. If s_7 (t_4) is removed from the graph, s_3 (t_2) will have higher probability (fault contribution) for the occurrence of s_v. Therefore, transition t_4 should be included in the error trace, although it does not lead to s_v. Similarly, the transitions leading to other correct states should also be included in the error trace. The outgoing transitions of these four states are considered as error traces π, i.e., $\pi = \{t_0, t_1, t_2, t_1, t_5, t_4, t_2, t_3, t_4\}$.

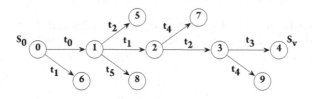

Fig. 7. Error Trace Example

The algorithm for enumerating all the error traces in the reachability graph is trivial, but the impact of state cycles in error traces needs to be discussed. The reachability graph in Fig. 8 contains a state cycle C_s ($s_1 \xrightarrow{t_1} s_3 \xrightarrow{t_4} s_4 \xrightarrow{t_3} s_1$).

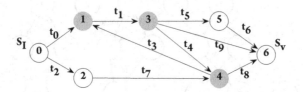

Fig. 8. Error Trace Example

The error traces passing through s_1 may loop in C_s. Take one error trace as an example, the trace passing through states s_0, s_1, s_3, s_4, s_6 is

$$s_0 \xrightarrow{t_0} \{s_1 \xrightarrow{t_1} s_3 \xrightarrow{t_4} s_4 \xrightarrow{t_3} s_1\}_n \xrightarrow{t_8} s_6$$

where n represents the times that the cycle repeats. The repetition of a cycle will not increase the fault contribution of the transitions in the cycle, because the system behavior is restricted to these states. Therefore, the cycle can be treated as a point with a chain of transitions (here $t1, t4, t3$). In other words, n is taken to be 1.

In the BCET case study, we construct error traces using the reachability graph in Fig. 6 and violation states s_{11} and s_{23}. The error traces are as follows:

$$\pi_1 : \{t_0, t_1, t_2, t_5, t_{10}, t_3, t_9, t_{10}\}$$
$$\pi_2 : \{t_0, t_1, t_2, t_4, t_{10}, t_7, t_9, t_{10}\}$$
$$\pi_3 : \{t_0, t_1, t_2, t_5, t_{10}, t_3, t_6, t_{10}, t_5, t_{10}, t_3, t_{10}, t_9\}$$

4.4   TC-ITC Algorithm

Fault contribution of the transition in error traces is measured by two factors, transition contribution and inverse trace contribution.

Definition 5 (Transition Contribution (TC)). *TC is a measure of the occurrence frequency of a transition t in an error trace π. It reflects a transition's contribution to violation state s_v in π. It is defined to be*

$$TC(t) = \frac{1}{M} \sum_{i=1}^{M} \frac{Q_i}{L_i} \tag{3}$$

where Q_i is number of occurrences of t in error trace π_i, L_i is the number of states from the initial state to the state before s_v, and M is the total number of error traces.

Definition 6 (Inverse Trace Contribution (ITC)). *ITC is a measure of whether a transition t is common or rare among all the error traces to all the violation states. It is defined to be*

$$ITC(t) = \log_2 \frac{M}{\sum_{i=1}^{M} X_i}, \tag{4}$$

where $X_i = \begin{cases} 1 & \text{if } t \text{ occurs at least one time in an error trace} \\ 0 & \text{otherwise} \end{cases}$ *and M is the total number of error traces.*

The weight `TC-ITC` is the product of the above two measures. In some cases, this product is 0, which does not mean it cannot be the fault source but only implies that the elements make the least contributions to the violation states and have the least probability comparing to the others. These elements usually should be checked at last.

It is expected that the ranking of fault contributions computed by the algorithm corresponds to manual analysis and human intuition. We use the `BCET` case study to illustrate how they are matched. The analysis results are provided in Fig. 9. The results show the fault contributions (normalized for comparing the trend) of each transition when T varies from 5 to 50. The explanation is provided as follows:

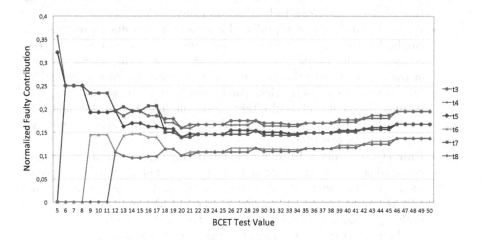

Fig. 9. Feedback of Fault Localization Example

- $1 \leq T < 5$: since the BCET of the system is 5, there will not be any violated state and accordingly no failure analysis will be launched.
- $T \geq 47$: since the WCET (Worst Case Execution Time) of the system is 47, the reachability graph will not have any change after this threshold, therefore the fault contribution of each transition will preserve the same value as $T = 47$.
- $5 \leq T < 47$: since T represents the expected BCET of the system, all execution with time inferior to T will be considered as violation. Without any other information, a reasonable heuristics can then be derived from this assertion: for BCET property, the less execution time a transition can contribute/has contributed to the violation of BCET, the higher risk it will be the failure cause. Another intuition-valid rule is: when an element holds a more complex function, it has a higher risk to cause design errors. To heuristically quantify the coefficient of these two different types of fault contribution is a subjective measure often context-dependent. In order to avoid this indecisive discussion, each time we encounter this situation in the case study, we will just explain the two aspects without trying to combine them into one score for matching the ranking. The statistical trends are then explained as follows:

  - **Topologically symmetric pair (t_3, t_4) has a higher risk to be the failure cause than (t_5, t_7) and (t_6, t_8).** This matches the heuristic rule because in whichever execution, t_3 and t_4 will only contribute once to the global execution time (i.e. [2,6] and [3,7] respectively), while t_5, t_6, t_7 and t_8 can at most execute twice and will contribute more (i.e [6,10], [2, 14], [8, 16] and [4, 12] respectively).
  - **In each symmetric pair of above, $t_3 \geq t_4$, $t_5 \geq t_7$ and $t_6 \geq t_8$.** This demonstrates that it is always the one with the smallest execution time that get more risk to be the faulty one.
  - **t_0, t_1, t_2 and t_9 are equally the least suspicious elements.** (To emphasize the other transitions, they are not shown in Fig. 9.) This conforms to the intuition because in all execution paths, whether is good or bad, t_0 and t_9 will always be executed therefore no information added for assessing their faulty risk. For t_1 and t_2 it is the similar situation, because a design fault will either be on the left side or the right side, and in all execution paths of the left (resp. the right) side, t_1 (resp. t_2) will always be executed.
  - **Pair (t_5, t_7) has a higher risk than (t_6, t_8).** Generally since t_6/t_8 has smaller execution time than t_5/t_7, it shall be more possible according to the first heuristic rule. However, since t_5 and t_7 play a role that not only postpone the execution (like t_6/t_8), but also branch the execution path (t_6/t_8 do not have this function), their risk to be the failure cause will be re-distributed and raised as the second rule is engaged.

5   Experiments

To assess the success of a fault localization algorithm, many important criteria should be measured, such as effectiveness, precision, informativeness, efficiency, performance, scalability and information usefulness. In our work, we assess our approach by using two significant criteria: effectiveness and efficiency.

Efficiency. The fault localization techniques in model checking, like other techniques, should terminate in a timely manner, limited by some resource constraints. The efficiency can be assessed by the scalability and the performance.

Effectiveness. An effective fault localization method should point out the origin of failure. The effectiveness can be evaluated by the precision. According to the survey [13], the effectiveness can be assessed by a score called EXAM in terms of the percentage of statements that have to be examined until the first statement containing the fault is reached. In this work, the EXAM score measures the percentage of transitions that have to be examined until the first faulty transition is found.

In order to assess the effectiveness and efficiency of the proposed method, we have designed an automated deadlock property test bed.

5.1 Automated Deadlock Property Test Bed

The test bed will randomly generate systems that might have deadlocks, then apply the proposed analysis algorithm to detect the introduced deadlocks. The main reason to use the deadlock as test property is because it is relatively easy to create a scalable system with deadlock heuristically. As the analysis in our method is based on the error traces and violation states in the reachability graph, it does not distinguish the property types in the model level. Although the test bed contains only one property, the effectiveness and efficiency evaluations will be meaningful for other safety properties.

For a given TPN system $S(P, R, M)$, P are processes which run infinitely and need a resource before the next task (a task is represented by a transition); R are resources shared by processes, but only accessible in an exclusive way; M is a matrix to decide whether process P_i needs to access resource R_j. We rely on the Coffman conditions [14] to build the deadlock test cases. Each process is designed to be moderately consuming the resource, i.e. it will use its resources consequently, always release one before locking another. The order in which a resource is accessed by processes is however random, which establishes the necessary condition of deadlock. In practice, the above conditions can be constructed statically when building test cases, while the circular wait condition (each process in a circular list or chain is waiting for a resource held by the next process in the list) can only be checked dynamically during the system execution. Therefore, the generated TPN will not systematically guarantee that a "real" deadlock will occur. To improve the success of creating deadlocks, we introduce another mechanism to enforce deadlocks: randomly let some processes during some tasks forget to release a used resource. These tasks are then considered as the failure cause of deadlocks. With a generated system and its already known faulty transitions (release-forgot tasks), the test bed will apply our method to compute the fault contribution of each task.

5.2 Evaluation of Efficiency

We have generated thousands of test cases by assigning P and R values from 5 to 20, creating 1 to 8 faulty transitions, with all the other parameters totally random. To create systems with deadlocks, we generate 10,000 cases for each fault number from 1 to 8. After examining the circular wait condition, most of these cases are deadlock-free, therefore the number of deadlock system is in fact much smaller than 10,000. The exact number of deadlock test cases is shown as the second column in Table 1.

The tests are performed on a 2,4 GHz Intel Core 2 Duo processor running Mac OS X 10.6.8. The average time for analyzing the deadlock cases is given in the evaluation column of the table. It shows that the approach is efficient.

Table 1. Efficiency Evaluation

System			Evaluation
Fault Num.	Test Num.	Average State/Transition	Average Time (s)
1	400	4949 / 15440	2.9092
2	517	2428 / 7130	1.1244
3	500	9884 / 31237	3.3533
4	402	8811 / 26663	2.5998
5	303	6756 / 18247	1.2196
6	504	27094 / 75808	5.064
7	757	104857 / 304741	15.0072
8	100	112306 / 283004	15.0289

5.3 Evaluation of Effectiveness

To evaluate the effectiveness, the **EXAM** score is calculated. Its value is the percentage of transitions that have to be examined until the first transition causing the deadlock fault is reached. The **EXAM** score measures the improvement of effectiveness with the help of ranking factor. Without ranking factors, in the worst case, the user needs to check the transitions one by one, until finally find the one with error.

We use an example to illustrated the evaluation method in Fig. 10. In a test case, assume there are 20 transitions in the system, and the transition t_2 is the only cause of failure. After applying the proposed failure analysis approach, the value of C_F ranking factor for each transition is calculated. As the transitions t_2, t_3 and t_4 have equal C_F values, the t_2 will be ranked either as the second position or the fourth position in the whole ranking list. The **EXAM** score is different in these two cases, respectively 10% and 20% We thus distinguish them by defining Fig. 10 (a) as a best case, and Fig. 10 (b) as a worst case.

The effectiveness evaluation is shown in Table 2. For each fault number (from 1 to 8) test cases, we give out **EXAM** score, **EXAM** score variance, rank, and rank variance for the best cases and worst cases, and then show the average **EXAM** score and average rank. The **EXAM** score varies from 2% to 13% for best cases, and varies from 4% to 18% for worst cases. In average, **EXAM** varies from 3% to 16% which

transition	C_F
t1	95%
(t2)	90%
t3	90%
t4	90%
t5	80%
...	...

(a) best case

transition	C_F
t1	95%
t4	90%
t3	90%
(t2)	90%
t5	80%
...	...

(b) worst case

Fig. 10. Illustration of Effectiveness Evaluation

Table 2. Effectiveness Evaluation

F. N.	Best Case				Worst Case				Average	
	EXAM	EXAM Var	Rank	Rank Var	EXAM	EXAM Var	Rank	Rank Var	EXAM	Rank
1	0,13335	0,00134	3,25	1,79	0,18603	0,00244	4,33	1,63	0,15969	3,79
2	0,04229	0,00219	1,1	1,75	0,09574	0,00213	2,11	1,75	0,069015	1,605
3	0,02108	0,00106	0,75	1,52	0,05892	0,0009	1,75	1,52	0,04	1,25
4	0,00722	0,0004	0,26	0,49	0,039	0,00042	1,26	0,49	0,02311	0,76
5	0,02044	0,0017	0,83	2,95	0,0478	0,00162	1,83	2,95	0,03412	1,33
6	0,05369	0,00336	2,46	7,36	0,0766	0,0033	3,46	7,36	0,065145	2,96
7	0,08857	0,00372	4,61	10,9	0,10822	0,0037	5,61	10,9	0,098395	5,11
8	0,13091	0,00099	7,3	3,95	0,14905	0,001	8,3	3,95	0,13998	7,8

corresponds to ranking results from 1 to 8. The stability is represented by the variance result. These experimental results shows our approach is effective.

6   Conclusion

Automated failure analysis in model checking is difficult to be computed exactly, due to semantics reduction caused by model abstraction. Yet, it is a key issue, as providing counterexamples is not enough to help designers in debugging faulty designs. It may require a great deal of human effort to locate faulty elements. Some works have provided good results by producing a set of suspicious faulty elements without particular ranking factor.

In our work, inspired by the theory of Kullback-Leibler Divergence and its successful application TF-IDF in text data mining, we start with comparing the similarity between information retrieval problem for documents and failure analysis problem for model checking, and propose an algorithm to compute the fault contribution of transitions on error traces. The fault contribution is the product of transition contribution (TC) and inverse trace contribution (ITC). The approach is illustrated using a BCET property case study, and then further assessed for its efficiency and effectiveness on a designed deadlock property test bed. The effectiveness is measured by the EXAM score.

The automated failure analysis relies on the reachability graph and violations states, thus can be applied to different verification models (TPN, timed automata, etc.) to provide helpful feedback for the assessment of safety properties. The liveness property asserts that something good eventually happens [5]. Examples of liveness properties include starvation freedom, termination and guaranteed service [6]. It will be interesting to study how to apply similar statistical methods to the failure analysis of liveness properties in the future work.

References

1. Alipour, M.A.: Automated fault localization techniques; a survey. Technical report, Technical report, Oregon State University (2012)
2. Ball, T., Naik, M., Rajamani, S.K.: From symptom to cause: localizing errors in counterexample traces. ACM SIGPLAN Notices 38(1), 97–105 (2003)
3. Groce, A., Visser, W.: What went wrong: Explaining counterexamples. In: Ball, T., Rajamani, S.K. (eds.) SPIN 2003. LNCS, vol. 2648, pp. 121–135. Springer, Heidelberg (2003)
4. Groce, A.: Error explanation with distance metrics. In: Jensen, K., Podelski, A. (eds.) TACAS 2004. LNCS, vol. 2988, pp. 108–122. Springer, Heidelberg (2004)
5. Lamport, L.: Proving the correctness of multiprocess programs. IEEE Transactions on Software Engineering (2), 125–143 (1977)
6. Alpern, B., Schneider, F.B.: Defining liveness. Information Processing Letters 21(4), 181–185 (1985)
7. Ge, N., Pantel, M.: Time properties verification framework for UML-MARTE safety critical real-time systems. In: Vallecillo, A., Tolvanen, J.-P., Kindler, E., Störrle, H., Kolovos, D. (eds.) ECMFA 2012. LNCS, vol. 7349, pp. 352–367. Springer, Heidelberg (2012)
8. Merlin, P., Farber, D.: Recoverability of communication protocols–implications of a theoretical study. IEEE Transactions on Communications 24(9), 1036–1043 (1976)
9. Berthomieu, B., Diaz, M.: Modeling and verification of time dependent systems using time petri nets. IEEE Trans. Softw. Eng. 17(3), 259–273 (1991)
10. Kullback, S., Leibler, R.A.: On information and sufficiency. The Annals of Mathematical Statistics 22(1), 79–86 (1951)
11. Baker, L.D., McCallum, A.K.: Distributional clustering of words for text classification. In: Proceedings of the 21st Annual International ACM SIGIR Conference on Research and Development in Information Retrieval, pp. 96–103. ACM (1998)
12. Jones, K.S.: A statistical interpretation of term specificity and its application in retrieval. Journal of Documentation 28(1), 11–21 (1972)
13. Wong, W.E., Debroy, V.: A survey of software fault localization. University of Texas at Dallas, Tech. Rep. UTDCS-45-09 (2009)
14. Coffman, E.G., Elphick, M., Shoshani, A.: System deadlocks. ACM Computing Surveys (CSUR) 3(2), 67–78 (1971)

A Model-Driven Methodology Approach for Developing a Repository of Models

Brahim Hamid

IRIT, University of Toulouse
118 Route de Narbonne, 31062 Toulouse Cedex 9, France
hamid@irit.fr

Abstract. To cope with the growing complexity of embedded system design, several development approaches have been proposed. The most popular are those using models as main artifacts to be constructed and maintained. The wanted role of models is to ease, systematize and standardize the approach of the construction of software-based systems. In order to enforce reuse and to interconnect the process of models' specification and the system development with models, we promote a model-based approach coupled with a repository of models. In this paper, we propose a Model-Driven Engineering methodological approach for the development of a repository of models and an operational architecture for development tools. In particular, we show the feasibility of our own approach by reporting some preliminary prototype providing a model-based repository of security and dependability (S&D) pattern models.

Keywords: Modeling artifact, Repository, Meta-model, Model Driven Engineering, Embedded Systems, Pattern.

1 Introduction

It is widely acknowledged that designers and developers of new-generation embedded systems are facing an exponential effort to manage the continuous increasing requirements of such systems [22]. Such systems come with a large number of common characteristics, including real-time and temperature constraints, security and dependability as well as efficiency requirements. In particular, the development of Resource Constrained Embedded Systems (RCES) has to address constraints regarding memory, computational processing power and/or energy consumption. The integration of these features requires the availability of both application domain specific knowledge and feature expertise at the same time. As a result, new recommendations should be considered to build novel methods capable of handling the complexity and reducing the cost of the development of these systems.

Model Driven Engineering (MDE) based solutions seem very promising to meet the needs of trusted embedded system applications development. The idea promoted by MDE is to use models at different levels of abstraction for developing systems. In other words, models provide input and output at all stages of system development until the final system itself is generated. MDE allows to increase software quality and to reduce the software systems development life cycle. Moreover, from a model, it is possible to

Y. Ait Ameur et al. (Eds.): MEDI 2014, LNCS 8748, pp. 29–44, 2014.

automatize some steps by model refinements and generate code for all or parts of the application. Domain Specific Modeling Languages (DSML) [8] has recently increased in popularity to cover a wider spectrum of concerns. As we will see, such a process reuses many practices from Model Driven Engineering. For instance, metamodeling and transformation techniques.

We believe that the use of a repository providing constructs for componentization of modeling artifacts can provide an efficient way to address these problems, improving the industrial efficiency and fostering technology *reuse* across domains (reuse of models at different levels), reducing the amount of effort and time needed to design a complex system. According to Bernstein and Dayal [3], a repository is a shared database of information on engineered artifacts. They introduce the fact that a repository has (1) a *Manager* for modeling, retrieving, and managing the components in a repository, (2) a *Database* to store the data and (3) *Functionalities* to interact with the repository. In our work, we go one step further: a model-based repository to support the specifications, the definitions and the packaging of a set of modeling artifacts to assist developers of trusted applications for embedded systems. Here, we describe a methodological approach for the creation of a flexible repository of modeling artifacts and for managing the models in that repository. To show the feasibility of our approach, we are developing an operational implementation in the context of the FP7 TERESA project [6]. Besides in this task some services dedicated to repository features will be developed. The goal is to integrate features together thanks to model-based repository engineering coupled with MDE technology; hence this will attempt to leverage reuse of model building blocks from the repository.

The rest of this paper is organized as follows. In Section 2, we discuss the modeling framework around a repository of modeling artifacts. Section 3 presents modeling language to support the design of the repository structure and its interfaces. In Section 4, we describe the approach for designing and exploiting the repository of modeling artifacts. Section 5 describes the architecture of the tool-suite and an example of an implementation of a repository. Section 6 describes the usage of the defined modeling framework in the context of FP7 TERESA project through the railway case study. In Section 7, we present a review of the most important related work. Finally, Section 8 concludes and draws future work directions.

2   The Framework for Software System Modeling Artifacts

The proposed approach promotes model-based development coupled with a repository of modeling artifacts. This approach aims to define an engineering discipline to enforce reuse and to share expertise. The main goal of this section is to define a modeling framework to support the packaging of a set of modeling artifacts for system software engineering. We start with a set of definitions and concepts that might prove useful in understanding our approach.

Definition 1 (Modeling Artifact.) *We define a modeling artifact as a formalized piece of knowledge for understanding and communicating ideas produced and/or consumed during certain activities of system engineering processes. The modeling artifact may be classified in accordance with engineering processes levels.*

Adapting the definition of pattern language given by Christopher Alexander [1], we define the following:

Definition 2 (Modeling Artifact System.) *A modeling artifact language is a collection of modeling artifacts forming a vocabulary. Such a collection may be skillfully woven together into a cohesive "whole" that reveals the inherent structures and relationships of its constituent parts toward fulfilling a shared objective.*

In our work, we promote a new discipline for system engineering around a model-based repository of modeling artifacts. The proposed framework addresses two kind of processes: the process of *modeling artifacts development* and *system development with modeling artifacts.* The main concern of the first process is designing modeling artifacts for reuse and the second one is finding the adequate modeling artifacts and evaluating them with regard the system-under-development's requirements. Therefore, we add a repository as a tier which acts as intermediate agent between these tow processes. A repository should provide a modeling container to support modeling artifacts life-cycle associated with different methodologies.

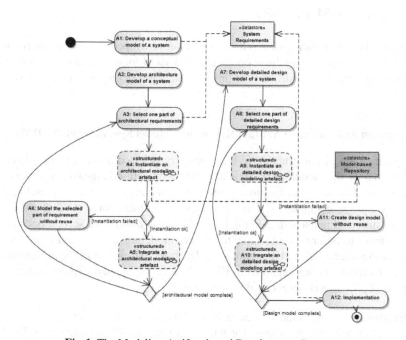

Fig. 1. The Modeling Artifact-based Development Process

Once the repository is available (the repository system populated with modeling artifacts), it serves an underlying engineering process. In the process model visualized in Fig. 1, as activity diagram, the developer starts by system specification (A1) fulfilling the requirements. In a traditional approach (non repository-based approach) the developer would continue with the architecture design, module design, implementation and

test. In our vision, instead of following these phases and defining new modeling artifacts, that usually are time and efforts consuming, as well as errors prone, the system
developer merely needs to select appropriate modeling artifacts from the repository and
integrate them in the system under development.

For each phase, the system developer executes the search/select from the repository
to instantiate modeling artifacts in its modeling environment (A4 and A9) and integrates
them in its models (A5 and A10) following an incremental process. The model specified
in a certain activity $An - 1$ is then used in activity An. In the same way, for a certain
development stage n, the modeling artifacts identified previously in stage (phase) $n - 1$
will help during the selection activity of a current phase. Moreover, the system developer can use a modeling artifact design process to develop their own solutions when the
repository fails to deliver appropriate modeling artifact at this stage. It is important to
remark that the software designer does not necessarily need to use one of the artifacts
stored in the repository previously included. He can define custom software architecture
for some modeling artifact (components), and avoid using the repository facilities (A6
and A11).

3   Repository Metamodel

Concretely, the repository system is a structure that stores specification languages, models and relationships among them, coupled with a set of tools to manage, visualize, export, and instantiate these artifacts in order to use them in engineering processes (see
Fig. 7).

3.1   System and Software Artifact Repository Model Specification(SARM)

The specification of the structure of the repository is based on the organization of its
content, mainly the modeling artifacts and the specification languages. Moreover, we
identified an *API* as a specification of the repository interaction system architecture.
That is, we propose a metamodel to capture these two main parts: the first one is dedicated to store and manage data in the form of *Compartments*, the second one is about
the *Interfaces* in order to publish and to retrieve modeling artifacts and to manage interactions between users and the repository. The principal classes of the metamodel are
described with the Ecore notations in Fig. 2. The following part depicts in details the
meaning of principal concepts used to specify the repository:

- SarmRepository. Is the core element used to define a repository.
- SarmCompartment. Is used for the categorization of the stored data. We have
  identified two main kinds of compartments:
  - SarmSpecLangCompartment. Is used to store the specification languages
    (SeSpecLang) of the modeling artifacts (SeArtefact).
  - SarmArtefactCompartment. Is used to store the modeling artifacts. To sim-
    plify the identification of a modeling artifact regarding the software develop-
    ment stage in which it's involved, an SeArtefact has an lifecycleStage typed
    with an external model library SeLifecycleStage.

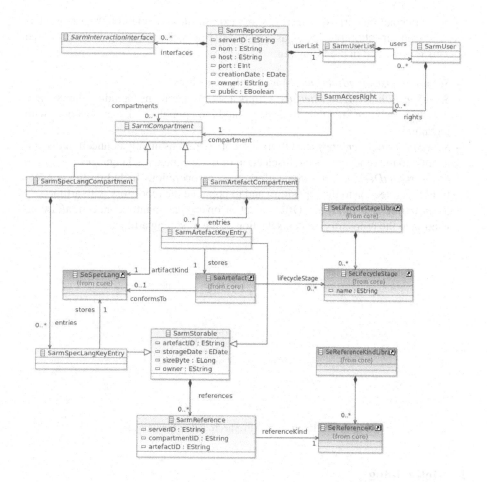

Fig. 2. The Repository Specification Metamodel (SARM)

- **SarmStorable.** Is used to define a set of characteristics of the model-based repository content, mainly those related to storage. We can define: *artefactURI*, *storageDate*, *sizeByte*, etc...
  In addition, it contains a set of references (**SarmReference**) to describe the different links with the other artifacts. The set of possible links is defined through and external model library **SeReferenceKind**.
- *SarmSpecLangKeyEntry.* Is the key entry to point towards a specification language model in the repository.
- *SarmArtefactKeyEntry.* Is the key entry to point towards a modeling artifact specification in the repository.
- *SarmAccesRight.* Is used to define the characteristics regarding the access right to the repository and its its content.
- *SarmUser.* Is used to define the user profile.
- *SarmUserList.* Is used to store the list of users in the repository.

For the interaction purposes, the repository exposes its content through a set of interfaces (**SarmInteractionInterface**), as depicted in Fig. 3. The meaning of the proposed concepts is presented in the following:

- *SarmAdministrationInterface*. Manages the repository.
- *SarmSpecLangDesignerInterface*. Offers a set of operations including the connection/disconnection to the repository and to populate the repository with metamodels.
- *SarmSpecLangUserInterface*. Offers a set of operations mainly connection/disconnection to the repository, search/selection of the specification languages.
- *SarmArtifactDesignerInterface*. Offers a set of operations including the connection/disconnection to the repository and to populate the repository with artifacts.
- *SarmArtefactUserInterface*. Offers a set of operations mainly connection/disconnection to the repository, search/selection of the modeling artifacts.

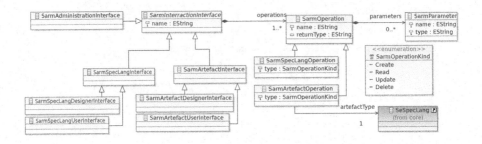

Fig. 3. The Repository API Specification Metamodel

4   Methodology

In this section, we describe a methodological approach for the creation of a flexible repository of modeling artifacts and for managing the models in that repository, such as visualized in Fig.4.

For illustration purpose, we will focus in the rest of the paper on the repository of security and dependability patterns, which acts as a specific demonstration for the TERESA resource constrained embedded systems, called *TeresaRepository*.

The following sections introduce the example of the *TeresaRepository* and describe in detail the process to be followed by the repository developers, including the designers of the metamodels of the artifacts and the modelers of these artifacts. The process describes the whole cycle from the creation of the artifacts' metamodels, the instantiation of the repository metamodel, the instantiation of these metamodels as modeling artifact for populating the repository, the management of the repository, and an overview on how the resulting repository software will support system engineering process.

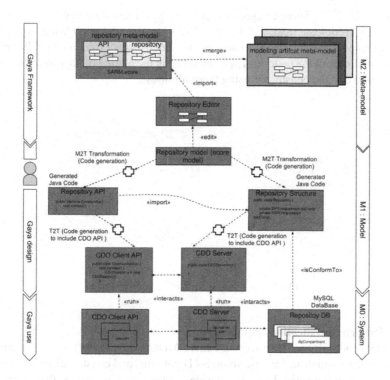

Fig. 4. Overview of the model-based repository building process

4.1 An S&D Pattern Repository

In the context of the TERESA project, we deal with three kinds of modeling artifacts: S&D patterns, S&D property models and resource property models. In this vision, the S&D pattern, derived from (resp. associated with) domain specific models, aims at helping the system engineer to integrate application S&D building blocks. Now, we briefly describe the modeling languages used to specify these artifacts. For more details, the reader is referred to [21] and [9] for property modeling language and for pattern modeling language, respectively.

4.1.1 Generic Property Modeling Language (GPRM)

The Generic PRoperty Metamodel (GPRM) [21], which is depicted with the Ecore notations in Fig. 5, is a metamodel defining a new formalism (i.e. language) for describing property libraries including units, types and property categories. For instance, security and dependability attributes [2] such as authenticity, confidentiality and availability are defined as categories. These categories require a set of measures types (degree, metrics, ...) and units (boolean, float,...). For that, we instantiate the appropriate type library and its corresponding unit library. These models are used as external model libraries to type the properties of the patterns. Especially during the editing of the pattern we define the properties and the constraints using these libraries.

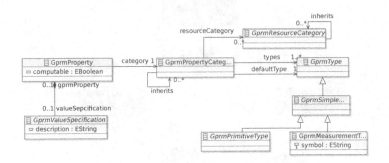

Fig. 5. The (simplified) GPRM Metamodel

4.1.2   Pattern Specification Metamodel

The System and Software Engineering Pattern Metamodel (SEPM) [9] is a metamodel defining a new formalism for describing S&D patterns, and constitutes the base of our pattern modeling language. Here we consider patterns as sub-systems that expose services (via interfaces) and manage S&D and Resource properties (via features) yielding a unified way to capture meta-information related to a pattern and its context of use. The following figure describes the principal concepts of the SEPM metamodel with the Ecore notations.

4.2   Model-Based Repository Building Process

(a) Create the artifacts' metamodel: Specify the metamodel of each artifact to be stored in the repository, as shown in the top part of Fig. 4. For instance, SEPM and GPRM metamodels are created and stored as Ecore models (Fig. 5 and Fig. 6).

(b) Create tools to support the repository modeling process: Write editors for the specification of the repository structure and APIs.

(c) Specify model libraries for classifications of artifacts: At each stage of the system engineering development process, identify the appropriate modeling artifacts to use by classifying them. In our context, we use the pattern classification of Riehle and Buschmann [17,5], which is (1) *System Patterns, Architectural Patterns, Design Patterns* and *Implementation Patterns* to create the model library SeLifecycleStage.

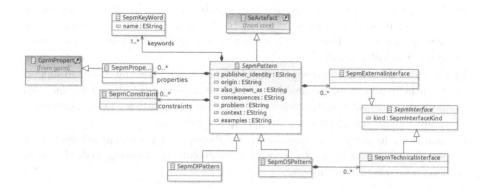

Fig. 6. The (simplified) SEPM Metamodel

(d) Specify model libraries for relationships between artifacts: At each stage n of the system engineering development process, the modeling artifacts identified previously in stage (phase) $n - 1$ will help during the selection activity of a current phase. For instance, a pattern may be linked with other patterns and associated with property models using a predefined set of reference kinds. For example *refines*, *specializes*, *uses* etc. Here, we create the SeReferenceKind model library to support specifying relationships across artifacts.

(e) Specify the repository structure: Use the editors, the metamodels and the model libraries to instantiate the SARM metamodel to create the model of the repository comprising the creation of metamodels' compartments, the artifacts' compartments, the users' list etc. The structure of the repository and its APIs are then available to modelers for populating and managing the repository (as seen in the middle part of Fig. 4). In our example, we define *TeresaRepository* as an instance of the SarmRepository: a model-based repository of S&D patterns and their related property models. To implement S&D pattern models and property models, we use a *MetamodelCompartment* as an instance of the SarmSpecLangCompartment, which has two instances of SarmSpecLangKeyEntry to store the pattern modeling language and the property modeling language. We also define a set of compartments to store the artifacts. In addition to the repository structure, we present define the model of interfaces (APIs) to exhibit the content of the repository and its management.

(f) Create tools for generating code: The resulting model is then used as input for the model transformations in order to generate the repository and APIs software implementation targeting a specific technological platform, for instance CDO [1] (as shown in the middle part of Fig. 4). Also, specify scripts to perform the installation and deployment of the resulted repository software system.

---

[1] http://www.eclipse.org/cdo/

(g) Specify views on the repository for access tools: Creating views on the repository according to its APIs, its organization and on the needs of the targeted system engineering process. For instance, a key word based-search access tool is implemented for the *TeresaRepository*.

(h) Create tools to support the populating of the repository: Creating editors to support the instantiation of the metamodels of artifacts. Furthermore, these tools includes mechanisms to validate the conformity of the modeling artifact and to publish the results into the repository using the appropriate interface.

(i) Create tools to support the administration of the repository: Creating editors to support the administration of the repository, the evolution of existing model libraries, users, artifacts relationships etc.

4.3   Exploitation of the Repository

We identified several roles. The modeling expert interacts with the repository to specify the modeling artifacts and then to store these artifacts, and the domain expert interacts with the repository in order to instantiate and then to reuse these artifacts. The repository manager is responsible for the repository administration. Finally, the system developer selects the modeling artifact for building an application. The following steps depicts the process to be followed to use the repository.

(a) Installation and deployment: The repository software system is deployed on an appropriate host while the accompanying development tools are installed in the user development environment.

(b) Define access security: Create users' list and grant them access rights to compartments.

(c) Create models: Create instances of the modeling artifacts metamodels and publish the results into the repository using appropriate editors. During this activity the pattern artifacts were built conforming to the pattern modeling language. An activity is added at this point to check the design conformity of the pattern.

(d) Generate reports and documentation: At this point, the modeling artifact designer may generate documentation. If the pattern has been correctly defined, i.e conforms the pattern modeling language, the pattern is ready for the publication to the model-based repository. Otherwise, we can find the issues from the report and re-build the pattern by correcting or completing its relevant constructs.

(e) Define relationships between models: Create instances of artifacts relationships model libraries. Also, each artifact is studied in order to identify its relationships with the other artifacts belonging to the same application domain with respect to the engineering process' activity in which it is consumed. The goal of this activity, in our case, is to organize patterns, to give them a structure of a set of pattern systems.

(f) Reuse of existing artifacts: Once the repository system is available, it serves an underlying trust engineering process through access tools, conforming to the process model visualized in Fig. 1.

5   Architecture and Implementation Tools

In this section, we propose an Model-Driven Engineering tool-chain supporting the repository system, and hence to assist the developers of software embedded systems. We provide four integrated sets of software tools: (i) *Tool set A* for populating the repository, (ii) *Tool set B* for retrieval from the repository, (iii) *Tool set C* as the repository software and (iv) *Tool set D* for managing the repository. The following details this software system from the specification, over target technology, evolution and maintenance for acquiring organizations, end-users and front-end support provider.

5.1   Tool-suite Architecture

To build our repository system, we use the well known architectural style: multitiered architectures as an alternative client-server organizations, as shown in Fig. 7.

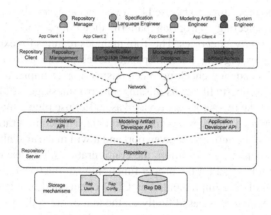

Fig. 7. An overview of repository system architecture

The server part (middle part of Fig. 7) is responsible for managing and storing the data interacting with storage mechanisms (down part of Fig. 7). In addition, the server part provides the implementation of the common APIs to interact with the repository content. For this, we identify a set of interfaces (APIs) for applications in order to create modeling artifact, in order to use them and in order to manage the repository. The user application part (top part of Fig. 7) is responsible for populating the repository and for using its content using the common APIs.

5.2   Implementation Details

Using the proposed metamodels, the Connected Data Objects (CDO) and the Eclipse Modeling Framework (EMF) [19], ongoing experimental work is done with SEMCOMDT [2] (SEMCO Model Development Tools, IRIT's editor and platform plugins). For our example, the tool-suite is composed of:

---
[2] http://www.semcomdt.org

- *Gaya.* for the repository platform (structure and interfaces) conforming to *SARM*,
- *Tiqueo.* for specifying models of S&D properties conforming to *GPRM*,
- *Arabion.* for specifying patterns conforming to *SEPM*,
- *Admin.* for the repository management,
- *Retrieval.* for the repository access.

The server part of *Gaya* is composed of two components: (1) *GayaServer* providing the implementation of the common API and (2) *GayaMARS* providing the storage mechanisms. The client part of *Gaya* provides interfaces, such as *Gaya4Pattern* (implements the API4PatternDesigner), *Gaya4Property* (implements the API4PropDesigner), *Gaya4Admin* (implements API4Admin) and *Gaya4SystemDeveloper* (implements the API4PatternUser). For pupulating purpose, we build two design tools, (1) The property designer (Tiqueo), to be used by a *property designer* and (2) The pattern designer (Arabion), to be used by a *pattern designer*. Tiqueo (resp. Arabion) interacts with the Gaya repository for publication purpose using the *Gaya4Property* (resp. *Gaya4Pattern* API).

For accessing the repository, to be used by a *system engineer*, the tool provides a set of facilities to help selecting appropriate patterns including *key word* search, *lifecycle stage* search and property categories. The Tool includes features for exportation and instantiation as dialogues targeting domain specific development environment. Moreover, the tool includes dependency checking mechanisms. For example, a pattern can't be instantiated, when a property library is missing, an error message will be thrown.

The server part of the repository is provided as an Eclipse plugin that will handle the launch of a CDO server defined by a configuration file. This configuration file indicates that a CDO server will be active on a given port and it will make available a CDO repository identified by its name. In addition, the configuration file is used to select which type of database will be used for the proper functioning of the CDO model repository.

The repository APIs are implemented as CDO clients and provided as an Eclipse plugin. The implementation is based firstly on the automatic code generation from the APIs model defined above. The generated Java code defines the different interfaces and functions provided by the repository APIs. The skeleton of the APIs implementations are then completed manually based on CDO technology.

The user applications for populating the repository are implemented as a set of EMF tree-based editors, to create patterns and the required libraries, and provided as Eclipse plugins. We also provide software, as a Java based GUI application, to manage the repository and for accessing. For more details, the reader is referred to [10].

6   Application of a Model-Based Repository of S&D Patterns to a Railway System Case Study

In the context of the TERESA project[3], we evaluated the approach to build an engineering discipline for trust that is adapted to RCES combining MDE and a model-based repository of S&D patterns and their related property models. We used the Tiqueo editor and Arabion editor to create the corresponding property libraries and the set of patterns, respectively. Arabion uses the property libraries provided by Tiqueo to type

---

[3] http://www.teresa-project.org/

the patterns property. Finally, we used the Gaya manager tool to set the relationships between the patterns. The TERESA repository contains so far (on January 2014):

- *Compartments*. 21 compartments to store artifacts of the TERESA domains.
- *Users*. 10 users.
- *Property Libraries*. 69 property model libraries.
- *Pattern Libraries*. 59 patterns.

One of the case studies acting as TERESA demonstrators is set in the railway domain throw the Safe4Rail demonstrator. Safe4Rail is in charge of the emergency brake of a railway system. Its mission is to check whether the brake needs to be activated. Most important, the emergency brake must be activated when something goes wrong.

The process flow for the example can be summarized with the following steps:

- Once the requirements are properly captured and imported into the development environment, for instance *Rhapsody*, the repository may suggest possible patterns to meet general or specific S&D needs (according to requirements and application domain): e.g. if the requirements contain the keywords *Redundancy* or *SIL4*, a suggestion could be to use a *TMR* pattern at architecture level. In addition, some diagnosis techniques imposed by the railway standard may be suggested:
  - TMR (suggested by the tool),
  - Diagnosis techniques (suggested by the tool),
  - Sensor Diversity (searched by the System Architect).
- Based on the selected patterns, the repository may suggest related or complementary patterns. For instance, if the TMR has been integrated , the following patterns may be proposed in a second iteration, for instance at design phase:
  - Data Agreement
  - Voter
  - Black Channel
  - Clock Synchronization

7 Related Work

In Model-Driven Development (MDD), model repositories [13,7,3] are used to facilitate the exchange of models through tools by managing modeling artifacts. Model repositories are often built as a layer on top of existing technologies (for instance, databases).

In order to ease the query on the repository, metadata can be added to select the appropriate artifacts. Therefore, there exist some repositories that are composed solely of metadata. For instance, as presented in the standard ebXML [15] and an ebXML Repository Reference Implementation [16], a service repository can be seen as a metadata repository that contains metadata about location information to find a service. In [13], the authors proposed a reusable architecture decision model for setting-up model and metadata repositories. They aimed to design data model and metadata repositories. In addition, some helpers are included in the product for selecting a basic repository technology, choosing appropriate repository metadata, and selecting suitable modeling levels of the model information stored in the repository. In [14], they proposed a repository implementation with storing and managing of artifacts support. The supported artifacts are: metamodels, models, constraints, specifications, transformation rules, code, templates, configuration or documentation, and their metadata.

Moogle [12] is a model search engine that uses UML or Domain Specific Language meta-model in order to create indexes that allow the evaluation of complex queries. Its key features include searching through different kind of models, as long as their meta-model is provided. The index is built automatically and the system tries to present only the relevant part of the results, for example trying to remove the XML tags or other unreadable characters to improve readability. The model elements type, attributes and hierarchy between model elements can be used as a search criteria. Models are searched by using keywords (Simple Search), by specifying the types of model elements to be returned (Advanced Search) and by using filters organized into facets (Browse). In order to properly use the advanced search engines, the user needs to know the metamodel elements. Moogle uses the Apache SOLR ranking policy of the results. The most important information of the results are highlighted to make them more clear to the user.

The MORSE project [11] proposes a Model-Aware Service Environment repository, for facilitating dynamically services to reflection models. MORSE addresses two common problems in MDD systems: traceability and collaboration. The model repository is the main component of MORSE and has been designed with the goal to abstract from specific technologies. MORSE focuses on runtime services and processes and their integration and interaction with the repository.

The work described in [4] is a general-purpose approach using graph query processing for searching repository of models represented as graphs. First the repository models are translated into directed graphs. Then, the system receives a query conforming to the considered DSL metamodel. In order to reduce the matching problem into a graph matching one, the submitted query is also transformed in a graph. Matches are calculated by finding a mapping between the query graph and the project graphs or sub-graphs, depending on the granularity. The results are ranked using the graph edit distance metric by means of the A-Star algorithm. The prototype considers the case of the domain-specific WebML language.

The work in [20] presents a survey of business process model repositories and their related frameworks. This work deals with the management of a large collections of business processes using repository structures and providing common repository functions such as storage, search and version management. It targets the process model designer allowing the reuse of process model artefacts. A comparison of process model repositories is presented to highlight the degree of reusability of artefacts.

Another issue is graphical modeling tool generation as studied in the GraMMi project [18]. In this project the repository is based on three levels of abstraction (metametamodel, metamodel and model). The repository stores both metamodels (notation definitions) and models (instantiation definitions). The repository access is made thanks to an interface provided by itself. GraMMi's Kernel allows to manage persistent objects. So this kernel aims at converting the objects (models) in an understandable form for the user via the graphical interface.

The metamodel and the methodology described in this paper may be used to specify the management and the use of these kinds of repositories. In fact, models aspects or the assets as a whole of the aforementioned repositories can be seen as artifacts supported by our metamodel. In return, the provided technologies to support repository implementations may be used in our work as targets platforms for repository generation.

8 Conclusion

Repositories of modeling artifacts have gained more attention recently to enforce reuse in software engineering. In fact, repository-centric development processes are more adopted in software/ system development, such as architecture-centric or pattern-centric development processes.

The proposed framework for building a repository is based on metamodeling, which allows to specify the structure of a repository and modeling artifacts at different levels of abstraction, and model transformation techniques for generation purposes. Moreover, we proposed an operational architecture for the implementation of a repository. In addition, the tool suite promotes the separation of concerns during the development process by distinguishing the roles of the different stakeholders. Mainly, the access to the repository is customized regarding the development phases, the stakeholder's domain and his system knowledge.

The approach presented here has been evaluated in in the context of the TERESA project for a repository of S&D patterns and property models, where we walk through a prototype with EMF editors and a CDO-based repository supporting the approach. Currently the tool suite named SEMCOMDT is provided as Eclipse plugins.

In a wider scope, new specification languages may be designed and stored with their related artifact in the repository. For instance, components, resources, analysis and simulations are important kinds of artifacts that we can consider in our framework to serve systematic construction of large complex systems with multiple concerns. As a result, specification languages, roles and compartments related to each of them can be clearly defined and applied in system development for more flexibility and efficiency.

As future work, we plan to study the automation of the search and instantiation of models and a framework for simpler specification of constraints would be beneficial. In addition, we will study the integration of our tooling with other MDE tools. Also, we will seek new opportunities to apply the framework to other domains.

References

1. Alexander, C., Ishikawa, S., Silverstein, M.: A Pattern Language. Center for Environmental Structure Series, vol. 2. Oxford University Press, New York (1977)
2. Avizienis, A., Laprie, J.-C., Randell, B., Landwehr, C.: Basic Concepts and Taxonomy of Dependable and Secure Computing. IEEE Transactions on Dependable and Secure Computing 1, 11–33 (2004)
3. Bernstein, P.A., Dayal, U.: An Overview of Repository Technology. In: Proceedings of the 20th International Conference on Very Large Data Bases, VLDB 1994, pp. 705–713. Morgan Kaufmann Publishers Inc. (1994)

4. Bislimovska, B., Bozzon, A., Brambilla, M., Fraternali, P.: Graph-based search over web application model repositories. In: Auer, S., Díaz, O., Papadopoulos, G.A. (eds.) ICWE 2011. LNCS, vol. 6757, pp. 90–104. Springer, Heidelberg (2011)
5. Buschmann, G., Meunier, R., Rohnert, H., Sommerlad, P., Stal, M.: Pattern-Oriented Software Architecture: a system of patterns, vol. 1. John Wiley and Sons (1996)
6. TERESA Consortium. TERESA Project (Trusted Computing Engineering for Resource Constrained Embedded Systems Applications), http://www.teresa-project.org/
7. France, R.B., Bieman, J., Cheng, B.H.C.: Repository for Model Driven Development (ReMoDD). In: Kühne, T. (ed.) MoDELS 2006. LNCS, vol. 4364, pp. 311–317. Springer, Heidelberg (2007)
8. Gray, J., Tolvanen, J.-P., Kelly, S., Gokhale, A., Neema, S., Sprinkle, J.: Domain-Specific Modeling. Chapman & Hall/CRC (2007)
9. Hamid, B., Gürgens, S., Jouvray, C., Desnos, N.: Enforcing S&D Pattern Design in RCES with Modeling and Formal Approaches. In: Whittle, J., Clark, T., Kühne, T. (eds.) MODELS 2011. LNCS, vol. 6981, pp. 319–333. Springer, Heidelberg (2011)
10. Hamid, B., Ziani, A., Geisel, J.: Towards Tool Support for Pattern-Based Secure and Dependable Systems Development. In: ACadeMics Tooling with Eclipse (ACME), Montpellier, France, pp. 1–6. ACM DL (2013)
11. Holmes, T., Zdun, U., Dustdar, S.: MORSE: A Model-Aware Service Environment (2009)
12. Lucrédio, D., de M. Fortes, R.P., Whittle, J.: MOOGLE: A model search engine. In: Czarnecki, K., Ober, I., Bruel, J.-M., Uhl, A., Völter, M. (eds.) MODELS 2008. LNCS, vol. 5301, pp. 296–310. Springer, Heidelberg (2008)
13. Mayr, C., Zdun, U., Dustdar, S.: Reusable Architectural Decision Model for Model and Metadata Repositories. In: de Boer, F.S., Bonsangue, M.M., Madelaine, E. (eds.) FMCO 2008. LNCS, vol. 5751, pp. 1–20. Springer, Heidelberg (2009)
14. Milanovic, N., Kutsche, R.-D., Baum, T., Cartsburg, M., Elmasgünes, H., Pohl, M., Widiker, J.: Model&Metamodel, Metadata and Document Repository for Software and Data Integration. In: Czarnecki, K., Ober, I., Bruel, J.-M., Uhl, A., Völter, M. (eds.) MODELS 2008. LNCS, vol. 5301, pp. 416–430. Springer, Heidelberg (2008)
15. Oasis. ebXML: Oasis Registry Services Specification v2.5 (2003)
16. Oasis. freebXML: Oasis ebxml registry reference implementation project (2007), http://ebxmlrr.sourceforge.net/
17. Riehle, D., Züllighoven, H.: Understanding and using patterns in software development. TAPOS 2(1), 3–13 (1996)
18. Sapia, C., Blaschka, M., Höfling, G.: GraMMi: Using a Standard Repository Management System to Build a Generic Graphical Modeling Tool. In: Proceedings of the 33rd Hawaii International Conference on System Sciences, HICSS 2000, p. 8058. IEEE Computer Society (2000)
19. Steinberg, D., Budinsky, F., Paternostro, M., Merks, E.: EMF: Eclipse Modeling Framework 2.0, 2nd edn. Addison-Wesley Professional (2009)
20. Yan, Z., Dijkman, R.M., Grefen, P.: Business process model repositories - framework and survey. Information & Software Technology 54(4), 380–395 (2012)
21. Ziani, A., Hamid, B., Trujillo, S.: Towards a Unified Meta-model for Resources-Constrained Embedded Systems. In: 37th EUROMICRO Conference on Software Engineering and Advanced Applications, pp. 485–492. IEEE (2011)
22. Zurawski, R.: Embedded systems in industrial applications - challenges and trends. In: SIES (2007)

Towards a Generic Framework
for the Initialization and the Observation
of Socio-environmental Models

Hasina Lalaina Rakotonirainy[1], Jean-Pierre Müller[2],
and Bertin Olivier Ramamonjisoa[1]

[1] EDMI, University of Fianarantsoa, Fianarantsoa, Madagascar
hasina.rakotonirainy@cirad.fr, bertinram@yahoo.fr
[2] GREEN, CIRAD, Campus international de Baillarguet, Montpellier, France
jean-pierre.muller@cirad.fr

Abstract. Researchers have sought to deal with the complexity of socio-ecosystems including biophysical and social dynamics, and their interactions. In order to cope with this complexity, they need increasingly complex models, whose initialization, and observation are becoming very difficult to implement. However, no generic framework has yet been developed to address this issue. Our objective is a generic framework for specifying and implementing the initialization from numerous heterogeneous data, and the observation producing the desired indicators. The contribution of the paper is the formulation of the initialization and observation as transformations among data and data structures. This formulation allows to use the Model Driven Engineering concepts in order to implement the generic framework and the corresponding domain specific languages. The expected result will be a set of domain specific languages and their tools for specifying and automatizing the whole model exploration process from the initialization to the production of the indicators.

1   Introduction

For around twenty years, researchers have sought to deal with all the complexity of socio-ecosystems [14] including biophysical and social dynamics, and their interactions. Modeling is an approach that is increasingly being used by researchers to understand those complex dynamics and interactions. In order to cope with this complexity, they are calling upon increasingly complex models. As the models are complex, to be able to initialize and parameterize them, they need a lot of heterogeneous data that are coming from socio-environmental systems, collected by the thematicians (ecologists, economists, sociologists, etc.). They have consequently both support heterogeneity (data-bases, excel files, shape files, XML, CSV, etc.) and semantic heterogeneity. It also becomes difficult to analyze and construct relevant indicators to understand the model behavior. More concretely, the simulation models are manipulating data structures that do not correspond to the data collected by the thematicians, nor to what they want to observe and monitor during and after the simulation. Two questions are raised, how to

Y. Ait Ameur et al. (Eds.): MEDI 2014, LNCS 8748, pp. 45–52, 2014.

effectively exploit the many heterogeneous data in order to facilitate the initialization of socio-environmental models, and how to construct indicators relative to both the questions of thematicians and the understanding of these models. Additionnaly, the data sources and the desired indicators evolve very often in the modeling process due to the system complexity, requiring continuous redesign of the initialization and observation processes.

In order to deal with these issues, [7] constructed a modular language that could be used to express the hierarchical structure of the specifications of the components in a system, in order to configure it. [4] constructed the XELOC language, based on the syntax of the XML language to configure and automatically initialize a multi-agent model from the maps provided by the thematicians.[15] proposed the SimExplorer tool, which can be used, among other things, to configure a model and to parameterize visualization of the model results during simulation. However, these approaches are relatively ad hoc. No general framework has yet been envisaged for initializing and observing complex models such as socio-environnemental models, providing the thematicians with the tools to easily specify how to initialize and to parameterize the model from the data they have as well as how to generate the observables of a model in a generic way.

In the process of building a socio-environmental model, we propose to see initialization and observation as the description of the heterogeneous data sources to generate the available data structures, the data structures of the model and those of the indicators, as well as the transformations between them. Hence, the model initialization and observation becomes a problem of transformations of data into data structures, data structures into other data structures, and data structures into data (Fig. 1). Our aim is to provide the thematicians with specific languages in order to flexibly specify these data, data structures and transformations. To implement these languages, we propose to use MDE (Model Driven Engineering) [10] that allows to build such languages called DSL (Domain Specific Language) and that allows to specify the relevant transformations. To be able to use MDE, we must formulate the preceding set of problems in terms of MDE.

Therefore, we first describe the concepts of MDE used to implement DSLs (section 2). We go on to show how they can be used to reformulate model initialization and observation questions (section 3). We show some preliminary results (section 4) and we deduce the work programme to be implemented on the basis of this proposal (section 5).

2   Succinct Description of MDE

According to [10], MDE (Model Driven Engineering) is a software design, development and manufacturing methodology based on models. It allows to build DSLs that are defined by tuples $\langle AS, CS^*, SD, Mac, Mas \rangle$ where AS is the abstract syntax that allows to model the studied system, CS^* are textual or graphical concrete syntaxes provided to the user to specify the model. SD is the semantic domain giving sense to AS, Mac is the set of mappings from CS to AS,

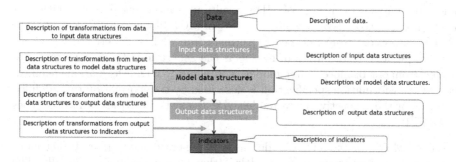

Fig. 1. An overview of a model initialization and observation process

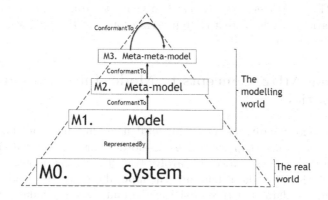

Fig. 2. OMG modelling pyramid [12]

and Mas is the mapping from AS to SD. To build DSLs and to relate them, MDE centers on four basic concepts: *models, meta-models, meta-meta-models* and *model transformations*.

1. Model: For [11], A is a model of a system B for an observer X, if manipulating A allows to answer questions of X on B. In reference to the DSL, A is specified by using an abstract syntax (AS) of a DSL using one of its CS, and B corresponds to the semantic domain SD.
2. Metamodel: A meta-model is a model to define the specification of a model. In OMG terms, the meta-model specifies the abstract syntax AS of the DSL. A model A is said to be "conform" to a meta-model AS if each of its elements is an instance of an element of the meta-model, and if it respects the properties expressed on the meta-model [10].
3. Meta-metamodel: A meta-meta-model defines the language to specify the meta-models. The OMG (Object Management Group) has defined the MOF (Meta-Object Facility) that is able to describe itself (meta-circularity) in order to limit the abstraction levels [12].

These fundamental concepts of MDE results in a modeling pyramid with four levels (Fig. 2). Nowadays, it exists a variety of MOF like EMOF (Essential MOF Model) [13], Ecore from Eclipse [3], Kermeta from IRISA [5], etc.

From [8], a transformation of models is the generation of one or more target models from one or more source models, compliant to a transformation specification. A transformation specification is described by transformation rules defined in terms of the respective meta-models AS; It exists two transformation types in MDE[10]:

- The "M2M" or Model To Model: used to generate one or more target models from one or more source models, either automatically or manually. The transformation can be *endogenous* when the source and target meta-models AS are the same, *exogeneous* otherwise.
- The "M2T" or Model To Text: used to generate from one or more source models various kinds of textual representations (XML, programming languages, etc. as particular CS).

3   Mapping MDE Concepts to Model Initialization and Observation

We propose to reformulate socio-environmental model initialization and observation questions as a problem of specifying transformations between data and data structures. In detail, these processes involve transformations between thematicians' data and the input data structure, the input data structure and that used for simulation, the data structure of the model and the output data structure, and lastly, the output data structure and the indicators (Fig. 1). In Minsky's terms, the systems B to model corresponding to M_0 in figure 2 are respectively the data sources, the data structures, the indicators and transformations among them.

Therefore, the models A are a detailed description of the data source content, of the resulting input data structures independently from the support, of the model data structure from which to extract the resulting output data structures and the indicator structures, as well as the transformations (M_1 in figure 2).

We must provide for each model an abstract syntax AS to be able to express these descriptions of data, data structures and transformations (M_2 in figure 2), as well as their related concrete syntaxes CS^*.

Finally, these meta-models must be specified using a meta-meta-model. Having chosen EMF, we will use an existing variant of the MOF called Ecore (M_3 in figure 2).

The complete mapping between our targeted implementation and the OMG pyramid is illustrated in the figure 3.

We need to specify the abstract syntax of the various DSLs using Ecore as illustrated in the figure 3:

1. Language $L1$: used to specify the different data sources and the semantics of the available data independently of their actual form. By default, the

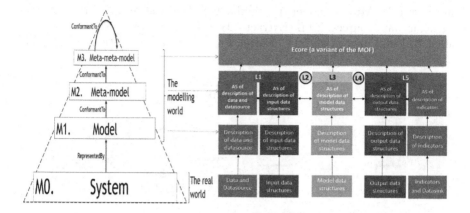

Fig. 3. Mapping the modeling pyramid to initialization and observation implementation

language $L1$ does not take into account the notion of time. The data from $L1$ is considered as the initial state, i.e. the data structure of the model at its initial date, as parameters or as explicit time series.

2. Language $L3$: used to specify the simulation model. The simulation model is seen as a partial specification of a continuous function of time into the data structures representing the model state at any given date. Therefore, a simulation is seen as a process of completion of this function of time on a given interval.
3. Language $L2$: used to specify the chain of possible transformations between the data described by $L1$ and the simulation model described by $L3$.
4. Language $L5$: used to specify the structure of the indicators that the user wishes to observe. In particular, it can be time series.
5. Language $L4$: used to specify the chain of possible transformations from the observables of the simulated model into the indicators. Many statistical tools to build specific indicators from the outputs of a model already exist. However, in the context of socio-environmental models, $L4$ allows to specify the chain of transformations to produce the desired indicators.

The next step consists in defining the semantic domain (SD), in our case the actual data and data structures as well as the transformation code, and the mapping Mas from the abstract syntax of each DSLs into SD. The expected outcome is the automatic generation of the code to actually generate the desired data structures and indicators, using the various transformations.

4   Preliminary Results

For the time being, we have fully specified $L1$ that aims at specifying the heterogeneous data sources in order to generate input data structures independent from the sources. For testing, it has been applied to set of heterogenous real data sources used by Mirana model [1]. Similar functionalities exist to manage heterogeneous data sources. ETL (Extract - Transform - Load) tools such as Informatica, Talend Open Studio, GeoKettle, Pentaho DataIntegration, CloverETL,

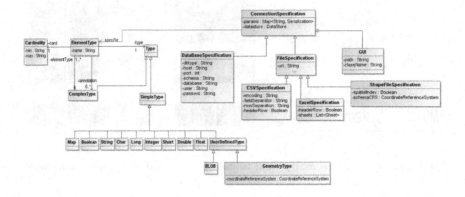

Fig. 4. The metamodel of the language L1

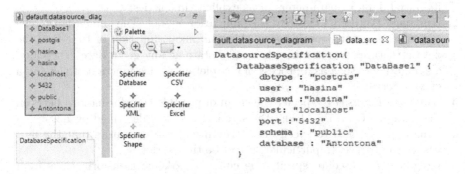

Fig. 5. Excerpt of the data source specification

```
ructure.dstruct ⊠

ElementType{ name "Antontona"    type ComplexType
    ElementType{
        name "Actions" type ComplexType
            ElementType{
                name "Duree"
                type Float
                }
            ElementType{
                name "Quantite"
                type Float
                }
            ElementType{
                name "Out"
                type String
                }
            ElementType{
                name "Action"
                type String
                }
```

Fig. 6. Exerpt of the generated input data structure

are used to extract, transform and automatically generate data from one set of data carriers to others. The Geotools project is a free and open source GIS toolkit developed in Java. It enables to access and manage different sources of data although it is focused on geographic information. In addition, [6] proposed a data integration architecture known as *mediator architecture* or *virtual integration*. The principle is to have a mediator that provides the overall scheme and a unique vocabulary to express user requests. [9], [16] and [2] presented the *data warehousing* or *materialized integration* architecture. While, for *virtual integration*, the data remain stored in the sources of origin, with *materialized integration*, the data are extracted from their original source and stored in a data warehouse. However, our specification has largely been inspired by these approaches and implemented using *EMF* [3].

Using Ecore, we have defined a meta-model (Fig. 4) :

1. A part of meta-model is used to specify heterogeneous data sources (databases, Excel files, shapefiles, CSV and even graphic interfaces from any kind of applications providing data).
2. The other part of meta-model is used to specify the data structures extracted from the various data sources into a representation independent from the sources.

Then we have defined a textual concrete syntax using the framework Xtext and a graphical concrete syntax using the GMF framework (Graphical Modeling Framework) in addition to the tree-like concrete syntax automatically generated by the EMF tools. These concrete syntaxes are provided to the thematicians to specify the data sources they are using in order to generate the generic data structures from the sources. The figure 5 shows the graphical and textual concrete syntax defined using the meta-model in order to generate the data structures from a PostgreSQL database with the port 5432 and the name "Antontona". Finally, the generated code is able to read the database content and generate the corresponding data structure (Fig. 6) to be later transformed into the model data structure using the transformations specified using L2.

5 Conclusion

We have shown in this paper that by using the concepts proposed by MDE, it is possible to formulate socio-environmental model initialization and observation problems generically. The language L1 is fully operational, however, much remains to be done, notably implementation of the other different specific languages L2, L3, L4 and L5.

In addition, "M2M" (Model To Model) and "M2T" (Model To Text) are the types of transformations proposed by MDE. They can be used to transform data structures into other data structures and data structures into textual concrete syntaxes of a language. However, in proposing the architecture (Fig. 3), we felt the need to consider other type of transformation that have not been dealt with by MDE, such as "M2G" (Model To Graphics) to transform model into graphical structures for visualization, including plots and graph tools.

Acknowledgements. The research is financed by a PhD grant from AIRD/CIRAD.

References

1. Aubert, S., Muller, J.-P., Ralihalizara, J.: MIRANA: a socio-ecological model for assessing sustainability of community-based regulations. In: International Congress on Environmental Modelling and Software Modelling for Environment's Sake, Ottawa, Canada, pp. 1–8. International Congress on Environmental Modelling and Software Modelling (2010)
2. Chrisment, C., Pujolle, G., Ravat, F., Teste, O., Zurfluh, G.: Entrepôts de données, Techniques de l'ingénieur, H3870 (2005)
3. Dave, S., Franck, B., Marcelo, P., Ed, M.: EMF: Eclipse Modeling Framework. The Eclipse Series, 2nd edn. (December 2008)
4. David, D., Payet, D., Courdier, R., Gangat, Y.: XELOC: Un support générique pour la configuration et l'initialisation de systèmes multi-agents, LIM IREMIA, Université de La Réunion (2009)
5. Drey, Z., Faucher, C., Fleurey, F., Mahé, V., Vojtisek, D.: Kermeta language: Reference manual. IRISA (2010)
6. Gio, W.: Mediators in the architecture of future information systems. IEEE Computer (1992)
7. Hill, G., Vickers, S.: A language for configuring multi-level specifications. In: Rattray, C., Maharaj, S., Shankland, C. (eds.) AMAST 2004. LNCS, vol. 3116, pp. 196–210. Springer, Heidelberg (2004)
8. Hubert, K.: Conception orienté objet guidée par les modèles. Dunod (2005)
9. Inmon, W.: Building the datawarehouse, 4th edn. Wiley (2005)
10. Jézéquel, J.M., Combemale, B., Vojtisek, D.: Ingénierie dirigée par les modèles - Des concepts à la pratique, p. 144. Editions Ellipses (2012)
11. Minsky, M.: Matter, mind, and models. In: Semantic Information Processing, pp. 425–432 (1968)
12. Object Management Group, Meta Object Facility (MOF) Specification, Version 1.4 (2002)
13. Object Management Group, Inc. Meta Object Facility (MOF), 2.0 Core Specification (2006)
14. Redman, C., Grove, M.J., Kuby, L.: Integrating Social Science into the Long Term Ecological Research (LTER) Network: Social Dimensions of Ecological Change and Ecological Dimensions of Social Change. Ecosystems 7(2), 161–171 (2004)
15. Truffot, J.: SimExplorer, une interface d'exploration de simulations en Java, Cemagref ISIMA, Nantes (2002)
16. Widom, J.: Research problems in data warehousing. In: Proceedings of the 1995 International Conference on Information and Knowledge Management (CIKM), Baltimore, Maryland (1995)

Context-Aware Verification
of a Cruise-Control System

Ciprian Teodorov, Luka Leroux, and Philippe Dhaussy

UEB, Lab-STICC Laboratory UMR CNRS 6285,
ENSTA Bretagne, France
`firstname.name@ensta-bretagne.fr`

Abstract. Despite the high-level of automation, the practicability of model-checking large asynchronous models is hindered by the state-space explosion problem. To address this challenge the Context-aware Verification technique relies on the identification and explicit specification of the environment (context) in which the system-under-study operates.

In this paper we apply this technique for the verification of a Cruise-control System (CCS). The asynchrony of this system renders traditional model-checking approaches almost impossible. Using the Context-aware Verification technique this task becomes manageable by relying on two powerful optimisation strategies enabled by the structural properties of the contexts: automatic context-splitting, a recursive state-space decomposition strategy; context-directed semi-external reachability analysis, an exhaustive analysis technique that reduces the memory pressure during verification through the use of external memory.

In the case of the CCS system, this approach enabled the analysis of up to 5 times larger state-spaces than traditional approaches.

Keywords: formal verification, context-aware model-checking, OBP, observer-automata.

1   Introduction

Since their introduction in the early 1980s, model-checking [17,5] techniques provide an automated formal approach for the verification of complex requirements of hardware and software systems. This technique relies on the exhaustive analysis of all states in the system to check if it correctly implements the specifications, usually expressed using temporal logics. However, because of the internal complexity of the systems studied, model-checking is often challenged with unmanageable large state-space, a problem known as the state-space explosion problem [6,15]. Numerous techniques, such as symbolic model-checking [3] and partial-order reduction [19], have been proposed to reduce the impact of this problem effectively pushing the inherent limits of model-checking further and further.

The Context-aware Verification has been recently introduced [9] as a new technique of state-space decomposition that enables compositional verification

Y. Ait Ameur et al. (Eds.): MEDI 2014, LNCS 8748, pp. 53–64, 2014.

of requirements. This technique reduces the set of possible behaviors (and thus the state-space) by closing the SUS with a well defined finite and acyclic environment. The explicit and formal specification of this environment enables at least three different decomposition axes: *a*) the environment can be decomposed in contexts, thus isolating different operating modes; *b*) these contexts enable the automatic partitioning of the state-space into independent verification problems; *c*) the requirements are focused on specific environmental conditions.

In this study we apply the Context-aware Verification technique for modelling and requirement validation of an automotive Cruise-control System, a system that automatically controls the speed of cars. Using this approach we verified three important requirements of the CCS, identifying one subtle concurrency bug that could lead to very dangerous situations. Furthermore, the importance of the Context-aware Verification approach is emphasised through the successful analysis of up to 4.78 larger state-space than traditional approaches. Result which was made possible by relying on the complementarity of two powerful optimisation strategies enabled by the explicit environment specification: a recursive state-space decomposition strategy and an exhaustive analysis technique that reduces the memory pressure during verification through the use of external memory.

This study starts by introducing the Context-aware Verification approach in Section 2 along with the CDL language (Section 2.1) and two innovative analysis techniques addressing the state-space explosion problem (Section 2.2). The CCS specifications are introduced in Section 3 and the CDL encoding of the requirements and environment are overviewed in Section 3.2 and Section 3.3. The verification results are presented in Section 3.4. Section 4 overviews related research emphasising the complementarity with the Context-aware Verification. Section 5 concludes this study presenting future research directions.

2   Context-Aware Verification

Context-aware Verification, focuses on the explicit modeling of the environment as one or more contexts, which then are iteratively composed with the system-under-study (SUS). The requirements are associated and verified in the contexts that correspond to the environmental conditions in which they should be satisfied, and automated context-guided state-space reduction techniques can be used to further push the limits of reachability analysis. All these developments are implemented in the OBP *Observation Engine* [9] and are freely available[1].

When verifying properties, through explicit-state model checking, the system explores all the behaviors possible in the SUS and checks whether the verified properties are true or not. Due to the exponential growth of system states relative to the number of interacting components, most of the time the number of reachable configurations is too large to be contained in memory. Besides using techniques like the ones described in Section 4, to alleviate this problem the system designers manually tune the SUS to restrict its behaviors to the ones

---

[1] OBP *Observation Engine* website: http://www.obpcdl.org

pertinent relative to the specified requirements. This process is tedious, error prone and poses a number of methodological challenges since different versions of the SUS should be kept sound, in sync and maintained.

To address these issues, Context-aware Verification technique proposes to restrict the model behaviors by composing it with an explicitly defined environment that interacts with the SUS. The environment enables a subset of the behaviors of the model. This technique reduces the complexity of the exploration by limiting its scope to a reduced set of behaviors related to specific environmental conditions. Moreover, this approach solves the methodological issues, since it decouples the SUS from its environment, thus allowing their refinement in isolation.

Context-aware reduction of system behaviors is particularly interesting in the case of complex embedded system, such as automotive and avionics, since they exhibit clearly identified operating modes with specific properties associated with these modes. Unfortunately, only few existing approaches propose practical ways to precisely capture these contexts in order to reduce formal verification complexity and thus improve the scalability of existing model checking approaches.

2.1   Environment Modeling with CDL Formalism

The *Context Description Language*[2](CDL) was introduced to formalize the environment specification [8]. The core of the CDL language is based on the concept of **context**, which has an acyclic behavior communicating asynchronously with the system. The environment is specified through a number of such contexts. The interleaving of these contexts generates a labelled-transition system representing all behaviors of the environment, which can be fed as input to traditional model-checkers. Moreover, the CDL enables the specification of requirements through properties that are verified by the OBP *Observation Engine*.

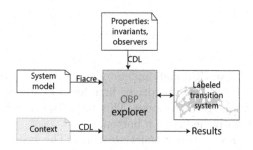

Fig. 1. OBP *Observation Engine* overview

Fig. 1 shows a global overview of the OBP *Observation Engine*. The SUS is described using the formal language Fiacre [11], which enables the specification of interacting behaviors and timing constraints through timed-automata.

---

[2] For detailed CDL syntax and semantics, see www.obpcdl.org.

The surrounding environment and the requirements are specified using the CDL formalism.

2.2 Context-Guided State-space Decomposition and Reachability

Automatic Context Splitting: OBP *Observation Engine* integrates a powerful context-guided state-space reduction technique which relies on the automated recursive partitioning (splitting) of a given context in independent sub-contexts [8]. This technique is systematically applied by OBP *Observation Engine* when a given reachability analysis fails due to lack of memory resources to store the state-space.

After splitting $context_i$, the sub-contexts are iteratively composed with the model for exploration, and the properties associated with $context_i$ are checked for all sub-contexts. Therefore, the global verification problem for $context_i$ is effectively decomposed into K_i smaller verification problems.

Context-directed semi-external reachability analysis: OBP *Observation Engine* also implements a new exhaustive analysis algorithm that reduces the memory consumption by using the external storage to store the "past-states" of the SUS [18]. This algorithm, named PastFree[ze], relies on the isolation of the acyclic components of the SUS, which are used to drive the reachability analysis. The nodes of the graph induced by the context identifies "clusters of states" that can be freed from memory and saved to disk.

3   Case Study: Cruise-Control System

This section provides a description and some of the requirements of an automotive Cruise-control System (CCS), which is the case study studied in this paper.

3.1   SUS Model

Functional Overview. The CCS main function is to adjust the speed of a vehicle. After powering the system on, the driver first has to capture a target speed, then it is possible to engage the system. This target speed can be increased or decreased by $5km/h$ with the tap of a button.

There are also several important safety features. The system shall disengage as soon as the driver hits the brake/clutch pedal or if the current vehicle speed (s) is off bounds ($40 < s < 180km/h$). In such case, it shall not engage again until the driver hits a "resume" button. If the driver presses the accelerator, the system shall pause itself until the pedal gets released.

Physical architecture. The CCS is composed of four parts (cf. Fig. 2). A *control panel* providing the controls needed to operate the system. An *actuation* that is able to capture the current speed and, once enabled, to adjust the vehicle speed

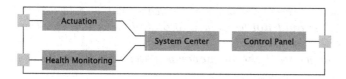

Fig. 2. CCS Physical Architecture

toward the defined target. A *health monitoring* component that detects critical events and relays them to the other components. A *system-center* component that acts as a controller.

The *control panel* provides the buttons needed by the driver to operate the system:

- PowerOn: Turns the system on;
- PowerOff: Turns the system off;
- Set: Capture the current speed of the vehicle as the target speed;
- Resume: Engage the control speed function of the system;
- Disengage: Disengage the control speed function of the system;
- Inc: Increments the current target speed by 5kmh;
- Dec: Decrements the current target speed by 5kmh.

The *control panel* is not responsible for handling those operations. However it should relay them to the *system-center*.

The *actuation* provides the tools for the system to interact with the vehicle. It can capture the current speed of the vehicle and set it as the new target speed. Once the CCS is enabled, the *actuation* is responsible for controlling the vehicle speed accordingly.

The *health monitoring* is responsible for monitoring the system and the vehicle for events that can potentially impact the behavior of the CCS:

- The driver hits the brake pedal (induces disengagement);
- The driver hits the clutch pedal (induces disengagement);
- The speed of the vehicle goes out of bounds (induces disengagement);
- The driver presses the accelerator pedal (pauses the speed control function);
- The driver releases the accelerator pedal (resumes the speed control function);

As for the *control panel*, this component is not responsible of handling the consequences of such events. However, it should relay them to the *system center* which shall handle them.

The *system center* is the "core" of the CCS. It is responsible for handling events detected by both the *control panel* and the *health monitoring* components. To do so, it shall be able to impact the behaviors of all other components.

3.2 Requirements

This section lists three requirements of the CCS system and shows how to model them using the CDL formalism.

REQ₁: **When** *an event inducing a disengagement is detected, the actuation component* **should not** *be allowed to control the vehicle speed* **until** *the system is explicitly resumed.*

REQ₂: *The target speed* **should never** *be lower than 40km/h nor higher than 180km/h.*

REQ₃: **When** *the system is powered off (PowerOff button), the target speed should be reset and be considered unset* **when** *the system is turned on again.*

REQ₁ can be encoded using the observer automaton presented in Fig. 3. To encode this observer using the CDL formalism we first need to introduce the events triggering the transitions.

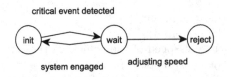

Fig. 3. Observer automaton for *Req₁*

Listing 1. Event declaration in CDL language

```
1   predicate disengageIsRequested is {
2       HealthMonitoring@DisengageRequested }
3
4   event criticalEventDetected is {
5       disengageIsRequested becomes true }
6
7   event systemAdjustingSpeed is {
8       send any from Actuation to Car }
9
10  event systemEngaged is {
11      SystemCenter@Engaged becomes true }
```

In Listing 1, *disengageIsRequested* is a predicate on the HealthMonitoring process returning true if the process is in DisengageRequested state. *disengageIsRequested* **becomes** *true* expresses a rising edge of the predicate, which is an observable event in OBP *Observation Engine*. Thus, the event *criticalEventDetected* expresses that the HealthMonitoring process just entered in DisengageRequested state from a different state. *systemAdjustingSpeed* (lines 7-8) expresses an observable event that triggers when the Actuation process sends any message to the Car process. Since, in our model, the only messages going through this channel are speed adjusting requests it matches an attempt from the actuation to control the speed. Using these events the observer automaton in Fig. 3 is specified in Listing 2.

Listing 2. The observer automaton for REQ₁ in CDL language

```
1   property REQ₁ is {
2       start     — criticalEventDetected –> wait;
3       wait      — systemAdjustingSpeed –> reject;
4       wait      — systemEngaged –> start }
```

REQ₂ can be encoded by declaring a predicate matching this property, see Listing 3 (lines 4-7). Since the requirements need to account for the SUS model, the allowed range for the target speed is extended to $[40..180] \cup \{Unset\}$.

Listing 3. Specifying REQ₂ as a predicate and REQ₃ as an observer automaton using CDL

```
1   predicate targetSpeedIsUnSet is {
2       Actuation@UnSet or Actuation@UnsetSetting }
3
4   predicate REQ₂ is {
5       (Actuation:targetSpeed >= 40
6        and Actuation:targetSpeed <= 180)
7       or  targetSpeedIsUnSet }
8
9   property REQ₃ is {
10      start — (not targetSpeedIsUnSet)
11            ∧ systemTurnsOn –> reject
12  }
```

The REQ₃ encoding is presented in Listing 3 (lines 9-12), and it can be interpreted as: "If the target speed is already set (*not targetSpeedIsUnset*) when the system turns-on (*systemTurnsOn*) the verification fails (*− > reject*)".

3.3   Environment Modeling

In the case of Context-aware Verification, the environment modeling should be seen as a methodological phase that needs to balance two important constraints while building the context. First the context has to cover enough behaviors to be considered valid for a given property. But at the same time it has to be small enough to be possible to exhaustively explore the product of its composition with the SUS. In the case of the CCS the environment, presented in Listing 4, is built from three distinct actors modeling: *a)* a nominal scenario, *b)* a pertubator *c)* and "ticks". The basic scenario can be seen as a linear use case of the CCS that covers all the functionality involved by the properties we aim to verify. The pertubator is a wide alternative including changes of the vehicle speed within the allowed range or not, pressions on the pedals and the panel buttons. The pertubator stresses the SUS against a number of possible unexpected behaviors of the environment. Once these two actors are composed, we get a wide range of variations of the basic scenario using the capabilities of the pertubator at all stages. A "tick" is an event sent to the car to trigger a broadcast of its speed to the involved components in the CCS. In other words, each tick allows the system to "read" the current speed once. The basic scenario we use involves 2 changes of speed, the pertubator can add another, so for the system to be able to react we need at least 3 "ticks". Adding a "tick" allows to see how the system reacts if there is no change of the current speed so it covers more possibilities. While 4 "ticks" is enough, the more "ticks" we add, while still being able to explore the behaviors of the system, the higher the coverage of the possible behaviors. We also use this variable (the number of "ticks") as a way to make the exploration bigger to stress our tools.

Listing 4. Context description and the corresponding LTS representation

```
1   cdl myContext is {
2       properties req1 , req3
3       assert req2
4       init is {
5           evtBtnStart
6       }
7       main is {
8           basic_scenario
9       || pertubator
10      ||
    loop 4 evtTick } }
```

3.4   Verification Results

This section presents the results obtained for the verification of the three requirements previously presented, emphasizing the importance of the Context-aware Verification approach, which through the use of the PastFree[ze] algorithm enabled the analysis of a 2.4 times larger state-space and through the joint use of PastFree[ze] and automatic split technique 4.78 times larger state-space compared to traditional breadth-first search (BFS) reachability algorithms.

The results presented in this study were obtained on a 64 bit Linux computer, with a 3.60GHz Intel Xeon processor, and 64GB RAM memory. We used OBP *Observation Engine* distribution version 1.4.6, which includes an implementation of the PastFree[ze] algorithm[3].

During the exploration, the observer encoding Req_1 reaches its reject state meaning the property is not verified. This happens because of a flaw in the model. Upon receiving a "tick" event, the car broadcasts its current speed to both Actuation and Health Monitoring. Both components will react, the former by sending back an adjusting request, the later by detecting this critical event and by requesting a disengagement. The model should be adjusted so that the Actuation doesn't not attempt to adjust the speed if out of bounds, for example by filtering it first via the Health Monitoring.

---

[3] The raw results presented in this study along with the source files and an OBP *Observation Engine* distribution are available for download on the OBP *Observation Engine* website at http://www.obpcdl.org

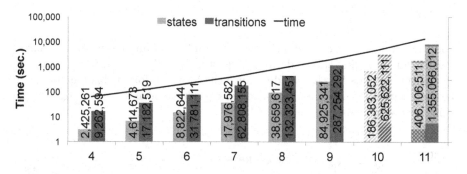

Fig. 4. Exploration results for contexts sending from 4 to 11 ticks

Exploration with BFS Search. Fig. 4 presents the results in terms of states, transitions and exploration time obtained for the CCS model by varying the number of "ticks" sent by the context presented in Listing 4 from 4 to 11. The traditional BFS reachability analysis algorithm failed to explore all the state-space in the case of 10 and 11 ticks.

Exploration with PastFree[ze]. The PastFree[ze] analysis successfully explored the 10 ticks case obtaining state-space 2.2 times larger than the 9 tick case. However with the 64GB memory limit this technique failed to finish the exploration for 11 ticks. The results shown in Fig. 4 for the 11 ticks case were obtained on a computer with 128GB memory and were included just as a reference for better understanding the advantages of the automatic-split state-space decomposition presented in the following paragraph.

Exploration with Splitting. To verify the three requirements for the 11 tick context we used the automatic-split technique which produced 9 sub-contexts which have been independently analysed by the OBP *Observation Engine* with the PastFree[ze] algorithm. The results of these explorations are presented in Fig. 5. It should be noted that in this case the traditional BFS algorithm would have failed to explore at least 3 of the obtained sub-contexts (the 1st, 2nd and 9th one) hence needing another split step for these cases, which was not needed for the PastFree[ze] technique. Another important observation is that while with the automatic-split technique the state-space was decomposed in 9 partitions these partitions are not disjoint. Hence their exploration analysed 779 739 813 states and 2 611 647 510 transitions which represents the analysis of 1.92 times more states and 1.93 more transitions than the exact state-space presented in Fig. 4 (the 11 ticks bars). Nevertheless, we believe that this is a small price to pay for the possibility of analysing a 4.78 times larger state-space without the need of doubling the physical memory of the machine.

4   Related Work

Model checking is a technique that relies on building a finite model of a system of interest, and checking that a desired property, typically specified as a temporal logic formula, holds for that model. Since the introduction of this technology in the early 1980s [17], several model-checker tools have been developed to help the verification of concurrent systems [14,1].

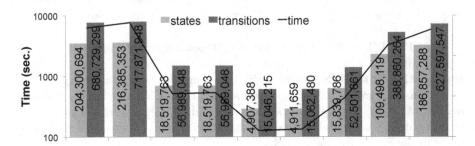

Fig. 5. Results for the analysis of the 9 partitions of the 11 tick context

However, while model-checking provides an automated rigorous framework for formal system validation and verification, and has successfully been applied on industrial systems it suffers from the state-space explosion problem. This is due to the exponential growth of the number of states the system can reach with respect to the number of interacting components. Since its introduction, model checking has progressed significantly, with numerous research efforts focused on reducing the impact of this problem, thus enabling the verification of ever larger systems. Some of these approaches focus on the use of efficient data-structures such as BDD [3] for achieving compact state-space representation, others rely on algorithmic advancements and the maximal use of the available resources such as external memories [10]. To prune the state-space, techniques such as partial-order reduction [13,16,19,13] and symmetry reduction [7] exploit fine-grain transition interleaving symmetries and global system symmetries respectively. Yet other approaches, like bounded model-checking [4] exploit the observation that in many practical settings the property verification can be done with only a partial (bounded) reachability analysis.

The successful application of these methods to several case studies (see for instance [2] for aerospace examples) demonstrates their maturity in the case of synchronous embedded systems. However, even though these techniques push the limits of model-checking ever further, the state-space explosion problem remains especially in the case of large and complex asynchronous systems.

Besides the previously cited techniques that approach the property verification problem monolithically, compositional verification [12] focus on the analysis of individual components of the system using assume/guarantee reasoning (or design-by-contract) to extract (sometimes automatically) the interactions that a component has with its environment and to reduce the model-checking problem to these interactions. Once each individual component is proved correct the composition is performed using operators that preserve the correctness.

Our approach can be seen as a coarse-grain compositional verification, where instead of analyzing the interactions of individual components with their neighboring environment we focus on the interactions of the whole system with its surrounding environment (context). Conversely to "traditional" techniques in which the surrounding environment is often implicitly modeled in the system (to obtain a closed system), we explicitly describe it separately from the model. By explicitly modeling the environment as one (or more) formally defined context(s) and composing it with the system-under-study we can conduct the full system verification.

5 Conclusion and Perspectives

In this paper we have used the Context-aware Verification technique for the analysis of three requirements of a Cruise-control System. The asynchrony of this system renders traditional model-checking approaches almost impossible. Using the environment reification through the CDL formalism this task becomes manageable by relying on two powerful optimisation strategies. These strategies rely on the structural properties of the CDL contexts and enable the reachability analysis of orders of magnitude larger models.

While the approach presented in this paper offers promising results, for this technique to be used on industrial-scale critical systems, we are currently working on a sound methodological framework that formalizes the context coverage with respect to the full-system behavior and assist the user on initial context specification.

References

1. Bengtsson, J., Larsen, K.G., Larsson, F., Pettersson, P., Yi, W.: UPPAAL — a Tool Suite for Automatic Verification of Real–Time Systems. In: Alur, R., Sontag, E.D., Henzinger, T.A. (eds.) HS 1995. LNCS, vol. 1066, pp. 232–243. Springer, Heidelberg (1996)
2. Boniol, F., Wiels, V., Ledinot, E.: Experiences using model checking to verify real time properties of a landing gear control system. In: Embedded Real-Time Systems (ERTS), Toulouse, France (2006)
3. Burch, J.R., Clarke, E.M., McMillan, K.L., Dill, D.L., Hwang, L.J.: Symbolic model checking: 10^{20} states and beyond. In: 5th IEEE Symposium on Logic in Computer Science, pp. 428–439 (1990)
4. Clarke, E., Biere, A., Raimi, R., Zhu, Y.: Bounded model checking using satisfiability solving. Formal Methods in System Design 19(1), 7–34 (2001)
5. Clarke, E., Emerson, E.A.: Design and synthesis of synchronization skeletons using branching time temporal logic. In: Kozen, D. (ed.) Logic of Programs 1981. LNCS, vol. 131, pp. 52–71. Springer, Heidelberg (1982),
http://dx.doi.org/10.1007/BFb0025774

6. Clarke, E., Emerson, E., Sistla, A.: Automatic verification of finite-state concurrent systems using temporal logic specifications. ACM Trans. Program. Lang. Syst. 8(2), 244–263 (1986)
7. Clarke, E., Enders, R., Filkorn, T., Jha, S.: Exploiting symmetry in temporal logic model checking. Formal Methods in System Design 9(1-2), 77–104 (1996)
8. Dhaussy, P., Boniol, F., Roger, J.C.: Reducing state explosion with context modeling for model-checking. In: 13th IEEE International High Assurance Systems Engineering Symposium (Hase 2011), Boca Raton, USA (2011)
9. Dhaussy, P., Boniol, F., Roger, J.C., Leroux, L.: Improving model checking with context modelling. Advances in Software Engineering ID 547157, 13 pages (2012)
10. Edelkamp, S., Sanders, P., Šimeček, P.: Semi-external LTL model checking. In: Gupta, A., Malik, S. (eds.) CAV 2008. LNCS, vol. 5123, pp. 530–542. Springer, Heidelberg (2008)
11. Farail, P., Gaufillet, P., Peres, F., Bodeveix, J.P., Filali, M., Berthomieu, B., Rodrigo, S., Vernadat, F., Garavel, H., Lang, F.: FIACRE: an intermediate language for model verification in the TOPCASED environment. In: European Congress on Embedded Real-Time Software (ERTS). SEE, Toulouse (January 2008)
12. Flanagan, C., Qadeer, S.: Thread-modular model checking. In: Ball, T., Rajamani, S.K. (eds.) SPIN 2003. LNCS, vol. 2648, pp. 213–224. Springer, Heidelberg (2003)
13. Godefroid, P.: The Ulg partial-order package for SPIN. In: SPIN Workshop (1995)
14. Holzmann, G.: The model checker SPIN. Software Engineering 23(5), 279–295 (1997)
15. Park, S., Kwon, G.: Avoidance of state explosion using dependency analysis in model checking control flow model. In: Gavrilova, M.L., Gervasi, O., Kumar, V., Tan, C.J.K., Taniar, D., Laganá, A., Mun, Y., Choo, H. (eds.) ICCSA 2006. LNCS, vol. 3984, pp. 905–911. Springer, Heidelberg (2006)
16. Peled, D.: Combining Partial-Order Reductions with On-the-fly Model-Checking. In: Dill, D.L. (ed.) CAV 1994. LNCS, vol. 818, pp. 377–390. Springer, Heidelberg (1994)
17. Queille, J.P., Sifakis, J.: Specification and verification of concurrent systems in cesar. In: Proceedings of the 5th Colloquium on International Symposium on Programming, pp. 337–351. Springer, London (1982)
18. Teodorov, C., Leroux, L., Dhaussy, P.: Past-free reachability analysis. reaching further with DAG-directed exhaustive state-space analysis. (submitted to) 29th IEEE/ACM International Conference on Automated Software Engineering (2014)
19. Valmari, A.: Stubborn sets for reduced state space generation. In: Rozenberg, G. (ed.) APN 1990. LNCS, vol. 483, pp. 491–515. Springer, Heidelberg (1991)

A Multi-Agent Based Approach for Composite Web Services Simulation

Fatma Siala[1], Idir Ait-Sadoune[2], and Khaled Ghedira[1]

[1] SOIE - ISG, University of Tunis, Tunis, Tunisia
[2] SUPELEC, Computer Science Department, Gif-Sur-Yvette, France
fatma.siala@gnet.tn, idir.aitsadoune@supelec.fr,
khaled.ghedira@isg.rnu.tn

Abstract. The Web service composition can be defined as the process of combining existing services to produce new ones. Indeed, composition to develop higher-level services, so-called composite services, by re-using existing services is Service Oriented Architectures (SOA) core capability. For this purpose, languages such as BPEL and platforms like the orchestration engine appeared for the specification and the implementation of service compositions. However, the expressiveness of these languages deals only with functional compositions and does not take into account the composite Web services properties validation and the tools associated to these languages do not support simulation of behavioural requirements.

Our contribution consists in using software agents to provide a simulation tool to BPEL, to observe agents behaviours and to evaluate properties. Simulation plays an important role by exploring "what-if" questions during the process composition phase. The proposed approach is implemented using JADE platform.

Keywords: Web services, Multi-Agent System, simulation, BPEL, JADE.

1 Introduction

Service-Oriented Architecture (SOA) consists of a set of design principles which enables defining and composing inter-operable services in a loosely coupled way. The value of SOA lies in ensuring that such compositions are easily and rapidly feasible with low costs. Thus, service composition is a key issue of SOA [14]. For this purpose, approaches [9] and languages such as BPEL (Business Process Execution Language) [3] appeared for the specification and the implementation of service compositions. However, their expressiveness doesn't take into account the relevant properties and the tools associated to this language doesn't support simulation of behavioral requirements. We have noticed that various problems related to Web services composition can occur, such as non-receipt of messages, concurrence and reaching deadlock freeness [15]. Indeed, since it is very expensive to modify compositions of Web services that have been deployed. It is desirable to have methods for the simulation of a composite Web service in the early design phases of the Web services composition design process.

Y. Ait Ameur et al. (Eds.): MEDI 2014, LNCS 8748, pp. 65–76, 2014.

Miller et al. [4] cite that simulation plays an important role by exploring "what-if" questions during the process composition phase. Their work on Workflows and simulation enables them to perceive how simulation can serve as a tool for the Web process composition problem. Moreover, well tested simulation models may be placed on the Web for others to use.

Our approach is based on Multi-Agent Systems (MAS) [6]. This technology handles simulations [8]. Based on the description of the W3C consortium: *"A Web service is an abstract notion that must be implemented by a concrete agent. The agent is the concrete piece of software or hardware that sends and receives messages"*. We claim that the behaviour of Web services composition can be operationalized as a MAS systems [16]. Indeed, while both approaches involve the exchange of messages, an agent based architecture will clearly introduce an enhanced level of interaction between Web services.

We propose in this paper, an approach based on BPEL as a service composition description language and MAS for modelling and for simulating Web services behaviours. Our contribution consists of simulating a Web service composition to observe the different exchanged messages and to detect the non acceptable behaviours due to contract and/or conditions violations, with evaluating properties (like deadlock, livelock and correct transformation of data). This simulation is based on MAS. Agents allow us to have a scenario close to reality avoiding execution of the real process (the BPEL). We propose several transformation rules of the BPEL constructs to a corresponding agent code, particularly by using the JADE (Java Agent DEvelopment) framework [7]. This framework supports agents negotiations and simulation.

This paper is structured as follows. The next section presents BPEL language, MAS system and JADE framework, section 3 proposes a complete set of transformation rules of BPEL constructs into MAS codes. Section 4 clarifies our approach by applying the proposed rules to a full case study. Section 5 presents an overview of the observation of Web services properties by simulation. Accordingly, section 6 presents a comparison with the major related work. Finally, we conclude the paper.

2   Definitions

Overview of BPEL. BPEL [3] is a standardized language for specifying the behaviour of a business process based on interactions between a process and its service partners. It defines how multiple service interactions, between these partners, are coordinated to achieve a given goal. Each service offered by a partner is described in a WSDL document through a set of operations and of handled messages.

A BPEL process uses a set of variables to represent the messages exchanged between partners. The content of these messages is amended by a set of activities which represent the process flow. BPEL offers two categories of activities: 1) simple activities representing the primitive operations performed by the process (invoke, receive, reply, assign, terminate, wait and empty activities) 2) and, structured activities obtained by composing primitive activities and/or other structured activities using the sequence, if, while and repeat Until composition operators that model traditional sequential control constructs, and The flow operator defining the concurrent execution.

The examples used in the following sections are based on the well-known case study of the Purchase Order BPEL specification [3]. Figure 1 shows a graphical representation of BPEL and describes how the *Purchase_Order_Process* is defined by a sequence of *Receive_Order*, *Purchase_Order_Processing* and *Reply_Invoice* activities. *Purchase_Order_Processing* is itself decomposed to three paths : *Production_Scheduling*, *Compute_Price* and *Arrange_Logistics* sub-processes. On receiving the purchase order from a customer, the process initiates the three paths concurrently. When these concurrent paths are completed, invoice processing can proceed and the invoice is sent to the customer.

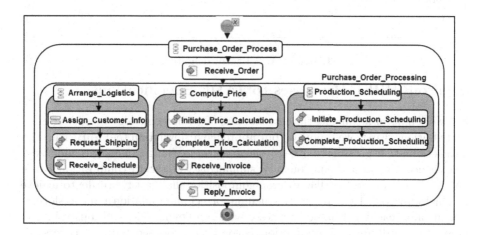

Fig. 1. BPEL representation of Purchase Order Process

Multi-Agent Systems (MAS). Since their introduction in the 80's, Multi-Agent Systems (MAS) [6] have been considered as "societies of agents". These societies are represented as a set of agents that interact together to coordinate their behaviours and often cooperate to achieve a given collective goal. Indeed, MAS focus on the level of the states of an agent and of the relation between these states and its overall behaviour. In this view, communications are seen as speech acts whose meaning may be described in terms of the mental states of an agent. The development of communication languages such as KQML (Knowledge Query and Manipulation Language)[1] and FIPA ACL (Agent Communication Language)[2] follows directly from this frame of mind. In order to make MAS ready for industrial applications, FIPA has proposed a set of standards[3] that designers should meet to make their MAS compatible with other systems.

---

[1] http://www.cs.umbc.edu/csee/research/kqml/

[2] http://www.fipa.org/repository/aclspecs.html

[3] http://www.fipa.org/repository/standardspecs.html

The JADE Platform. JADE (Java Agent DEvelopment) [7] is a software framework fully implemented in Java language. It simplifies the implementation of MAS through a middleware that complies with the FIPA specifications and through a set of graphical tools that supports the debugging and deployment phases. The agent platform can be distributed across machines and the configuration can be controlled via a remote GUI (Graphical User Interface). The configuration can be even changed at run-time by moving agents from one machine to another when required.

In JADE framework, an agent is defined by a Java class that extends Agent class (Listing 1.1). The behaviour of the defined agent is detailed in a method named setup.

```
public class sampleAgent extends Agent {
    ...
    public void setup(){
        ...
    }
}
```

Listing 1.1. An agent definition

3   From BPEL Processes to JADE Specifications

Our work aims at advancing the current state of art in technology by adding three contributions. First, we report on our approach a simulation tool to BPEL. The idea is to make it possible to observe the different exchanged messages and to detect the non acceptable behaviours. By simulating Web service composition we are able to observe properties that a service composition shall satisfy in order to achieve its functional goal. These properties include correct manipulation and transformation of data, reaching deadlock freeness, liveness, obeying rules and constraints on interactions ordering and termination. Second, the proposed approach covers different static and dynamic parts of BPEL specification and can be generalized to the all constructs of this specification. Finally, error tracing is considered.

The translation of a BPEL description to JADE specifications is managed by the BPEL process structure. Each BPEL element is represented by its corresponding element in JADE. The transformation of a BPEL description into JADE code has two parts : static and dynamic. The first part concerns the content of the various WSDL files that include definitions of data types, messages and profiles of operations used by Web services participants. This part is encoded into Java classes. The second part concerns the content of the BPEL file with the definition of the BPEL process state and its behaviour. This part is encoded by agents. The process associated to these two parts is presented in the following subsections.

3.1   JADE Translation of the BPEL Static Part
A WSDL specification usually contains the declaration of data types, messages, port types (the profile of supported operations), bindings and services. Since a BPEL process references only the messages and the operations of the port types, solely the rules for encoding these elements in JADE are defined.

1- The different exchanged messages are declared in the *message* element. In JADE, a *message* is encoded by a Java class. Each *part* of the message, is declared as an attribute having the same type. For example, the *POMessage* message of Listing 1.2 is encoded by a *POMessage* Java class. The *customerInfo* and *purchaseOrder* elements are represented by attributes in the *POMessage* class having respectively *customerInfoType* and *purchaseOrderType* types (Listing 1.3).

```
<wsdl:message name="POMessage">
  <wsdl:part name="customerInfo" type="sns:customerInfoType"/>
  <wsdl:part name="purchaseOrder" type="sns:purchaseOrderType"/>
</wsdl:message>
```

Listing 1.2. Representation of a message in BPEL

```
class POMessage{
   CustomerInfoType customerInfo;
   PurchaseOrderType purchaseOrder ;
   // Constructor
   public POMessage(CustomerInfoType ci, PurchaseOrderType po) {
      this.customerInfo = ci;
      this.purchaseOrder = po;
   }
}
```

Listing 1.3. Translation of a message in JADE

2- The different services operations of each partner are declared in the *portType* element that contains a set of *operation* elements. An *operation* describes the published interface (input and output parameters types) of the partner Web service. In JADE, a *portType* is encoded by a Java class and an *operation* by a Java "static method"[4]. As an example, the *purchaseOrderPT portType* containing the *sendPurchaseOrder operation* (Listing 1.4), is encoded in JADE by the *purchaseOrderPT* Java class containing a method named *sendPurchaseOrder* having the same input and output parameters types (Listing 1.5).

```
<wsdl:portType name="purchaseOrderPT">
  <wsdl:operation name="sendPurchaseOrder">
    <wsdl:input message="pos:POMessage" />
    <wsdl:output message="pos:InvMessage" />
  </wsdl:operation>
</wsdl:portType>
```

Listing 1.4. Example of an operation in BPEL

```
class purchaseOrderPT {
   public static InvMessage sendPurchaseOrder (POMessage input) {
      InvMessage output;
      //initiatePriceCalculation method's code
      return output ;
   }
}
```

Listing 1.5. Translation of an operation in JADE

---

[4] Static Method definition:
  http://docs.oracle.com/javase/specs/jls/se7/html/jls-8.html#jls-8.4.3.2

3.2   JADE Translation of the BPEL Dynamic Part

This section addresses the description of the dynamic part of a BPEL process definition. The JADE description process is inductively defined on the structure of the BPEL definition. All BPEL variables are encoded as attributes in a Java class and correspond to a state of an agent, and each BPEL activity becomes an agent of the MAS system. The following rules are set-up.

1- A Java class named *BPELState* is created and all BPEL *variable* elements are represented by "static attributes"[5] declarations in the *BPELState* class. These attributes are typed using the same type of the BPEL variables. For example, in Listing 1.6, the variable named *PO* of the BPEL specification that have as type the *POMessage* message, is encoded in the JADE specification by the *PO* attribute of the *BPELState* class (Listing 1.7).

```
<variables>
    <variable name="PO" messageType="POMessage"/>
    <variable name="Invoice" messageType="InvMessage"/>
    <variable name="shippingRequest"
        messageType="shippingRequestMessage"/>
    <variable name="shippingInfo" messageType="shippingInfoMessage"/>
    <variable name="shippingSchedule" messageType="scheduleMessage"/>
</variables>
```

Listing 1.6. Example of variables in BPEL

```
public class BPELState {
    static POMessage PO;
    static InvMessage Invoice;
    static shippingRequestMessage  shippingRequest;
    static shippingInfoMessage  shippingInfo;
    static scheduleMessage shippingSchedule;
}
```

Listing 1.7. Translation of variables in JADE

2- There are three classes of BPEL simple activities. The activities related to the communication with Web services (invoke, receive, reply), the activities related to the data manipulation (assignment and modification of a variable content) and the control activities (wait, empty, exit). Due to space limitation we will only explain one simple activity which represents the communication with Web services (*invoke* activity).

Each simple activity is encoded by an agent as described in the listing 1.1. Listing 1.9 presents a JADE implementation of an invoke activity defined in Listing 1.8. This activity invokes a Web service defined by *initiatePriceCalculation* operation. This activity is encoded in an agent named *initiatePriceCalculation-Agent* that calls the *ComputePricePT.initiatePriceCalculation* method having *BPELState.PO* as an input variable.

---

[5] Static Field definition:
   http://docs.oracle.com/javase/specs/jls/se7/html/jls-8.html#jls-8.3.1.1

```
<invoke name="initiatePriceCalculation" partnerLink="invoicing"
    portType="lns:computePricePT"
    operation="initiatePriceCalculation" inputVariable="PO" />
```

Listing 1.8. Example of an invoke activity in BPEL

```
public class initiatePriceCalculationAgent extends Agent {
    public void setup(){
        ComputePricePT.initiatePriceCalculation(BPELState.PO);
        ...
    }
}
```

Listing 1.9. Translation of an invoke activity in JADE

3- Each BPEL structured activity (flow, sequence, for each, if then else) can be encoded in different ways by combining the behaviours of the involved agents. In the case of the *sequence* activity that activates A_1 and A_2 activities in sequence, the agent corresponding to the A_1 activity creates and starts its successor agent corresponding to the A_2 activity after executing its own behaviour. For example, in the listing 1.10, the two activities *initiatePriceCalculation* and *sendShipping-Price* are activated in sequence order. In JADE, the code of the *initiatePrice-CalculationAgent* agent, given in listing 1.9, is completed at the end by a Java code that allows the creation and the starting of the *sendShippingPriceAgent* agent (Listings 1.11).

```
<sequence name="ComputePrice">
    <invoke name="initiatePriceCalculation" .../>
    <invoke name="sendShippingPrice" .../>
    ...
</sequence>
```

Listing 1.10. A sequence of BPEL activities

```
public class initiatePriceCalculationAgent extends Agent{
    public void setup() {
        ...
        AgentContainer c = (AgentContainer)getContainerController();
        AgentController ac = c.createNewAgent("sendShippingPriceAgent",
            "sendShippingPriceAgent", null);
        ac.start();
    }
}
```

Listing 1.11. The *initiatePriceCalculationAgent*

Let us consider the *flow* activity as the parallel activation of A_1 and A_2 activities. In JADE, the agent that encodes the *flow* activity creates two agents corresponding to the A_1 and A_2 activities and starts them in an indifferent order. JADE framework manages A_1 and A_2 agents as two Java threads and executes them in parallel.

4   Application to the Case Study

This section addresses the Multi-Agents System obtained from the case study presented on Figure 1. After encoding the *PurchaseOrder* BPEL process into JADE,

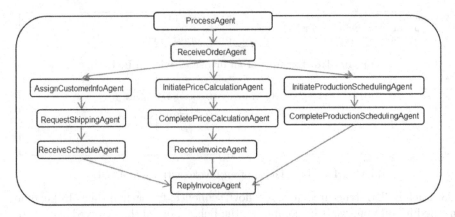

Fig. 2. The MAS representation of Purchase Order Process

we obtain the following structure (Figure 2): the *ProcessAgent* is the main agent, it creates and starts the *ReceiveOrderAgent* agent; the *ReceiveOrderAgent* agent receives the purchase order from a customer and creates three agents (*InitiatePrice-CalculationAgent, AssignCustomerInfoAgent,* and *InitiateProductionSchedulingAgent*) and starts them in parallel; *InitiatePriceCalculationAgent* agent and its successors agents calculate the final price for the order, *AssignCustomerInfoAgent* and its successors agents select a shipper, and *InitiateProductionSchedulingAgent* and its successors agents schedule the production and shipment for the order; When the three concurrent paths are completed, *ReplyInvoiceAgent* agent is created and started to send the invoice to the customer.

5   Validation of Web Services' Properties by Simulation

When the MAS system corresponding to the BPEL description is obtained, we can simulate and observe the behaviour of the described composed Web service with the JADE framework. By simulation, we can observe the different exchanged messages and detect the non acceptable behaviour. More precisely, regarding the simulation process, our contribution is summarized in the following points.

5.1   Correct Manipulation of Data

Since we have encoded data type and messages manipulated by the BPEL process in the MAS system, we can observe if these messages are correctly manipulated. In the case of the *PurchaseOrder* process described on the figure 1, the simulation helped us to detect errors in the BPEL description.

The *completeProductionScheduleAgent* agent (Listing 1.12) encodes an *invoke* activity that calls the *sendShippingSchedule* Web service using the *shippingSchedule* message. This message is initially empty (null), and when we look at the BPEL description, we find that this message is initialised by the *ReceiveSchedule* activity encoded by the *ReceiveScheduleAgent* agent. Notice that the *completeProductionScheduleAgent* agent and the *ReceiveScheduleAgent*

agent are executed in parallel. The simulation of the obtained MAS system causes a null pointer error on the *processState.shippingSchedule* variable because the *completeProductionScheduleAgent* agent was executed before *ReceiveScheduleAgent* agent (this scenario is possible). Thus, in the side of the BPEL description, the order of executing *completeProductionSchedule* and *ReceiveSchedule* activities must be corrected.

```
public class completeProductionScheduleAgent extends Agent {
    public void setup(){
        schedulingPT.sendShippingSchedule(processState.shippingSchedule);
        ...
    }
}
```

Listing 1.12. Beginning of the *completeProductionScheduleAgent* code

5.2 Error Tracing

As shown in the previous section, the simulation of the MAS system helps us to observe the different exchanged messages and to detect the non acceptable behaviours. In the case of an undesired behaviour, the BPEL elements that cause this behaviour can be found and corrected.

For example, in the previous section we have detected that the order of executing the *completeProductionScheduleAgent* agent and the *ReceiveScheduleAgent* agent causes a null pointer error and the order of executing *completeProductionSchedule* and *ReceiveSchedule* BPEL activities must be corrected. Because *completeProductionSchedule* and *ReceiveSchedule* activities are executed in parallel, we can synchronise them by using the *link* BPEL element that defines dependency between the two activities. This defines an execution order between the two activities. This synchronisation is shown as an arrow between the two activities in Figure 3.

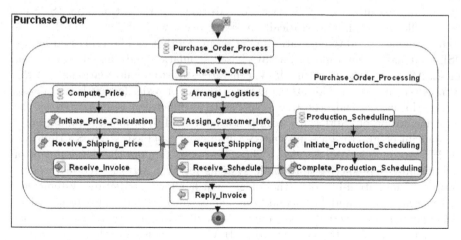

Fig. 3. BPEL representation of a corrected Purchase Order Process

5.3 Observation of Live-Lock and Deadlock Behaviours

When we simulate the obtained MAS system, we can observe some undesired behaviours like live-lock and deadlock. The deadlock freeness property expresses that a BPEL process never stops during its execution and the no live-lock property expresses that there is no BPEL activity that takes control indefinitely.

If we observe during simulation that the behaviour of the MAS system does not progress, it has not reached its final state, and there is no agents that run, we can conclude that it's possible that the BPEL process comes to a deadlock. In the same manner, if we observe that the behaviour of the MAS system does not progress and there is an agent or a set of agents that runs indefinitely, we can conclude that it's possible that the BPEL process live-locks.

Notice that if we do not observe any undesired behaviours, we cannot conclude that there is no errors in the BPEL process description because we cannot simulate all the possible scenarios. In this case, we can use a formal method to validate a Web services composition as in [1].

6 Comparison with Related Work

Several research efforts have adopted simulation as a testing technique for analysing the efficiency of composite Web services.

Narayanan et McIlraith [12] have proposed a model-theoretic semantics as well as distributed operational semantics that can be used for simulation, validation, verification, automated composition and enactment of DAML-S [2]. To provide a fully service description, Narayanan and McIlraith use the machinery of situation calculus and its execution behaviour described with Petri Nets. They use the simulation and modeling environment KarmaSIM [11] to translate DAML-S markups to situation calculus and Petri Nets. This work is only interested to the semantic aspect of Web services.

Use of simulation for Web services is described also by Chandrasekaran et al. [4]. This work focused on problems related to Web service specification, evaluation and execution using Service Composition and Execution Tool (SCET). SCET allows to compose statically a WS process with WSFL (Web Services Flow Language) and to generate simulation model that can be processed by the JSIM simulation environment, a Java-based simulation and animation environment. After its simulation run, JSIM generates statistical information about the completed simulation. This statistical information provides feedback on the process performance. Only the QoS response time dimension is supported by the implementation of JSIM. This work is not interested to properties validation.

Mancini et al. [10] have presented a framework, named MAWeS (MetaPL/ HeSSE Autonomic Web Services) whose aim is to support the development of self-optimizing predictive autonomic systems for Web service architectures. It adopts a simulation-based methodology, which allows predicting system QoS in different status and load conditions. These authors have also proposed in [13] a general architecture of a framework for SLA management identifying the requirements implied by the simulation. However, in this case, their approach is adopted to cloud.

Driss et al. [5] have proposed a simulation approach which assures the evaluation of composite Web services performance under different context status. They have adopted a discrete-events simulation to test and verify Web services compositions. They have introduced a modeling approach for composite Web services. This approach enables analytical description of composite Web services and allows QoS predictions in different status and conditions of the execution context.

All these cited works are not interested to static part of composition and do not consider properties validation. Our work consists in using an agent based semantics to validate a Web service composition and to observe behaviours.

Our work includes four contributions. First, it is based on agents' simulation. In fact, observing composite Web service properties' using an agent at each service does not only suggest improvements to the BPEL artifact under test, but also points to reliability improvements in each service being simulated. Agents allow us to simulate and / or animate our model. Therefore, we are able to visualize the attitude of execution paths, particularly of the selected composite Web services. Based on simulation, we obtain a scenario that is close to reality without executing the real process (the BPEL).

Second, we are able to observe undesirable behaviours, to observe the exchanged messages, and to ensure correct manipulation of data. The correct transformation of data is not considered by the other approaches. Third, it covers different static and dynamic BPEL language parts and can be generalized to the all constructs of the BPEL specification. Finally, it addresses the error tracing.

7 Conclusion

In this paper, we have presented agent based models for Web services compositions simulation implemented with the JADE framework. We have used BPEL as Web services description language and defined a set of translation rules to encode BPEL constructs with JADE. So, the obtained MAS system and the JADE framework provide a simulation tool to the BPEL process. The simple Web services, manipulated messages, and the behaviour of the composed Web service described with BPEL are respectively encoded within Java classes and agents. Moreover, the simulation process allows us to observe undesirable behaviours and the exchanged messages, and to ensure correct manipulation of data. Our approach is implemented and applied on the well-known case study of the Purchase Order. We conclude that simulating a Web service composition using an agent behaviour at each service does not only improve the BPEL artefact under test, but also points to reliability improvements in each service being simulated by an agent.

In the future, this work can be pursued in five main directions. The first one is related to propose a new tool BPEL2JADE that automatizes the implementation of the translation process from BPEL to JADE. The second direction concerns the investigation of QoS properties and others that are relevant to the services compositions' definitions like transaction-based properties. The third direction is devoted to the generalization of our approach by applying it in another area such as teleconferencing, where there are emerging properties. Finally, since our approach observe properties, the fourth direction is interested to complete it with a formal method for the verification of the observed properties.

References

1. Aït-Sadoune, I., Ameur, Y.A.: A proof based approach for modeling and verifying-web services compositions. In: ICECCS, pp. 1–10 (2009)
2. Ankolekar, A., Burstein, M.H., Hobbs, J.R., Lassila, O., Martin, D.L., McIlraith, S.A., Narayanan, S., Paolucci, M., Payne, T.R., Sycara, K.P., Zeng, H.: Daml-s: Semantic markup for web services. In: The Emerging Semantic Web (2001)
3. BPEL. Business process execution language (2007), http://docs.oasisopen.org/wsbpel/2.0/OS/wsbpel-v2.0-OS.html
4. Chandrasekaran, S., Miller, J.A., Silver, G.A., Arpinar, I.B., Sheth, A.P.: Performance analysis and simulation of composite web services. Electronic Markets 13(2) (2003)
5. Driss, M., Jamoussi, Y., Jézéquel, J.-M., Ghézala, H.H.B.: A discrete-events simulation approach for evaluation of service-based applications. In: ECOWS, pp. 73–78 (2008)
6. Ferber, J.: Les systmes multi-agents. vers une intelligence collective. In: Inter Editions (1995)
7. JADE. Java agent development framework (2011), http://sharon.cselt.it/projects/jade/
8. Lajmi, S., Ghedira, C., Ghédira, K., Benslimane, D.: Wescocbr: How to compose web services via case based reasoning. In: ICEBE, pp. 618–622 (2006)
9. Mancini, E., Villano, U., Rak, M., Torella, R.: A simulation-based framework for autonomic web services. In: ICPADS (2), pp. 433–437 (2005)
10. Narayanan, S.: KARMA: Knowledge-based Action Representations for Metaphor and Aspect. University of California, Berkeley. thesis (1997)
11. Narayanan, S., McIlraith, S.A.: Simulation, verification and automated composition of web services. In: WWW, pp. 77–88 (2002)
12. Rak, M., Cuomo, A., Villano, U.: A proposal of a simulation-based approach for service level agreement in cloud. In: AINA Workshops, pp. 1235–1240 (2013)
13. Siala, F., Ghedira, K.: How to select dynamically a QoS-driven composite web service by a multi-agent system using CBR method. International Journal of Wireless and Mobile Computing, u- and e-Service, Science and Technology 7(4) (2014)
14. ter Beek, M.H., Bucchiarone, A., Gnesi, S.: Web service composition approaches: From industrial standards to formal methods. In: ICIW, p. 15 (2007)
15. Wan, W., Bentahar, J., Hamza, A.B.: Modeling and verifying agent-based communities of web services. In: IEA/AIE, pp. 418–427 (2010)
16. Wooldridge, M.J.: Introduction to multiagent systems. Wiley (2002)

Model-Driven Generation of Multi-user and Multi-domain Choreographies for Staging in Multiple Virtual World Platforms

Emanuel Silva[1,2], Nuno Silva[1], and Leonel Morgado[3]

[1] School of Engineering, Polytechnic of Porto, Porto, Portugal
[2] University of Trás-os-Montes e Alto Douro, Vila Real, Portugal
{ecs,nps}@isep.ipp.pt
[3] INESC TEC (formerly INESC Porto) / Universidade Aberta, Lisbon, Portugal
leonel.morgado@uab.pt

Abstract. This paper presents an approach that enables the staging of choreographies for education and training purposes in multiple virtual world platforms. Choreography is the description of a set of actions that must or may be executed by a group of participants, including the goals to be achieved and any restrictions that may exist. For capturing and representing multi-actor multi-domain choreographies an approach based on ontologies with distinct levels of abstraction is adopted. Further, this paper proposes a modelling driven approach and a set of processes that, through mappings between ontologies, enable the automatic construction of a platform-specific choreography from a platform-independent one, thus reducing the time and effort of the choreography development. For this, the MDA paradigm was adopted and adapted in a way where models can reflect two dimensions of independence: platform independence and application domain independence. We also point the guidelines for staging the choreography in a virtual world platform.

Keywords: virtual worlds, training, choreography, multi-user, model-driven, ontology, mapping, transformation.

1   Introduction

Virtual worlds have achieved significant levels of interest for supporting teaching and learning activities [1], [2] since they provide educators with tools for creation of immersive environments where multiple characters together can develop skills in a simulated context sharing a common virtual space [3], [4]. Choreographies of virtual actors are a specific type of content that represent the set of actions that can be performed simultaneously by human-users and virtual computer-controlled actors thus enabling human trainees/students to play roles as part of teams or within a simulated social context. In this sense, a choreography is the description of a set of actions that must or may be executed by a group of participants, including the goals to be achieved and any restrictions that may exist.

Y. Ait Ameur et al. (Eds.): MEDI 2014, LNCS 8748, pp. 77–91, 2014.

Designing a choreography is a resource-intensive effort so, it is important that the result will not stay tied to a specific virtual world platform (VWP) but available to be applied on any VWP. However, as virtual platforms are very heterogeneous in terms of (e.g.) functionalities, data models, execution engines and programming/scripting languages or APIs, deploying a platform-based choreography into another VWP is difficult and time-consuming [5]–[8].

In this paper we present an approach that provides a contribution that facilitates the development, sharing and generation of choreographies aimed to be staged in different virtual platforms. For this, we suggest an approach where the conceptual representation model of the choreography is captured in the form of ontologies, and its adaptation to a particular virtual world follows a set of model transformation processes, similar to that suggested by the Model Driven Architecture (MDA) paradigm [9]. The proposed ontology-based definition of choreographies can capture not only the physical aspects as objects but more complex content such as procedures, consisting of sets of actions and conditions in which the actors can perform them.

Thus, this paper presents an approach that deals with the representation of platform-independent multi-user choreographies, and their deployment to different VWPs using a set of transformation processes based on ontologies and alignments. The rest of the paper comprehends six more sections. In section 2 the work related with our ideas is described. In section 3 we present the background knowledge necessary to understand better the transformation process. In Section 4 is described how to transform a choreography to a specific VWP and the corresponding algorithm is presented. Further, a validation of the choreography's feasibility is proposed. In section 5 aspects related to the execution of the choreography are described. Section 6 describes the developed experiments. Finally, Section 7 summarizes our ideas and suggests future directions.

2   Related Work

In the literature there is relevant work addressing the description of plans to represent training procedures to be staged by a single actor or by several elements, and how actions are distributed among them. However, most approaches design a choreography to be staged on a particular VWP. This creates strong dependencies with this VWP, making it difficult or even impossible to apply to other virtual worlds. Thus, related work can be categorized according to three dimensions: modeling independence, VWP independence and number and type of the actors.

Some approaches use separate models to represent the specification of procedures and scene [7], [10], [11]. They address team training scenarios but they are strongly dependent on the characteristics of the VWP. Some other approaches attempt to bridge the gap between the representation of procedures and its execution in distinct VWP. However, such approaches are only focused on a single user not allowing the representation of teamwork [12]–[14].

The representation of a choreography is very similar to what the W3C working group calls a task model (e.g. EOFM, AMBOSS, CTT, GOMS) [15]. These approaches propose hierarchical tree models in which tasks are successively decomposed into subtasks until an atomic level, where tasks represent actions that can be performed directly.

We intend to explore the ability to generate actions plan (using existing planners) for team members controlled by the computer, so we adopt a more simplified task model with a STRIPS-like representation [16] instead of a Hierarchical Task. Regarding the hierarchical models we can compare them to our STRIPS-like approach as follows: a choreography represents one task composed of a set of actions that represent subtasks. Thus, this model can be seen as a hierarchical structure with only one depth level.

Theoretically, models with hierarchical representation have a higher expressiveness than STRIPS. However, hierarchical models have severe limitations in their practical application since they can become undecidable, even under strong constraints and therefore being computationally unsuitable due to excessive computation time required to calculate action plans. In practice, restrictions are applied to restrict the size of the plan to make it finite, reduce the depth of the hierarchy (the number of levels of subtasks) and set order among tasks in order to establish a sequence between them.

By applying this set of constraints, the hierarchical model becomes very close and can even be expressed in STRIPS. So, it can be considered that in practice the expressivity of STRIPS and hierarchical models are similar [17].

We try bringing together all these features and present an approach capable of representing teamwork choreographies involving multi-users, capturing conceptually in a unique ontology model the actions and scene. We present also how to adapt the choreography to potentially any VWP and how to stage it.

3   Background Knowledge

To deal with VWP with different characteristics, we argue that choreographies should be clearly separated from the technical characteristics of the execution in the VWP [18]. To represent choreographies, we adopt a model based on ontologies instead of MOF/OCL metamodels for the following main reasons:

- ontologies are possibly the best way to represent conceptual information in order to bring the intelligent systems closer to the human conceptual level [19];
- ontologies allow different ways of describing classes. Can be defined which are the necessary conditions, i.e., conditions that must be met for an instance belonging to this class, and the necessary and sufficient conditions, i.e., the conditions that once fulfilled make an instance belongs to this class (cf. example of section 3.2);
- ontologies provide additional constructs like transitive closure for properties or represent disjoint classes;
- ontologies enable and automated reasoning, namely the dynamic classification of instances based upon class descriptions and automatic consistency checking when operated with a reasoner (cf. example of section 3.2).

Hence, the core of the proposal is a "generic high-level ontology" that captures the choreography in a conceptual and abstract model, so it is independent from the staging/deployment VWP. The data model of every virtual world must be captured by the so-called "platform-specific ontology", and a mapping must be defined between these two ontologies. The mapping will provide the means to transform the platform-independent choreography into a platform-dependent one.

To address this, the MDA software-development paradigm [9] was adopted and adapted. Based on the concept of model independence and model transformation of MDA, we adopt an approach based on two first-class citizen dimensions: the VWP dimension and the choreography's domain dimension. In fact, unlike in MDA, in our approach the model is not only independent from the VWP but also independent from the (choreography's) domain. Fig. 1 depicts the MDA one-dimensional approach (Fig. 1 a) in comparison with the two-dimensional envisaged approach (Fig. 1 b).

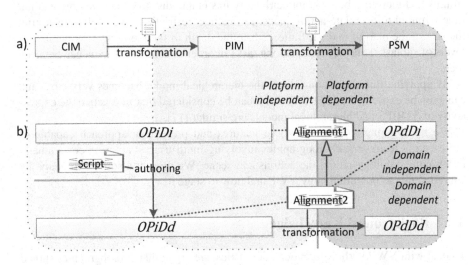

Fig. 1. Model-Driven representation according to: a) MDA and b) Our approach

The nomenclature O_{PxDx} refers to Ontology, Platform and Domain, with "x" assuming "d" and "i" values for "dependent" and "independent", respectively.

Taking into account the characteristics of ontologies described earlier, we claim that ontologies are then the adequate knowledge representation model for bridging the gap between the human requirements and the computational requirements [19]–[22], thus able to play the role of both Computation-Independent Model (CIM) and Platform-Independent Model (PIM). Following MDA, the ontology-based choreography representations are successively transformed through a set of processes until the platform-specific choreography (O_{PdDd}) that is intended to be executed in a specific VWP. The proposed architecture is depicted in Fig. 3, and comprehends four models (ontologies) and five processes.

3.1   Choreography Models

We use four different models to represent different abstractions of the choreography that are represented by the following ontologies:

- O_{PiDi} is the generic high-level ontology representing the core concepts of a choreography independent of any implementation platform, also designated as the foundational choreography [23]. Fig. 2. depicts its current status.

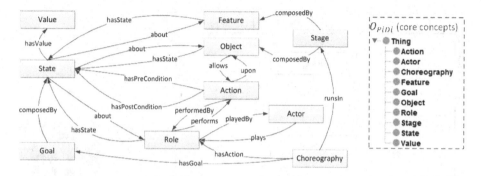

Fig. 2. The Foundational Choreography Ontology (O_{PiDi}): representation of concepts, properties and relations between concepts

- O_{PdDi} represents the core concepts of a choreography for a specific VWP. It is developed only once, but may have to be adapted in the future to reflect the evolution of the VWP. This ontology should capture the interpretation of a choreography for a VWP in a private way in order to best fit its characteristics, but must capture every concept corresponding to those defined in the foundational ontology to represent the same semantic knowledge, so that is possible to establish semantic relations between them.
- O_{PiDd} is a choreography resulting from the authorship of O_{PiDi}. It captures the representation of a complete choreography for a specific application domain, without any commitment to the technical specificities of any platform.
- O_{PdDd} is the representation of a choreography for a specific VWP.

3.2   Processes

The adaptation of a generic choreography to a specific choreography of a particular VWP is conducted through a set of five processes that execute successive transformations of the models representing different abstractions of choreography.

Authoring. It is a user-based process in which the choreographer authors a domain dependent choreography in the form of an ontology.

   The foundation ontology (O_{PiDi}) is extended and refined semantically to describe the choreography entities specific to an application domain, giving rise to O_{PiDd}, but the modifications applied cannot change the semantics defined in O_{PiDi}. For that, the following assumptions must be guaranteed:

- No axioms defined in O_{PiDi} can be removed;
- No contradictions can be added, i.e., O_{PiDd} must be logically consistent;
- No new root elements are allowed. I.e. new entities (classes and properties) are defined as sub entities of those existing in O_{PiDi} and should not create new root elements.

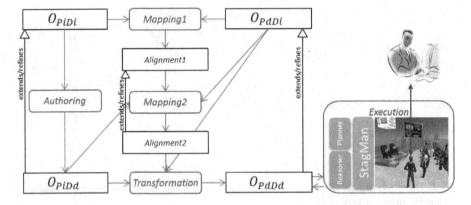

Fig. 3. The system architecture with the processes of authoring, mappings, transformation and execution

In this process, new concepts are added as well as restrictions to define the type of action actors can perform. Restrictions are associations between roles (that actors can play) and actions, and has a dual purpose: (1) to allow an actor performing an action if he plays a role compatible with it, and (2) to assign dynamically a role to an actor according to the type of action he performs.

For a better understanding, an illustrative example for these two possible constraints is presented.

1. Assuming that the type of action Drop_SDM1 can only be performed by an actor who plays the role T1, the specification of the constraint using the Manchester syntax can be as the following:

```
Class: Drop_SDM1
    SubClassOf:
        upon some SDM1,
        hasPostCondition some s13,
        hasPreCondition some s12,
        performedBy some T1,
        performedBy only T1
```

2. It is intended that, when a Technician performs any of the actions: Drop_SDM1, Go_P1, Grab_SDM1 or Lift_Screw1, his/her role is automatically changed to role

T1. The rule that specifies this assignment can be defined using the Manchester syntax as follows:

```
Class: T1
    EquivalentTo:
        Technician
        and ((performs some Drop_SDM1)
        or (performs some Go_P1)
        or (performs some Grab_SDM1)
        or (performs some Lift_Screw1))
    SubClassOf:
        Technician
```

Mapping1. It is the process that establishes correspondences between the representations of the two choreographies abstractions represented by $O_{P_iD_i}$ and $O_{P_dD_i}$ (Alignment1).

Mapping2. It is the process that establishes correspondences between the domain choreography (O_{PiDd}) and a VWP ontology (O_{PdDi}), i.e. Alignment2. Alignment2 profits from (and extends) Alignment1, thus promoting reuse and reducing effort.

Transformation. It is the process that creates the VWP choreography (O_{PdDd}) from O_{PiDd} and O_{PdDi} and according to the Alignment2.

This is a fully automatic process that "copies" the O_{PiDd} concepts and constraints to the O_{PdDd}. This process is described in section 4. Despite this being an automatic process, choreographers can edit the resulting O_{PdDd} ontology for additional adjustments to better fit the implementation platform.

Execution. It is the process that stages the choreography in a VWP through a Staging Manager (StagMan in Fig. 3) that is a computer program compatible with the VWP. It has the following responsibilities: (1) monitors the VW and the behavior of actors, (2) updates the Knowledge Base (KB) according to the changes to the states of VW and the actions performed by actors, (3) validates the actions triggered by actors comparing them with those described in the choreography, and (4) gives feedback to actors about the actions they triggered through the VW interface.

4   Generating a Choreography

Running the aforementioned transformation process generates a choreography to a specific VWP. This fully automatic process gives rise to the O_{PdDd} by performing a novel ontology transformation algorithm. This process may be defined by the function $f: transformation(O_{PiDd}, O_{PdDi}, A_2) \rightarrow O_{PdDd}$ such that A_2 is the alignment resulting from the alignment of the O_{PiDd} and O_{PdDi} ontologies. The transformation process consists of the following steps:

1. The taxonomy of each O_{PiDd} ontology concept (hierarchical structure considering the concept as root) added during the authoring process is replicated into the O_{PdDd} according to the correspondences in A_2. The whole sub-taxonomy of the concept is copied to ensure that all expressiveness and restrictions developed in the authoring process will be available in the target ontology.
2. For each copied sub-concept in the target ontology (O_{PdDd}), their properties and relations will be set based on the alignments. Simultaneously, the restrictions applied to each source sub concept are also replicated in the corresponding target sub concept in accordance to the defined alignments.

The algorithm executed in this process is depicted in Fig. 4. Consider CB and PB as correspondences (or semantic relations/bridges). CB (Concept Bridge) represents the correspondence between one concept from the source ontology and one concept from the target ontology. PB (Property Bridge) represents the correspondence between one property from the source concept and one property from the target concept.

```
1. Transformation(Alignment A2) {
2.      processConceptBridges(A2)
3.      processPropertyBridges(A2)
4.  }
5.  //[step 1]
6.  processConceptBridges(Alignment A2) {
7.      for each CB in A2.getListOfConceptBridges() {
8.          SC = CB.getSrcConcept()
9.          TC = CB.getTgtConcept()
10.         createConceptHierarchy(SC, TC)
11.     }
12. }
13. createConceptHierarchy(SC, TC) {
14.     for each srcSubConcept in SC.getListOfSubConcepts(){
15.         if(not A2.existCBforSrcConcept(srcSubConcept)){
16.            tgtSubConcept = TC.createSubConcept(srcSubConcept)
17.            createConceptHierarchy(srcSubConcept, tgtSubConcept)
18.         }
19.     }
20. }
21. //[step 2]
22. processPropertyBridges(Alignment A2) {
23.     for each CB in A2.getListOfConceptBridges() {
24.         SC = CB.getSrcConcept()
25.         TC = CB.getTgtConcept()
26.         for each srcSubConcept in SC.getListOfSubConcepts() {
27.            if(not A2.existCBforSrcConcept(srcSubConcept)){
28.               tgtSubConcept = TC.getCrrsSubConcept(srcSubConcept)
```

Fig. 4. The transformation process algorithm

```
29.              listPB = CB.getListOfPropertyBridges()
30.              for each PB in listPB) {
31.                SP = PB.getSrcProperty()
32.                TP = PB.getTgtProperty()
33.                TC.createProperty(TP)
34.              }
35.              if(srcSubConcept.hasRestrictions()){
36.                TR = tgtSubConcept.createRestriction()
37.                for each SR in srcSubConcept.getListOfRstrcts() {
38.                  TR.copyRestriction(SR)
39.                }
40.              }
41.            }
42.          }
43.        }
44. }
```

Fig. 4. *(continued)*

To better understand how the transformation process works, we present a small example. Let us assume that in the authoring process it is intended to represent only two types of action: GrabScrewDriver and SayStart. For the sake of organization, Grab-ScrewDriver is considered as a subtype of ManipulateAction and SayStart a subtype of commandAction. There are two distinct types of roles: Supervisor and Mechanic which in turn has a subtype M1. The type ManipulateAction must be performed by Mechanic and the type CommandAction by Supervisor.

The choreography will be transformed for a messaging platform (developed in-house) and OpenSim[1] (OpenSim). The messaging platform only models one action (Write) and OpenSim models the types: Touch, Chat, Detach, Attach and Go. The rest of example will address the messaging platform only.

In Alignment1 CBs and PBs are defined to link the elementary concepts and properties of O_{PiDi} and O_{PdDi}, e.g., CB1 links O_{PiDi}:Action with O_{PdDi}:Action, CB2 links O_{PiDi}:Role with O_{PdDi}:Role, and PB1 links O_{PiDi}:performedBy with O_{PdDi}:writtenBy.

In Alignment2 are defined new alignments for the types of action that have been added during the authoring. In the messaging platform there is only one action, hence all new types of action of O_{PiDi} should be aligned with it (simply align the new top concepts). We define two CBs (CB1.1 and CB1.2) to align the two new types of action (O_{PiDi}:ManipulateAction and O_{PiDi}:CommandAction) with O_{PdDi}:Write.

Running the transformation algorithm, and based on the defined alignment (Alignment2), the processing of CBs and PBs creates new concepts and properties in O_{PdDd}, described as follows:

1. In the first step are processed the concepts. For each CB, is created in O_{PdDd} ontology the hierarchy of the concept of O_{PiDd} that is aligned. This is done by the method *createConceptHierarchy(SC, TC)* ([step1] lines 6-12 of the algorithm);

---

[1] http://opensimulator.org/

2. In the second step the properties are processed. For each CB, all sub-concepts of the O_{PiDd} concept are scanned, and according to all PBs associated with this concept, the corresponding property in O_{PdDd} ([step2] lines 30-34) is created and after that, the existing restrictions are added ([step2] lines 35-40).

Although this is an automatic process, choreographers can intervene and edit the resulting O_{PdDd} ontology for additional adjustments. Thus, the O_{PdDd} ontology may be further tweaked to best suit the implementation platform. Fig. 5 depicts an extract of a O_{PdDd} ontology for Messaging and OpenSim platforms resulting from the concept-bridge transformation process.

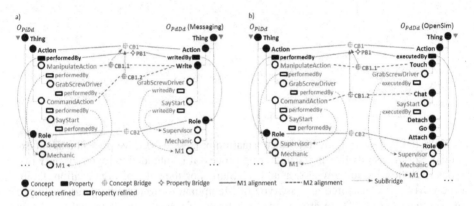

Fig. 5. An extract of O_{PdDd} ontology for a) Messaging and b) OpenSim

Given the representation of a choreography it is important to check the feasibility of its staging. Some factors may lead to the impossibility of its execution, e.g. the virtual world can be in a state incompatible with the choreography or actions having cross dependences between them causing deadlock situations.

The validation of the feasibility of the choreography is performed using a planner that, from the current state of the virtual world and the representation of actions of the choreography (with pre and post conditions) calculates a plan of actions capable of achieving the set of goals. When a solution for the problem is not found, it means that you cannot proceed with the execution of the choreography, or the choreography goals have been achieved in the meantime. The validation of the choreography can be done earlier after the transformation process, and later during its staging when there are suspicions of passivity or deadlocks.

The validation of choreography can be performed at an early stage after the transformation process or at any time during its staging, especially when there are no progresses. In this case the validation can be used to check if there are deadlocks or simply passive actors.

5   Executing a Choreography

Another important key point is to ensure that during the staging of a choreography the ontology remains consistent, i.e., semantically valid. The staging in each of the virtual worlds is controlled by StagMan that continuously monitors the state of the world and the behavior of actors, and when it senses that the behavior of an actor corresponds to a type of action of the choreography, it performs a progressive validation following the next three steps:

1. Checks the KB whether the necessary pre-conditions for this type of action are met;
2. Creates an instance of this action in the KB relating it to the actor that requested it;
3. Apply the post-conditions described by this type of action.

The result of the validation is communicated to the actor responsible for the action through the VWP interface, and is one of the following messages: (1) "Preconditions are not met" when step 1 fails, (2) "Unauthorized Action" when step 2 or step 3 fails, and (3) "Correct" when the three steps are successful.

The consistency checking of the model is automatic and permanent. This procedure is carried out by a reasoning tool, which is coupled to the StagMan component. Any changes made inside the KB, i.e. insertion or removal of facts and changes in relationships automatically trigger the execution of the reasoner that checks if the semantic integrity of the KB remains consistent. When the attempting to execute an action causes inconsistencies in the KB, the action is ignored and the changes associated with it are canceled and the information is restored to the state prior to the action.

6   Experiments

To evaluate our approach we deployed several real-world choreographies that were staged in three different multiuser platforms with very distinct characteristics. We selected examples involving quite different application domains, such as maintenance of military equipment, sports games and children's stories. After authoring the choreographies, the resulting ontologies undergo the remaining processes (Mapping1, Mapping2, Transformation) and staged in different VWP, as depicted in Fig. 6 and Fig. 7.

We used OpenSim, to create a realistic multiuser 3D environment, SmartFoxServer[2] (SmartFox) that allow creating massive multiplayer applications with an isometric environment 2.5D using OpenSpace[3] engine and as a counterpart system, we developed for testing purposes a messaging platform. This messaging platform has characteristics that differ greatly from OpenSim and SmartFox, since it does not allow the graphical representation of scene objects, but enables the development of a team's choreography nonetheless. In the messaging platform interface, the actions activation of the choreography are presented in the form of Buttons, thus the interaction is done

---

[2] http://www.smartfoxserver.com/
[3] http://www.openspace-engine.com/

by pressing them, and when an action is performed successfully by the team member, it is communicated to all other team members by means of a text log (Fig. 6 a).

In OpenSim platform, (i) the actions that can be performed on an object are presented in the form of a menu when an actor selects the object, (ii) verbal actions are implemented through the existing Chat mechanism of the virtual world, and (iii) the movement of avatars is known through sensors placed on the stage.

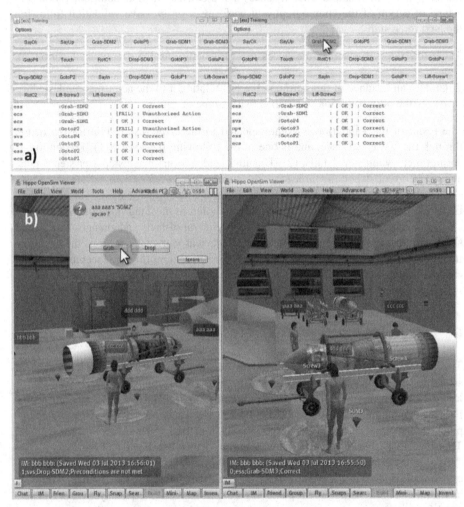

Fig. 6. The staging of the procedures to insert an engine into an aircraft in a) Messaging and b) OpenSim platforms

In SmartFox platform, non-verbal actions are associated with buttons in the interface, verbal actions are interpreted through public messages that actors exchange between them, and actions related to movement of avatars are determined by sensors placed on the stage.

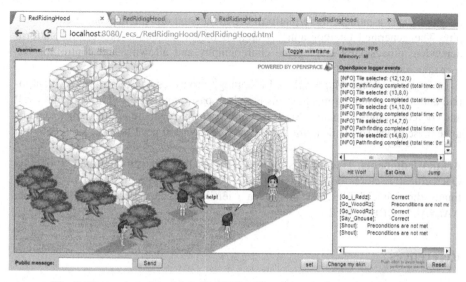

Fig. 7. The staging of the Little Red Riding Hood story in SmartFox platform

Authoring is obviously the most time-consuming and creative process (the expressivity of the ontologies authored during the experiments range between $\mathcal{ALCHI}(\mathcal{D})$ and $\mathcal{SHOIN}(\mathcal{D})$ Description Logics expressivity), the Mapping1 and Mapping2 semi-automatic processes require reduced time and effort. Once these processes are performed, the transformation and execution processes are fully automatic.

7 Conclusions and Future Work

In this paper we propose an approach that allows the development of choreographies and its adaptation and staging in potentially any VWP. For that, based on the concept of MDA and the assumption that the use of ontologies is possibly the best way to represent the conceptual information to approximate the intelligent systems to the human conceptual level, we propose an ontology to capture the semantics of a generic choreography independent of any application domain and VWP. Further, for each VWP is adopted an ontology representing its specific features that is mapped with the generic one.

Moreover, ontologies allow the integration in the same model of all the modeling information related to the choreography, i.e. the definition of procedures related to teamwork and the information about the scene.

The use of alignments between ontologies enables the automation of the adaptation of the generic ontology to the specific target ontology, hence contributing to reduce development time and resources.

We describe a sequence of processes that uses alignments between ontologies and allows adapting a choreography of a specific domain into a choreography capable of being staged in potentially any VWP. In particular this paper presents the fully automatic algorithm for transforming a platform independent yet domain dependent choreography (i.e. a model) into a platform dependent and domain dependent choreography. The generated choreography is applied by the execution process (a platform dependent process) for staging the choreography and allowing and controlling the user interaction.

In future work the Mapping1 and Mapping2 processes can be refined to incorporate automatic matching mechanisms based on past experiences with the same VWP and choreographies' domains. So, it would be possible to increase the ability to automate these processes while at the same time it reduces the need for user intervention.

Acknowledgments. This work is supported by FEDER Funds through the "Programa Operacional Factores de Competitividade - COMPETE" program and by National Funds through FCT "Fundação para a Ciência e Tecnologia" under the project AAL4ALL (QREN13852).

References

1. De Freitas, S.: Serious virtual worlds, Scoping Guide JISC E-Learn. Programme Jt. Inf. Syst. Comm. JISC UK (2008)
2. Morgado, L., Varajão, J., Coelho, D., Rodrigues, C., Sancin, C., Castello, V.: The attributes and advantages of virtual worlds for real world training. J. Virtual Worlds Educ. 1(1) (2010)
3. Kapahnke, P., Liedtke, P., Nesbigall, S., Warwas, S., Klusch, M.: ISReal: An open platform for semantic-based 3D simulations in the 3D internet. In: Patel-Schneider, P.F., Pan, Y., Hitzler, P., Mika, P., Zhang, L., Pan, J.Z., Horrocks, I., Glimm, B. (eds.) ISWC 2010, Part II. LNCS, vol. 6497, pp. 161–176. Springer, Heidelberg (2010)
4. Pinheiro, A., Fernandes, P., Maia, A., Cruz, G., Pedrosa, D., Fonseca, B., Paredes, H., Martins, P., Morgado, L., Rafael, J.: Development of a Mechanical Mainte-nance Training Simulator in OpenSimulator for F-16 Aircraft Engines. Procedia Comput. Sci. 15, 248–255 (2012)
5. 'Media Grid: Open File Formats Technology Working Group (OFF.TWG) Charter', http://mediagrid.org/groups/technology/OFF.TWG/ (accessed: October 14, 2013)
6. Mollet, N., Arnaldi, B.: Storytelling in virtual reality for training. In: Pan, Z., Aylett, R.S., Diener, H., Jin, X., Göbel, S., Li, L. (eds.) Edutainment 2006. LNCS, vol. 3942, pp. 334–347. Springer, Heidelberg (2006)
7. Gerbaud, S., Mollet, N., Ganier, F., Arnaldi, B., Tisseau, J.: GVT: a platform to create virtual environments for procedural training. In: IEEE Virtual Reality Conference, VR 2008, pp. 225–232 (2008)
8. Vernieri, T.M.: A web services approach to generating and using plans in configurable execution environments (2006)
9. Alhir, S.: Methods & Tools - Understanding the Model Driven Architecture (MDA). Martinig & Associates (fall 2003)
10. Edward, L., Lourdeaux, D., Lenne, D., Barthes, J., Burkhardt, J.M.: Modelling autonomous virtual agent behaviours in a virtual environment for risk. IJVR Int. J. Virtual Real. 7(3), 13–22 (2008)

11. Lopes, A., Pires, B., Cardoso, M., Santos, A., Peixinho, F., Sequeira, P., Morgado, L.: System for Defining and Reproducing Handball Strategies in Second Life On-Demand for Handball Coaches. Education

12. Young, R.M., Riedl, M.O., Branly, M., Jhala, A., Martin, R.J., Saretto, C.J.: An architecture for integrating plan-based behavior generation with interactive game environments. J. Game Dev. 1(1), 1–29 (2004)

13. Young, R.M., Thomas, J., Bevan, C., Cassell, B.A.: Zócalo: A Service-Oriented Architecture Facilitating Sharing of Computational Resources in Interactive Narrative Research (2011)

14. Cash, S.P., Young, R.M.: Bowyer: A Planning Tool for Bridging the gap between Declarative and Procedural Domains. Artif. Intell., 14–19 (2009)

15. MBUI - Task Models, http://www.w3.org/TR/task-models/ (accessed: July 9, 2014)

16. Fikes, R.E., Nilsson, N.J.: STRIPS: a new approach to the application of theorem proving to problem solving. In: Proceedings of the 2nd international Joint Conference on Artificial intelligence, San Francisco, CA, USA, pp. 608–620 (1971)

17. Lekavỳ, M., Návrat, P.: Expressivity of STRIPS-like and HTN-like planning. In: Agent Multi-Agent Syst. Technol. Appl., pp. 121–130 (2007)

18. Silva, E., Silva, N., Morgado, L.: Staging Choreographies for Team Training in Multiple Virtual Worlds Based on Ontologies and Alignments. In: Presented at the HCI International 2014, Heraklion, Crete, Greece (accepted for publication, 2014)

19. Obrst, L., Liu, H., Wray, R.: Ontologies for Corporate Web Applications. AI Mag. 24(3), 49 (2003)

20. Gruber, T.R., et al.: A translation approach to portable ontology specifications. Knowl. Acquis. 5(2), 199–220 (1993)

21. Fensel, D.: Ontologies: a silver bullet for knowledge management and electronic commerce. Springer, Heidelberg (2004)

22. Gruninger, M., Lee, J.: Ontology Applications and Design-Introduction. Commun. ACM 45(2), 39–41 (2002)

23. Silva, E., Silva, N., Paredes, H., Martins, P., Fonseca, B., Morgado, L.: Development of platform-independent multi-user choreographies for virtual worlds based on ontology combination and mapping. In: 2012 IEEE Symposium on Visual Languages and Human-Centric Computing (VL/HCC), pp. 149–152 (2012)

Adapting Aerial Root Classifier Missing Data Processor in Data Stream Decision Tree Classification

Oussama Lachiheb and Mohamed Salah Gouider

Laboratoire SOIE, Institut Superieur De Gestion, Tunis University
oussama.lachiheb@gmail.com,
ms.gouider@yahoo.fr

Abstract. This work has contributed to the development of a classification method that can deal with the missing data problems. This method called ARC-CVFDT was developed in order to adapt the Aerial Root Classifier missing data processor to the Data Stream decision tree classification method. it offers a higher level of accuracy and adaptation with most of DSM challenges such as Concept Drifting.

Keywords: Missing data, Classification, Decision Tree, Data Stream, Machine Learning.

1 Introduction

In recent years,new technologies and material evolution have facilitated the ability to collect data continuously; using credit card, road sensors, mobile calls and browsing web have all lead to a large and a continue flow of data.

Data Stream mining DSM is a new kind of data mining which handles continuous data streams. We have many DSM methods, classification using real-time decision tree is one from the favorite methods because it is useful in applications that requires instant decision-making.

Sometimes, sensor malfunction or interruption on a flow of data communication signals can give rise to missing data in the input of the Miner which can affects classification results. There are several techniques to deal with missing values in traditional data mining such as eliminating records having missing attributes, or using statistic approach to estimate those values, these techniques does not work with DSM because the testing and training in DSM is done dynamically with a moving data and not with a complete dataset.

We propose in this work our approach called ARC-CVFDT which adapts the aerial root classifier missing data processor to Concept adapting Very Fast Decision Tree.

This work will be followed by an experimental study using JAVA to show the obtained results which help us evaluate this approach.

Y. Ait Ameur et al. (Eds.): MEDI 2014, LNCS 8748, pp. 92–99, 2014.

2   Related Works

In traditional Data Mining algorithms, the presence of missing data may not affect the quality of output, they can be simply ignored or replaced by a mean value, but in the case of Data Stream Mining, any algorithm scans data only one time because of the high speed nature of Data Streams, so the problem of incomplete data is more impactful in this case.

Many previous works was based on dealing with the incomplete data problem, in [4], authors have proposed a new method called WARM (Window Association Rule Mining) for dealing with the problem of incomplete data, this approach estimate missing values that can result from sensors errors or malfunction.

This method has been extended in 2007, authors have called the new approach FARM [12].

In 2011, Hang, Fong and Chen have proposed in [7] a solution for predicting missing values in data stream mining, and especially for the classification task, this method is called ARC-HTA and it can perform data stream mining in the presence of missing values.

HTA (Hoeffding tree classifier). This approach offers a high level of classifcation accuracy.

In 2013, Authors on [6] have proposed a new approach that performs Data interpolating in the presence of missing readings.

Their method is based on a novel probabilistic interpolating method and three novel deterministic interpolating methods, the experimental results demonstrate the feasibility and effectiveness of the proposed method.

3   Background

3.1   Traditional Decision Tree Classification

Decision trees are a simple yet successful technique for supervised classification learning. They have the specific aim of allowing us to predict the class of an object given known values of its attributes.

Traditional Decision Tree construction algorithms such as ID3 [11] and C4.5 [5] need to scan the whole data set each time to split the best attribute, they need to scan the data set again in order to update the obtained model, which cannot be useful with the Data Stream case.

3.2   Data Streams Decision Tree Classification

Classification task of Data Streams has several challenges such as high speed nature, the concept drifting, the unbounded memory requirement and the tradeoff between the accuracy and the efficiency.

During last years, researchers have proposed many classification methods and models that can deal with data stream challenges such as Hoeffding tree Algorithm (HTA)[7], Very Fast Decision Tree (VFDT) [8] and Concept-adapting Very Fast Decision Tree (CVFDT)[9].

3.3   Methods for Dealing with Missing Values

The problem of incomplete data can happen with most of real world data sources, as shown in [10], several methods have been proposed in order to deal with this problem.

In this section, we will present a brief overview of existing methods for dealing with missing data, and comment on their suitability for the equipment maintenances databases such as described in previous section.

- Ignoring and Discarding Incomplete Records and Attributes
- Parameter Estimation in the Presence of Missing Data

4   Predicting Missing Values within CVFDT Classification

Data stream mining algorithms handles a flow of continuous data stream and classify target values on the fly, sometimes, examples may include incomplete data due to sensor malfunction or generator error which can affect directly the quality and the accuracy of the output.

As detailed above, missing data is more impactful in the case of data stream mining, so we have to include a method that predicts incomplete data with a high level of accuracy.

This section is focused on the presentation of the new approach that enables predicting missing values before running the main CVFDT classifier, we first give some motivations to develop this method, then we define the new structure of the data stream within the sliding window model.and we finally report the algorithm of our approach.

4.1   Sliding Window Model

Sliding window is a model that enables storing a part of data stream; as a result, for each task we can scan a part of data because of the unbounded nature of the sensor data stream.

The main issue is which part of the data stream will be selected for the processing; there are different data stream processing models, such as fixed model, land mark and sliding window.

Fixed model scans the whole data stream in a fixed start time and end time, the landmark model capture the historical behavior of the data streams, and the sliding window model contains always the most recent data streams in an interval of time or for N records.

4.2   Adapting Aerial Root Classifier to CVFDT

Initialization Step
In the beginning, a sequence of data is loaded from the stream in order to construct the data set that will be used in the classification process.

Due to the huge amount of data generated from sensors, its sufficient to use just a number of samples in order to choose the split attribute at each decision node, this statistical method is called hoeffding bound.

Let us consider $\varepsilon = \sqrt{\frac{R^2 ln(\frac{1}{\delta})}{2N}}$

For N independants observations, we consider G as information gain function, the difference between the two highest information gain functions $\triangle G$ must be higher than ε in order to split the attribute Xi into decision node.

Estimating Missing Values

We will use in this work the Aerial root classifier (ARC), ARC is a classification model that work parallel with the main classifier and predicts all missing values that the dataset may contain.

This method checks all attributes in the loaded dataset; if an attribute has some missing values, it builds a parallel classification model (with the main classifier) that consider this attribute as class attribute and predicts its value using other attributes values.

Let $X = \{X_1, X_2, ..., X_n\}$

We have n attributes for each sample, the number of ARCs that our method builds is $0 \preceq N \preceq n$.

More generally, the idea is to use all attributes to build an ARC expect Xk if Xk in the sliding window has missing values.

CVFDT Classification

The last step of our approach is to run the main classifier algorithm, as mentioned above, we have many ARCs that work in parallel in order to predict all missing values, then the complete dataset is used to build the main decision tree (Concept adapting Very Fast Decision Tree).

CVFDT system works by keeping the model consistent with the sliding window of examples, the method enables resolving the concept drift problems, as a result, at any time, we cant have an outdated model.

4.3   Reducing the Computation Cost of the Algorithm

ARC-CVFDT offers a high classification accuracy, but in the experimental studies, we have identified that this method has several pass in building ARCs models and in estimating missing values, so we have to reduce the computational cost of this approach.

Theres many method that can reduce the computational cost of our approach such as the ID4 algorithm and the feature selection method.

The ID4 algorithm constructs a decision tree incrementally, it updates the decision tree automatically when new instances are loaded into the sliding window instead of re building it, this algorithm reduce the complexity of ARC missing values processor. The second method is to use feature selection, it gives a rank to each attribute during computing the information gain function, then we calculate E as ARC performance indicator. If E is beyond to a predefined bound, then we use the current ARC.

$$\omega_i = \frac{Rank_i}{\sum_{i=1}^{n} Rank_i} \tag{1}$$

$$\sum_{i=1}^{n} \omega_i e_i \tag{2}$$

$$e = \frac{CorrectClassifiedInstances}{TotalInstances} \tag{3}$$

ARC-CVFDT Algorithm

```
VAR
  ARC: Aerial Root Classifier;
  S: a sequence of instances;
  WS: Window size (the number of instances);
  X:a set of attributes;
 begin
 Repeat

  If ((ARC empty)) then
   BuildARC(X,WS);
  else
   UpdateARC(X,WS);
  end If
  until xi=n
  Use ARC to predict the missing values in Xi;
  Until no attribute has missing values in X;
  Run CVFDT to build decision tree;
  Update Weight();
 end
Return CVFDT
```

Build ARC procedure

```
Procedure BuildARC(X,WS)
Repeat
 If ((xk has missing value)) then
 Use WS instances in S excluding xk to build ARC;
 end If
Until xi=X.Length in S
Return ARC;
```

5   Performance Study and Experiments

Implementing our methods for predicting missing values within CVFDT classification allows us have an idea concerning the performance of our presented method.

In addition to the different implemented programs, other simulation and test results will be shown; these results are done in real databases taken from the U.C.I repository.

In this section, we will detail our experimental setup before describing different simulation and test results.

6   Experimental Setup

Our algorithm was written in Java and compiled using eclipse integrated development environment, all our experiments were performed on a PC equipped 3.2 Ghz intel core i3 and a 4 GB memory, the operating system was windows seven.

All these experiments were run without any other user on the machine.

6.1   Simulations and Results

Simulations on Synthetic Datasets
In order to illustrate the ability of our proposed algorithm, synthetic datasets are generated to test the scalability and the efficiency of the method.

Different datasets generated are described in the table below:

Table 1. Synthetic datasets

Name	Attributes Nbr	Att values	Class Nbr	Instance Nbr
LED7	7	Nominal	10	100.000
LED24	24	Nominal	10	100.000

In this experiment, we want to see the direct impact of missing data in the accuracy of CVFDT classification, for this reason, missing data are randomly added near the end parts of the data stream (figure 1).

Simulations on Real Datasets
In this experiment, we have downloaded a dataset which is KDD cup 98 provided by the paralyzed Veterans of America, this learning dataset have 481 attributes both in numeric and nominal, it contains 95412 instances.

Using this dataset, we have compared the classification accuracy of our proposed approach ARC-CVFDT, complete data stream and the WEKA method that replaces missing values with the mean, we have obtained results shown in the figure 2.

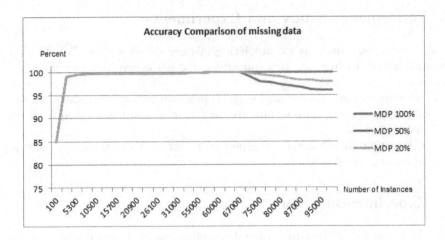

Fig. 1. Accuracy comparison of missing values in LED7 dataset

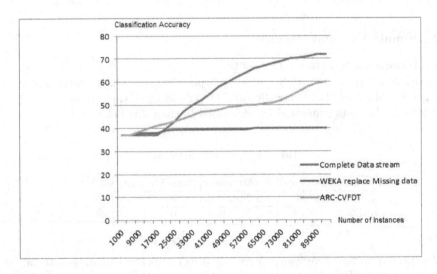

Fig. 2. CUP98 dataset comparing classification accuracy

7   Conclusion

Because of unexpected error and malfunction, datasets containing incomplete data is becoming relevant, which can affect the quality of any mining and knowledge discovery process; however, existing methods in Data Stream Mining have not proposed enough consideration to this problem. Our method called ARC-CVFDT can perform Data Stream classification with the presence if missing readings.

In order to evaluate our approach, we have proposed an experimental study based on both real and simulated data, we got promising results that encourages us to complete our research with other real datasets.

As future work, since our approach was providing encouraging results, this work can be extended by adapting the missing data processor ARC to other classification models instead of decision trees in order to compare different results, ARC can also be adapted to clustering techniques in order to estimate missing values which increase the quality of the process results.

References

1. Domingos, P., Hulten, G.: Mining highspeed data streams. Journal of Computer Science and Technology (2000)
2. May, P., Ehrlich, H.C., Steinke, T.: ZIB Structure Prediction Pipeline: Composing a Complex Biological Workflow through Web Services. In: Nagel, W.E., Walter, W.V., Lehner, W. (eds.) Euro-Par 2006. LNCS, vol. 4128, pp. 1148–1158. Springer, Heidelberg (2006)
3. Foster, I., Kesselman, C.: The Grid: Blueprint for a New Computing Infrastructure. Morgan Kaufmann, San Francisco (1999)
4. Halatchev, M., Le Gruenwald: Estimating missing values in related sensor data streams. In: The University of Oklahoma, School of Computer Science (2005)
5. Quinlan, J.R.: Programs for machine learning. Morgan Kaufmann series in machine learning.Kluwer Academic Publishers (1993)
6. Xiao, Y., Jiang, T., Li, Y., Xu, G.: Data Interpolating over RFID Data Streams for Missed Readings. In: Gao, Y., Shim, K., Ding, Z., Jin, P., Ren, Z., Xiao, Y., Liu, A., Qiao, S. (eds.) WAIM 2013 Workshops 2013. LNCS, vol. 7901, pp. 257–265. Springer, Heidelberg (2013)
7. Yang, M., Simong, F., Wei, C.: Aerial root classifiers for predicting missing values in data stream decision tree classifcation. Journal of Emerging Technologies in Web Intelligence (2011)
8. Domingos, M., Hulten, G.: Mining highspeed data streams. Journal of Computer Science and Technology (2000)
9. Domingos, M., Hulten, G., Spencer, L.: Mining timechanging data streams. In: Knowledge Discovery and Data Mining (2001)
10. Kamashki, L., Steven, A., Samad, T.: Imputation of missing data in industrial databases. Applied Intelligence Archive 11(3) (1999)
11. Quinlan, J.R.: Induction on decision tress. In: Machine Learning, vol. 1, pp. 81–106 (1986)
12. Gruenwald, L., Chok, H., AbouKhamis, M.: Using Data mining to estimate missing sensor data. In: Seventh IEEE International Conference on Data Mining Workshops (ICDMW 2007), pp. 207–212 (2007)

Leveraging Concepts and Semantic Relationships for Language Model Based Document Retrieval

Lynda Said Lhadj[1], Mohand Boughanem[2], and Karima Amrouche[1]

[1] National High School for Computer Science (ESI),
Algiers, Algeria
{l_said_lhadj,k_amrouche}@esi.dz
[2] IRIT, 118 route de Narbonne, 31062 Toulouse Cedex 9, France
bougha@irit.fr

Abstract. During the last decades, many language models approaches have been proposed to alleviate the assumption of single term independency in documents. This assumption leads to two known problems in information retrieval, namely polysemy and synonymy. In this paper, we propose a new language model based on concepts, to answer the polysemy issue, and semantic dependencies, to handle the synonymy problem. Our purpose is to relax the independency constraint by representing documents and queries by their concepts instead of single words. We consider that a concept could be a single word, a frequent collocation in the corpus or an ontology entry. In addition, semantic dependencies between query and document concepts have been incorporated into our model using a semantic smoothing technique. This allows retrieving not only documents containing the same words with the query but also documents dealing with the same concepts. Experiments carried out on TREC collections showed that our model achieves significant results compared to a strong single term based model, namely uni-gram language model.

Keywords: Information Retrieval, Language Modeling, semantic smoothing, Concept, Semantic Relatonships.

1 Introduction

Language models (LM) have shown so far more significant performances compared to some traditional Information Retrieval (IR) models, such as probabilistic and vector space model [6, 21]. This is particularly due to their simplicity and well-founded theoretical setting relying on probabilities. In fact, the relevance score of a document (D) to a query (Q) is simply given by the conditional probability $P(Q|D)$ [20, 13]. Several works have been proposed to estimate $P(Q|D)$ [6, 20, 13]. Most of them are based on the assumption that words are independent from each other. Such an assumption is in contrast with natural language where terms are related to each other. Thereby the two long-standing problems in IR, namely the synonymy and the polysemy phenomena are still arising in language models. To address these problems, a new generation of language modeling approaches based on n-grams or concepts has been developed [1, 9, 19, 23].

Y. Ait Ameur et al. (Eds.): MEDI 2014, LNCS 8748, pp. 100–112, 2014.
© Springer International Publishing Switzerland 2014

In this generation, two main underlying categories can be distinguished. The first one attempts to capture term dependencies directly from texts using statistical methods or learning techniques [1, 9, 20, 17, 18]. The second category use external semantic resources, such as ontologies to capture terms dependencies [3, 5, 8, 19].

The model presented in this paper is in the cross-road of both categories. It is intended as a novel language model that allows matching documents and queries at concept level to handle the polysemy issue. We assume that a concept can be a single word or a frequent collocation in the text. The latter can be either ontology entries or not. In addition, we exploit a semantic smoothing technique [6] to integrate semantic relationships between concepts in our retrieval model. This means that the model is capable to retrieve documents that contain not only the same concepts as a query but also those containing related concepts, such as synonyms, hypernyms, hyponyms.

The rest of this paper is organized as follows: Section 2 describes the general language model principle. Section 3 highlights previous LM approaches dealing with the issue of word independency assumption. In Section 4 we present our document retrieval model. Finally, we describe the experiment and the results in section 5. Section 6 summarizes the contribution and suggests some perspectives.

2   Related Work

The main idea behind LM is to assume that a document is generated by a statistical model. The relevance of a query with respect to a document is given by the conditional probability of the query to be generated by the language model of the document D. Therefore, the score of relevance is so given by the formula 1:

$$Score(Q, D) = P(Q|D) \tag{1}$$

In order to estimate $Score(Q, D)$, document words are assumed to be independent. This assumption has been widely adopted in IR, specifically in probabilistic models. Obviously, it simplifies the model estimation but there is a contradiction with the reality of natural language. Thus, two problems arise from this assumption. First, the problem of synonymy, for example, given a query containing the word "car", documents containing synonyms or related words as "automobile" or "vehicle" would not be retrieved even though they deal with the query concept. Second, the problem of polysemy, for queries containing ambiguous (polysemic) word such as "java" (programming language, island), irrelevant documents containing the same word but with a different meaning could be returned. These issues have been widely discussed in Information Retrieval. Particularly, in language models, most of works has attempted to address these issues by introducing some term dependencies into language models. According to [8], there are two kinds of dependencies can be considered, the ones within query words or within document ones, for example bi-grams, bi-terms or concepts. The intuition is that the combinations of words are less ambiguous than single words[16, 1, 17]. The second kind concerns dependencies between query words and document ones, they are generally semantic such as synonyms [6, 8]. Both mentioned kinds are helpful for IR and many approaches have been proposed to integrate them into language models. They can be classified into tow categories : 1) the one capturing dependencies extracted directly within text and the approach and 2) the approaches integrating dependencies extracted from external resources

2.1   Integrating Dependencies from Text

In this approach, terms dependencies are captured by mean of different statistical techniques such as, word collocations. The earliest work have been proposed by Song and Croft [16]. They extended the uni-gram (single word) model to the bi-grams (sequences of two ordered words) one. The results were not successful since bi-grams cannot cover all words dependencies; In addition, bi-grams introduce noise because of adjacency constraint [9]. Srikanth and Srihari [17] proposed a bi-term language model to relax the constraints of term order and term adjacency in the bi-gram model. In their work presented in [18], authors focus on a higher level of dependencies in queries: a query is seen as a sequence of concepts identified using a syntactic parser. Each concept is a sequence of words co-occurring in the documents. The performance of their concept based uni-gram language model has been consistently better than the bi-grams model and bi-terms models. However none relation between query concepts (words) and documents concepts (words) have been exploited. For their part, Hammache and al. [10] proposed to combine single words and filtered bi-grams into a language model. In their approach bi-grams are selected and weighted by considering both their own occurrence in the document and the occurrence of their component terms. The results of these approaches are better than the single word model and some state of the art models. In the same purpose, Gao and al. [9] modelled dependencies between query terms pairwise as a hidden linked variable. The latter is undirected acyclic graph which express the most distant and robust dependencies among query words. The results have shown that the incorporation of this type of dependency has a positive impact on retrieval performance. Moreover, the dependence model outperforms the uni-grams, bi-grams and the co-occurrence ones. Results of these approaches are mixed: the bi-gram language model has shown lower results than the uni-gram model. Nevertheless, this model has been further enhanced by relaxing the constraint order and adjacency in bi-grams or by considering more distant relations [17, 18, 9]. However there are implicit and important dependencies such as synonymy or any semantic relation which are not captured.

2.2   Integrating Dependencies Extracted from External Resources

A number of extension of the LM approach have attempted improve retrieval performance using semantic information a priori defined in external resources such as WordNet[8, 3], UMLS [23] and Wikipedia[?]. One of the main work in LM framework which incorporates relationships between query words and document ones has been proposed by Cao and al. [8], they have proposed a language model framework which incorporates relationships between query words and document words. Accordingly, a relationship can be identified in two ways: direct connection when words are identical and/or indirect connection through co-occurrences and WordNet relations. The relationships between words are exploited in the smoothing ...of the proposed language model. Their results were better than the uni-gram model. In the same spirit, Bao and al [3] proposed a Language Sense Model (LSM) based on WordNet senses. They have also used the linear interpolation in order to integrate hyponyms and hypernyms. The experiments did not highlight strong conclusions [3]. However the combination of terms and their respective senses have improved retrieval effectiveness especially for long queries (having more than 20 words). Other works [23] proposed a semantic smoothing of the document model using topic signatures. The latter corresponds to sets of synonyms, senses, contextual information and collocations extracted from documents. For this purpose, MaxMatcher[1] and XTRACT[2] have been used. The model was tested on a domain collection (TREC Genomic) and results were significant. Xinhui and al. [19] used Wikipedia title articles as topic signature with the same smoothing model of [23] and results were also successful.

In this paper, we propose to go beyond single words representation by assuming that document and queries are represented by mean of concepts which may be a single word, or frequent word collocations. The latter might be an ontology entry. Indeed, documents as well as queries should contain potential concepts which are not available in the ontologies, such as neologisms or proper names. Our definition of a concept joins the one described in [5]. Our belief is that a robust IR model should take into account all these elements and integrates them in a weighting schema proportionally to their importance in the text. Unlike the models proposed in [8, 3], both kinds of dependencies mentioned previously are integrated into our model, namely : 1) dependencies within the document and ones within throughout frequent collocation and ontology concepts to answer the polysemy issue. Indeed, multi-words are less ambiguous than single words. 2) Higher level dependencies are integrated in LM throughout relationships between query concepts and document ones. There are two intuitions behind integrating concepts relationships into the language model: the first one is to retrieve relevant document containing the same concepts whereas they are written with different words. The second one is to increase the concept weight with its related concepts such as hyponyms, hypernyms. The translation model of Berger and Lafferty [6], also known as a semantic smoothing model, seems to be the well adapted one to take into account our intuitions. Accordingly, the centrality of a concept, viewed as an important factor of relevance [7], is taken into account in a retrieval model.

---

[1] UMLS concepts extraction tool.

[2] Collocation extraction tool.

3   Concept Based Language Model

Let us consider query Q, document D and Ontology O where query Q and document D are respectively represented by concepts based modeling: $Q = c_1, c_2, ...c_m$ and $D = c_1, c_2, ...c_n$, where c_j is a concept which may be a single word or a multi words which corresponds also to an ontology entry or to a frequent collocation in the document collection. The relevance score RSV(Q,D) of a document to a query is estimated as mentioned in the formula 2.

$$RSV(Q, D) = P(Q|D)) = \prod_i^n P(c_i|D) \qquad (2)$$

Formula 2 can be considered as an abstraction of the Ponte and Croft unigram model [13], where $P(c_i|D)$ is the probability of concept c_i in document D expressed as:

$$P(c_i|D) = \begin{cases} P(c_i|D, \bar{O}) & if c_i \notin O \\ P(c_i|D, O) & otherwise \end{cases} \qquad (3)$$

For a better clarity, probability $P(c_i|D)$ can be reformulated as:

$$P(c_i|D) = P(c_i|D, \bar{O}) + P(c_i|D, O) \qquad (4)$$

$P(c_i|D, \bar{O})$ corresponds to the probability of c_i in D given the information that c_i is ont an ontology entry.
$P(c_i|D, O)$ is the probability of c_i an ontology entry in the document model.
These probabilities are complementary since events O and $\bar{O}$ are complementary. We assume that a concept c_i is an ontological entry, its probability is estimated by taking into account its related concepts in the ontology and in the document. Therefore, it should model the fact that c_i should be seen effectively in the document model or represented by its related concepts.

$$P(c_i|D, O) = \sum_{c_j \in D} P(c_i|c_j) \; P_{sem}(c_j|D)) \qquad (5)$$

This formulation is based on the translation model[6]. Our aim, here, is to integrate semantic relationships between query and document concepts. This can be seen as "Semantic Smoothing". Thus, the weight of query concepts are enhanced with those of related concepts (Synonyms, hypernyms or hyponyms). Therefore, estimating $P(c_i|D, O)$ in this way highlights the centrality of query concepts in the documents. The centrality of a concept c_i is defined by the number of its related concepts in D [7]. Notice that in our model, the centrality is implicitly taken into account and corresponds to the number sequences of the sum in formula (5).
The global score of relevance is expressed by the following formula:

$$P(Q|D) = \prod_{c_i \in Q} \left[P(c_i|D, \bar{O}) + \sum_{c_j \in Q} P(c_i|c_j, O) \; P_{sem}(c_j|D) \right] \qquad (6)$$

where the three probabilities $P(c_i|D,\bar{O})$, $P_{sem}(c_j|D,O)$ and $P(c_i|c_j,O)$ are described below

The Probability $P(c_i|D,\bar{O})$ of c_i Given D
In the case where a query concept c_i is not in the ontology, its probability in D is given by using the Dirichlet prior smoothing.

$$P_{Dir}(c_i|D,\bar{O}) = \frac{count(c_i,D) + \mu P_{ML}(c_i|C)}{\sum_{c_k} count(c_k,D) + \mu}$$

where $Count(c_i,D)$ is c_i frequency in the document D, μ is the Dirichlet smoothing parameter and $P_{ML}(c_i|C)$ corresponds to the background collection language model by the maximum likelihood estimator as follows:

$$P_{ML}(c_i|C) = \frac{count(c_i,C)}{\sum_{c_k} count(c_k,C)} \tag{7}$$

The Semantic Probability $P_{sem}(c_j|D,O)$ of c_j Given D
This probability is called "semantic probability" since it estimates the likelihood of the ontological entry c_j and the one of its component sub concepts (sc) corresponding to WordNet entries. The intuition is the following : usually, authors tend to use sub-concepts to refer to the multi-term concepts that they have previously used in the same document[4]. For example, in TREC documents, the concept "coup" occurs after the multi-word concept "military coup d'etat" used more than once. Therefore, the component sub-concept "coup" is very likely to refer to "Military coup d'etat" than to another one. Therefore, $P_{sem}(c_j|D,O)$ is expressed as follow:

$$P_{sem}(c_j|D,O) = \theta P(c_j|D) + (1-\theta) \sum_{sc \in sub_{C}oncepts(c_j)} \frac{length(sc)}{length(c_j)} P(sc|D) \tag{8}$$

where $length(sc)$ is the size of sc in words, Sc is a sub-concept of c_j that corresponds to an ontology entry. θ is $\in [0,1]$. The probabilities $P_{ML}(c_j|D)$ and $P_{ML}(sc|D)$ are respectively estimated using the Dirichlet smoothing like formula (7). We notice that formula (8) is equivalent to the CF-IDF weighting formula proposed by Baziz and al. [?]

The Probability $P(c_i|c_j,O)$ of c_i Given c_j
This probability estimates the relationship degree between concepts c_i and c_j. Several ways have been proposed to estimate the probability of a term given another. In general, they are based on relationships such as co-occurrences, mutual information, fuzzy relationships [1], or ontological relationships like synonymy, hypernymy or hyponymy [8, 23]. For our part, we estimate $P(c_i|c_j,O)$ using the degree of relation between c_i and c_j in the ontology compared to the whole relationship degrees between query concepts and document ones. Thus, $P(c_i|c_j,O)$ est estimated as follow

$$P(c_i|c_j, O) = \begin{cases} \dfrac{Rel(c_i, c_j)}{\sum_{c_k \in Q} Rel(c_k, c_j)} & if \quad c_i \neq c_j \\ \\ 1 & otherwise \end{cases} \tag{9}$$

where $Rel(c_i, c_j)$ is relationship degree between concepts c_i and c_j, estimated using Resnik Semantic Similarity [14] as:

$$Rel(c_i, c_j) = sim_{res*}(c_i, c_j)$$

Resnik Similarity is based on the is-a relationship and Information Content (IC) metric proposed in Seco and al.[15].

$$sim_{res*}(c_i, c_j) = max_{c \in S(c_i, c_j)} IC_{wn}(c))$$

$S(c_i, c_j)$ is the set of concepts that subsumes c_i and c_j. The Information Content IC_{wn} is based on the following principle: the more a concept has descendants, the less is its Information Content. Therefore, concepts that are leaves (specific concepts) have more IC than ones situated up in the hierarchy. In fact, Resnik Similarity based on IC highlights specificity defined in [7].

$$IC_{wn}(c) = 1 - \frac{\log(hypo(c)) + 1}{\log(max_{wn})}$$

where $hypo(c)$ returns the hyponyms number of concept c and max_{wn} is a constant corresponding generally to the maximal number of concepts in the taxonomy. In the version 2.1 of WordNet, $max_{wn} = 117659$.

4   Experimental Evaluation

To evaluate the effectiveness of our retrieval model, we used two datasets issued from TREC [3] collections and WordNet 2.0 [11] a linguistic ontology to detect ontological concepts and relationships. We carried out a threefold objective-based experiment:

a) Evaluating the impact of combining ontological concepts and the non-ontological ones in a language modeling approach.
b) Highlighting the impact of integrating concept relationships (hyponymy, hyponymy) in the retrieval model.
c) Comparing our model with a strong single word language model, namely the uni-gram model.

---

[3] trec.nist.gov

4.1   Datasets and Experimental Setting

As mentioned above, experiments were carried out on two datasets of TREC (issued from disk 1 & 2) namely WSJ 86-87 (Wall Street Journal) and AP 89 (Associated Press News). Each dataset is a collection of news. In addition, a set of topics constituting the queries and the relevance judgement are provided for each dataset.

Document Processing
In our approach each document in both datasets is processed using the following approach:

a) Terms and multi-terms of different sizes are detected using Text-NSP tool [2] and saved in a list.
b) Detected terms of that list are then processed to remove all terms beginning or ending with a stop word. Terrier [12] stop word list is used for this purpose. We underline that unlike almost related work, we avoid pretreatment of the text before detecting multi-terms in order to keep potential concepts such as "Ministry of justice", "Bureau of investigation "[4]. This type of concepts is called "complex phrases"[22] and are frequently monosemic.
c) For validating that a given multi-term concept, we only keep those occurring at least twice.
d) We check whether a concept occur or not in WordNet. For those having an entry, they are selected and represented by their Synset Number. For instance, the concepts "coup", "coup d'etat", "takeover" and "putch" are grouped in the synset with number 01147528.
e) When a given concept has several entries (polysemy) in WordNet, the default first sense is selected.
f) The remainder of concepts is kept as the non WordNet entries and weighted with simple count of occurrences.

   TREC Topics have been used as queries. Each topic is composed of three parts: Title part which is a short query, Description part, which is a long (verbose) query and Narrative part, describing in detail previous parts and precisely what relevant documents should contain. In this evaluation, we used the Title part of topics as queries since they are as short as user queries.
The value of Dirichlet prior parameter μ is set to 2500 for all datasets and models.

4.2   Results and Evaluation

In this section, we present the results obtained throughout our experimental evaluation. For this purpose, we used the following metrics $P@x$ precision at the point $x \in \{10, 20\}$ [5] and the MAP.

---

[4] These examples are taken from TREC documents.

[5] P@x, is the ratio evaluating the number of relevant document at the top x retrieved documents and the Mean average precision

Analysing the impact of combining WordNet terms and non Word-Net terms. We aim here at evaluating the impact of combining terms (single words, phrases non corresponding to WordNet entries, and those belonging to WordNet). First, we test the retrieval model corresponding to formula (2) using all detected collocations and without filtering WordNet concepts. Thus $P(c_i|D)$ is estimated using Dirichlet smoothing (see formula (7)). Second, the model was tested by considering only WordNet concepts and finally the combined model of WordNet concepts and frequent collocations (the whole fromula (6)). Fig.1 illustrates changes in MAP for the three tests mentioned above. It can be clearly seen

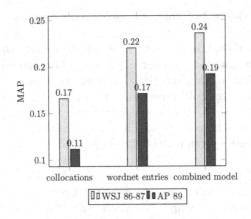

Fig. 1. The variation of MAP

in Fig.1 that the combined model outperforms the two other models. It achieves a MAP value of $0,24$ for WSJ 86-87 dataset and $0,19$ for AP 89 dataset. Accordingly, the combined model noted CLM_0 is used in the remaining experiments and compared to the uni-gram model noted ULM.

Table.1 compares the obtained results of the evaluation of CLM_0 and ULM. Gain (%) line denotes the percentage of improvement regarding the ULM. The reported precisions show that CLM_0 generally outperforms ULM with significant improvement equal to the value of $+3,21\%$ for WSJ 86-87 dataset. For AP 89 dataset, the improvement is not as significant as for WSJ 86-87. Nevertheless, at $P@10$ and $P@20$, the improvements are statistically significant with the p-value is lower to $0,5$ according to t-test.

Indeed, we have performed a more in-depth analysis on some queries such as " Military Coup d'Etat" (topic-62). We observed that ULM achieved an Average Precision (AP) of $0,1446$ while our model CLM_0 reached an AP of $0,3956$. To show the reason of this improvement in AP for that query, we have checked how both models have ranked some relevant documents[6]. For example, document "WSJ870526-0068" was promoted from rank 114 with ULM to rank 22 with

---

[6] The list of relevant documents is taken from Relevance judgement file.

Table 1. Comparison between performances of the uni-gram model(ULM) and the combined concept based model CLM_0. Test significance : + for p-value < 0.05 and ++ p-value < 0.01.

Collection	Evaluated model	Performance evaluation		
		$P@10$	$P@20$	MAP
WSJ (86-87)	ULM	$0,3280$	$0,2790$	$0,2302$
	CLM_0	$0,3640$	$0,3030$	$0,2376$
	Gain (%)	$+10,98^{++}$	$+8,60^{++}$	$+3,21^{+}$
AP (89)	ULM	$0,3160$	$0,2810$	$0,1924$
	CLM_0	$0,3280$	$0,2910$	$0,1925$
	Gain (%)	$+3,80^{+}$	$+3,56^{+}$	$+0,05$

our model. When examining manually the document content, we found that it does not contain exactly the concept "coup dtat", but synonyms such as "coup" and "takeover occur respectively 7 and 6 times. The same has been observed for query "Iran-contra affair" (Topic 99) for which our model reached an AP value of $0,2832$ and ULM achieved an AP of 0.0069. This enhancement in AP is due to the fact that the query itself is a frequent collocation in WSJ 86-87 dataset. However, for AP 89 dataset, the noticed enhancement is less important. However, both models perform nearly equally for AP 89 dataset. They achieved respectively AP values of 0.3212 and 0.3209. This result is due to the fact that "Iran contra affair" and "Iran-contra" are frequent collocations in WSJ 86-87 dataset in contrast with AP 89 dataset. This highlights the importance of considering various concepts (single words, collocations and WordNet entries) in the retrieval model.

Analysing the Impact of Incorporating Concepts Relations. We perform a further analysis evaluation in order to show the impact of integrating concepts relations into the retrieval model. This evaluation concerns the model named CLM_1 expressed in the formula 6 where we only integrated "is a" relationships namely the hypernymy and hyponymy.

We can see in table2 that for WSJ dataset, we notice that CLM_1 overpasses generally CLM_0 and the ULM. As of AP 89 collection, the improvements are not as significant as those achieved for WSJ 86-87 collection but they are statistically significant on P@10 and P@20. Indeed, t-test shows that our results are significant since the p-value $< 0,01$.

We performed the same analysis as the previous experiment with the same query (topic-62). We notice that ULM, CLM_0 and CLM_1 achieve respectively average precisions with value of $0,1446, 0,2911$ and $0,4342$. The analysis of a relevant document, for example WSJ870526-0068, showed that it is promoted from ranks 8 and 6 under ULM and CLM_0 respectively to the rank 2 because it contains a direct hypernym of "military" which is "forces" and it occurs 4 times

Table 2. Comparison between uni-gram model ULM and concept based models CLM_1. Test significance : $+$ for p-value < 0.05 and $++$ for p-value < 0.01 .

Collection	Evaluated model	Performance evaluation		
		$P@10$	$P@20$	MAP
WSJ (86-87)	ULM	$0,3280$	$0,2790$	$0,2302$
	CLM_0	$0,3640$	$0,3030$	$0,2376$
	Gain (%)	$+10,976^{++}$	$+8,60^{++}$	$+3,21^{+}$
	CLM_1	$0,3642$	$0,3266$	$0,2380$
	Gain (%)	$+11,04^{++}$	$+17,06^{++}$	$3,39^{++}$
AP (89)	ULM	$0,3160$	$0,2810$	$0,1924$
	CLM_0	$0,3280$	$0,2910$	$0,1925$
	Gain (%)	$+3,80^{+}$	$+3,56^{+}$	$+0,05$
	CLM_1	$0,33140$	$0,2900$	$0,1932$
	Gain (%)	$+8,23^{++}$	$+4,63^{+}$	$+0,51$

in the document. So the probability of "military" is boosted with that of its related concept "forces". These statements lead us to conclude that integrating concepts, semantic relations in the retrieval model enhanced document retrieval.

5   Conclusion and Future Work

In this paper we introduced a concept-based language model for enhancing document retrieval. The intuition is to build a rich document representation through single words, ontological concepts, their relationships available in an ontology and collocations which are not ontological concepts. The latter can be either proper names or neologisms. Moreover, through integrating relationships between query and document concepts, our model allows to take into account of related concepts to those of the query. This is carried out through smoothing part of the proposed language model. The empirical results on TREC collections show that our model outperforms the uni-gram one. Indeed, this highlights the effectiveness of combining statistical collocations and WordNet concepts and their relationships namely "is-a" relation in a language modeling approach. These results are also encouraging to mix further evidence sources of concepts to estimate richer and more precise document model. Our model could be further improved by integrating additional NLP rules for filtering collocations and other resources such as Wikipedia. We also plan to test the impact of other semantic relationships on retrieval.

References

[1] Bai, J., Song, D., Bruza, P., Nie, J.Y., Cao, G.: Query expansion using term relationships in language models for information retrieval. In: Proceedings of the 14th ACM International Conference on Information and Knowledge Management, CIKM 2005, pp. 688–695. ACM (2005)

[2] Banerjee, S., Pedersen, T.: The design, implementation, and use of the ngram statistics package. In: Gelbukh, A. (ed.) CICLing 2003. LNCS, vol. 2588, pp. 370–381. Springer, Heidelberg (2003)

[3] Bao, S., Zhang, L., Chen, E., Long, M., Li, R., Yu, Y.: LSM: Language sense model for information retrieval. In: Yu, J.X., Kitsuregawa, M., Leong, H.-V. (eds.) WAIM 2006. LNCS, vol. 4016, pp. 97–108. Springer, Heidelberg (2006)

[4] Baziz, M., Boughanem, M., Passi, G., Prade, H.: An information retrieval driven by ontology from query to document expansion. In: Large Scale Semantic Access to Content (Text, Image, Video, and Sound), RIAO 2007, pp. 301–313 (2007)

[5] Bendersky, M., Croft, W.B.: Modeling higher-order term dependencies in information retrieval using query hypergraphs. In: Proceedings of the 35th International ACM SIGIR Conference on Research and Development in Information Retrieval, SIGIR 2012, pp. 941–950. ACM (2012)

[6] Berger, A., Lafferty, J.: Information retrieval as statistical translation. In: Proceedings of the 22nd Annual International ACM SIGIR Conference on Research and Development in Information Retrieval, SIGIR 1999, pp. 222–229. ACM (1999)

[7] Boughanem, M., Mallak, I., Prade, H.: A new factor for computing the relevance of a document to a query. In: Proceedings of the International Conference on Fuzzy Systems, pp. 1–6. IEEE (2010)

[8] Cao, G., Nie, J.Y., Bai, J.: Integrating word relationships into language models. In: Proceedings of the 28th Annual International ACM SIGIR Conference on Research and Development in Information Retrieval, SIGIR 2005, pp. 298–305. ACM (2005)

[9] Gao, J., Nie, J.Y., Wu, G., Cao, G.: Dependence language model for information retrieval. In: Proceedings of the 27th Annual International ACM SIGIR Conference on Research and Development in Information Retrieval, SIGIR 2004, pp. 170–177. ACM (2004)

[10] Hammache, A., Boughanem, M., Ahmed Ouamar, R.: Combining compound and single terms under language model framework. In: Knowledge and Information Systems, pp. 329–349 (2013)

[11] Miller, G.A.: Wordnet: A lexical database for english. Communications of the ACM 38(11), 39–41 (1995)

[12] Ounis, I., Amati, G., Plachouras, V., He, B., Macdonald, C., Johnson, D.: Terrier information retrieval platform. In: Losada, D.E., Fernández-Luna, J.M. (eds.) ECIR 2005. LNCS, vol. 3408, pp. 517–519. Springer, Heidelberg (2005)

[13] Ponte, J.M., Croft, W.B.: A language modeling approach to information retrieval. In: Proceedings of the 21st Annual International ACM SIGIR Conference on Research and Development in Information Retrieval, SIGIR 1998, pp. 275–281. ACM (1998)

[14] Resnik, P.: Using information content to evaluate semantic similarity in a taxonomy. In: Proceedings of the 14th International Joint Conference on Artificial Intelligence, IJCAI 1995, pp. 448–453. Morgan Kaufmann Publishers Inc. (1995)

[15] Seco, N., Veale, T., Hayes, J.: An intrinsic information content metric for semantic similarity in wordnet. In: ECAI, vol. 4, pp. 1089–1090 (2004)

[16] Song, F., Croft, W.B.: A general language model for information retrieval. In: Proceedings of the Eighth International Conference on Information and Knowledge Management, CIKM 1999, pp. 316–321. ACM (1999)

[17] Srikanth, M., Srihari, R.: Biterm language models for document retrieval. In: Proceedings of the 25th Annual International ACM SIGIR Conference on Research and Development in Information Retrieval, SIGIR 2002, pp. 425–426. ACM (2002)

[18] Srikanth, M., Srihari, R.: Incorporating query term dependencies in language models for document retrieval. In: Proceedings of the 26th Annual International ACM SIGIR Conference on Research and Development in Informaion Retrieval, SIGIR 2003, pp. 405–406. ACM (2003)

[19] Tu, X., He, T., Chen, L., Luo, J., Zhang, M.: Wikipedia-based semantic smoothing for the language modeling approach to information retrieval. In: Gurrin, C., He, Y., Kazai, G., Kruschwitz, U., Little, S., Roelleke, T., Rüger, S., van Rijsbergen, K. (eds.) ECIR 2010. LNCS, vol. 5993, pp. 370–381. Springer, Heidelberg (2010)

[20] Victor, L., Croft, W.B.: Relevance based language models. In: Proceedings of the 24th Annual International ACM SIGIR Conference on Research and Development in Information Retrieval, SIGIR 2001, pp. 120–127. ACM (2001)

[21] Zhai, C., Lafferty, J.: A study of smoothing methods for language models applied to ad hoc information retrieval. In: Proceedings of the 24th Annual International ACM SIGIR Conference on Research and Development in Information Retrieval, SIGIR 2001, pp. 334–342. ACM (2001)

[22] Zhang, W., Liu, S., Yu, C., Sun, C., Liu, F., Meng, W.: Recognition and classification of noun phrases in queries for effective retrieval. In: Proceedings of the Sixteenth ACM Conference on Information and Knowledge Management, CIKM 2007, pp. 711–720. ACM (2007)

[23] Zhou, X., Hu, X., Zhang, X.: Topic signature language models for ad hoc retrieval. IEEE Trans. on Knowl. and Data Eng. 19(9), 1276–1287 (2007)

The Multidimensional Semantic Model of Text Objects(MSMTO): A Framework for Text Data Analysis

Sarah Attaf[1], Nadjia Benblidia[1], and Omar Boussaid[2]

[1] LRDSI Laboratory, Saad Dahlab University BP 270 Soumaa-Blida, Algeria
sarah.attaf@gmail.com, benblidia@yahoo.com
[2] ERIC Laboratory, University of Lyon 2,5
AV. P. Mends-France 69676 Bron Cedex Lyon, France
Omar.Boussaid@univ-lyon2.fr

Abstract. The modeling process for text-data type used for analysis purposes is to give a special representation for this kind of unstructured data. The given representation offers a formal description for text data to enable an effective use of the information contained in the text. In this context, and in order to perform analysis on this unstructured data type, we propose the multidimensional semantic model (MSMTO). The proposed model is based on the object paradigm. The model integrates a new concept *Semantic Content Object* used to represent and organize the semantic of text data in a hierarchical format, to enable a semantic analysis at different levels of granularity. Our modeling approach considers the internal composition of text documents as a structural hierarchy, which allows the user to perform analysis on different hierarchical levels. Our model offers also flexibility, by considering the semantic content of text-data as a measure, a fact or even a dimension.

Keywords: Text warehouse Modeling, Semantic Content, Structural hierarchy, Semantic hierarchy, Flexibility, Text data.

1 Introduction

Nowadays, electronic documentation is part and parcel of the information and communication strategy of any contemporary Organization. In fact, it is understood that more than 80% [10] of the data needed for organizations operations are encapsulated in documents, and not just in operational databases. These textual data remain out of reach of decision support systems, which indicates that much of the information remains inaccessible.

Classical decision support systems used in analyzing simple data, have already given good results. However, these systems are not adapted for text documents analysis, which highlights the need to create new multidimensional models for text data. The storage of this type of data remains today as one of the major difficulties which involve many challenges regarding their modeling and integration on the one hand and analysis on the other. Text warehouses have emerged as a

Y. Ait Ameur et al. (Eds.): MEDI 2014, LNCS 8748, pp. 113–124, 2014.

new solution for text data analysis. The complex nature of these data requires a particular treatment, taking into account their semantics. In the literature, methods of information retrieval and data mining have yielded good results for textual data exploration. The key idea behind text warehouses is to link data mining and information retrieval techniques, with OLAP techniques. The existing text warehouse models, such as topic cube [10] and text cube [6], proposed a first solution to this problem by integrating a semantic dimension. However, it still remains untapped, each model propose a specific semantic type (terms, topics...) which could limit analysis possibilities.

Flexibility represents another challenge in the analysis of text data. In classical business intelligence systems, a fact represents a predefined analysis subject. A fact definition from the outset reduces the flexibility in the analysis for the decision maker is forced to use these facts as subjects. In order to ensure more flexibility, some works have proposed to delete the fact concept, to avoid constraining the analysis by pre-defined facts. In this study, we tackle the problem of flexibility in the analysis by identifying, the semantic content of text data can as an analytical measurement as well as a fact. In other words, an object is considered as a measurement for a given set of data and an axis for the analysis of another set of data. To our knowledge, this dual role, in order to ensure a good analysis flexibility, is not used by existing work.

The modeling approach we propose focuses particularly on the following aspects: (i) the inclusion of the text data structure, (ii) the inclusion of the semantic aspects of text data, and finally (iii) the analysis flexibility. In this context, we propose the multidimensional semantic model of text objects (MSMTO), which is based on the object paradigm, a choice justified by the representative capacity of object-oriented models. The aim of this work is to design a warehouse model that can represent any text data and make multidimensional analysis based on the information contained in these warehouses (structure and semantic content) providing a good analysis flexibility. The main contributions for this paper are: (1) the introduction of a multidimensional semantic model of text objects and (2) the development of an operator to construct semantic text cubes.

2   Related Works

Multidimensional modeling is to organize data so that OLAP applications will be efficient and effective. The existing warehouse models offer a framework for a multidimensional modelling of simple data, but they are not suitable for text data. To address this problem several studies have being developed. These studies can be grouped into two categories [1]. The first category includes extensive models, which have proposed to extend the traditional warehouse models to enable analysis on textual data. They are based on the two basic concepts: fact and dimension. Some of these models have proposed to extend the classical data cube by integrating a semantic dimension, like a topics hierarchy in Topic cube [10], terms hierarchy in text cube [6] and an AP-Structure based on the frequent items named AP-sets in [2]. Other works have based their models on the classification technique; two major representative works in this group are Doc cube [7] and microtextcluster [11]. These models were able to treat the semantics of text data by integrating a semantic dimension. The structural aspect was not taken into account however, which does not support analysis on different structural levels, such as analyzing a specific section (ex: sports) in a journal. Models in this category are based on the traditional warehouse model, leading to a lack of flexibility in the analysis. The second category includes models with new concepts, in this later, new models based on new concepts were proposed. The two best known models are: galaxie model [9] and Complex objects model [4]. The first one is based on the generalization of the concept of constellation [5]. The second model is based on complex object concept. This model allows an analysis at different levels of granularity of each complex object, while the semantic aspect of complex data is not supported. Models in this category consider the structural aspects of the documents which allow an analysis in different structural levels, while the semantic aspect is still untapped. These models offer good analysis flexibility, but they do not allow defining the semantic content as a measure or a dimension at the same time.

3   MSMTO: Multidimensional Semantic Model of Text Objects

In our modeling approach we focused on three aspects: (i) the text data structure, (ii) the text data semantic and (iii) the flexibility of the analysis. Our model offers a deep analysis on different semantic and structural levels through two kinds of hierarchies, structural hierarchy and semantic hierarchy. It also provides analysis flexibility by means of our operator for semantic text cube construction.

3.1   Concepts Definition

In this section, we will present the basic concepts defined for our model:

Text Object (TObjt): a text object is an entity representing a text element (ex: text document) that can be analyzed as a fact or an analysis dimension. A text object is defined by a set of simple attributes which are UML class attributes. Text object attributes represent data extracted from textual documents.

Definition 1. *A text object is noted TObjt and is defined as follows:*

$$TObjt = (IDTObjt, SATObjt) \tag{1}$$

$$With : SATObjt = \{ATObjt_1, ATObjt_2, ..., ATObjt_n/n \in \mathbb{N}\}$$

where: IDTObjt represents the identifier of the text object and SATObjt represents the set of its attributes.

Content Object (SCObjt): This is an entity representing the semantic content of a text object. It is obtained by applying a method to extract semantic of the target text object. Relevant terms or topics are examples of semantic content object. This later is defined by an attributes set and a single semantic aggregation method, that operates on it in order to produce other semantic content objects with highest granularity. For example, Class terms object represents a semantic content object with highest granularity level. It is obtained by applying *AVG KWD* aggregation function [9] to the semantic content object Terms. It should be noted that the semantic content object of the lowest level of granularity is associated with the 0 level, in the precedent example Terms object is associated with the 0 level.

Definition 2. *A semantic content object is noted SCObjt and is defined as follows:*

$$SCObjt = (IDSCObjt, SASCObjt, MSCObjt) \tag{2}$$

$$With : SASCObjt = \{ASCObjt_1, ASCObjt_2, ..., ASCObjt_n\}/n \in \mathbb{N}\}$$

Where IDSCObjt represents the identifier of the semantic content object, SASCObjt represents the set of its attributes and MSCObjt represents an aggregation method.

Figure 1 shows the multidimensional semantic meta model of text objects described by UML class diagram.

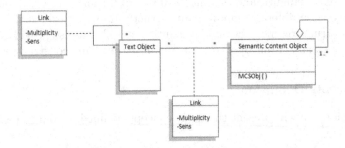

Fig. 1. The semantic meta model of text objects

This model is described as follows:

- The text object class represents the text object
- The Semantic content object class represents the semantic content object
- The association *Link(TObjt, TObjt)* represents the link between different text objects such as aggregation, association, composition...
- The association *Link(SCObjt, SCObjt)* represents the aggregation link between semantic content objects.
- The *association(TObjt, SCObjt)* represents the link that associate each text object to its semantic content object.

Example: An example of a text object is a press journal. A press journal can be described by an attributes set, such as journal name, type, publisher... etc. A journal can be described by a set of text objects as: section, articles. Topics associated to text objects (Journal, section, articles) are an example of semantic content object. An example of the link (SCObjt,SCObjt) is the aggregation relation between the semantic content object *topics* and the semantic content object *topics family*. The *AVG KW* [8] method used to group keywords into ones more general is an example of an aggregation method applied to the object *Terms*.(Fig.2)

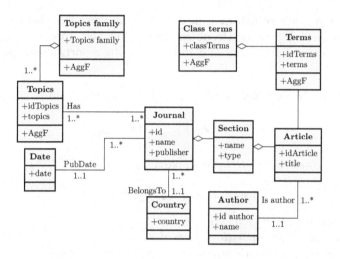

Fig. 2. Representation of a journal by the multidimensional semantic model of text objects

Complex relation: this relation models the links between text objects beyond those of aggregation, generalization and composition on the one hand, and the links between text objects and semantic content objects on the other hand. It's complexity lies in the fact that it defines the analysis axis and the analytical measure of certain objects by reports of others.(Fig.3)

Definition 3. *A Complex relation is noted R and is defined as follows:*

$$R = (TObjt^R, Object^R) \tag{3}$$

$$Where: \quad Object \in \{TObjt, SCObjt\}$$

$$And \quad R \notin \{Aggregation, composition, generalisation\}$$

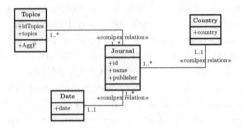

Fig. 3. An example of complex relation for Journal object

Extended complex relation: it models the non-direct links between objects, for example the link between the object articles and the object date in figure 2. It also defines the analysis axis of certain objects by reports of others.

Definition 4. *An extended complex relation is noted ER and is defined as follows:*

$$ER = (Tobjt_{Source}^{ER}, TObjt_{Cible}^{ER}) \tag{4}$$

$$Such\ that:\quad Relation(Tobjt_{Source}^{Relation}, TObjt_{x}^{Relation})$$

$$And\quad R(objt_{x}^{R}, TObjt_{Cible}^{R})$$

Where: R is a complex relation (see (3))
ER ∉ {Aggregation, composition, generalisation}
and   Relation ∈ {Aggregation, composition, generalisation}

Structural hierarchy: it is defined between multiple text objects. It allows performing aggregation operations between text objects according to their structure. Structural hierarchy defines a partial order between some text objects according to their degree of granularity.(Fig.4)

Definition 5. *Structural hierarchy is noted StH and is defined as follows:*

$$StH = \{TObjt_1, TObjt_2, ..., TObjt_n / n \in \mathbb{N}\} \cup \{AllObjt\} \tag{5}$$

Where: AllObjt is an artificial object with the lowest granularity.

Semantic hierarchy: a semantic hierarchy is defined between multiple semantic content object. It is a particular type of hierarchy that establishes semantic aggregations between semantic content objects. We define a function SCObjtLevel(SCObjt; SH), which returns the level of each semantic content object in the semantic hierarchy. We suppose that the level of the more detailed object of the hierarchy is assigned to 0, this object is associated to a text object. (Fig.5)

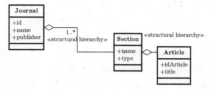

Fig. 4. An example of structural hierarchy

Definition 6. *A Semantic hierarchy is noted SH and is defined as follows:*

$$SH = \{SCObjt_1, SCObjt_2, ..., SCObjt_n / n \in \mathbb{N}\} \qquad (6)$$

$$Such that: R(TObjt^R, SCObject^R) \implies SCObjtLevel(SCObjt, SH) = 0$$

And AllObjt is an artificial object with the lowest granularity.

Fig. 5. An example of semantic hierarchy

3.2   Semantic Text Cube (ST-Cube)

In order to perform multidimensional analysis in our model, we define a semantic text cube as follows: A semantic text cube is constructed based on the multidimensional semantic model of text objects; it can model an analysis subject called FactObject defined by several text object dimensions $TODim_i, i \in [1..*]$ and semantic object dimensions $SODim_j, j \in [1..*]$. A text object dimension includes attributes $TA =< ta_1, ta_2, .., ta_* >$ and it is associated to a structural hierarchy composed of text objects $StH =< to_1, to_2, .., to_* >$. A semantic object dimension includes attributes $SA =< sa_1, sa_2, .., sa_* >$ and it is associated to a semantic hierarchy composed of semantic objects $SO =< so_1, so_2, .., so_* >$. A semantic text cube is defined by a set of textual dimensions objects, semantic dimensions objects, fact object and a measure set. Drill down and roll-up along textual dimensions objects will allow users to make analyses on different hierarchical levels. Drill down and roll up along semantic dimensions objects will enable a semantic analysis at different levels of granularity. Our semantic text cube may store different kind of measure: numerical measure, textual measure, semantic measure.

ST-Cube Construction Operator. The proposal model offers good analysis flexibility, not just by giving users the ability to define the fact over the cube construction operator, but by giving the possibility to consider the semantic content of text data as : an analysis axis, a fact or even a measure for a textual fact object. The semantic text cube building process is to: (i) select an object from the multidimensional semantic model of text objects and assign it the role of fact, this object will be called fact object. (ii) Select a set of objects and assign them the role of dimensions, these objects will be called dimensions objects. The fact object may be: a text object or a semantic content object which gives us two cases:

a. **Case 1:** the fact object may be a text object or a semantic content object which gives us two possibilities:
   - The measure is a simple attribute of the fact object. In this case the semantic content object related to the text object(selected as fact) by a complex relation will be considered as an analysis axis.
   - The measure is a content semantic object. In this case the complex relation between the text object and the semantic content object(selected as measure)is not supported when selecting dimension objects.
b. **Case 2:** the fact object is a semantic content object. In this case the measure will be a simple attribute of the semantic content object.

For graphic representation, we use UML package diagram to represent our ST-Cube, where:

- A package representing a fact object contains the fact object and the analysis measure.
- A package representing a dimension object contains the dimension object.
- The links between package are called complex relation and extended complex relation. Figure 6 shows a multidimensional schema for journal analysis. It is obtained by applying ST-Cube construction operator and selecting journal object as a fact object and a journal attribute as a measure. In this case the topics object will be considered as a dimension object. The schema in figure 7 present another analysis possibility, it results by applying ST-Cube construction operator, defining articles object as fact object and terms object as measure. The resulting the fact object in this case is shown in figure 7.

ST-Cube Construction Operator Algorithm. The algorithm takes as input a list of text objects and semantic content objects which will be called $Object_{List} = \{Obj_1; Obj_2; Obj_3; ...; Obj_n\}/n \in \mathbb{N}$. It outputs a semantic text cube. The algorithm uses the following functions and procedures:

- **GetHDimension (DimensionObject)**: is a function that takes as input a dimension object and returns a set of objects that have a direct link with it such that: $Relation(Object^{Relation}; DimensionObject^{Relation})$ (see (4))
- **GetDimensionSet(FactObject)**: is a function that takes as input a fact Object and returns the set of objects related to this object through a complex relation defined in (3) and an extended complex relation defined in (4).

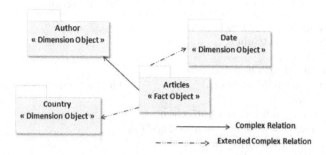

Fig. 6. An example for a multidimensional schema for articles object

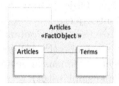

Fig. 7. A detailled package representing the fact object articles

- **SetAgregationFunction(Function)**: is a function that attribute for each analytical measure an aggregate function "Function".
- **Select (mesure, AttributeSet)**: is a function that attribute to the measure a value from the AttributeSet.

Algorithm 1. ST-Cube Construction Part 1(Called functions)

1: **function** GETHDIMENSIONSET(DimensionObject)
2:     **for** each object **From** $Object_{List}$ **do**
3:         **if** $Relation(Object^{Relation}, DimensionObject^{Relation})$ **then**
4:             HDimensionObject.add(Object);
5:         **end if**
6:     **end for**
7: **end function**
8: **function** GETDIMENSIONSET(Object)
9:     **for** each object **From** $Object_{List}$ **do**
10:        **if** $R(Object^{R}, DimensionObject^{R})$ **then**
11:            DimensionObject.add(Object);
12:        **end if**
13:    **end for**
14: **end function**

Algorithm 1. ST-Cube Construction Part 2 (Main Program)

Input: $Object_{List} = \{Obj_1, Obj_2, ..., Obj_n\}$
Output: Semantic TextCube
begin
FactObject:=SelectFact($Object_{List}$);
if FactObject = TextObject **then**   ▷ The fact object is a text object
   Define measure ;
   if measure is TextObjectAttribute **then**
      DimensionSet:=GetDimensionSet(FactObject);
      for all DimensionObject in DimensionSet **do**
         GetHDimension(DimensionObject);
      end for
   else
      if measure is SemanticContentObject **then**
         object:=SemanticContentObject;
         measure:= Select(measure,SemanticContentObjectAttributes);
         DimensionSet:=GetDimensionSet(FactObject)-{object};
         for all DimensionObject in DimensionSet **do**
            GetHDimension(DimensionObject);
         end for

      end if
   end if
else   ▷ the FactObject is a semanticContentObject
   measure:= Select(measure,SemanticContentObjectAttributes);
   DimensionSet:=GetDimensionSet(FactObject);
   for all DimensionObject in DimensionSet **do**
      GetHDimension(DimensionObject);
   end for
   measure.setAgreegationFunction(Function);
end if
End

3.3   Experiments

In order to validate our multidimensional semantic model of text object and the
st-cube constructor operator, we have implemented a text warehousing framework (Fig.8) based on two modules: an ETL(Extract,Transform and Load) module and a semantic text cube specification module.(1) The ETL module ensure:(i)
a mechanic feeding which allows extracting documents meta-data and feeding
text objects. (ii) a semantic feeding which consists of extracting and organizing
topics hiding in text documents in hierarchical format. This later is made by developing a new method based on LDA (latent Dirichelet Allocation) [3]. (2)The
semantic text cube specification module implements the st-cube construction
operator. For the warehouse and the cube storage, we used Postgresql, which is
an ORDBMS (Object Relational Database Management System). The choice of
this later is justified by its power to deal with complex data. Then, for functional

validation, we applied our approach on data set composed of 1970 press articles from Europe Topics[1]. Table 1, presents an example of a ST-Cube cell. This later answers an analysis query in which the decision maker wants to analyze press articles (Art) for $Time = \{"2001","2002","2003"\}$, $Location = "London"$, and $Topics = \{"Baseball","Soccer","Tax"\}$.

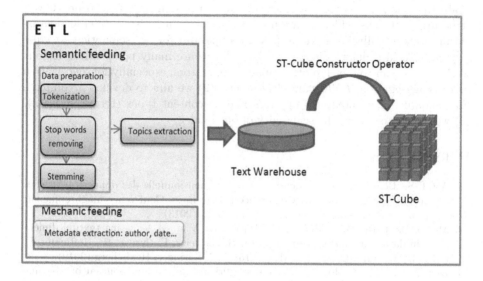

Fig. 8. System architecture

Since the semantic content could be considered according to the MSMTO model, as an analytical measurement as well as fact, our system can also answers queries, in which topics are considered as measure, such as analyze topics for: $Time = \{"2001","2002","2003"\}$, $Location = "London"$. Experiments shows that the proposed model gives good flexibility and could answer different analytical needs.

Table 1. An example of cell in semantic text cube

	London		
	2001	2002	2003
BaseBall	Art_3 ,Art_7,Art_{32}	Art_{41},Art_{23},Art_{12}	Art_{13} ,Art_{27},Art_{22}
Soccer	Art_{24},Art_{33},Art_{25}	Art_{34},Art_{26}	Art_{39} ,Art_7
Tax	Art_{19},Art_{11},Art_{21}	Art_{18} ,Art_{23},Art_6	,Art_{10},Art_{29}

---

[1] http://www.eurotopics.net/fr/home/presseschau/aktuell.html

4 Conclusion

In this paper we defined a new model for text data analysis. The modeling approach we propose focuses particularly on the inclusion of the text data structure, its semantic aspect and the analysis flexibility. The proposed model is based on the object paradigm. It integrates a new concept, *semantic content object*, used to represent and organize the semantic of text data in hierarchical format, to enable a semantic analysis at different levels of granularity. It also provides a structural hierarchy which allows users to perform analysis on different hierarchical levels. Finally We have proposed an operator for the semantic text cube construction in order to display its data. There are many perspectives for our work; (1) we aim to develop other analysis operators, especially for aggregation and dis-aggregation, *Rollup* and *Drilldown*. (2) we aim to develop a complete ETL module, that integrates others semantic content types (terms,phrases..). (3) we plan to evaluate the scalability of our model.

References

1. Attaf, S., Benblidia, N.: Modelisation multidimensionnelle des donnees textuelles ou en sommesnous? In: ASD Conference Proceedings, Conference maghrebine sur les avancees des systemes decisionnels, pp. 3–25 (2013)
2. Martín-Bautista, M.J., Molina, C., Tejeda, E., Vila, M.A.: Using textual dimensions in data warehousing processes. In: Hüllermeier, E., Kruse, R., Hoffmann, F. (eds.) IPMU 2010. CCIS, vol. 81, pp. 158–167. Springer, Heidelberg (2010)
3. Blei, D.M., Ng, A., Jordan, M.: Latent dirichlet allocation. Journal of Machine Learning Research 3(2), 993–1022 (2003)
4. Boukraa, D., Boussaid, O., Bentayeb, F., Zegour, D.: Modle multidimensionnel d'objets complexes: Du modele d'objets aux cubes d'objets complexes. Ingénierie des Systèmes d'Information 16 (2011)
5. Kimball, R.: The data warehouse toolkit: Practical Techniques for Building Dimensional Data Warehouses. John Wiley and Sons (1996)
6. Lin, C.X., Ding, B., Han, J., Zhu, F., Zhao, B.: Text cube: Computing ir measures for multidimensional text database analysis. In: Proceedings of the 2008 Eighth IEEE International Conference on Data Mining, pp. 905–910 (2008)
7. Mothe, J., Chrisment, C., Dousset, B., Alaux, J.: Doccube: Multi-dimensional visualisation and exploration of large document sets. Journal of the American Society for Information Science and Technology 54, 650–659 (2003)
8. Park, B.-K., Han, H., Song, I.-Y.: Xml-olap: A multidimensional analysis framework for xml warehouses. In: Tjoa, A.M., Trujillo, J. (eds.) DaWaK 2005. LNCS, vol. 3589, pp. 32–42. Springer, Heidelberg (2005)
9. Tounier, R.: Analyse en ligne (OLAP) de documents. Thèse de doctorat, Université Toulouse III. Paul Sabatier (2007)
10. Zhang, D., Zhai, C., Han, J.: Topic cube: Topic modeling for olap on multidimensional text databases. In: SDM 2009: Proceedings of the 2009 SIAM International Conference on Data Mining, Sparks, NV, USA, pp. 1124–1135 (2009)
11. Zhang, D., Zhai, C., Han, J.: Mitexcube:microtextcluster cube for online analysis of text cells. In: The NASA Conference on Intelligent Data Understanding (CIDU), pp. 204–218 (2011)

A Full Service Approach
for Multimedia Content Retrieval

Sid Ahmed Djallal Midouni[1,2], Youssef Amghar[2], and Azeddine Chikh[1,3]

[1] Département d'informatique
Université Abou Bekr Belkaid,
Tlemcen B.P.230, Tlemcen 13000, Algérie
djallal.midouni@gmail.com
[2] Université de Lyon. CNRS
INSA-Lyon. LIRIS. UMR5205, F-69621, France
youssef.amghar@insa-lyon.fr
[3] Information Systems Department,
College of Computer Science, King Saud University, Riyadh, Saudi Arabia
az☐chikh@ksu.edu.sa

Abstract. The present paper tackles the access problem to distributed and heterogeneous data sources. In this context we propose a full service approach for composing a new pattern of services. This pattern, called multimedia web services (MaaS: Multimedia as a Service): is able to retrieve data regarding their type (image, video, audio, text). The composition of WSM allows to resolve user requests. The proposed approach for MaaS composition is based on two main principles: the clustering and the filtring of WSDL data.

Keywords: Semantic web, web services, service composition, multimedia data.

1   Introduction

The diversity of distributed data sources and their heterogeneity are among the main difficulties encountered by users of the Web [1]. Heterogeneity is due to the data types of sources (structured sources such as relational databases, semi-structured or unstructured sources). The semantic web can address this problem by providing mechanisms for accessing distributed and heterogeneous data sources, in standardized and comprehensive way for both machines and humans [2]. The semantic web is also a paradigm which can address information retrieval with new formalisms, tools and techniques. To illustrate the problem we address, let us consider the medical field. A patient is described by images of IRM or radiology stored on site 1, and or XML documents containing the reports of these stored images on a site 2, audio -visual tracing of stored medical operation of the patient on a site 3, and also other multimedia documents treating diseases or epidemiological studies stored on a site 4. The need to access a semantically unified information becomes quite legitimate in this case.

Y. Ait Ameur et al. (Eds.): MEDI 2014, LNCS 8748, pp. 125–137, 2014.

Data integration approaches have been the first approaches to partially solve the having been applied to relational data or at most to more data of same type. A data integration system is an information system that integrates data from different sources providing users with uniform and centralized views of distributed data.

One of the latest techniques used in the context of data integration is the use of web services [3]. The approach we propose is based on the composition of a set of web services allowing the access to distributed multimedia data sources in order to respond to user requests.

In addition to this introduction, we present in section 2 the motivations and challenges of this work. In section 3, we define our multimedia web services and we describe our matching process. In section 4, we present our composition approach of multimedia services. In section 5, we present an illustrative example to evaluate our approach. The last section is devoted to the conclusion and future works.

2   Motivation and Challenges

Multimedia systems have become indispensable on the web. Thus, we find it quite natural, now, to integrate video, sound or music in various applications: educational, scientific, technical, medical, administrative, commercial, cultural and artistic.

Access to multimedia data in distributed systems poses new challenges due to many system parameters: volume, diversity of interfaces, representation format, location, etc. In addition, the growing need of users and applications to incorporate semantics in the information retrieval poses new issues to handle. Current solutions to these issues are based on integration or interoperability. They are often unsatisfactory or at least only partially meeting these needs and the requirements of globally controlling the multimedia content flows.

In a full-service approach, the discovery of a new type of service to access multimedia data in the context of distributed and heterogeneous data systems is the basis for building services architecture. The state of the art provides many formal tools to describe data access services (in the sense of relational databases), we talk about DaaS (Data as a Service) [3, 4], but obviously we lack tools to describe multimedia web services (MaaS: Multimedia as a Service). Our work is located at the intersection of the RI and Services communities.

The literature review revealed that the existing works separately deal with each type of multimedia data and there are few works that are simultaneously interested to several types of data. Regarding multimedia services, they focus on materializing the treatment of multimedia content as web services. In the field of image retrieval, for example, web services are used for operations in image processing [5, 6]. Authors of [5] proposed an algorithm for image deconvolution accessible via a web portal using web services. Authors of [6] developed an application that uses a set of Amazon Web Services (AWS) to load and process images.

In the same domain, web services are also used to search images by content [7, 8]. Authors of [7] present a solution based on WSMO ontology [9] to semantically describe the web services interface supporting multimedia indexing. The solution considers the possibility to combine several services to get richer descriptors. The idea was to use a generic XML format that covers the formats of existing multimedia metadata to describe the functionality of such a web service in terms of metadata provided after indexing. Similarly, authors of [8] designed an architecture of image retrieval system (CBIR: Content-Based Image Retrieval) based on web services. The solution presented consists of two parts: a graphical user interface for query formulation and a search engine exploring the images database to calculate the similarity between the visual features of images and the visual descriptors of query.

Other works use web services to achieve a very specific operation or process, for instance, [10] which focuses on the improving of universal access to multimedia content in the context of mobile devices using web services and concepts of the semantic web based on OWL-S ontology [11].

To our knowledge there are relatively few works that are based on multimedia Web services, to respond to user queries in the context of heterogeneous and distributed data, as we envision. We propose an approach of multimedia web services composition capable of performing syntactic and semantic mediation to meet user needs.

3   Formalization

3.1   MaaS Services – Notation

Before detailing our approach of multimedia web services composition, we formally define ontology, MaaS service and user query.

- **Definition 1 (ontology)**

  Formally, ontology is defined by 6-tuple $O: = (C, P, A, H^C, prop, att)$ [12] where:

  - C is a set of concepts,
  - P is a set of relationships,
  - A is a set of attributes,
  - H^C is a relationship $(C \times C)$, representing a hierarchy of concepts. For example, let $c_1, c_2 \in C$, $c_1 H^C c_2$ means that c_2 *subsumes* c_1,
  - *prop* is a function that connects a concept with another concept, each function has its prop domain and co-domain (range) in C. For example, let $c_1, c_2 \in C$, $prop(P)=(c_1, c_2)$ (denoted also $c_1 P c_2$) means that c_1 is connected to c_2 by P,
  - *att* is a function that connects a concept with an attribute, each *att* function has a domain in C and a co-domain in A.

- **Definition 2 (MaaS service)**

We have extended the work of Vaculin and al. [4], which defines a service as a pair of inputs and outputs, by the addition of ontological concepts annotating the inputs and outputs of services. A MaaS web service is a 5-tuple :

$$MaaS = (I, O, \mathcal{O}, IC, OC), \text{ where}$$

— *I* is the set of inputs, $I=\{(?v,T) \mid ?v \in Var, T \in metierType\}$,
— *O* is the set of outputs, $O=\{(?v,T) \mid ?v \in Var, T \in multimediaType\}$,

Var is the set of inputs and outputs names, *metierType* and *multimediaType* are two types of XML Schema defined in this work. The first type, *metierType* defines XSD domain types of inputs and it is specific to the process domain of MaaS services (medical, commerce, etc). The second type, *multimediaType* defines XSD types of outputs, it represents the four types of multimedia data (Image, Video, Audio, and Text). The *multimediaType* and an example of MaaS Service defining a *metierType* used are respectively defined in Appendix 1 and 2.

— $\mathcal{O}$ is the ontology used to annotate the inputs and outputs of services,
— *IC* is the set of concepts annotating the inputs of the service, $IC \subset C$,
— *OC* is the set of concepts annotating the outputs of the service, such as :

- $\forall x \in OC, x \, H^c \, y \mid y \in IC$ or
- $\forall x \in OC, x \, P \, y \mid y \in IC$

means that *OC* is a sub-concept of *IC* or a concept linked to *IC* by a relation *P*.

- **Definition 3 (Query)**

  In the same way as MaaS services, we represent the query Q as :

  $$Q = (I_q, O_q, \mathcal{O}, IC_q, OC_q)$$

  Each term of Q has the same signification as term of MaaS.

3.2   Semantic Matching Mechanism

Given a set of MaaS and a user query, how to find services satisfying the query in the best way? To answer this question, one approach could be to identify a degree of similarity between semantic concepts annotating MaaS services and those annotating the query. Such an evaluation mechanism is called: matching. Generally, web service matching is similar to the matching problems of other areas, such as database matching, text matching and software pattern matching of programming languages [13]. But these matching problems are still different from web service matching, so the research achievements on these areas are not suitable for our study.

In the literature, we identify three web service matching approaches [14]:

- **IO-matching:** also called "IO-matching service profile". This type of match is determined from semantic data service parameters: inputs (I) and outputs (O).
- **PE-matching:** determined from matching on pre-conditions (P) and effects (E) of services and queries.
- **IOPE-matching:** determined from matching semantic data of inputs (I), outputs (O), pre-conditions (P) and effects (E) of services and queries.

Our approach is based on an IO-matching, i.e. a matching process that considers only the inputs and outputs. The matching of these elements is summarized in a matching between the annotated concepts. We assume, for simplicity, that each input and output are both annotated by a single concept. The similarity between two concepts $(c_1, c_2 \in C)$ is evaluated by a matching degree. The different matching degrees used in our approach are:

— "Exact": if the first concept (c_1) and the second concept (c_2) are the same (or equivalent)
— "Subsumed" : if the first concept (c_1) is a sub-concept of the second concept (c_2),
— "Subsumed-by": if the first concept (c_2) is a sub-concept of the second concept (c_1),
— "Has-Relation": if the two concepts $(c_1$ and $c_2)$ are linked by a relation,
— "Has-same-Hierarchy": if the two concepts $(c_1$ and $c_2)$ belong to the hierarchy of the same concept,
— "Unknown" : if one of the concepts $(c_1$ or $c_2)$ is not specified,
— "Fail": If no relationship can be determined between the two concepts.

We have extended the existing works of matching services by adding two degrees: "Has-Relation" and "Has-same-Hierarchy" that are specific to our approach.

We associate with these degrees of matching the numeric values between [0,1] (Table 1) representing similarity degrees, enabling the calculation of the similarity function *SIM* between a MaaS service and query.

Table 1. Similarity degrees

Matching Degree	Exact	Subsumes	Subsumes-by	Has-Relation	Has-same-Hierarchy	Unknown	Fail
Similarity Degree	1	4/5	4/5	3/5	2/5	1/5	0

A similarity degree equal to 1 means that the matching is correct or equivalent, whereas a similarity degree equal to 0 means a failure of matching. We consider the two matching degrees "Subsumes" and "Subsumes-by" having the same similarity degree that equal to 0.8.

Similarity (SIM) is calculated based equally on the similarity of inputs (SIM$_I$) and similarity of outputs (SIM$_O$), the similarity function is given by the following formula: $SIM = (SIM_I + SIM_O) / 2$.

4   MaaS Services Composition Approach

Our approach is based on a four-phase process: description, filtering, clustering and restitution. In this full service approach the data sources are queried by a set of web services whose purpose is to find a solution (a combination of MaaS web services) that best meets the user's request. Figure 1 shows our MaaS services composition approach.

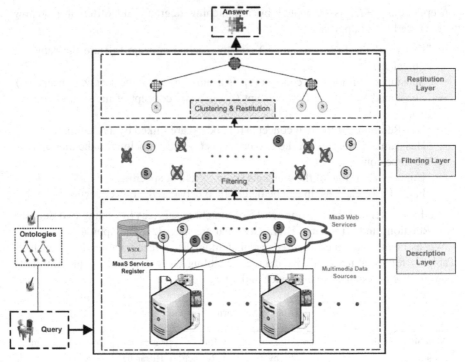

Fig. 1. MaaS services composition approach

The four phases of our approach are:

- **Description Phase.** The purpose of this phase is to semantically describe MaaS services accessing distributed multimedia resources. The functionality provided by these web services, input and output for each feature, and the protocol adopted for communication are described by WSDL files. The lack of semantics is one of the main criticisms of the WSDL standard.

To overcome the lack of semantics, many languages and approaches have been developed with the aim to describe semantic web services. We distinguish two main classes of these approaches. Approaches of the first class are based on adding annotations, such as WSDL [15], SAWSDL [16] and USDL [17]. Approaches of the second class are based on using of high-level ontology such as OWL-S [11] or WSMO [9], thus avoiding the problems of semantic heterogeneity that may occur. These last approaches use domain ontology to add semantic concepts in their description; they are a "closed approach": on the one hand, they manipulate a language ontology specification, e.g. OWL for OWL-S and WSML to WSMO. On the other hand, they specify very limited set of concepts that are not easily extensible. However, SAWSDL remains an independent approach to language semantic representation through the separation between the mechanisms of semantic annotation and representation of the semantic description. Without such a mechanism, developers do not have enough flexibility to select their favorite semantic representation of languages or to reuse their own ontology to annotate services [14]. For all these reasons, we chose the SAWSDL language to annotate semantically MaaS services.

SAWSDL provides mechanisms to reference the concepts of models defined outside the WSDL document. This is done through the attribute "SAWSDL." There are three extensions of this attribute. The first is *modelReference* for associating a WSDL or XML Schema component to a concept of ontology. The two other attributes are *liftingSchemaMapping* and *loweringSchemaMapping* allowing the specification of the mapping between semantic data and XML elements. The annotation interfaces, operations, input / output and simple XML types is done associating their concept in an ontology through the *modelReference* attribute. However, the annotation of complex XML data types may require more a Schema Mapping. An extract from the SAWSDL description of MaaS service is given in appendix 2.

- **Filtering Phase.** It focuses on the identification of MaaS relevant services to meet the user's request. This refinement is done by applying our matching mechanism (defined in section 3.2) between the query and the candidates MaaS services. In this work, we assume that MaaS services and the query are annotated using the same ontology. The concepts of input and output MaaS services and the query are extracted from their SAWSDL files. Assuming we have a set of services MaaS $\{S_1, S_2, ..., S_n\}$ and a query Q, we adopt the following principle to filter relevant MaaS services:

1. We calculate the similarity (SIM_I) between the input concept of service S_1 and the input concept of the query Q,
2. We calculate the similarity (SIM_O) between the output concept of service S_1 and the output concept of the query Q,
3. The global similarity function is calculated, $SIM = (SIM_I + SIM_O) / 2$,
4. The same process is repeated for all remaining MaaS service$_s$ $\{S_2, S_3, ..., S_n\}$ and the results are sorted in descending order,
5. We only retains the services that have a similarity measure SIM greater or equal than a threshold θ (θ is a numerical value chosen by the user, $\theta \in [0,1]$).

- **Clustering Phase.** This phase aims to put the similar MaaS services (results of filtering phase) together. It provides two types of clustering: **structural** clustering and/or **semantic** clustering. We can either choose one of two types, namely enchained to put together similar services. For the first type of clustering, it is simply to create four clusters depending on the type of multimedia services. For the second type of clustering, services are divided into clusters according to the meaning of services based on their semantic similarity. The similarity between two MaaS services is computed applying our semantic matching mechanism between concepts annotating these two services. The services to compare are the results services of filtering phase, which are the closest to the user request.

A service S_i is inserted into the same cluster with another service S_j if their input similarity degrees or their output similarity degrees are higher than or equal to 0.8 ($SIM_I \geq 0.8$ ou $SIM_O \geq 0.8$). We consider that the semantically closest services are those that have a matching degree between their input or output concepts equal to: *Exact, Subsumes, Subsumes-by*.

- **Definition 4 (cluster)**

A cluster is a logical grouping of services with the same meaning. A cluster is represented by its input and output concepts.

$$cls = (IC_{cls}, OC_{cls})$$

Assuming we have a set of Maas services, representing the result of the filtering phase $\{S_1, S_2, ..., S_m\}$ *(m<n / n:* number of services before the filtering phase) , we adopt the following principle to put MaaS services in semantic clusters:

1. We calculate the similarity (SIM_I) between the input concept of the S_1 and the input concept of S_2,
2. We calculate the similarity (SIM_O) between the output concept of the S_1 and the output concept of S_2,
3. If the similarity ($SIM_I \geq 0.8$) or ($SIM_O \geq 0.8$), we create a first cluster cls_1 which contains the services S_1 and S_2. The input and output concepts of this cluster cls_1 are the union of input and output concepts of S_1 with the input and output concepts of S_2,
4. If not ($SIM_I < 0.8$) and ($SIM_O < 0.8$) we create two clusters cls_1 and cls_2 containing respectively S_1 and S_2. The input and output concepts of clusters cls_1 and cls_2 are the input and output concepts of S_1 and S_2 (respectively),
5. Then, we calculate the similarity (SIM_I) between the input concept of service S_3 and the input concepts of clusters already created,
6. We also calculate the similarity (SIM_O) between the output concept of service S_3 and the output concept of clusters already created,
7. If the similarity ($SIM_I \geq 0.8$) or ($SIM_O \geq 0.8$) with one of the clusters, S_3 is added to this cluster and their input concepts and their output concepts are added together with those of the service S_3,
8. If not ($SIM_I < 0.8$) and ($SIM_O < 0.8$) we create a new cluster that contains the service S_3. The input and the output concepts of cluster are the same of the service S_3.
9. The steps 5,6,7 and 8 are repeated for all the remaining MaaS services $\{S_4, S_5, ..., S_m\}$,
10. We obtain at the end a set of clusters $\{cls_1, cls_2, ..., cls_k\}$ with $k < m$.

- **Restitution Phase.** It aims to restitute to the user what provide the services such as data. These services are grouped into homogeneous clusters to provide to the user coherent and ranked results. We recall that the outputs of MaaS services are modeled by *multimediaType* (XSD type shown in Appendix 1). A MaaS service can return one or more image, video, audio or text files.

5   Illustrative Example

Our approach will be evaluated in the medical field. We are particularly interested in this illustrative example, on cancerous diseases data.

Assuming that a student in medecine wants to know and gather all kinds of data on a cancerous disease, lung cancer for instance. He wants to have as a result all kinds of information and resources talking about this disease: its symptoms, its diagnostic methods, its different stages and its possible treatments. Let us assume that this student has a set of MaaS services (Table 2) to respond to his request.

Table 2. MaaS web services

Services	Functionalities	IC	OC	SIM$_I$	SIM$_O$	SIM
S$_1$	Returns text files describing the different treatments for small cell lung cancer	Small_cell	LC_ Treatment	0.8	1	0.9
S$_2$	Returns videos that shows the progress of a fiberoptic bronchoscope of a patient suffering from lung cancer	Lung_ Cancer	Medical_ Imaging	1	0.8	0.9
S$_3$	Returns images of a colonoscopy showing a tumor in the colon	Colon_ Cancer	CC_ Diagnoses	0	0	0
S$_4$	Returns audio files made by experts describing the common symptoms of lung cancer	Lung_ Cancer	LC_ Symptom	1	1	1
S$_5$	Returns images visualizing the different causes of lung cancer	Lung_ Cancer	LC_ Causes	1	0	0.5
S$_6$	Returns courses video on possible treatments of prostate cancer	Prostate_ Cancer	PC_ Treatment	0	0	0
S$_7$	Returns audio files discussing the different possible treatments for non-small cell lung cancer	Non_Small_ cell	LC_ Treatment	0.8	1	0.9
S$_8$	Returns text files containing a list of tests and exams to do in case of symptoms of lung cancer	LC_ Symptom	LC_ Diagnoses	0.6	1	0.8

The answer to the student query cannot be satisfied by single web service, the integration and the composition of multiple web services is required. The answer must be constructed by invoking and combining the different services in Table 2 in order to offer the user a complete and appropriate answer. To achieve this goal, we apply and follow our approach.

The first phase of our approach is the description phase in which the MaaS services are semantically described. We have developed for this purpose, an ontology "*canceronto*" (Figure 2) to semantically annotate MaaS services. At the end of this phase, MaaS services are annotated using SAWSDL language with concepts of *canceronto* ontology. We are interested, as we have already mentioned, by the annotation of input and output services. The third and fourth columns of Table 2 represent the ontological concepts annotating respectively inputs and outputs of services. Taking for example, the S_2 service that returns a video showing the progress of a fiberoptic bronchoscope of a patient suffering from lung cancer, knowing that fiberoptic bronchoscope is an imaging test that can diagnose a patient case. So we annotate the input that is lung cancer by the concept "*Lung_cancer*" and the output that is fiberoptic bronchoscope by the concept "*Medical_Imaging*".

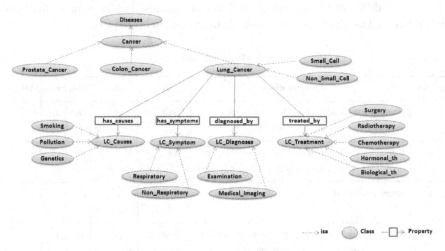

Fig. 2. Canceronto ontology

Using the same principle, we annotate the inputs and outputs of the user query, the result of this annotation is :

IC_q = {*Lung_Cancer*} ; OC_q={*LC_Symptom, LC_Diagnoses, LC_Stages, LC_Treatment*}.

In the second phase of our approach, we filter out services that meet the user's query. Assuming that the user has specified a threshold θ to 0.7, it means that he wants to get the services with a similarity measure greater than 0.7. Therefore the following services {S_1, S_2, S_4, S_7, S_8} will be obtained.

In the clustering phase, we aim to group similar services together in order to return to the user a homogenize response. We have chosen in the case of this example, a semantic clustering. So we get to the end of this phase the following clusters: cls_1{S_1,S_7}, cls_2{S_2,S_8}, cls_3{S_4}.

In the last phase of our approach, it is simply to return to the user that provides services of the three clusters found. The results are shown in three groups giving the user types, URI, and other metadata (defined in the *multimediaType*) of different types of multimedia data.

6   Conclusion

In this article, we presented a new type of service: the MaaS service whose interest is to collect multimedia data in an environment of distributed and heterogeneous data. For this service, we propose to annotate the inputs and outputs of multimedia web services by ontological concepts to allow their matching with input and output concepts annotating query terms. We then proposed a full service approach to compose MaaS for multimedia data researching. This approach gives a relevant answer to the user based on a 4-phase process: description, filtering, clustering and restitution. As a future work we plan to optimize and implement our process for combining and composing MaaS services.

References

1. Stollberg, M., et al.: A semantic web mediation architecture. Canadian Semantic Web, pp. 3–22. Springer, US (2006)
2. Berners-Lee, T., Hendler, J., Lassila, O.: The semantic web. Scientific American 284(5), 28–37 (2001)
3. Barhamgi, M.: Composing DaaS web services: application to eHealth. Diss. Lyon 1 (2010)
4. Vaculín, R., et al.: Modeling and discovery of data providing services. In: IEEE International Conference on Web Services, ICWS 2008. IEEE (2008)
5. Almeida, F., et al.: IDEWEP: Web service for astronomical parallel image deconvolution. Journal of Network and Computer Applications 32(1), 293–313 (2009)
6. Fronckowiak, J., Myer, T.: Processing Images with Amazon Web Services (2008), http://www.tripledogs.com/../2008_Processing_Images_with_Amazon_Web_Services.pdf
7. Brut, M., et al.: Adapting Indexation to the Content, Context and Queries Characteristics in Distributed Multimedia Systems. In: 2011 Seventh International Conference on Signal-Image Technology and Internet-Based Systems (SITIS). IEEE (2011)
8. Giro-i-Nieto, X., et al.: System architecture of a web service for content-based image retrieval. In: Proceedings of the ACM International Conference on Image and Video Retrieval. ACM (2010)
9. WSMO: Web Service Modeling Ontology (2005), http://www.w3.org/Submission/WSMO
10. Wagner, M., Kellerer, W.: Web services selection for distributed composition of multimedia content. In: Proceedings of the 12th Annual ACM International Conference on Multimedia. ACM (2004)
11. Martin, D., et al.: OWL-S: Semantic markup for web services. W3C member submission 22 (2004); 2007-04
12. Maedche, A., Zacharias, V.: Clustering ontology-based metadata in the semantic web. In: Elomaa, T., Mannila, H., Toivonen, H. (eds.) PKDD 2002. LNCS (LNAI), vol. 2431, p. 348. Springer, Heidelberg (2002)
13. Wu, Z., Dou, Z., Song, C.: Web Service Matching for RESTful Web Services Based on Parameter Semantic Network. In: 3rd International Conference on Computer Science and Service System. Atlantis Press (2014)
14. Chabeb, Y.: Contributions à la description et la découverte de services web sémantiques. Diss. Institut National des Télécommunications (2011)

15. Chinnici, R., et al.: Web services description language (wsdl) version 2.0 part 1: Core language. W3C recommendation 26, 19 (2007)
16. Lausen, H., Farrell, J.: Semantic annotations for WSDL and XML schema. W3C recommendation, W3C (2007)
17. Simon, L., et al.: A universal service description language.In: IEEE 20th International Conference on Web Services (2013)

Appendix 1: MultimediaType

```
1   <?xml version="1.0" encoding="ISO-8859-1"?>
2   <xs:schema xmlns:xs="http://www.w3.org/2001/XMLSchema"
3            xmlns="http://localhost/maas/MediaType"
4            targetNamespace="http://localhost/maas/MediaType" >
5   <!-- common attributes -->
6   <xs:complexType name="multimediaAtt">
7       <xs:attribute name="source" type="xs:anyURI" use="required" />
8       <xs:attribute name="format" type="xs:string" use="optional" />
9   </xs:complexType>
10  <!-- Image Type -->
11  <xs:element name="images">
12      <xs:complexType>
13          <xs:sequence>
14              <xs:element name="image" minOccurs="0" maxOccurs="unbounded">
15                  <xs:complexType>
16                      <xs:extension base= "multimediaAtt">
17                          <!-- To define here the specific attributes to the image type -->
18                      </xs:extension>
19                  </xs:complexType>
20              </xs:element>
21          </xs:sequence>
22      </xs:complexType>
23  </xs:element>
24  <!-- Video Type -->
25  <xs:element name="videos">
26      <xs:complexType>
27          <xs:sequence>
28              <xs:element name="video" minOccurs="0" maxOccurs="unbounded">
29                  <xs:complexType>
30                      <xs:extension base= "multimediaAtt">
31                          <!-- To define here the specific attributes to the video type -->
32                      </xs:extension>
33                  </xs:complexType>
34              </xs:element>
35          </xs:sequence>
36      </xs:complexType>
37  </xs:element>
38  <!-- Audio Type -->
39  <xs:element name="audios">
40      <xs:complexType>
41          <xs:sequence>
42              <xs:element name="audio" minOccurs="0" maxOccurs="unbounded">
43                  <xs:complexType>
44                      <xs:extension base= "multimediaAtt">
45                          <!-- To define here the specific attributes to the audio type -->
46                      </xs:extension>
47                  </xs:complexType>
48              </xs:element>
49          </xs:sequence>
50      </xs:complexType>
51  </xs:element>
52  <!-- Text Type -->
53  <xs:element name="texts">
54      <xs:complexType>
55          <xs:sequence>
56              <xs:element name="text" minOccurs="0" maxOccurs="unbounded">
57                  <xs:complexType>
58                      <xs:extension base= "multimediaAtt">
59                          <!-- To define here the specific attributes to the text type -->
60                      </xs:extension>
61                  </xs:complexType>
62              </xs:element>
63          </xs:sequence>
64      </xs:complexType>
65  </xs:element>
66  <!-- Multimedia Type -->
67  <xs:complexType name="multimediaType">
68      <xs:choice>
69          <xs:element ref= "images" />
70          <xs:element ref= "videos" />
71          <xs:element ref= "audios" />
72          <xs:element ref= "texts" />
73      </xs:choice>
74  </xs:complexType>
75  </xs:schema>
```

Appendix 2: SAWSDL File of Service S2

```xml
1   <?xml version="1.0" encoding="UTF-8"?>
2   <wsdl:description
3     xmlns="http://schemas.xmlsoap.org/wsdl/"
4     targetNamespace="http://localhost/maas/LungCancerServices/"
5     xmlns:wsdl="http://www.w3.org/ns/wsdl"
6     xmlns:xs="http://www.w3.org/2001/XMLSchema"
7     xmlns:sawsdl="http://www.w3.org/ns/sawsdl"
8     xmlns:tns="http://localhost/maas/LungCancerServices/"
9     xmlns:mt="http://localhost/maas/MediaType"
10    name="LungCancerSymptomWebService">
11    <wsdl:types>
12      <xs:schema targetNamespace="http://localhost/maas/LungCancerServices/"
13              xmlns="http://localhost/maas/LungCancerServices/" >
14        <!-- Import the MultimediaType schema -->
15        <xs:import namespace="http://localhost/maas/MediaType"
16                schemaLocation="MultimediaType.xsd" />
17        <!-- Define the CancerType schema -->
18        <xs:element name="causes" type="xs:string"/>
19        <xs:element name="symptoms" type="xs:string" />
20        <xs:element name="diagnoses" type="xs:string" />
21        <xs:element name="stages" type="xs:string" />
22        <xs:element name="treatment" type="xs:string" />
23        <xs:complexType name="cancer">
24            <xs:all>
25                <xs:element ref="causes"/>
26                <xs:element ref="symptoms" />
27                <xs:element ref="diagnoses" />
28                <xs:element ref="stages" />
29                <xs:element ref="treatment" />
30            </xs:all>
31        </xs:complexType>
32        <xs:element name="lungCancer" type="cancer" />
33      </xs:schema>
34    </wsdl:types>
35    <wsdl:interface name="LungCancerSymptomServiceInterface">
36      <wsdl:operation name="getImagesSymptomLC">
37          <wsdl:input element="tns:lungCancer"
38              sawsdl:modelReference="http://localhost/canceronto#Lung_Cancer"/>
39          <wsdl:output element="mt:images"
40              sawsdl:modelReference="http://localhost/canceronto#Medical_Imaging"/>
41      </wsdl:operation>
42    </wsdl:interface>
43    <wsdl:binding name="LungCancerSymptomServiceSOAPBinding"
44      interface="tns:LungCancerSymptomServiceInterface" ...> ... </wsdl:binding>
45    <wsdl:service name="LungCancerSymptomWebService"
46      interface="tns:LungCancerSymptomServiceInterface">
47      <wsdl:endpoint name="LungCancerSymptomServiceEndpoint"
48        binding="tns:LungCancerSymptomServiceSOAPBinding"
49        address="http://localhost/LungCancerSymptomWebService/" />
50    </wsdl:service>
51  </wsdl:description>
```

Ontology-Based User Modeling
for Handicraft Woman Recommendation

Maha Maalej[1], Achraf Mtibaa[1], and Faiez Gargouri[2]

[1] National School of Electronic and Telecommunications of Sfax, Tunisia
[2] Higher Institute of Computer Science and Multimedia of Sfax, Tunisia
{maha.maalej,achrafmtibaa,faiez.gargouri}@gmail.com

Abstract. Intelligent systems are good in presenting adapted information and services to the systems users' contexts. In fact, they are often based on contextual and profiling information. Thus it is necessary for these systems to have an explicit model for the user profile as well as for the user context. Ontology-based user profile and context modeling is especially important for reasoning systems that can benefit from inference on ontology representing different knowledge. In this paper, we propose an ontology-based user model to represent both user profile and context. Then, we give some rules for users' recommendation in the handicraft domain which is the domain of research project that we are involved in. The aim of the research project is to help handicraft women from emerging countries to use new technologies in order to improve their socio-economic level. Our ontology enriched by SWRL (Semantic Web Rule Language) rules has the advantage to infer adapted services to handicraft woman through a system.

Keywords: Ontology, Profile, Context, User model, SWRL rules, Handicraft.

1   Introduction

The information personalization is established by a set of individual preferences, by schedules of criteria or specific semantic rules for each user or user community [1]. These specification modes are used to describe the user interest, the quality of the data he wants or the presentation modalities of these data. All of this information is shown in a model of user often called profile. Context-awareness was introduced by Schilit [10] to develop software that adapts according to its locations of use, the collection of nearby people and objects, as well as changes to those objects over time. According to Dey [3] the context contains any information that can be used to characterize the situation of an entity. This work is involved in the BWEC (Business for Women of Emerging Countries) project that treats handicraft women from emerging (Tunisian and Algerian) countries. In this context, in order to improve the socio-economic situation of these women, an interactive system will be built based on many works. Project steps are cited in previous work [13]. Our contribution focuses in the second step which is "Ontology-based analysis and modeling of contextual and profiling knowledge".

Y. Ait Ameur et al. (Eds.): MEDI 2014, LNCS 8748, pp. 138–145, 2014.

In the context of the project we should model the handicraft woman needs, context and profile. The handicraft woman may have several needs by interacting with a personalized system. Indeed, she may seek raw materials having suitable price. She can also search for a supplier that is not far from her home to buy them. She can as well look for a particular training to improve her skills. In order to satisfy handicraft woman needs, we tried to model his profile as to have a specific model which can be used to effectively meet her needs. Several sides of handicraft woman should be specified as production, sale, knowledge and skills, use of new technologies and training. In order to cover these sides the user model has to be complete and extensible. The user model contains diverse information. Some of them are related to personal side of the user which represents the user profile. This information is related to age, name, study level, intellectual level, marital status, etc. Other information is related to business domain which will represent the commerce and in particular handicraft domain. The last type of information will represent the time, location, activity, etc. which represents the contextual information related to the user context. For representing all these information we proceed to use ontology. The later is defined by Gruber [4] as "an explicit specification of a conceptualization". Ontology is proved to be an important tool in modeling user model. In fact, Han [5] have already pointed out the advantage of using ontologies for user models. In this context, formal representation of ontologies in a common data model on the web can represent a foundation for adaptive web technologies. In fact, the system may represent the user's personal interests. Moreover, ontologies allow effective reasoning by means of rules and reasoners. The benefit acquired from their use is to infer new and implicit knowledge from explicit and existing one which requires sometimes complex inferences. In this context, we improve our user model ontology by adding SWRL1 rules.

In the rest of this paper, we present, in section 2, we give some related works. In section 3, we propose an ontology for user model representation enriched with some rules for personalization and recommendation purposes. In the last section, we conclude by summarizing our contributions and giving our future works.

2   Related Works

In the domain of representing user knowledge, several user models arise which are based on ontology in literature. Panagiotopoulos [9] proposed to model the User profile information by ontology as static user information. The dynamic user information depends on contextual information is also modeled. Stan [12] proposed ontology where the main class is Person uses many concepts to create a profile applicable in any kind of domain or application. Hella [6] proposed to model a profile in three main parts. The first category is termed personal information. The second category is termed long term interests. Therefore, the third category is termed temporary interests. Skillen [11] proposed a user profile ontology that provides an extensible user profile model which focuses on the modeling of dynamic and static user aspects,

---

1   www.w3.org/Submission/SWRL/

facilitating its primary use in context-aware applications. Cretton [2] created a user model ontology (GenOUM) in order to provide a domain independent description and understanding of the user. GenOUM ontology contains three components User's knowledge, Content's knowledge and User's personality. User's profiles represent in which context does the user do something or know something. In [7] authors proposed solutions that are specific teachings/trainings and which are offered by specialized educative teams using technical platforms based on ontologies and patterns. In fact, they started with us in the project, but we propose an alternative solution such as using SWRL rules. In our work, we proposed a user model which has three part user profile, user context and domain related concepts. Thus profile presents static information about the user and context represents dynamic information about him. Our user model will be the subject of the next section.

3   Ontology-Based User Modeling

One of the main goals of intelligent systems is to provide services to users based on their activity in order to achieve a specific user objective. For that, knowledge about users must be collected and structured. To this aim, we employed interviews directly with handicraft women. The women interviewed are in fact representative of handicraft woman population thanks to the diversity of their business, age, intellectual level, socio-economic situation, etc. and their origin from different cities from Tunisian and Algerian countries. As a preliminary step we have 80 interviews that we will increase later. In order to create an ontology we followed some steps that are necessary to have an accurate and validated ontology. These steps are concepts representation, relationships determination, axioms definition, ontology populating and finally ontology enrichment with rules. In the first step, we create concepts that are pertinent in our model. Thus, we should have concepts related to handicraft domain and handicraft woman context and profile modeling. In the second step we create relationships between the created concepts. The third step permits to define restriction on the concepts i.e. axioms. The fourth step should be the ontology populating with instances. In the final step, we define some rules to allow service adaptation and handicraft woman recommendation. In the following sub sections, we will present these steps.

3.1   Concepts Representation

The proposed ontology for user model is presented in Fig. 1. It contains the relevant concepts that we have extracted from the interviews. In fact, user model encloses the core element of this model that is *Handicraft_woman*. The secondary elements are *Context, Profile, Coordination_tool, Supplier, Customer, Product, Raw_material and Production_tool*. The *Context and Profile* classes are needed to describe user context and profile information for adaptation purposes. The *Supplier and Customer* classes are needed to determine the contacts of the *Handicraft woman* to sell product. The *Raw_material and Production_tool* classes describe the tools and raw materials for her production. The *Product* class describes the products she makes with her hands. Finally, ***Coordiantion_tool*** class is needed to represent the tools she uses to sell her products. These tools can be either directly with customers, through a whole-saler or through a distribution channel. The ontology editor that we used is Protégé[2]. Figures 2 and 3 below are visualized using Jambalaya[3] plug-in. ***Profile*** concept has relationships with five concepts namely ***Personal_Characteristics, Capability, Skills, Interest and Preferences***. The ***Capability*** concept is sub-divided into two kinds ***Writing_capability and Reading_capability***. The ***Skills*** concept is necessary to know what the handicraft woman skills are. It may contain the job that she is competent in, etc. The ***preferences*** concept is necessary to recognize the preferred things of the handi-craft woman like places (touristic zone, sea and beach, mountain, desert, etc.), hob-bies (swimming, reading, shopping, etc.). ***Interest*** corresponds to the interest of the handicraft woman which is related to the trade fair, exhibition places, training, etc. ***Personal_Characteristics*** contains personal information about the user which are ***date_of_birth, location_of_residence, marital_status, name, number_of_children place_of_birth, age*** and ***spoken_language. Context*** is a primordial concept to define in order to adapt the system services to the user's needs. For that purpose, in previous works, we have defined the context notion by five parameters [8]. In fact, in order to detect the context, we need to know the contextual parameters. The contextual para-meters were User, Location, Time, Activity and Physical environment.

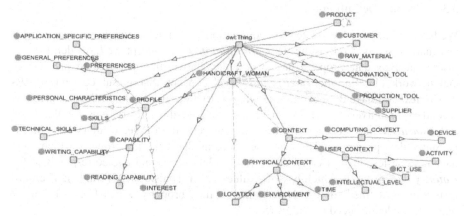

Fig. 1. Ontology-based user model for handicraft woman

In this work, we sub-divided the context into three classes which are ***Us-er_Context, Computing_Context and Physical_Context***. The ***User_Context*** is cha-racterized by the user ***Activity, Intellectual_level and ICT_Use***. The ***Compu-ting_Context*** characterized by the ***Devices*** used by the user. The ***Physical_Context*** is related to user ***Environment, Time and Location*** of the interaction of the user with the system. When we examine the state of the art, the important concepts are related to task (activity), device, location and time. We think that adding some concept like

---

[2] Protege.stanford.edu/

[3] Protegewiki.stanford.edu/wiki/Jambalaya

ICT use and intellectual level can better define the user context jointly with the first concepts.

3.2   Relationship Determination

In this sub-step, we expose the relationships between relevant concepts presented in the last sub-step (Fig.1). The **Handicraft_Woman** concept has the central role in this ontology. It has relationships with eight concepts. The **Handicraft_Woman** is related to **Raw_material** by "buys_raw_material" relationship. Besides this concept has relationship with **Production_tool** by "uses_tool" relationship. Moreover, **Handicraft_Woman** concept has relationships with **Coordination_tool** by "uses_coord_tool" relationship, with **Product** by means of "creates_product" relationship and with **Profile** by means of "has_profile" relationship. It also has relationship with **Context** by "has_context" relationship. **Handicraft_Woman** has relationship with **Customer** and with **Supplier** by "has_contact_with_client" and "has_contact_with_supplier" respectively. The concept **Product** has a reflexive relationship which is "composed_of_product". In the next sub-step, we will define some axioms which contain statements invoked as a priori knowledge.

3.3   Axioms Definition

We have defined axioms related to coordination_tool, intellectual_level, age, country and marital_status. Concerning the **Coordination_tool** concept we have defined one restriction: *type* data property has to be either phone, internet, face_to_face or social_network (1). For the **Intellectual_Level** concept that is sub-concept of **User_Context**, we have defined the following restriction. It would be illiterate, primary, secondary or university (2). We have also defined three restrictions for the **Personal_Characteristics** concept. Restrictions are related to Age, Country and Marital_Status data properties. The first one concerns the **Age** data property which must have a value less than or equal 60 years old (3). The second one corresponds to the **Country** data property which has two values either Tunisia or Algeria (4). The third restriction is defined for the **Marital_Status** data property which has to be either married, single, divorced or widow (5).

$$\text{type has "\{phone or internet or face\_to\_face or social\_network\}"} \tag{1}$$

$$\text{intellectual\_level has "\{illiterate or primary or secondary or university\}"} \tag{2}$$

$$\text{age max 60} \tag{3}$$

$$\text{country has "\{tunisia or algeria\}"} \tag{4}$$

$$\text{marital\_status has "\{single or married or divorced or widow\}"} \tag{5}$$

Once concepts, relationships and axioms are defined, we pass to ontology populating.

3.4   Ontology Populating

As input to this sub-step, we have semi-structured interviews described in natural language. Thus, we have instantiated the ontology with instances from 80 treated interviews. This step consists mainly in filling the concepts individuals. An example of Handicraft woman "fatma" which has activity "searching" for a trade fair (*Interest*) at a given date (*Time*) is located in tunisia (*Location*). This woman is able to read and write (*Capability*) and can use new technologies (*ICT_Use*). She has *Technical_Skills* "pottery". She is using personal computer (*Device*).

3.5   Rules Definition for Handicraft Woman

As the ontology created requires some rules to adapt the user query result we have defined some SWRL rules. In the following we present two kinds of rules: rules based on user profile criteria and rules based on user context dimensions. For simplification reasons, we express some of these rules in SWRL and the rest are in natural language. Below we consider rules that have as conclusion "propose" are recommendation rules. We consider other rules as adaptation rules. The proposed rules are related to some features of profile and some features of context.

Rules Based on User Profile Criteria

As profile criteria, we choose reading and writing Capabilities, Preferences (color) and Interests (trade fair). For example if the handicraft woman can read and write then we can ask her to choose the language of the result display. If she is not able to read and write then we adapt the display of result to be in the form of image. If the preferred color is blue then we would change the text color or the font color to blue. If the interest of the handicraft woman is in searching trade fair we would propose to her the nearest one to her location.

— Handicraft woman ∧ (reading =yes) ∧ (writing =yes) → ask for kind of display language
— Handicraft woman ∧ (reading =no) ∧ (writing =no)→ display the result as an image

```
HANDICRAFT_WOMAN (?x)  ∧  composed_of_capability
(?x,?y)  ∧  READING_CAPABILITY (?y)  ∧  com-
posed_of_capability (?x,?z)  ∧  WRITING_CAPABILITY (?z)
∧  swrlb:equal(?y,"no")  ∧  swrlb:equal(?z,"no") ∧
uses(?x, ?a)  ∧  DEVICE(?a)     ∧  display_type (?a,?b)→
swrlb:equal(?b, "image")
```

— Handicraft woman ∧ (preference: color = blue) → display the result in blue color.
— Handicraft woman ∧ (preference : nearest market) ∧ location → propose a nearby market

Rules Based on User Context Dimensions

The contextual information is important to define the suitable display or the suitable element to propose to the handicraft woman. For example, taking into account the computing context side (device) the rules would be: if she is using a mobile phone then the display resolution is set to "400*240". Else if she is using a personal computer then the resolution should be bigger and set to 1024*768. If we take the user context side (activity) then the rules would be: if she is interested in learning then we can propose training session to her. If she is interested in searching a question in the system then we propose to her result for the query she wanted. If we take the physical context, another rule related to location would be if the location is "Sajnane" then the system would propose a market for natural raw material. If the woman is located at Tunis she would be searching for ready to use raw materials (with transformation) then we propose to her a market for transformed raw materials.

— Handicraft woman ∧ (device= mobile) → result display with resolution= 400*240

```
HANDICRAFT_WOMAN (?x)   ∧   uses (?x,?y)   ∧   DEVICE (?y)
∧  device_description (?y,?b)   ∧  resolution (?y,?c) ∧
swrlb:equal(?b,"mobile")  →   swrlb:equal(?c,"400*240")
```

— Handicraft woman ∧ (device= PC)   → result display with resolution= 1024*768
— Handicraft woman ∧ (activity = learning) → propose training
— Handicraft woman ∧ (activity = searching) → ask for information
— Handicraft woman ∧ (location = Sajnane) → propose market natural raw materials
— Handicraft woman ∧ (location = Tunis) → propose market for transformed raw materials
— Handicraft woman ∧ (time= day) → luminosity of the screen display will be reduced
— Handicraft woman ∧ (temps= night) → luminosity of the screen display will be increased

4   Conclusion

The main goal of the current study was to determine the utility of using ontologies to represent user profile and user context i.e. user model. This study has shown that rules are appropriate to provide useful recommendations to handicraft women and adapt the system interface display, according to handicraft woman context. It was also shown that our ontology together with rules can therefore be integrated in a useful inference-based system. In our further work, we aim at improving these rules, so as to provide better solutions to handicraft women and to ameliorate their situations. We aim at building a prototype to support the proposed ontology and the associated rules.

Acknowledgements. We are very thankful to the Algerian Tunisian Project dealing with the improvement of handicraft women business in emerging countries through affordable technologies and social networks.

References

1. Bouzeghoub, M., Kostadinov, D.: Personnalisation de l'information: aperçu de l'état de l'art et définition d'un modèle flexible de profils. In: CORIA, pp. 201–218 (2005)
2. Cretton, F., Calvé, A.L.: Generic ontology based user model: GenOUM. Technical report, Université de Genève (June 2008)
3. Dey, A.K., Hamid, R., Beckmann, C., Li, I., Hsu, D.: a CAPpella: Programming by demonstration of context-aware applications. In: ACM Conference on Human Factors in Computing Systems (CHI), Vienna (2004)
4. Gruber, T.R.: A translation approach to portable ontologies. Knowledge Acquisition 5(2), 199–220 (1993)
5. Han, L., Chen, G., Li, M.: A method for the acquisition of ontology-based user profiles. Advances in Engineering Software 65, 132–137 (2013)
6. Hella, L., Krogstie, J.: Personalisation by Semantic Web Technology in Food Shopping. In: WIMS, p. 34. ACM (2011)
7. Monfort, V., Khemaja, M.: Bridging Ontologies and Patterns to Overcome Socio-Cultural Lags. International Journal of Advanced Research in Computer Science and Software Engineering 3(10), 179–189 (2013)
8. Mtibaa, A., Maalej, M., Gargouri, F.: Contextual dimension in ontology dedicated to requirement specification. In: IADIS International Conference Information Systems, pp. 41–48 (2012) ISBN: 978-972-8939-68-7
9. Panagiotopoulos, I., Seremeti, L., Kameas, A.: An alignable user profile ontology for ambient intelligence environments. In: Proceeding of 7th International Conference on Intelligent Environments (IE), Nottingham, pp. 270–276. IEEE (2011)
10. Schilit, B., Theimer, M.: Disseminating active map information to mobile hosts. IEEE Network 8(5), 22–32 (1994)
11. Skillen, K.L., Chen, L., Nugent, C.D., Donnelly, M.P., Burns, W., Solheim, I.: Ontological User Profile Modeling for Context-Aware Application Personalization. In: Bravo, J., López-de-Ipiña, D., Moya, F. (eds.) UCAmI 2012. LNCS, vol. 7656, pp. 261–268. Springer, Heidelberg (2012)
12. Stan, J., Egyed-Zsigmond, E., Maret, P., Daigremont, J.: Personalization in Mobile and Pervasive Computing. In: User Modeling, Adaptation, and Personalization conference (UMAP) Workshop on Personalization in Mobile and Pervasive Computing, Italy (2009)
13. Yangui, R., Maalej, M., Mtibaa, A., Nabli, A., Mhiri, M., Gargouri, F.: Towards Ontology-Based Clustering of Handicraft Women. In: 8th Edition of the Conference ASD 2014, Hammamet, Tunisia, pp. 29–31 (May 29-31, 2014)

Stability Assess Based on Enhanced Information Content Similarity Measure for Ontology Enrichment

Karim Kamoun[1] and Sadok Ben Yahia[2]

[1] Higher School of Digital Economy, University of Mannouba, Tunis, Tunisia
karim.kamoun@gmail.com
[2] University of Tunis El Manar, LIPAH, Faculty of Sciences of Tunis, Tunisia
Sadok.benyahia@fst.rnu.tn

Abstract. Ontology assessment is an important issue that has to be addressed during evolution process. It aims at evaluating the quality of ontology in different aspects. One of key aspects is the ontology stability. To compute the stability value of evolved ontology, we rely on a battery of semantic similarity measures especially those based on information content. These measures deal only with the subsumption relationship to compute similarity between two concepts of the same ontology. However, using only this relationship has been shown to be, very often, insufficient. To palliate such shortness, we advocate taking into account other types of relationships, that could improve the semantic relation. In this respect, we introduce a new information content based similarity measure that consider the property relationship in addition to the subsumption one. We show the advantages of this measure and how they asses stability of evolved ontology using our ontology enrichment procedure.

Keywords: semantic similarity measures, Ontology Stability, Ontology enrichment, Ontology Evolution, Ontology assessment.

1 Introduction

Assessing the quality of evolved or enriched ontologies has received more attention. In fact, it can help ontology engineers to better control the management and the development of ontology-based systems and significantly reduce the risk of project failures. Several ontology evolution approaches exist in literature. Most of them tried to follow an evolution process defined by AIFB (Institute of Applied Informatics and Formal Description Methods), and based on 6 steps: change capturing, change representation, semantics of change, change propagation, change implementation and change validation. However, most of ontology evolution approaches focus on one or two steps. One of the first tools that integrate the evolution process is the KAON[1] system. The authors of this tool proposed an

---

[1] KAON (KArlsruhe ONtology and Semantic Web infrastructure):
http://kaon.semanticweb.org.

Y. Ait Ameur et al. (Eds.): MEDI 2014, LNCS 8748, pp. 146–153, 2014.
© Springer International Publishing Switzerland 2014

overall process for managing evolution of KAON ontologies [1], specifying the semantics of changes and maintaining the structural consistency. Other approaches focus on the first step of AIFB process which is change capturing. As approach of Trousse et al [2] which is based on data mining using extraction techniques of the knowledge. There are also approaches that focus on the forth step which is change propagation as CCOE (Collaborative and Contextual Ontology Editor) [3]. Indeed, it allows the construction and evolution of ontologies ensuring the changes propagation to the semantic referencing resources. However, most of evolution approaches override one important step of ontology evolution process which is change validation in assessing the quality of evolved ontology. Otherwise, assessing quality of evolved ontology enables developers to recognize and specify what parts of the ontology might cause problems and decrease its quality after an evolution process. By having several possibilities to evolve existing ontology, the assessment of the ontology quality allow users to compare these different evolved ontologies and select from it the higher quality one to be used. Several approaches put the focus on ontology quality assessment. These are those proposed within the Semantic Web (SW) community [4] and those proposed by ontology engineers of software engineering (SE) community [5]. Both SW and SE community propose a wealthy number of metrics to assess ontology. These metrics differ in the way and the criteria chosen to evaluate the ontology. We can classify these metrics in six categories of approaches: lexical approaches, domain approach, application based approach, human judgment approach, structural approach and multi-criteria approach [6]. In the remainder, we follow the application based approach category since we believe that it's more reliable to assess ontology with respect to its actual use in real application and test its performance against expected results by users. However, there are some disadvantages of this approach such as the result is often based on a specific task and could not easily be generalized and comparing several ontologies can only be done if they are used by the same application. These inconveniences are due to the lack of quality measure processing to more general aspect and can be applied to any ontology used by different applications. Our work tackles this issue by proposing a more general aspect of quality which is stability. We proposed, therefore, an ontology enrichment approach which assesses this aspect of quality by computing stability metric [7]. The majority of proposed metrics provided by different approaches for assessing ontology's quality relies on measures that allow evaluating the semantic similarity or the semantic relatedness between ontology concepts. We showed in previous work[9], the advantages of measures based on information content to assess the semantic similarity between concepts in hierarchical structure such as ontology. We demonstrated the positive impact of this type of measure especially that of Wu&Palmer (wup) [8] on our enrichment approach and how it can assess the stability of enriched ontology [9]. However, this measure only handle subsumption relationship between concepts which sometimes seems insufficient and it become necessary to consider other type of relationship such as property between concepts. In this work, we propose new similarity measure based on information content which enhances the wup measure by taking into account the property relationship in addition to the subsumption one. We integrate this measure in our enrichment approach and we illustrate its benefits in better assessing the stability of enriched ontology. The remainder of this paper is organized as follows. Section 2 introduces our enrichment approach based on stability assessment. In section 3 we describe our proposal measure which enhances WUP. Then, in section 4 we illustrate through an example of ontology the application of our new measure to compute semantic similarity between its concepts. Before concluding, we present in section 5 the experimental results of simulation carried out to evaluate the contribution of our new measure to keep stability of enriched ontology.

2   Ontology Enrichment Approach Based on Stability Assessment

According to [10], we define ontology stability as follows: *"Ontology is considered stable if the results of user requests, obtained in its initial state, are not lost after enrichment."*
The ontology structure can considerably change after several enrichment processes and so the relationships between ontology's concepts may significantly vary. Stability notion can be used to assess change's degree of enriched ontology regarding its initial state. This assessment is based on semantic relationship between ontology's concepts which can be represented in the spectrum of ontology. Thus, the ontology is considered stable as far as maintains the same spectrum even after enrichment. The spectrum of ontology is performed with frequencies of similarity measures values between ontology concepts [10]. To compute theses frequencies we use a well-defined semantic similarity measure. Evaluating ontology stability consists in computing the distance similarity between spectra of ontologies in initial state and after enrichment. This distance similarity is obtained with a measure called Global Stability Measure (SimStab$_{Glob}$)as following:

$$SimStab_{Glob}(O_1,O_2) = \sum_{i=1}^{\lfloor \frac{1}{\Delta s} \rfloor} \frac{\left| SpectN_{O_1}^{SimM}(s_i) - SpectN_{O_2}^{SimM}(s_i) \right|}{\lfloor \frac{1}{\Delta s} \rfloor} \qquad (1)$$

where $SpectN_{O_i}^{SimM}$ is the normalized spectrum of ontology O_1 with regard to similarity measure between concepts denoted $SimM$, Δs is the size of each interval used to determine ontology spectrum and $S_i = i * \Delta s$ and $S_i \in [o,1]$. If the value obtained with $SimStab_{Glob}$ is close to 0, then we infer that ontologies spectra are quite similar and conclude, therefore, that the stability of initial ontology O_1 was maintained even after its enrichment to O_2. we used $SimStab_{Glob}$ in our enrichment procedure. This latter operates in three steps [9] as sketched by figure 1. During the first step, we look for different position possibilities to add the new concept in the ontology. Note that the new concept will always be added as a child of an existing concept in the ontology. In the second step, the different possible enriched ontologies will be constructed, according to insertion positions defined in previous step. The third step allows choosing the best enriched ontology based on stability assess. This choice is based on global stability measure (SimStab$_{Glob}$) which relies on elementary measure such as those based on information content. Starting with hierarchical structure, Resnik defines in [11] the

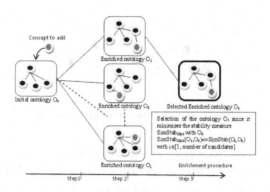

Fig. 1. Enrichment procedure

information content of a concept C_i by:$\psi(C_i) = -logP(C_i)$ where $P(C_i) \in [0, 1]$ is the probability for a generic instance of C_i to belong to the overall instances set. To compute this probability, we distinguish two approaches. Those based on textual corpus and others based on ontology structure. There is little number of ontologies carried by a textual corpus. That's why we followed the second type of approaches which exploit ontology structure to define the information content of each concept. Several similarity measures are proposed following this type. In the sequel, we focus on measure highlighted in a previous work [9] which is the redefinition of Wu & Palmer measure [8]. The redefinition of the Wu&Palmer measure (wup) by considering the information content notion is given by the following formula:

$$wup\,(C_i, C_j) = \frac{2.\psi(C_{ij})}{\psi_p(C_i) + \psi_p(C_j)} \qquad (2)$$

with ψ_p is the information content with hypothesis or approximation P_p Owe to the latter, the probability for an instance to be associated with a concept $C_i$decreases exponentially with respect to the depth of C_i [8].

3   Enhanced of Information Content Similarity Measure

In this section, we present our proposed generalization of wup measure. This generalization takes into account the property relationship as well as the subsumption one. Thus, each measure is composed of two parts. The first one is dedicated to the similarity measure relative to the inheritance relationship,

whereas the second is specific to the similarity measure of the property relationship. As described above, Wu & Palmer similarity measure (wup) between
two concepts of the same ontology takes the form of Dice measurement and is
based on their information contents as well as the information content of the
nearest common ancestor. Figure 2 shows an example of an ontology structure.
Let's consider concepts C_2 and C_3 which we want to compute the similarity

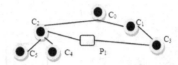

Fig. 2. Example of ontology structure

measure wup. We note that the nearest common ancestor denoted C_{23} is the
root of the tree C_0. The measurement is given by $wup(C_2, C_3) = \frac{2.\psi(C_{23})}{\psi_p(C_2)+\psi_p(C_3)}$
This equation totally disregards the information content induced by the prop-
erty P_1 between C_2 and C_3. In order to extend the wup measure, we assume
that the property relationship is important enough to be comparable to the subsumption relation. The information content of P_1(denoted $\psi_p(P_1)$) is given by:
$\psi_p(P_1) = \psi_p^{prop}(C_{23}) = Min(\psi_p(C_2), \psi_p(C_3))$ where $\psi_p^{prop}(C_{23})$ is the informational content of the property P_1 between C_2 and C_3 which is considered as a
virtual common ancestor C_{23}. It should be noted that the information content
value of that virtual common ancestor must be less or equal to the information
content of its sons. We approximate this value to the minimum informational
content of its sons. In general case, if we have a property that directly connect
or through their ancestors two concepts C_i and C_j. The information content of
the property is given by the following formula:

$$\psi_p^{prop}(C_{ij}) = Min(\psi_p(C_i), \psi_p(C_j)) \tag{3}$$

Then if there are several properties between two concepts C_i and C_j, the overall
information content is, thus, equal to:

$$\psi_p^*(C_{ij}) = \psi_p^{inherit}(C_{ij}) + \alpha.\frac{\sum_{prop \in E_{prop}} \psi_p^{prop}(C_{ij})}{|E_{prop}|} \tag{4}$$

where E_{prop} is the set of existing properties between concepts C_i and C_j directly or through their ancestors and α is a weighting parameter which reflects
the importance level of information content regarding the property relationship
compared to the inheritance information content. Considering the overall information content, the enhanced Wu&Palmer measure (Ewup) is given by the
following expression:

$$Ewup(C_i, C_j) = Min\left(\frac{2.\psi_p^*(C_{ij})}{\psi_p(C_i) + \psi_p(C_j)}, 1\right) \tag{5}$$

4   Application on Real Ontology

In order to show the interest of our proposal measure that improves the *wup* measure, we have to apply it in concrete example of ontology. We have chosen the ontology Wonders[2] which is in OWL format. This ontology is described in French; we translate it in English for more clearness. The Wonders ontology describes list of various wonders in the world, their location, their civilization, etc.. It is composed of 32 concepts and 8 properties (ObjectProperty). We present in the following table some similarities values of *wup* measure before and after enhancement between the main concept Wonder and some others concepts of the ontology. The similarity values presented in bold (Table 1) illustrate the

Table 1. values of similarity obtained with Wu&Palmer measure(*wup*)and enhanced wup (*Ewup*)

	Wonder	
	wup	*Ewup*
Wonder	1	1
Civilization	0	**0.666**
Country	0	**0.5**
Monument	0.5	0.5

differences between similarity values obtained with initial Wu& Palmer measure (*wup*) and those obtained with our new proposal for a generalization and enhancement of this measure (*Ewup*). For example, the pair of concepts ("Wonder","Civilization"), its similarity measure obtained with *wup* measure is equal to 0. Thanks to the enhanced measure, the value becomes 0.666. This significant change in the similarity value of this pair of concepts as well as others ensures and increases the ontology's coherence. Indeed, the relationship between concepts "Civilization" and "Wonder" should be close, since a wonder is necessary created at a civilization era. Initial measures Wu&Palmer totally ignore this relationship and consider that these two concepts are completely disjoint. However, our enhanced measure (*Ewup*) gives us much more reasonable similarity values. These changes are owe to the fact that the initial measures Wu & Palmer only consider the inheritance relationship and ignore therefore, any other type of relationship between concepts such as the property relationship "hasCivilization" which connects concepts "Wonder" and "Civilization". Note also that there are pairs of concepts whose similarity value has not changed, as the case of concepts ("Wonder", "Monument"). The similarity value was maintained before and after enhancement of measure. This can be explained by the lack of any property relationship between both concepts.

---

[2] The ontology was developed and implemented in this reference website :
    http://www.semanticweb.org/ontologies/2008/9/5/Ontology1223234403343.owl

5   Experimental Results

To better assess the benefits of our new information content similarity measure, we need to apply it with different structures of ontologies in significant sizes. In this section, we show the impact of our proposal measure in our ontology enrichment procedure and we evaluate whether this measure preserve the ontology stability after enrichment procedure described in section 2. In order to exploit different ontologies structures, we implement an automatic generator of random ontologies structures in the OWL format. This generator takes five input parameters which are: number of concepts or nodes in the ontology, number of property (ObjectProperty), depth of the tree representing the ontology, maximum and minimum number of sons per node, except leaves. This generator also allows enriching an existing ontology by a number of concepts or properties. The simulation starts firstly with creating a random initial ontology which having the following features: the number concepts is 100, the number of properties is equal to 10, the maximum number of concepts sons is 6, the minimum number of concepts sons is 2 and the depth of the tree representing the ontology is 6. The values of these different criteria provide fairly balanced tree structures of

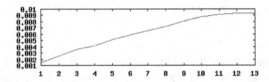

Fig. 3. Assessing stability of the enriched ontology using enhanced Wu&Palmer measure ($Ewup$)

ontology. Then, we make on this ontology 13 successive enrichments based on our enrichment procedure steps. In each enrichment, we consider 5 new concepts and only one property to add and we also assume that there are 10 possibilities to add it. The selection of the further stable ontology compared to the initial one is done through the stability measure $SimStab_{Glob}$ presented in equation 1. This latter will be computed based on our new information content similarity measure which enhance wup measure. Since ontologies are randomly constructed, our simulation is repeated 10 times to get averaged results. To investigate whether our enrichment approach maintains the quality of enriched ontology and more precisely the stability aspect, we draw the representative curves (figure 3) of stability measure values obtained in 13 enrichment iterations. We note the little change of stability values. It reaches 0.00935 with $Ewup$ measure after 13 successive enrichment iterations. This variation becomes smaller in the last three iterations. This implies that our enrichment approach keeps the stability of enriched ontology even relying on our new measure as a basis to compute the stability measurement.

6 Conclusion

To assess the quality of evolved ontology, we use enrichment procedure which based on evaluating stability of enriched ontology by computing a global stability measure. In order to handle other types of relationships between concepts especially the property relationship, we propose new information content similarity measure which enhance Wu& Palmer measure. We used it in our enrichment procedure and we have demonstrated via simulation that our approach preserves the stability of enriched ontology.

References

1. Stojanovic, L.: Methods and Tools for Ontology Evolution. PhD thesis, University of Karlsruhe (2004)
2. Trousse, B., Aufore, M.A., Le Grand, B., Lechevakier, Y., Masseglia, F.: Web Usage Mining for ontology management in Data mining Mining with ontologies imlementations, finding, and frameworks. ch. 3, pp. 37–64 (2009)
3. Luong, P.H., Dieng-Kuntz, R.: A Rule-based Approach for Semantic Annotation Evolution. The Computational Intelligence Journal 23(3), 320–338 (2007)
4. Gangemi, A., Catenacci, C., Ciaramita, M., Lehmann, J.: Modelling ontology evaluation and validation. In: Sure, Y., Domingue, J. (eds.) ESWC 2006. LNCS, vol. 4011, pp. 140–154. Springer, Heidelberg (2006)
5. Orme, A.M., Yao, H., Etzkorn, L.H.: Complexity metrics for ontology based information. International Journal of Technology Management 47(1-3), 161–173 (2009)
6. Brank, J., Grobelnik, M., Mladenic, D.: A Survey of Ontology Evaluation Techniques. In: Proc. of the Conference on Data Mining and Data Warehouses (SiKDD 2005), Ljubljana, Slovenia, pp. 165–170 (2005)
7. Kamoun, K., Ben Yahia, S.: Automatic Approach for Ontology Evolution based on Stability Evaluation. In: Proc. of 8th International Conference on Web Information Systems and Technologies (WEBIST 2012), Porto, Portugal, pp. 452–455 (April 2012)
8. Blanchard, E., Harzallah, M., Kuntz, P.: A generic framework for comparing semantic similarities on a subsumption hierarchy. In: Proc. of 18th European Conference on Artificial Intelligence (ECAI), Patrace, Greece, pp. 20–24 (2008)
9. Kamoun, K., Ben Yahia, S.: Information content similarity measure to assess stability during ontology enrichment. International Review on Computer and Software (IRECOS) 7(3) (May 2012)
10. Kamoun, K., Ben Yahia, S.: A Novel Global Measure Approach based on Ontology Spectrum to Evaluate Ontology Enrichment. International Journal of Computer Applications 39(17), 23–30 (2012)
11. Resnik, P.: Semantic similarity in a taxonomy: An information based measure and its application to problems of ambiguity in natural language. Journal of Artificial Intelligence Research 11, 95–130 (1999)

Algebraic Graph Transformations
for Merging Ontologies

Mariem Mahfoudh, Laurent Thiry, Germain Forestier, and Michel Hassenforder

MIPS EA 2332, Université de Haute Alsace,
12 rue des Frères Lumière 68093 Mulhouse, France
{mariem.mahfoudh,laurent.thiry,
germain.forestier,michel.hassenforder}@uha.fr

Abstract. The conception of an ontology is a complex task influenced by numerous factors like the point of view of the authors or the level of details. Consequently, several ontologies have been developed to model identical or related domains leading to partially overlapping representations. This divergence of conceptualization requires the study of ontologies merging in order to create a common repository of knowledge and integrate various sources of information. In this paper, we propose a formal approach for merging ontologies using typed graph grammars. This method relies on the algebraic approach to graph transformations, SPO (Simple PushOut) which allows a formal representation and ensures the consistence of the results. Furthermore, a new ontologies merging algorithm called GROM (Graph Rewriting for Ontology Merging) is presented.

Keywords: Ontologies Merging, Typed Graph Grammars, Algebraic Graph Transformations, GROM.

1   Introduction

With the emergence of ontologies [1] and their wider use, several ontologies have been developed to model identical or related domains leading to partially overlapping representations. As an example, we can cite the domain of Large Biomedical Ontologies which contains more than 370[1] ontologies with some famous ontologies : Foundational Model of Anatomy (FMA) [2], SNOMED CT[2], National Cancer Institute Thesaurus[3] (NCI), etc. This multitude of ontologies motivates the study of their merging to integrate and compose the different sources of knowledge.

Merging ontologies becomes more and more necessary and represents an important area of research. It is defined by Klein [3] as *"Creating a new ontology from two or more existing ontologies with overlapping parts, which can be either*

---

[1] http://bioportal.bioontology.org
[2] http://www.ihtsdo.org/snomed-ct
[3] http://ncit.nci.nih.gov

Y. Ait Ameur et al. (Eds.): MEDI 2014, LNCS 8748, pp. 154–168, 2014.
© Springer International Publishing Switzerland 2014

virtual or physical". The creation of the new ontology (also called the *global ontology*) is generally a complex task and requires considerable adaptation and a rigorous formalism to control the various steps of the construction. In this context, this paper proposes a formal approach for merging ontologies using typed graph grammars with algebraic graph transformations. Typed Graph Grammars (*TGG*) are a mathematical formalism which permits to represent and manage graphs. They are used in several fields of computer science such as software systems modelling, pattern recognition and formal language theory [4]. Recently, they started to be used in the ontology field, in particular for the formalization of the operations on ontologies like the alignment, merge and evolution [5,6,7,8,9,10]. In our previous work [10], we used *TGG* to formalize and implement ontology changes. They allow, thanks to their application conditions, to control the evolution process and to avoid inconsistencies.

In this paper, we use the same formalism to describe a formal approach of ontologies merging. The proposed approach has been implemented and a new tool called GROM (Graph Rewriting for Ontology Merging) is introduced. An application is presented on two ontologies developed in the frame of the CCAlps European project. Thus, the main contribution of this work is to take advantage of the graph grammars domain and the algebraic graph transformations to define and implement the process of merging ontologies.

The rest of this paper is structured as follows: Section 2 presents an overview of the typed graph grammars and algebraic graph transformations. Section 3 proposes an approach of ontology merging. Section 4 presents an example of application. Section 5 discusses some properties of the proposed approach. Section 6 shows some related work. Finally, a conclusion summarizes the presented work and gives some perspectives.

2   Typed Graph Grammars

This section reviews the fundamental notions involved in typed graph grammars and algebraic graph transformations.

Definition 1 (Typed graph grammars). A typed graph grammar is a formalism that is composed of a type graph (*TG*), a start graph (*G* also called host graph) and a set of production rules (*P*) called graph rewriting rules (or graph transformations). In this article, we consider the typed attributed graphs. Thus, $TGG = (G, TG, P)$ where:

- $G = (N, E, src : E \rightarrow N, tgt : N \rightarrow E, att : N \cup E \rightarrow \mathcal{P}(att))$ is a graph composed of : 1) a set of nodes (N); 2) a set of edges (E); 3) two functions, *src* and *tgt*, which specify the source and target of an edge; 4) a set of attributes (*att*) which are associated to the edges and nodes.
- $TG = (N_T, E_T, src : E_T \rightarrow N_T, tgt : N_T \rightarrow E_T, att_T)$ is a graph which represents the type of the elements of the graph G. The typing of a graph G over TG is given by a total graph morphism $t : G \rightarrow TG$ defined by 3 functions $t_E : E \rightarrow E_T$, $t_N : N \rightarrow N_T$ and $t_{att} : att \rightarrow att_T$. Figure 1 shows

an example of type graph and host graph. The TG represents two nodes "Conference" and "Emplacement" which have respectively two attributes "name" and "description" and linked by an edge "hasPlace". The host graph G represents an instance of the TG.

- P is a set of production rules which permit the replacement of one sub-graph by another. It is defined by a pair of graphs patterns (LHS, RHS) where:

  - LHS (Left Hand Side) represents the preconditions of the rewriting rule and describes the structure that has to be found in G.
  - RHS (Right Hand Side) represents the postconditions of the rule and must replaces LHS in G.

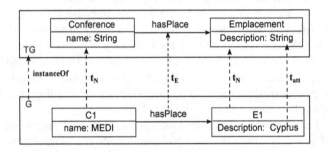

Fig. 1. Example of Type Graph and Host Graph

Moreover, the rules are allowed to have negative application conditions ($NACs$). A NAC is another graph pattern that specify the graph that should not occur when matching a rule. This means that rewriting rule cannot be applied if NAC exists in G. In this way, a graph transformation defines how a graph G can be transformed to a new graph G'. More precisely, there must exist a morphism that replaces LHS by RHS to obtain G'. To apply this replacement, different graph transformations approaches are proposed [11]. In this work, we use the algebraic approach [12] based on Category Theory [13] with the *pushout* concept.

Definition 2 (Category Theory). A category [14] is a structure consisting of: 1) a collection of objects O; 2) a set of arrows (also called morphism M) and a function $s : M \rightarrow O \times O$ such as $s(f) = (A, B)$ is written $f : A \rightarrow B$; 3) a binary operation called composition of morphisms $(\circ) : M \times M \rightarrow M$; 4) an identity morphism for each object $id : O \rightarrow O$. The composition operator is associative and $id(O)$ is the neutral element, i.e. if $m : A \rightarrow B$ then $m \circ id(A) = m = id(B) \circ m$. In our work, we consider the category of *Graph* where the objects are the graphs and the arrows are the graph morphisms.

Definition 3 (Pushout). Given three objects A, B and C and two morphisms $f : A \rightarrow B$ and $g : A \rightarrow C$, the pushout of B and C consists of: 1) an object D and two morphisms $f' : B \rightarrow D$ and $g' : C \rightarrow D$ where $f' \circ f = g' \circ g$; 2) for any morphisms $f'' : B \to E$ and $g'' : C \to E$ such that $f \circ f'' = g \circ g''$, there is a unique morphism $k : D \to E$ such that $f' \circ k = f''$ and $g' \circ k = g''$.

Algebraic approaches are divided into two categories: the *Single PushOut*, *SPO* [15] and the *Double PushOut*, *DPO* [16]. Applying a rewriting rule to an initial graph (G) with the SPO method consists in (Figure 2):

1. Finding a matching of LHS in G by defining a morphism $m : LHS \to G$.
2. Deleting $m(LHS) - m(LHS \cap RHS)$ from G.
3. Adding $m(RHS) - m(LHS \cap RHS)$ to G to give new version G'.

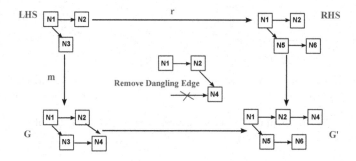

Fig. 2. Graph rewriting rule with SPO

The DPO approach consists of two pushouts and requires an additional condition called the dangling condition. This condition states that the transformation is applicable only if its application will not lead to dangling edges. For example, for the host graph G of the Figure 2, the rewriting rule is forbidden by the DPO approach because it breaks the dangling condition. If we want to apply this rule, the host graph G should not contain the edge $E(N3, N4)$. In the SPO approach, the dangling edges are removed. This allows to write transformations that do not allow DPO approach which is limited by the dangling condition. For this reason, we only consider the SPO approach in this work.

3   Merging Ontologies with Typed Graph Grammar

3.1   Ontologies with Typed Graph Grammars

As mentioned above, a typed graph grammar is defined by $TGG = (TG, G, P)$. By adapting this definition to the ontology field, we obtain:

- G is the host graph which represents the ontology. Figure 3 shows two examples of host graphs. They are sub-ontologies from the EOCCAlps (Event Ontology CCAlps) and COCCAlps (Company Ontology CCAlps) which are

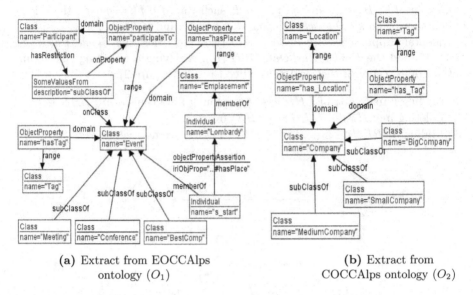

(a) Extract from EOCCAlps ontology (O_1)

(b) Extract from COCCAlps ontology (O_2)

Fig. 3. Example of ontologies represented as a host graph

developed in the frame of the European project CCAlps[4]. The EOCCAlps ontology represents events. They can be a "Conference", "Meeting" or a "BestComp" and should takes place in the Alpine space. The COCCAlps ontology represents companies and is used to describe those which will be participate to the events.

– TG is the type graph which represents the meta-model of the ontology (see [10]). The OWL meta-model was chosen because it is the standard proposed by the W3C and the language usually adopted to represent ontologies. Thus, the types of nodes, $N_T = \{Class, Property, Individual, DataType, Restriction\}$ and the type of edges are the axioms, $E_T = \{subClassOf, domain, ...\}$.

- Classes (C) model the set of individuals. For example, for EOCCAlps ontology, $C = \{$"Event", "Meeting", "Participant", ...$\}$.
- Individuals (I) represent the instances of classes, $I = \{$"Lombardy", "It's − Start"$\}$.
- Properties (P), for each class $C_i \in C$, there exists a set of properties $P(C_i) = DP(C_i) \cup OP(C_i)$, where DP are datatype properties and OP are object properties. If a property relates a class C_i to an entity E_i (*Class* or *Datatype*), then C_i is called the *domain* of the property and E_i is called the *range* of the property. For example, $OP = \{$"hasTag"$\}$, $domain($"hasTag"$) = \{$"Event"$\}$, $range($"hasTag"$) = \{$"Tag"$\}$.
- Datatypes (D) represent the type of data value. They can be string, boolean, etc.

---

[4] http://www.ccalps.eu

- Restrictions (R), for each property $p \in P(C_i)$ there exists a set of restrictions on the value or cardinality. For example, there is a value restriction on the property "participateTo" which states that some value for the "participateTo" should be an instance of the class "Participant".
- Axioms (A) specify the relations between the ontologies entities. For example, $subClassOf$ represents the subsumption relation between classes.

Note that both nodes and the edges can contain attributes. For example, among the attributes of the nodes of types C, I and P, we found the attribute *name* which specifies their local names and the *iri* which identifies them. In the figures of this article, the *iri* has not represented for readability reasons.

- P are the rewriting rules corresponding to the ontology changes (*AddClass*, *RemoveDataProperty*, *RenameIndividual*, etc.). An ontology change is defined by $CH = (Name, NACs, LHS, RHS, DCHs)$ where: 1) *Name* specifies the type of change; 2) *NACs* define the conditions which must not be true to apply the rewriting rule; 3) *LHS* represents the precondition of the rewriting rule; 4) *RHS* defines the postcondition of the rewriting rule; 5) *DCHs* are the Derived CHanges. They are additional rewriting rules that are attached to *CH* to correct its possible inconsistencies.

Figure 4 shows an example of a rewriting rule for the *RenameClass* change. This rule renames a node of type *Class* "Company" to "Enterprise" while avoiding redundant elements by the *NAC*.

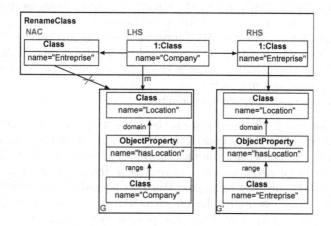

Fig. 4. Rewriting rule for the *RenameClass* change

After introducing how to use typed graph grammars to represent ontologies and their changes, we present now an approach for merging ontologies. This consists mainly of three steps presented in the following sections: 3.2) similarity search; 3.3) merging ontologies; 3.4) global ontology adaptation (Figure 5).

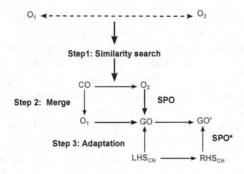

Fig. 5. Approach of merging ontologies with algebraic graph transformations

3.2 Similarity Search

In order to establish a correspondence between the ontologies, it is necessary to identify the relationship (similarity) between their entities. In the literature, several techniques have been proposed to determine these similarities [17]. They can be divided into five categories:

1. lexical techniques, consider the name of the entities and compare them as String, e.g. Levenshtein distance [18];
2. structural techniques, consider the structure of the ontologies to detect the subsumption relations, e.g. Children and Leaves [19];
3. strategies that use an external resource like ontology linguistic (e.g. Wordnet [20]), dictionary, thesaurus or other ontology for the same domain;
4. strategies that compare ontologies through their usage traces (ex. annotations of the same resources);
5. combination of the previous techniques.

Despite this multitude of techniques, the domain of similarity search has still several challenges [21]. Thus, considering that our main goal is merging ontologies, we chose to work with a simple, but efficient, combination of lexical techniques and external resource. Thus, Levenshtein distance is used for detecting the common and equivalent terms and WordNet is used to recognize the semantic correspondences essentially the synonym terms. The subsumption relations ($IsaN$) are defined manually. Then, the process of the similarity search takes two ontologies (O_1 and O_2) as input and compares their components (class by class, property by property and individual by individual). Then, it generates:

- $CN = \{N_i|(N_i \in N(O_1)) \wedge (\exists N_j \in N(O_2) \cdot (N_{iT} = N_{jT}) \wedge$
  $(Levenshtein(N_i.name, N_j.name) = 0))\}$ is the set of common nodes between the nodes of ontology O_1 ($N(O_1)$) and those of ontology O_2 ($N(O_2)$) where the type of nodes can be *Class*, *Property* (*DP* or *OP*) or *Individual*;
- $EN = \{(N_i, N_j)|(N_i \in N(O_1)) \wedge (N_j \in N(O_2)) \wedge (N_{iT} = N_{jT}) \wedge$
  $(Levenshtein(N_i.name, N_j.name) < threshold))\}$ is the set of the equivalent nodes;

- $SN = \{(N_i, N_j) | (N_i \in N(O_1)) \wedge (N_j \in N(O_2)) \wedge (N_{iT} = N_{jT}) \wedge (N_i.name \in (synsetWordNet(N_j.name)\}$ is the set of the nodes sharing a semantic relation.

3.3 Merging Ontologies

The process of ontologies merging is based on SPO approach which offers a rigorous and simple way to glue the graphs. It encapsulates the complex details of the ontologies structures by considering them as objects of a suitable abstract category. Thus, this step is divided into three sub-steps (see Figure 6). The first one aims at minimizing the differences between the two ontologies. Thus, its role is to replace the entities of the ontology 1 by their equivalent in the ontology 2. This replacement is applied by the rewriting rule $RenameNode$ (N_i, N_j) where N_i is a node of O_1 and N_j is its equivalent in O_2. So, for this SPO:

- the host graph is the ontology O_1;
- the LHS is the graph composed by the set of nodes $\{N_i \in EN\}$;
- the RHS is the graph composed by $\{N_j \in EN\}$.

An example of the $RenameClass$ rule is already presented in Figure 4.

Then, the second step consists in creating the Common Ontology (CO). This is the common sub-graph between the two ontologies. It is constructed by the common nodes (CN) and the edges that they share.

The third and last step merges the ontologies with the $MergeGraph(CO, O_2)$ rewriting rule. This SPO is defined as following:

- its host graph is the ontology O_1 after modification (O'_1);
- its LHS is the Common Ontology CO;
- its RHS is the ontology O_2.

The role of this pushout is the merge of the two ontologies by linking them by their common entities. Thus, this step provides a global ontology (GO) which will be enriched by the integration of semantic and subsumption relations.

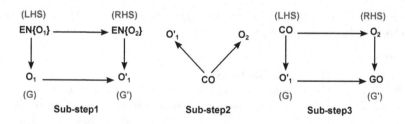

Fig. 6. The three sub-steps of the ontologies merging

3.4 Global Ontology Adaptation

Given that the graph transformation requires the presence of the match (i.e a morphism m) between LHS and the host graph, the addition of the semantic and the subsumption relations should be applied after the creation of the global ontology. Thus, this section presents the $AddEquivalentEntity$ and $AddSubClass$ rewriting rules which can enrich the global ontology without affecting its consistency. The checking of the inconsistencies is done by using the $NACs$.

The $AddEquivalentEntity$ rewriting rule adds an equivalent axiom between two entities (two classes or two properties). Figure 7 presents the rewriting rule of the $AddEquivalentClasses$ (C_1, C_2) which is defined:

- NACs :
  1. $C_1 \equiv C_2$, condition to avoid redundancy;
  2. $C_1 \sqsubseteq \neg C_2$, two classes cannot be disjoint and equivalent at the same time;
- LHS : $\{C_1, C_2\}$, the classes should exist in the ontology.
- RHS : $(C_1 \equiv C_2)$, the axiom will be added to the ontology.
- DCH : $\emptyset$.

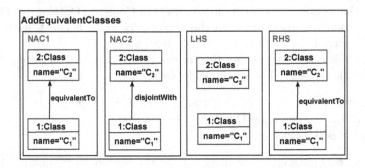

Fig. 7. Rewriting rules for the $AddEquivalentClasses$ change

The $AddSubClass$ (C_1, C_2) rewriting rule adds a $subClassOf$ axiom between two classes (Figure 8) and it is defined by:

- NACs :
  1. $C_1 \sqsubseteq C_2$, to avoid redundancy.
  2. $C_2 \sqsubseteq C_1$, the subsumption relation cannot be symmetric;
  3. $C_1 \sqsubseteq \neg C_2$, classes which share a subsumption relation cannot be disjoint;
  4. $\exists C_i \in C(O) \cdot (C_1 \sqsubseteq C_i) \wedge (C_i \sqsubseteq C_2)$, if exist a class C_i which is the $subClassOf$ the class C_2 and the $superClass$ of C_1, then, C_1 is already a $subClass$ of C_2;
  5. $\exists (C_i, C_j) \in C(O) \cdot (C_i \sqsubseteq C_1) \wedge (C_j \sqsubseteq C_2) \wedge C_i \sqsubseteq \neg C_j$, classes which share a subsumption relation cannot have subClasses that are disjoint;

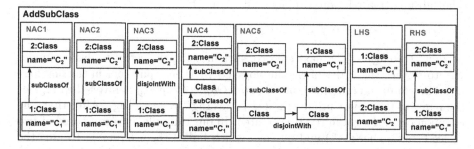

Fig. 8. Rewriting rule for the *AddSubClass* change

- LHS : $\{C_1, C_2\}$, the classes should exist in the ontology.
- RHS : $(C_1 \sqsubseteq C_2)$, the axiom will be added to the ontology.
- DCH : $\emptyset$.

4 Implementation and Example

In order to implement the proposed method, we have developed a Java program called GROM (Graph Rewriting for Ontology Merging). GROM is based on AGG (Algebraic Graph Grammar) API[5] that supports the algebraic graph transformations (SPO and DPO approaches) and manipulates the typed attributed graph grammars. The tool take as input two ontologies in AGG format (.ggx), a mapping in XML and outputs the merged ontology in AGG format (.ggx). Note that the semantic relations, in the mapping process, are identified by the RitaWN[6] that provides access to the WordNet ontology.

The following presents a merging example of the two ontologies presented in Figure 3. The ontologies were created in OWL using Protégé. They were converted into AGG graphs using the software OWLToGGx [10]. In the following, the word "ontology" is used to refer to its corresponding graph[7].

Similarity Search The first step of the proposed approach is the detection of the similarities between the ontologies entities. By considering the ontologies example O_1 and O_2, the Levenshtein distance returns the following correspondences:

- $CN = \{\text{"Tag"}\}; \qquad EN = \{(\text{"hasTag"}, \text{"has\_Tag"})\}.$

Wordnet detects the synonym terms:

- $SN = \{(\text{"Emplacement"}, \text{"Location"})\}.$

---

[5] http://user.cs.tu-berlin.de/~gragra/agg

[6] http://rednoise.org/rita/wordnet/documentation

[7] All the materials used in this example (ontologies in OWL and in graph (GGX format) along with the Java implementation) are available for download under open source licence here: http://mariem-mahfoudh.info/medi2014/

The subsumption relations are manually defined:

– $IsaN = \{(\text{``Company''}, \text{``Participant''})\}$.

Merging Ontologies The next step consists in using the set of equivalent nodes EN to replace the nodes of the ontology O_1 by their equivalent in the ontology O_2. Therefore, the rewriting rule *RenameObjectProperty* is invoked to replace the name of the object properties (OP) "hasTag" by "has_Tag". After that, the common ontology graph (CO) is created. In our example, it is composed of two nodes ("tag", "hasTag") and an edge which linked them (*range*). To glue the ontologies, the rewriting rule *MergeGraph* is executed. It takes the ontology O_1 as a host graph, CO as a *LHS* and O_2 as a *RHS*. Finally, it returns as an output the global ontology (GO). Note that all this process if is fully automatic and only takes as parameter the correspondences found in the previous step.

Global Ontology Adaptation The global ontology does not yet represent the semantic and subsumption relations. Thus, it is necessary to execute the rewriting rules: 1) *AddEquivalentClasses* ("Emplacement", "Location"); 2) *AddSubClass* ("Company", "Participant"). Figure 9 presents the global ontology resulting of the merging ontologies O_1 and O_2. Once again, this process is automatic. Finally, the resulting ontology can be easily converted back to OWL[8].

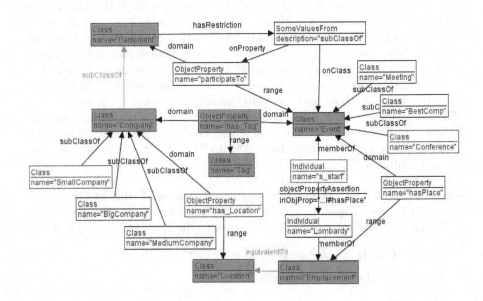

Fig. 9. Result of merging the ontologies O_1 & O_2

---

[8] http://mariem-mahfoudh.info/ksem2013

5   Discussion

Symmetry of the approach. Raunich and al. [22], have presented a state of the art of ontology merging and have distinguished two types of approaches: 1) Symmetric approaches preserve both input ontologies even the redundant data; 2) Asymmetric approaches take one of the ontologies as the source and merge the other as a target. In this type of approach, only the concepts of the source ontology are preserved. Our approach is an asymmetric one with:

$$Merge(O_1, O_2) \neq Merge(O_2, O_1),$$
$$Merge(O_1, O_2) = Merge(O_2, Merge(O_1, O_2)) \text{ and}$$
$$Merge(O_2, O_1) = Merge(O_1, Merge(O_2, O_1)).$$

However, if the set of equivalent nodes is empty ($EN = \emptyset$) and there is no conflicts between the ontologies, then the "sub-step1" of the ontologies merging is not executed and the approach, in this case, is symmetric. Thus, we have:

$$Merge(O_1, O_2) = Merge(O_2, O_1) = Merge(O_1, Merge(O_1, O_2)) =$$
$$Merge(O_2, Merge(O_1, O_2)) = GO.$$

Coverage. The coverage (Cov) is a criteria to evaluate the quality of merge results. It is is related to the degree of information preservation and measures the share of input concepts preserved in the result. Coverage values is between 0 and 1 [22]. In our approach, we distinguish two cases:

1. if $EN = \emptyset$, then, $Cov = 1$. All the ontologies concepts are preserved but with the advantage that the redundant data (*e.g.* the multiple inheritance) are dropped (thanks to the application of the $NACs$ in the rewriting rules).
2. if $EN \neq \emptyset$, then, $Cov = 1 - \frac{card(EN(O_1))}{card(N(O_1)+N(O_2))}$. Only the equivalent nodes of the ontology source (O_1) are lost.

Complexity. The most demanding step in time and resource is the recognition of the LHS from the host graph G. This research is an NP-complete problem. More precisely, a search of a sub-graph composed of k elements in a graph compound of n elements has a complexity of $O(n^k)$. However, the cost of calculation remains quite acceptable if the size of the LHS graph is limited [23]. In the most examples of transformations, this condition is satisfied.

Conflicts management. In this article, ontologies are expected to be correct and there is no strong contradictions between them. However, as they conceptualize identical or related domains, ontologies may have some conflicts. Therefore, another step should be added to detect the possible conflicts. Thus, the addition of axioms into the target ontology should be sequential and the user intervention may be required. Several cases can be found. We present in this section how to add individuals axioms of the target ontology without affecting the source ontology. In particular, the rewriting rule $AddObjectPropertyAssertion(I_1, I_2, OP)$ is discussed. It adds an $ObjectPropertyAssertion$ between two individuals and it is defined as follow:

– NAC :

1. $(I_1, I_2) \in OP$, to avoid redundancy.
2. $\exists I_i \in I(O) \cdot (I_i \neq I_2) \wedge ((I_1, I_i) \in OP)^9 \wedge (\top \sqsubseteq 1OP)$, if there is an individual I_i which different to I_2 and it is linked to I_1 by OP, where OP is a functional property, then the addition of the assertion is not allowed;
3. $\exists \leqslant nOP \cdot (\exists I_i \in I(O)) \wedge \{(I_1, I_i) \in OP\} = n$, if there is a restriction (OP maxCardinality(n)) and the count of the assertion individuals is equal to n, then, the adding of other assertion is not allowed.

– LHS : $\{I_1, I_2, OP\}$, I_1, I_2 and OP should exist in the ontology.
– RHS : $((I_1, I_2) \in OP)$, the assertion should be added to the ontology.
– DCH : $\emptyset$.

6 Related Work

A limited number of approaches were proposed for merging ontologies. They can be classified into two main categories: the approaches based on semantic web technologies [24,25,26,27,28] and the approaches based on algebraic specification and Category Theory [29,5,7].

The aim of our work is to present a formal approach for ontologies merging and show that typed graph grammars can be a good formalism to manage ontology changes (evolution and merging). Therefore, we have studied the existing propositions in the domain of algebraic specifications. Thus, Zimmermann et al., [5] have presented a categorical approach to formalize ontologies alignment. They proposed two formalisms: the V-alignment and W-alignment which use the "span" concept of the Category Theory. This work is an important reference as it presents the foundations of using categories in the field of semantic web. However, it is focused on the problem of ontologies alignment and it studied the merge only as an operation of alignment. Later, Cafezeiro et al., [7] have proposed to use the concepts of Category Theory ("limit", "colimit" and "pushout") to formalize the ontology operations. This work defines merge and composition operations but only considers ontologies which are composed of classes, hierarchies of classes and relations. It does not consider neither the individuals nor the axioms. Finally, these approaches have not been implemented. In our work, we use the algebraic approach and category theory in the frame of graph grammars formalism. This allowed us to implement the proposed approach (GROM) and to benefit the application conditions (e.g. NACs) to avoid inconsistencies. Furthermore, our approach is more general because it treats individuals and axioms.

7 Conclusion

In this paper, we presented a formal approach for merging ontologies using typed graph grammars. It is divided into three steps. The first searches correspondences

---

[9] I_1 and I_i are linked by the objectProperty OP.

between nodes from the ontologies. It is based on lexical techniques (Levenshtein distance) and an external resource (the linguistic ontology WordNet). The second step merges the structures of the ontologies using the correspondences computed in the previous step, by using the SPO approach. The last step, enriches the merged ontology with subsumption and semantic relations. It used for that the rewriting rules of some basic ontology changes (*AddEquivalentEntity*, *AddSubClass*, etc.). To validate our proposals, we have implemented a new tool, GROM that given two ontologies and their mapping, it is able to generate the global ontology automatically. As it is based on the the algebraic graph transformations, it allows to define a simple and formal way to merge ontologies while encapsulating the complex details of their structures.

For future work, we intend to study the different conflicts which can affect the result of the merge. Then, we plan to improve the alignment result and explore other techniques of similarity search specially the structural techniques. The current test case study includes small ontologies, we are currently considering larger ontologies in order to perform a better evaluation of the method.

Acknowledgment. The authors would like to thank the European project CCAlps which funded this work (project number is 15-3-1-IT).

References

1. Staab, S., Studer, R.: Handbook on ontologies. Springer (2010)
2. Rosse, C., Mejino Jr., J.L.: A reference ontology for biomedical informatics: the foundational model of anatomy. Journal of Biomedical Informatics 36(6), 478–500 (2003)
3. Klein, M.: Combining and relating ontologies: an analysis of problems and solutions. In: IJCAI-2001, Workshop on Ontologies and Information Sharing, pp. 53–62 (2001)
4. Ehrig, H., Montanari, U., Rozenberg, G., Schneider, H.J.: Graph Transformations in Computer Science. Geschäftsstelle Schloss Dagstuhl (1996)
5. Zimmermann, A., Krotzsch, M., Euzenat, J., Hitzler, P.: Formalizing ontology alignment and its operations with category theory. Frontiers in Artificial Intelligence and Applications 150, 277–288 (2006)
6. d'Aquin, M., Doran, P., Motta, E., Tamma, V.A.: Towards a parametric ontology modularization framework based on graph transformation. In: WoMO (2007)
7. Cafezeiro, I., Haeusler, E.H.: Semantic interoperability via category theory. In: 26th International Conference on Conceptual Modeling, pp. 197–202. Australian Computer Society, Inc. (2007)
8. De Leenheer, P., Mens, T.: Using graph transformation to support collaborative ontology evolution. In: Schürr, A., Nagl, M., Zündorf, A. (eds.) AGTIVE 2007. LNCS, vol. 5088, pp. 44–58. Springer, Heidelberg (2008)
9. Javed, M., Abgaz, Y.M., Pahl, C.: Ontology change management and identification of change patterns. Journal on Data Semantics 2(2-3), 119–143 (2013)
10. Mahfoudh, M., Forestier, G., Thiry, L., Hassenforder, M.: Consistent ontologies evolution using graph grammars. In: Wang, M. (ed.) KSEM 2013. LNCS, vol. 8041, pp. 64–75. Springer, Heidelberg (2013)

11. Rozenberg, G.: Handbook of graph grammars and computing by graph transformation, vol. 1. World Scientific (1999)
12. Ehrig, H., Pfender, M., Schneider, H.J.: Graph-grammars: An algebraic approach. In: Switching and Automata Theory (SWAT), pp. 167–180. IEEE (1973)
13. Barr, M., Wells, C.: Category theory for computing science, vol. 10. Prentice Hall, New York (1990)
14. Fokkinga, M.M.: A gentle introduction to category theory — the calculational approach. In: Lecture Notes of the STOP 1992 Summerschool on Constructive Algorithmics, pp. 1–72. University of Utrecht (1992)
15. Löwe, M.: Algebraic approach to single-pushout graph transformation. Theoretical Computer Science 109(1), 181–224 (1993)
16. Ehrig, H.: Introduction to the algebraic theory of graph grammars (a survey). In: Claus, V., Ehrig, H., Rozenberg, G. (eds.) Graph Grammars 1978. LNCS, vol. 73, pp. 1–69. Springer, Heidelberg (1979)
17. Ivanov, P., Voigt, K.: Schema, ontology and metamodel matching - different, but indeed the same? In: Bellatreche, L., Mota Pinto, F. (eds.) MEDI 2011. LNCS, vol. 6918, pp. 18–30. Springer, Heidelberg (2011)
18. Levenshtein, V.I.: Binary codes capable of correcting deletions, insertions and reversals. In: Soviet physics doklady, vol. 10, pp. 707–710 (1966)
19. Do, H.H., Rahm, E.: Coma: a system for flexible combination of schema matching approaches. In: 28th International Conference on Very Large Data Bases (VLDB), VLDB Endowment, pp. 610–621 (2002)
20. Miller, G.A.: Wordnet: A lexical database for english. Communications of the ACM 38(11), 39–41 (1995)
21. Shvaiko, P., Euzenat, J.: Ontology matching: state of the art and future challenges (2012)
22. Raunich, S., Rahm, E.: Towards a benchmark for ontology merging. In: Herrero, P., Panetto, H., Meersman, R., Dillon, T. (eds.) OTM-WS 2012. LNCS, vol. 7567, pp. 124–133. Springer, Heidelberg (2012)
23. Karsai, G., Agrawal, A., Shi, F., Sprinkle, J.: On the use of graph transformations in the formal specification of computer-based systems. In: IEEE TC-ECBS and IFIP10. 1 Joint Workshop on Formal Specifications of Computer-Based Systems, pp. 19–27 (2003)
24. Noy, N.F., Musen, M.A.: Algorithm and tool for automated ontology merging and alignment. In: 17th National Conference on Artificial Intelligence (AAAI), pp. 450–455. AAAI Press/The MIT Press (2000)
25. Nováček, V., Smrž, P.: Empirical merging of ontologies — A proposal of universal uncertainty representation framework. In: Sure, Y., Domingue, J. (eds.) ESWC 2006. LNCS, vol. 4011, pp. 65–79. Springer, Heidelberg (2006)
26. Li, G., Luo, Z., Shao, J.: Multi-mapping based ontology merging system design. In: 2nd International Conference onAdvanced Computer Control (ICACC), vol. 2, pp. 5–11. IEEE (2010)
27. Raunich, S., Rahm, E.: Atom: Automatic target-driven ontology merging. In: 27th International Conference on Data Engineering (ICDE), pp. 1276–1279. IEEE (2011)
28. Fareh, M., Boussaid, O., Chalal, R., Mezzi, M., Nadji, K.: Merging ontology by semantic enrichment and combining similarity measures. International Journal of Metadata, Semantics and Ontologies 8(1), 65–74 (2013)
29. Hitzler, P., Krötzsch, M., Ehrig, M., Sure, Y.: What is ontology merging? In: American Association for Artificial Intelligence (2005)

SOIM: Similarity Measures on Ontology Instances Based on Mixed Features

Rania Yangui[1], Ahlem Nabli[2], and Faiez Gargouri[1]

[1] Sfax University, Institute of Computer Science and Multimedia, BP 1030, Tunisia
yangui.rania@gmail.com, faiez.gargouri@isimsf.rnu.tn
[2] Sfax University, Faculty of Sciences, BP 1171, Tunisia
ahlem.nabli@fsegs.rnu.tn

Abstract. Clustering has been widely applied to various domains to explore the useful patterns inside data. Clustering quality can be improved using Knowledge represented by ontology. Nevertheless, most traditional ontology-based clustering algorithms are limited to handle categorical instances. But in real case study, ontology contains both numerical and categorical attributes. In this paper, we propose a new method for clustering knowledge contained in the ontology based on mixed features. The main contribution is the proposition of new similarity measures that combine numerical and nominal variables along different dimensions (instances, attributes, and relation-ships). Three kinds of similarity measures are so defined: *instances-based similarity IS*, *relations-based similarity RS* and *attributes-based similarity AS*. These three measures are then combined into an overall similarity measure. This combined measure is used for clustering.

1 Introduction

Clustering is a popular data mining technique that aims to divide objects into groups in such a way that objects inside a group are similar, and objects belonging to different groups are dissimilar. In order to obtain a more accurate clustering, a large number of features are often used to describe objects. The knowledge provided by ontology serves as perfect input data for clustering. As defined by Gruber an ontology is "a set of representational primitives with which to model a domain of knowledge or discourse. The representational primitives are typically classes (or sets), attributes (or properties), and relationships (or relations among class members)" [1].

In the literature, various ontology-based clustering algorithms are designed to focus mainly on categorical data [2-6]. But in real case, ontology contains both numeric and categorical attributes. The transformation of numerical attributes to categorical ones can generate a loss of information and degrade the clustering quality.

Motivated by these issues, the main thrust of this paper is the definition of new method that extends the hierarchical clustering algorithm to cluster knowledge contained in the ontology based on mixed features. Our method relies on a set of similarity measures that allow computing similarities between semantically linked instances along different dimensions (instances, attributes, and relation-ships).

Y. Ait Ameur et al. (Eds.): MEDI 2014, LNCS 8748, pp. 169–176, 2014.
© Springer International Publishing Switzerland 2014

The remainder of this paper is organized as follows: Section 2 presents our research context. Section 3 reviews some related work. Section 4 introduces our method (SOIM). Experimental results are presented in section 5. Finally, section 6 gives a conclusion and future research directions.

2   Research Context

We are involved in the BWEC (Business for Women of Emerging Country) research project that treats women from rural and urban areas of Tunisian and Algerian countries. The project aim is to improve the socio-economic situation of these women by providing true technological means in concordance with the women habits. However, the number of handicraft women is increasing every day so it is impossible to define for every woman the appropriate solution. This growing number of handicraft women has made a strong need to analyze the information about these women and divide them into groups in order to define the affordable solution fitted to each group. To perform our analysis, a set of interviews are realized with 320 handicraft women in many areas of Tunisian and Algerian countries. Finally, relevant concepts are extracted from interviews and represented through ontology.

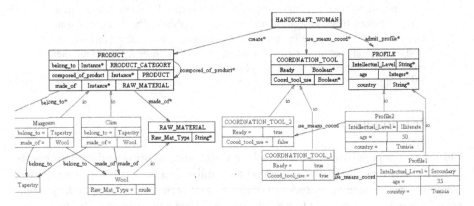

Fig. 1. Ontology except

As shown in Fig1, Handicraft women concept is related to three concepts *Coord_Tool_Use*, *Profile* and *Product* that can be used as features for the clustering. Note that features may be numerical such as *Coord_Tool_Use* or categorical like *Profile* and *Product*. Therefore, it is difficult to apply traditional clustering algorithm directly into these kinds of data. Traditional similarity measures, such as the Euclidian distance, can be perfectly used to compute similarity on ontology instances based on numerical features. Some categorical values which are ordinal can be easily transformed to numerical ones such as *Intellectual_Level* ("Illiterate"<= "1", "Primary"<= "2", "Secondary"<= "3" and "University"<= "4"). However, other categorical values cannot be ordered. In the case where categorical instances cannot be ordered like "Jebba", "Clim", "Zarbiya", "Margoum", "Chechia" and "Barnous", a new similarity measure is recommended. For that, we suggest to use composed similarity measure where similarity between components checks the contexts in which it appears. For example two *products* instances are considered similar if they have the same *category* values and their respective sets of *raw materials* values are similar. Or *Category* and *raw materials* represent two concepts linked to *product* concept via *belong_to* and *made_of* relations-ship. So, a new similarity measure based on relationship must be defined. Another example, concerning *profile* feature, two *profiles* instances are considered similar if they have similar *age, intellectual level* and *country* values. These criteria represent attribute (data-properties) in the *product* concept. So, a new similarity measure based on attributes can be useful.

Hence, we need to define similarity measures that handle mixed data while taking advantages of the ontology structure. So, an extension of hierarchical clustering algorithm can be proposed based on these measures.

3   Related Work

3.1   Ontology-Based Clustering

In the literature, some data mining techniques have been used for the analysis of knowledge contained in the ontology. Several works have applied clustering techniques for grouping objects based on ontological instances. For example, [2, 3] proposed an approach for grouping ontology instances based on a set of similarity measures. They distinguished between three measures of similarity: concept similarity, relation similarity and attribute similarity. In the same context, [4, 5] proposed methods for grouping semantically annotated resources in order to facilitate the ontology management. These methods define similarity measures which takes advantage of semantics in the ontology. Otherwise, [6] proposed a measure-based clustering method for ontology. The similarity between individuals is defined by a semi-similarity measurement reflecting the similarity of these individuals. All research cited above compute similarity on ontology instances based on only categorical features. But, in real case, ontology contains both categorical and numerical attributes.

3.2   Clustering Mixed Variables

During the past decades, some works try to find a unified similarity measure for categorical and numerical attributes. These approaches are classified into four main groups. The first group proposes to divide data set into two sub-sets such that each sub-set contain either numerical or categorical data, then apply separate clustering algorithm on each sub-set [7]. The second group proposes the discretization of categorical attributes (converting categorical attribute into numerical ones) and apply numerical attribute clustering algorithm [8]. The third group suggests discriminating the numerical attributes and then applying categorical based clustering algorithm [9]. The forth group propose to convert the categorical attributes into binary ones and apply any numerical based clustering algorithm [10].

Due to the fundamental differences in two data types, the unification of categorical attribute and numerical values may not be perfect and not semantically meaningful. In fact, the loss of information in the conversion process decreases the clustering results. One of the most important motivations of our method is to adjust similarities between objects described by mixed semantically linked instances. In the next section we will detail our method (SOIM) of combining numeric and nominal variables in calculating the similarity between ontology instances along different dimensions.

4   SOIM: Similarity Measures on Ontology Instances Based on Mixed Features

As input to our clustering method, we have ontology that contains information about handicraft women profiles, their productions and their ability to use new technologies. In our specific case objects W (Woman) are described via features set F = $\{f_1, f_2, ...,$ $f_n\}$. Each feature is represented by instances that serve as input for measuring similarities. F contains both numeric and categorical attributes.

4.1   SOIM Process

For clustering mixed numerical and categorical datasets, we proposed a new method called SOIM for measuring similarity on ontology instances based on mixed features. First, (1) features set is divided into two sub-features sets: the pure categorical features set and the pure numeric features set. (2) Categorical features set are subdivided on ordered and nominal ones. Next, (3) ordinal categorical features instances are mapped to numerical ones and moved to the numerical features set. Domain experts should be involved in the conversion process to provide a better conversion. Numeric attributes' values are then normalized into the range of zero and one. (4) For each object, separate similarity measures are then calculated based on numeric and nominal features, and are then (5) combined into an overall similarity measure. The similarity matrix is so generated. Finally, (6) we use the hierarchical clustering algorithm with the combined similarity function to cluster instances.

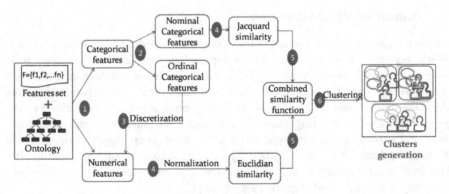

Fig. 2. Steps of SOIM method

4.2   Similarity Functions

Recall that, in our specific case objects W are described via features set $F = \{f_i\}$. Each feature f_i is represented by a set of instances I.

Notations

- $I_{W_j}^{f_i}$: The instance of the feature f_i for woman w_j.
- $Sim(w_1, w_2)$: The similarity between two objects w_1 and w_2 in the ontology.
- $Sim\left(I_{W_1}^{f_i}, I_{W_2}^{f_i}\right)$: The similarity between two instances of the same features concerning two different women.

According to the feature kind, the similarity measure between two objects can be described via a simple measure (*IS*) or a composed measure (*RS* or *AS*). We define three similarity measures: *instances-based similarity*, *attributes-based similarity* and *relations-based similarity*.

Instances-Based Similarity (IS): Computes the similarity between two instances on the basis of their corresponding categorical or numerical values. It consists on measuring the Jacquard similarity between two nominal (no-ordinal) categorical instances and the Euclidean similarity between two standardized numerical instances.

$$IS\left(I_{W_1}^{f_i}, I_{W_2}^{f_i}\right) = \begin{cases} JIS\left(I_{W_1}^{f_i}, I_{W_2}^{f_i}\right) = \dfrac{|V_1 \cap V_2|}{|V_1 \cup V_2|} \; if \; I_{W_1}^{f_i} and \; I_{W_2}^{f_i} are \; categorical \quad (1) \\[4mm] EIS\left(I_{W_1}^{f_i}, I_{W_2}^{f_i}\right) = 1 - \sqrt{Stand\left(I_{W_1}^{f_i}\right) - Stand\left(I_{W_2}^{f_i}\right)^2} \\[2mm] if \; I_{W_1}^{f_i} and \; I_{W_2}^{f_i} are \; numerical \quad\quad\quad\quad\quad\quad\quad (2) \end{cases}$$

Where $V_j = \{v_{j_1}, \dots, v_{j_k}\}$ is the values set that compose $I_{W_j}^{f_i}$ and

$$Stand\left(I_{W_j}^{f_i}\right) = \frac{I_{W_j}^{f_i} - min\left(I_{W_j}^{f_i}\right)}{max(I_{W_j}^{f_i}) - min\left(I_{W_j}^{f_i}\right)} \quad (3)$$

In JIS, we use terminological relations (= identical, ≡ synonymous, ≠ different) represented in the ontology to measure the similarity between two values.

Attributes-Based Similarity (AS): Computes the similarity between two instances based on their attributes values. This similarity is expressed using formula (4).

$$AS\left(I_{W_1}^{f_i}, I_{W_2}^{f_i}\right) = \frac{\sum_{j=1}^{n} IS\left(A_{1j}^{f_i}, A_{2j}^{f_i}\right)}{n} \quad (4)$$

Where $A_k^{f_i}$ is the attributes values set concerning f_i feature with w_k.

Relations-Based Similarity (RS): Computes the similarity between two categorical instances on the basis of their relations to other instances. This similarity is expressed using Formula (5).

$$RS\left(I_{W_1}^{f_i}, I_{W_2}^{f_i}\right) = \frac{\sum_{j=1}^{n} IS\left(R_{1j}^{f_i}, R_{2j}^{f_i}\right)}{n} \tag{5}$$

Where $R_k^{f_i}$ is the instances values set to which f_i is related concerning w_k object.

Based on the similarity measures introduced above we present a common measure to compute similarity between ontology instances during an   iteration.

$$Sim(W_1, W_2) = \sum_{i=1}^{n} \left(Sim\left(I_{W_1}^{f_i}, I_{W_2}^{f_i}\right)\right)$$

$$= \frac{\sum_{i=1}^{k} \left(IS\left(I_{W_1}^{f_i}, I_{W_2}^{f_i}\right)\right) + \sum_{a=k+1}^{l} \left(AS(I_{W_1}^{f_a}, I_{W_2}^{f_a})\right) + \sum_{r=l+1}^{n} \left(RS(I_{W_1}^{f_r}, I_{W_2}^{f_r})\right)}{n}$$

Where k is the number of features using *instances-based similarity* measure, (l-a) is the number of features applying *attributes-based similarity* measure and (n-r) is the number of features for which we apply *relations-based similarity* measure.

4.3   SOIM Algorithm

Steps followed during implementation of ontology-based hierarchical clustering algorithm are described by the following algorithm.

```
Input: O ← ontology, F ← a set of N features set
Output: C ← Generated clusters
Begin
    1. Features set F={f_i} upload from O
    2. Splitting F into two subsets, FN for numerical fea-
       tures and FC for categorical features.
    3. Identify ordinal categorical features OCF
    4. Convert OCF instances to numerical ones OCN
    5. FN<- FN U OCN
    6. Similarity matrix initialization with 0
    7. For each w_i ∈ O
        For each w_j ∈ O
            For each feature f_n in FN do:
                -Normalise I_{W_i}^{f_n} et I_{W_j}^{f_n}
                -Calculate sim(I_{W_i}^{f_n}, I_{W_j}^{f_n})
                -SimMatrix[i,j]= SimMatrix[i,j]+ sim(I_{W_i}^{f_n}, I_{W_j}^{f_n})
            End for each
            For each feature f_c in FC do:
                - Calculate sim(I_{W_i}^{f_c}, I_{W_j}^{f_c})
                - SimMatrix[i,j]= SimMatrix[i,j]+sim(I_{W_i}^{f_n}, I_{W_j}^{f_n})
            End for each
```

```
            End For each
        End For each
     8. SimMatrix[i,j] = SimMatrix [i,j]/n
     9. Cluster data according to SimMatrix
End
```

5   Experimental Results

To evaluate the effectiveness and efficiency of our SHICOW method, we carried out extensive experiments. For that, we will apply our method in our case study and then compare obtained results with those obtained by standard hierarchical clustering. In order to evaluate the performance of the proposed method, we calculated three measures of quality (Tabel 1): the precision (P), the recall (R) and the F-score (F).

Table 1. Effectiveness of the SOIM method

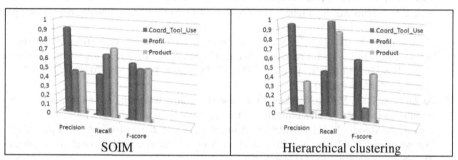

As shown in Tabel 1, the average of precision of SOIM method in our example is equals to 91%, 46% and 45% respectively for **Coord_Tool_Use**, **Profile** and **Age** features. Similarly, the values of recall metric is associated to the same criterion are equals to 44%, 66% and 73%. Thanks to the proposed similarity measures use, we have obtained these approved results (F-score = 56% while 42% for simple hierarchical clustering).

6   Conclusion and Future Works

In this paper, we proposed a new method called SOIM, for clustering knowledge contained in the ontology based on mixed features. The main contribution of our method is the proposition of three similarity measures: instances-based similarity, relations-based similarity and attributes-based similarity. The carried out experimental results showed that the method has the advantages of efficiency improvement of clustering quality. In terms of perspectives, we aim use the proposed similarity measures accompanied with weighting and ordering features based clustering in order to obtain a higher clustering quality. We also aim testing SOIM method on a large number real case of handicraft women.

Acknowledgements. We are very thankful to the Algerian Tunisian Project dealing with the improvement of handicraft women business in emerging countries through affordable technologies and social networks.

References

1. Gruber, T.: Ontology. In: Encyclopedia of Database, Berlin, Heidelberg, pp. 1963–1965 (2009),
   http://tomgruber.org/writing/ontology-definition-2007.htm
2. Maedche, A., Zacharias, V.: Clustering Ontology-based Metadata in the Semantic Web. In: Elomaa, T., Mannila, H., Toivonen, H. (eds.) PKDD 2002. LNCS (LNAI), vol. 2431, p. 348. Springer, Heidelberg (2002)
3. Kim, J.-M., Park, Y.-T.: Study of Ontology-based Incremental Clustering Technique in Semantic Web. Proceedings of the International Conference on Next Generation Web Services Practices (NWeSP 2005). IEEE (2005)
4. Esposito, F., Fanizzi, N., d'Amato, C.: Conceptual Clustering Applied to Ontologies. In: Raś, Z.W., Tsumoto, S., Zighed, D.A. (eds.) MCD 2007. LNCS (LNAI), vol. 4944, pp. 42–56. Springer, Heidelberg (2008)
5. Mikroyannidi, E., Iannone, L., Stevens, R., Rector, A.: Inspecting regularities in ontology design using clustering. In: Aroyo, L., Welty, C., Alani, H., Taylor, J., Bernstein, A., Kagal, L., Noy, N., Blomqvist, E. (eds.) ISWC 2011, Part I. LNCS, vol. 7031, pp. 438–453. Springer, Heidelberg (2011)
6. de Amorim, R.C., Mirkin: Minkowski, B.: metric, feature weighting and anomalous cluster initializing in K-Means clustering. Pattern Recognition 45(3), 1061–1075 (2012)
7. Jagannatha Reddy, M.V., Kavitha, B.: Clustering the Mixed Numerical and Categorical Dataset using Similarity Weight and Filter Method. International Journal of Database Theory and Application 5(1) (March 2012)
8. Shih, M.-Y., Jheng, J.-W., Lai, L.-F.: A Two-Step Method for Clustering Mixed Categorical and Numeric Data. Tamkang Journal of Science and Engineering 13(1), 11–19 (2010)
9. He, Z., Xu, X., Deng, S.: Scalable algorithms for clustering mixed type attributes in large datasets. International Journal of Intelligent Systems 20(10), 1077–1089 (2005)
10. Ralambondrainy, H.: A conceptual version of the k-means algorithm. Pattern Recognition Letters 16(11), 1147–1157 (1995)

Analysis of Trajectory Ontology Inference Complexity over Domain and Temporal Rules

Rouaa Wannous[1], Jamal Malki[1], Alain Bouju[1], and Cécile Vincent[2]

[1] University of La Rochelle, L3i laboratory, France
[2] University of La Rochelle, LIENSs/UMR 7372 laboratory, France
{rwannous,jmalki,abouju,cvincent}@univ-lr.fr

Abstract. Capture devices rise large scale trajectory data from moving objects. These devices use different technologies like global navigation satellite system (GNSS), wireless communication, radio-frequency identification (RFID), and other sensors. Huge trajectory data are available today. In this paper, we use an ontological data modeling approach to build a trajectory ontology from such large data. This ontology contains temporal concepts, so we map it to a temporal ontology. We present an implementation framework for declarative and imperative parts of ontology rules in a semantic data store. An inference mechanism is computed over these semantic data. The computational time and memory of the inference increases very rapidly as a function of the data size. For this reason, we propose a two-tier inference filters on data. The primary filter analyzes the trajectory data considering all the possible domain constraints. The analyzed data are considered as the first knowledge base. The secondary filter then computes the inference over the filtered trajectory data and yields to the final knowledge base, that the user can query.

Keywords: Trajectory ontology modeling, Ontology inference, Domain rules, Temporal rules, Data filter algorithm.

1 Introduction

Advances in information and communication technologies have encouraged collecting spatial, temporal and spatio-temporal data of moving objects [6]. The raw data captured, commonly called trajectories, traces moving objects from a departure point to a destination point as sequences of data (sample points captured, time of the capture). Raw trajectories do not contain goals of traveling nor activities accomplished by the moving object. Large datasets need to be analyzed and modeled to tackle user's requirements. To answer user's queries we also need to take into account the domain knowledge.

This paper deals with marine mammals tracking applications, namely seal trajectories. Trajectory data are captured by sensors included in a tag glued to the fur of the animal behind the head. The captured trajectories consist of spatial, temporal and spatio-temporal data. Trajectories data can also contain some meta-data. These datasets are organized into sequences. Every sequence, mapped to a temporal interval, characterizes a defined state of the animal. In our application, we consider three main states of a seal: *hauling out, diving* and *cruising*. Every state is related to a seal's activity. For example, a foraging activity occurs during the state diving.

Y. Ait Ameur et al. (Eds.): MEDI 2014, LNCS 8748, pp. 177–192, 2014.

Our goal is to enrich trajectory data with semantics to extract more knowledge. In our previous work [18], we tackled trajectory data connected to other temporal and spatial sources of information. We directly computed the inference over these data. The experimental results addressed the running time and memory problems over the ontology inference computation. Furthermore, we tried to solve these problems by defining some domain constraints, time restrictions in [12] and inference refinements in [17]. The proposed refinements enhanced the inference computation, however, they did not fully solve the problems.

In the present work, we introduce two-tier inference filters on trajectory data. In other words, two distinct operations are performed to enhance the inference: primary and secondary filter operations. The primary filter is applied to the captured data with the consideration of domain constraints. The primary filter allows fast selection of the analyzed data to pass along to the secondary filter. The latter computes the inference over the data output of the primary filter. The global view of this work is detailed as the following steps:

- Semantic trajectory data is an RDF dataset based on an ontology trajectory;
- For analyzing the data, filtering or indexing could be applied. In our case, we carry out a place-of-interest process to analyze data. The analyzed data are stored in a knowledge repository;
- The secondary filter computes inferences over the data with the consideration of domain knowledge;
- The semantic trajectory data and the new data inferred are stored in the knowledge repository.

This paper is organized as follows. Section 2 summarizes recent work related to trajectory data modeling using ontology approach and some introduced solutions to tackle the problem of the inference complexity using data filtering. Section 3 illustrates an overview of the domain data model used. Section 4 shows an overview of the semantic domain model used. This trajectory ontology contains temporal concepts mapped to W3C OWL-Time ontology [10] in Section 5. Section 6 details the implementation of the trajectory ontology, the domain ontology rules and the temporal rules. Section 7 addresses the complexity of the ontology inference over the domain and temporal rules. Section 8 introduces the primary filter over trajectory data based on a place-of-interest process. Section 9 evaluates the ontology inference over the filtered data. Finally, Section 10 concludes this paper and presents some prospects.

2   Related Work

Data management techniques including modeling, indexing, inferencing and querying large data have been actively investigated during the last decade [19,13,11]. Most of these techniques are only interested in representing and querying moving object trajectories [20,18,3]. A conceptual view on trajectories is proposed by Spaccapietra et al. [16] in which trajectories are a set of stops, moves. Each part contains a set of semantic data. Based on this conceptual model, several studies have been proposed such as [2,20]. Alvares et al. [2] proposed a trajectory data preprocessing method to integrate trajectories with the space. Their application concerned daily trips of employees from home to work and back. However, the scope of their paper is limited to the formal definition of semantic trajectories with the space and time without any implementation and evaluation. Yan et al. [20] proposed a trajectory computing platform which exploits a spatio-semantic trajectory model. One of the layers of this platform is a data preprocessing layer which cleanses the raw GPS feed, in terms of preliminary tasks such as outliers removal and regression-based smoothing.

Based on a space-time ontology and events approach, Boulmakoul et al. [4] proposed a generic meta-model for trajectories to allow independent applications. They processed trajectories data benefit from a high level of interoperability, information sharing. Their approach is inspired by ontologies, however the proposed resulting system is a pure database approach. Boulmakoul et al. have elaborated a meta-model to represent moving objects using a mapping ontology for locations. In extracting information from the instantiated model during the evaluation phase, they seem to rely on a pure SQL-based approach not on semantic queries. Taking these limitations into account, we defined and implemented two tier inference filters over trajectory data to clean and analyze the data and solve the inference computation problem.

3   Domain Data Model

3.1   Trajectory Data Model

This paper considers trajectories of seals. Trajectories of seals between their haulout sites along the coasts of the English Channel or in the Celtic and Irish seas are captured using GNSS systems provided by the Sea Mammal Research Unit (SMRU, University of St Andrews, UK). The captured spatio-temporal data, seal trajectories, can be classified into three main states: haulout, cruise and dive. Figure 1 shows the three states, the transitions and their guard conditions. From the analysis of the captured data, we define a seal's trajectory model that we connect to the trajectory domain package (Figure 2). The latter model is our trajectory pattern used in many moving object applications. In the seal trajectory package, the CTD (Conductivity-Temperature-Depth) and Summary classes are metadata about, respectively, marine environment and deployment's conditions of the sensor. Table 1 gives a dictionary of the trajectory pattern's classes.

Table 1. Dictionary classes of the trajectory domain

Classe	Description
Trajectory	logical form to represent sets of sequences
Sequence	spatio-temporal interval representing a capture
GeoSequence	spatial part of sequence
Specific Sequence	metadata associated of a capture

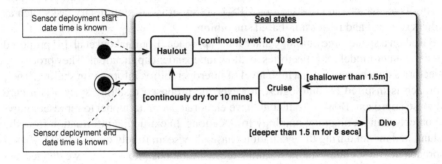

Fig. 1. The three states of seal trajectory

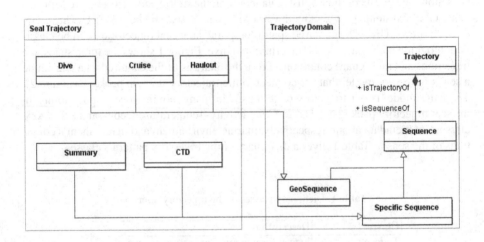

Fig. 2. Seal Trajectory connected to Trajectory Domain

3.2   Trajectory Ontology

In this work, we propose a modeling approach based on ontologies. To define the seal trajectory ontology, we use model transformation techniques introduced by the Model Driven Engineering (MDE) community. For this, we choose an automatic transformation from UML class diagram into a formal ontology in OWL. We use transformer tool called *uml2owl Eclipse* [8]. This transformer, based on the meta-model *eCore Eclipse*, takes as input a UML class diagram and turns it into OWL-DL ontology. So, we transform the UML class diagram of trajectory data model (Figure 2) to an OWL ontology called `owlSealTrajectory`, Figure 3 presents an extract of it. The concepts of this ontology keep the same definition as the domain's dictionary (Table 1). Besides these concepts, the ontology `owlSealTrajectory` defines trajectory domain relationships, such as:

1. `isSeqOf`: object property to say that a sequence is a kind of trajectory;

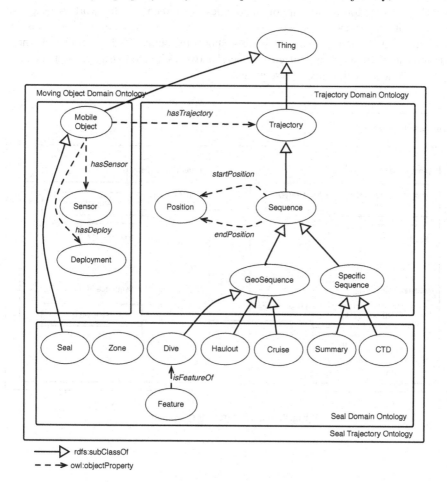

Fig. 3. Overview of the Seal trajectory ontology

2. `startPosition` and `endPosition`: object properties to represent the points captured which form the end and the beginning of a `GeoSequence`;
3. `long` and `lat`: data properties for longitude and latitude values of a point;
4. `dive_dur`, `sur_dur` and `max_depth`: data properties for dive duration, surface duration and maximum depth of a dive, respectively;
5. `TAD`: data properties for the "Time Allocation at Depth" index which defines the shape of a seal's dive [5].

4   Semantic Domain Model

4.1   Semantic Data Model

The semantic data model is the result of integrating semantic layers to data models. Several approaches are interested in semantic integration as statistical methods [7] or probabilistic [15] for the description of complex phenomena. In this work, we suppose that semantic layers can be defined using semantic annotations. Therefore, we consider annotations as domain activities. Figure 4 shows the semantic domain model where semantic annotations are organized as general activities linked to trajectory, and a hierarchy of basic activities linked to sequences.

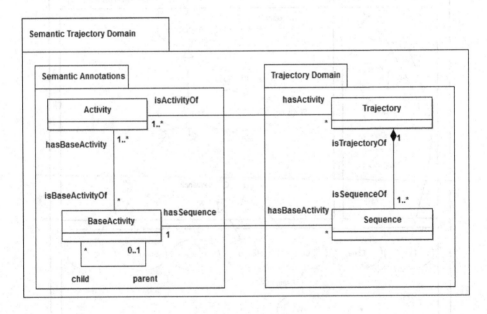

Fig. 4. Semantic trajectory domain

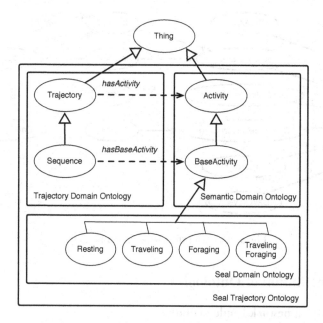

Fig. 5. Overview of the semantic Seal trajectory ontology

4.2 Semantic Trajectory Ontology

In this work, we consider the seal's activity performed during its dives. The instances of the classes `Haulout` and `Cruise` are related to the concept of travel and are actually not taken into account in this work. According to the domain expert, instances of the `Dive` class are associated with three main activities: resting, traveling, foraging and traveling-foraging. In view of the domain semantics and using the same models transformation technique cited above over the semantic trajectory domain (Figure 4), we define a new version of the seal trajectory (Figure 5)

5   Time Ontology

The seal trajectory ontology includes concepts that can be considered as temporal. For example, the concept `Sequence` is a temporal interval. To integrate temporal concepts and relationships in the seal trajectory ontology, we choose a mapping approach between our ontology and the `OWL-Time` [1] ontology [10] developed by the World Wide Web Consortium (W3C). This mapping is detailed in our previous work [18]. An extract of the declarative part of this ontology is shown in Figure 6 described in detail in [10]. We are mainly interested in the `ProperInterval` concept and its two properties `hasBeginning` and `hasEnd`.

---

[1] http://www.w3.org/2006/time

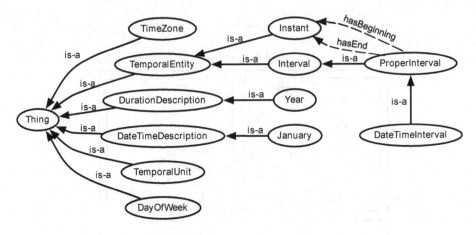

Fig. 6. A view of the OWL-Time ontology

6   Implementation of Ontologies

6.1   General Framework Implementation

For the implementation of the ontologies, we use Oracle Semantic Technologies. These technologies have evolved since Oracle DBMS version 10g, 11g and take the name of "Oracle Spatial and Graph - RDF Semantic Graph" in Oracle DBMS version 12c. This system provides support for persistence, inference and querying ontologies through implementation of RDF, RDFS and a large part of OWL standards. The DBMS defines a core in its metabase to support technologies related to ontological data. It stores the ontology declaration with data as RDF triples in the system under the scheme MDSYS. Each triple {subject, predicate, object} is handled as a basic data object. Detailed description of this technology can be found in Oracle Semantic Technologies Developer's Guide [14]. Our steps for creating declarative and imperative parts of the seal trajectory and time ontologies in Oracle Semantic Data Store are:

1. Create the declarative parts of the ontologies;
2. Create instances and population of the trajectory and time ontologies;
3. Consistency checking of the ontological instances;
4. Create the imperative parts of the ontology (seal trajectory ontology rules and temporal rules).

6.2   Seal Trajectory Ontology Rules

The seal trajectory ontology (Figure 5) is dealing with the seal's activities. Each seal activity has both a declarative part and an imperative corresponding part. The imperative parts of the activities are defined as rules in the ontology. A rule is an object that can be used by an inference process to query semantic data.

Oracle Semantic Technologies is a rule-based system where rules are based on IF-THEN patterns and new assertions are placed into working memory. Thus, the rule-based system is said to be a deduction system. In deduction systems, the convention is to refer to each IF pattern an antecedent and to each THEN pattern a consequent. User-defined rules are defined using the SEM_APIS.CREATE_RULEBASE procedure in a rulebase. Our rulebase is called sealActivities_rb. The system automatically associates a view called MDSYS.SEMR_rulebase-name to insert, delete or modify rules in a rulebase.

According to the domain expert, there is a correlation between the geometrical shape of dives and activities. To classify geometric shapes of dives, the TAD index is computed over a set of data. For this classification, we can distinguish three patterns:
- dive shaped V: if $0 <= TAD < 0.7$;
- dive shaped U+V: if $0.7 <= TAD < 0.9$;
- dive shaped U: if $0.9 <= TAD < 1$.

In addition to the geometric shape of dives, according to the domain expert, we take into account the maximum dive depth and surface ratio which is the ratio between surface duration and dive duration. The decision Table 2 summarizes conditions of the IF parts of rules associated with activities. Based on this table, Code 1.1 gives an example of rule definition, foraging_rule, in the system. From line 4 to 10 of Code 1.1, we construct a subgraph and necessary variables needed by the IF part of foraging_rule. Line 11 gives the THEN part of the rule. Line 12 defines the namespace of ontology.

Table 2. Decision table of IF parts of seal activities

Rules	Max dive depth (meter)	Dive shape or TAD	Surface ratio = surface dur/dive dur
Resting	< 10	>0.9	> 0.5
Travelling	> 3	< 0.7	$<$ all
Foraging	> 3	> 0.9	< 0.5

```
1  EXECUTE SEM_APIS.CREATE_RULEBASE('sealActivities_rb');
2  INSERT INTO mdsys.semr_sealActivities_rb
3  VALUES( 'foraging_rule',
4  '(?diveObject rdf:type   s:Dive        )
5   (?diveObject s:max_depth ?maxDepth  )
6   (?diveObject s:tad        ?diveTAD   )
7   (?diveObject s:dive_dur   ?diveDur   )
8   (?diveObject s:surf_dur   ?surfaceDur )
9   (?diveObject s:seqHasActivity ?activityProperty )',
10 '(maxDepth > 3) and (diveTAD > 0.9) and (surfaceDur/diveDur < 0.5)',
11 '(?activityProperty rdf:type s:Foraging )',
12 SEM_ALIASES(SEM_ALIAS('s','owlSealTrajectory#')));
```

Code 1.1. Implementation of the foraging rule

6.3 Time Ontology Rules

The OWL-Time ontology declares the 13 temporal interval relationships based on Allen algebra [1]. We implement the rule base owlTime_rb to hold the interval temporal relationships. For example, Code 1.2 presents the implementation of the imperative part of the `intervalAfter_rule` based on operations defined in the table `TM_RelativePosition` of the ISO/TC 211 specification about the temporal schema [9]. In Code 1.2, line 10 expresses the condition that the beginning of the reference interval is bigger than the end of the argument interval. Line 10 expresses the condition that the beginning of the reference interval is bigger than the end of the argument interval, as explained in the following condition. Line 11 is the consequent of the rule.

$$sself.begin.position > other.end.position$$

where

$$\begin{cases} self & = tObj2 \\ other & = tObj1 \\ self.begin.position = beginTime2 \\ other.end.position = endTime1 \end{cases}$$

```
1  EXECUTE SEM_APIS.CREATE_RULEBASE('owlTime_rb')
2  INSERT INTO mdsys.semr_owltime_rb
3  VALUES('intervalAfter_rule',
4  '(?tObj1 rdf:type  ot:ProperInterval  )
5  (?tObj2 rdf:type owltime:ProperInterval )
6  (?tObj1 ot:hasEnd ?end1         )
7  (?end1   :inXSDDateTime ?endTime1 )
8  (?tObj2 ot:hasBeginning ?begin2    )
9  (?begin2 ot:inXSDDateTime ?beginTime2 )',
10 '(beginTime2 > endTime1          )',
11 '(?tObj2 owltime:intervalAfter ?tObj1   )',
12 SEM_ALIASES(SEM_ALIAS('ot','http://www.w3.org/2006/time#')));
```

Code 1.2. Implementation of the `intervalAfter` rule

7   Trajectory Ontology Inference

Inferencing is the ability to make logical deductions based on rules defined in the ontology. Inferencing involves the use of rules, either supplied by the reasoner or defined by the user. At the data level, inference is a process of discovering new relationships, in our case, new triples. Inferencing, or computing entailment, is a major contribution of semantic technologies that differentiates them from other technologies.

In Oracle Semantic Technologies, an entailment contains precomputed data inferred from applying a specified set of rulebases to a specified set of semantic models. Code 1.3 creates an entailment over the seal trajectory and time models. This entailment uses a subset of OWL rules called `OWLPrime` [14], the seal trajectory and time ontologies rules. Other options are also required like the number of rounds that the inference engine should run. When applying user-defined rules `USER_RULES=T`, the number of rounds should be assigned as default to `REACH_CLOSURE`.

```
1 SEM_APIS.CREATE_ENTAILMENT('owlSealTrajectory_idx',
2 SEM_MODELS('owlSealTrajectory','owlTime'),
3 SEM_RULEBASES('OWLPrime','sealActivities_rb', 'owlTime_rb'),
4 SEM_APIS.REACH_CLOSURE, NULL, 'USER_RULES=T');
```

Code 1.3. Entailment over the `owlSealTrajectory` and `owlTime` ontologies

In our experiment, we measure the time needed to compute the entailment (Code 1.3) for different sets of real trajectory data for one seal. Its movements are captured from 16 June until 18 July 2011 and we have got 10 000 captured data. In this experiment, the seal activity rulebase contains only the foraging rule. The input data for this entailment are only dives. Figure 7 shows the experiment results for the computation time in seconds needed by the entailment. For example, for 450 dives, the inference takes around 60 000 seconds ($\simeq$ 16.6 hours).

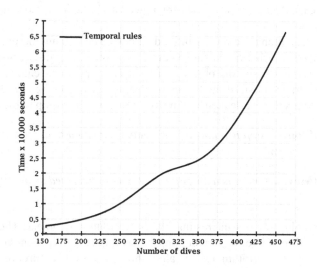

Fig. 7. Entailment computation time with all temporal rules and the foraging activity

8   Place of Interest over Trajectory Data

We introduce a two-tier inference refinement on trajectory data. In other words, two distinct operations are performed to enhance the inference: primary and secondary inference operations. Figure 8 shows the two-tier inference filter refinement. The primary filter is applied to the captured data to classify them into a set of interested places, called area-restricted search (ARSs). The primary filter allows fast selection of the classified data to pass along to the secondary inference. The latter computes the inference mechanism considering the ARS. Then, instead of annotating each sequence in the model, we annotate the ARSs with the expert knowledge activity model. The inference process is

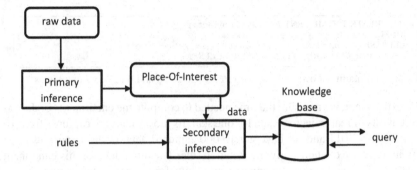

Fig. 8. Two-tier inference filter refinement

computed for each ARS. The secondary inference yields the final knowledge data that the user can query.

Our proposal is to analyze the captured data before computing the ontology inference. This analysis is achieved thanks to our primary filter. This filter considers trajectories that are segmented by the object positions. These positions change and remain fixed. Spaccapietra [16] named the former moves and the latter stops. For this reason, a trajectory is seen as a sequence of moves going from one stop to the next one.

Definition 1 (Stop). *A stop is a part of a trajectory having a time interval and represented as a single point.*

Definition 2 (Move). *A move is a part of a trajectory represented as a spatio-temporal line.*

The primary filter defines interesting places for a moving object. The interesting places are related to where the moving object stays more and visits more often. This filter is explained in Algorithm 1. This algorithm takes the two parts of a trajectory (move and stop) data as input and gives as output interesting places. The following definitions are used by this algorithm:

Definition 3 (Neighbors). *Neighbors for a point (p_i) are a list of points from the Move data where the distance between p_i and any neighbor point is smaller than a fixed radius. $Neighbor(p_i) = \{(p_j)_{j=1}^n : p_i, p_j \in Move, distance(p_i, p_j) < radius\}$.*

Definition 4 (Peak). *A $peak_i$ is a cardinality of the list $Neighbor(p_i)$. $(peaks_i)_{i=1}^n = \#(Neighbor(p_i))_{i=1}^n$.*

Definition 5 (Points_Neighbors). *Points_Neighbors are a list of points and their neighbors. $Points\_Neighbors = \{(p_i, Neighbors_i)_{i=1}^n : p_i, Neighbors_i \in Move\}$.*

Definition 6 (Places). *$Place_i$ is an interesting place which contains the $Neighbor(p_i)$ and number of its visits (nVisits) by the moving object. $Places = \{(Neighbors_i, nVisits_i)_{i=1}^n : Neighbors_i \in Move, nVisits_i \in number\}$.*

The first step of the primary filter, Algorithm 1 lines 5-9, gathers the move data into groups of neighbors. These groups are defined with respect to a *radius*. This radius is a fixed distance between two points to calculate the neighbors. The candidate of the radius is related to the application view of a trajectory, and is an input for this algorithm. The output of the first step is *Points_Neighbors*, from which the second step starts.

---

input : *Move*
input : *Stop*
input : *radius*
output: *Places*
1 initialization;
2 $Neighbor \leftarrow \phi$;
3 $Points\_Neighbors \leftarrow \phi$;
4 $Places \leftarrow \phi$;
5 **for** *each* $p_i \in Move$ **do**
6   calculate $Neighbor(p_i)$;
7      $Points\_Neighbors \leftarrow (p_i, Neighbors(p_i))$;
8      $Move \leftarrow Move - Neighbor(p_i)$;
9 **end**
10 **for** *each* $p_i \in Points\_Neighbors$ AND *condition*$(p_i, peaks_i)$ AND
    condition$(distance(p_i, Stop) > radius)$ **do**
11   **if** $distance(p_i, Places[j]) > radius$ **then**
12          $Places[k] \leftarrow (Neighbors_i, 1)$;
13   **else**
14          $Places(Neighbors_j, nVisits_j) = ([Neighbors_j, Neighbors_i], nVisits_j + 1)$;
15   **end**
16 **end**

Algorithm 1. The Place Of Interest algorithm

Lines 10-16, the second step, defines the interesting places. In general, we can consider all the members of *Points_Neighbors* or we can apply a condition over the *Peaks*. For example, the application view could be interesting in places that have 60 points and over, or could be interesting in any place having at least a point. For defining a place, the coordinates of the neighbors could be an interesting place after applying two conditions. Every point that belongs to a place should be far from the stop data more than the fixed radius. Any place should not have any neighbor within the radius distance, otherwise we merge the two coordinates and increase the visits number. The result of this step is the output *Places* of this algorithm.

To analyze our data, we consider the same datasets in Sect. 7. We pass these data to the Place Of Interest algorithm. This algorithm analyzes the data and gives as output the places and their visits, as shown in Fig 9 interesting places (1). Finally, the results of the primary filter are decreased the captured data from 10 000 into 6 170 interesting raw trajectories organized in places.

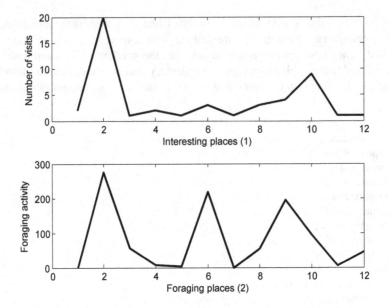

Fig. 9. Interesting and foraging places

9   Experimental Results

We analyze the trajectory data and define the interesting places. However, the main goal is to define foraging places among them. This is the objective of the secondary filter. The secondary filter computes the entailment over the interesting places. This filter specifies foraging places and determines the number of foraging activity for each place, as shown in Figure 9 foraging places (2). We can notice that the places 1, 4, 5, 7 and 11 are not considered as foraging places. Places 2, 6 , 9 and 10 are the significant foraging places.

By the normal inference ontology computation results, we could not be able to consider all the captured data. We computed the inference just for 500 raw data. However, using the primary filter and defining the interesting places helped us to define foraging places over all the captured data. These inferred data are considered as the final knowledge data that the user can query.

10   Conclusion and Future Work

In this work, we propose a modeling approach based on ontologies to build a trajectory ontology. Our approach considers three separated ontology models: a general trajectory domain model, a domain knowledge or semantic model and a temporal domain model. We map the spatial concepts in the trajectory ontology to the spatial ontology. To implement the declarative and imperative parts of the ontologies, we consider the framework of Oracle Semantic Data Store. To define the thematic and temporal reasoning, we implement rules related to the considered models. The thematic rules are based on the domain trajectory activities and the temporal rules are based on Allen relationships.

Then, we define and apply two-tier inference filters. In other words, two distinct operations are performed to enhance the inference: primary and secondary filter operations. The primary filter analyzes the trajectory data into places of interest. The secondary filter computes the ontology inference over the semantic trajectories using the ontology domain and temporal rules. The latter filters the interesting places into domain activity places.

The main contributions of this work are:

- How to use an ontological approach modelling for semantic trajectories;
- How to define inferences on semantic trajectories to answer user queries;
- What are the costs of these inferences;
- What can we do to face and reduce the inferences costs.

The experimental results show that we are able with the two-tier filters to consider all the captured data, whereas we could not even compute the ontology inference. For the evaluation, we use a PC with Linux system over a processor i5-250M, 2.5GHz and 8G memory. For the future work, we look for a server PowerVault NX400 with processor E5-2420 at 1.90GHz 6 cores and 16Gb ram with 4 drives TB.

References

1. Allen, J.F.: Maintaining knowledge about temporal intervals. Commun. ACM 26(11), 832–843 (1983)
2. Alvares, L.O., Bogorny, V., Kuijpers, B., Macedo, A.F., Moelans, B., Vaisman, A.: A model for enriching trajectories with semantic geographical information. In: Proceedings of the 15th Annual ACM International Symposium on Advances in Geographic Information Systems, pp. 22:1–22:8. ACM (2007)
3. Baglioni, M., Macedo, J., Renso, C., Wachowicz, M.: An ontology-based approach for the semantic modelling and reasoning on trajectories. In: Song, I.-Y., et al. (eds.) ER Workshops 2008. LNCS, vol. 5232, pp. 344–353. Springer, Heidelberg (2008)
4. Boulmakoul, A., Karim, L., Lbath, A.: Moving object trajectories meta-model and spatio-temporal queries. International Journal of Database Management Systems (IJDMS), 35–54 (2012)
5. Fedak, M.A., Lovell, P., Grant, S.M.: Two approaches to compressing and interpreting time-depth information as collected by time-depth recorders and satellite-linked data recorders. Mar. Mamm. Sci., 94–110 (2001)
6. Güting, R., Schneider, M.: Moving Objects Databases. Morgan Kaufmann (2005)
7. Halevy, A.Y.: Structures, semantics and statistics. In: Proceedings of the Thirtieth International Conference on Very Large Data Bases, VLDB 2004, vol. 30, pp. 4–6. VLDB Endowment (2004)
8. Hillairet, G., Bertrand, F., Lafaye, J.Y.: MDE for publishing data on the semantic web. In: International Workshop on Transformation and Weaving Ontologies and Model Driven Engineering (TWOMDE) at MODELS 2008 (2008)
9. ISO/TC_211. Geographic information – temporal schema, ISO 19108 (2002)
10. Jerry, R.H., Feng, P.: An ontology of time for the semantic web. ACM Transactions on Asian Language Information Processing, 66–85 (2004)
11. Malki, J., Bouju, A., Mefteh, W.: An ontological approach modeling and reasoning on trajectories. taking into account thematic, temporal and spatial rules. In: Technique et Science Informatiques, TSI, vol. 31, pp. 71–96 (2012)

12. Malki, J., Wannous, R., Bouju, A., Vincent, C.: Temporal reasoning in trajectories using an ontological modelling approach. Control and Cybernetics, 1–16 (2012)
13. Matthew, P.: A framework to support spatial, temporal and thematic analytics over semantic web data. PhD thesis, Wright State University (2008)
14. Oracle. Oracle Database Semantic Technologies Developer's guide 11g release 2 (2012)
15. Predoiu, L., Stuckenschmidt, H.: Probabilistic Extensions of Semantic Web Languages - A Survey
16. Spaccapietra, S., Parent, C., Damiani, M., Demacedo, J., Porto, F., Vangenot, C.: A conceptual view on trajectories. In: Data and Knowledge Engineering, pp. 126–146 (2008)
17. Wannous, R., Malki, J., Bouju, A., Vincent, C.: Modelling mobile object activities based on trajectory ontology rules considering spatial relationship rules. In: Amine, A., Mohamed, O.A., Bellatreche, L. (eds.) Modeling Approaches and Algorithms. SCI, vol. 488, pp. 249–258. Springer, Heidelberg (2013)
18. Wannous, R., Malki, J., Bouju, A., Vincent, C.: Time integration in semantic trajectories using an ontological modelling approach: A case study with experiments, optimization and evaluation of an integration approach. In: Pechenizkiy, M., Wojciechowski, M. (eds.) New Trends in Databases & Inform. AISC, vol. 185, pp. 187–198. Springer, Heidelberg (2012)
19. Yan, Z., Chakraborty, D., Parent, C., Spaccapietra, S., Aberer, K.: SeMiTri: A framework for semantic annotation of heterogeneous trajectories. In: Proceedings of the 14th International Conference on Extending Database Technology, pp. 259–270. ACM (2011)
20. Yan, Z., Parent, C., Spaccapietra, S., Chakraborty, D.: A hybrid model and computing platform for spatio-semantic trajectories. In: Aroyo, L., Antoniou, G., Hyvönen, E., ten Teije, A., Stuckenschmidt, H., Cabral, L., Tudorache, T. (eds.) ESWC 2010, Part I. LNCS, vol. 6088, pp. 60–75. Springer, Heidelberg (2010)

Ontology-Based Context-Aware SLA Management for Cloud Computing

Taher Labidi[1], Achraf Mtibaa[1], and Faiez Gargouri[2]

MIRACL Laboratory
[1] National School of Electronic and Telecommunications, University of Sfax, Tunisia
[2] Higher institute of computing and multimedia, University of Sfax, Tunisia
{taherlabidi,achrafmtibaa,faiez.gargouri}@gmail.com

Abstract. Cloud Computing represents a new on-demand computing approach that tries to provide resources responding to some pre-set non-functional proprieties specified and negotiated by means of Service Level Agreement (SLAs). In order to avoid costly SLA violations and to duly react to failures and environmental changes, it is necessary to implement some advanced SLA enactment strategies. However, contextual information of the cloud consumer, which has not been deeply elaborated yet, may change at any time, which would significantly affect the Quality of Service (QoS). Therefore, in this paper, our aim is to ameliorate SLA by considering the semantic meaning of SLA concepts and contextual information from cloud consumers. In this regard, we propose a new ontology-based context-aware SLA management for cloud computing. Our approach aims to dynamically adapt cloud services to different variations of consumer's context while meeting their needs using the benefits of inference in ontology. This maintains a reliable QoS and respects the SLA parameters. The efficiency and effectiveness of the proposed approach is demonstrated in this paper through a simulation.

Keywords: Cloud Computing, Service Level Agreement, Quality of service, Ontology, Context.

1 Introduction

Cloud computing has been recently a hot topic in the research community. It offers on demand computing elements in a pay-as-you-go manner. In cloud computing, everything is provided as a service. Consequently, the service provider answers the user's requests by providing him with all the resources in a way to meet his requirements.

The U.S. National Institute of Standards and Technology (NIST) proposes the following definition: "Cloud computing is a model for enabling convenient, on-demand network access to a shared pool of configurable computing resources (e.i., networks, servers, storage, applications, and services) that can be rapidly provisioned and released with minimal management effort or service provider interaction" [1]. This definition was adopted by most researchers and seems to be a common consent on cloud computing.

Y. Ait Ameur et al. (Eds.): MEDI 2014, LNCS 8748, pp. 193–208, 2014.

Nowadays, many enterprises rely more and more on cloud computing in shaping their portfolio. Therefore, fulfilling the promises that cloud services offer is becoming all the more elementary. Hence, one of the fundamental problems that remains unsolved is the assurance of Quality of Service (QoS). Service Level Agreements (SLA) is the principal means of control which includes QoS requirements and penalties in case there is a QoS violation and defines the terms of engagement for the participating entities.

However, NIST identified cloud SLAs as an important gap that needs further clarification [1]. Thus, although they are elementary, most cloud providers do not consider SLAs important. In fact, we can distinguish three types of cloud providers. Some providers do not raise the issue of SLAs during the phase of trade negotiations, unless the client does. Others limit discussion on the available time for SLAs ignoring other vital aspects, such as the performance of services, incident response, security, etc. However, others propose an SLA that can be unsuited to their clients' needs. In order to address these shortcomings; we decided to work on cloud computing SLAs.

In addition, some providers in cloud computing are compelled to reject consumers' requests of resources when the SLA is not respected [2]. This is due to the consumer's extensive demand which can negatively affect the QoS and cause inconsistencies with the agreements negotiated in the SLA. For this reason and in the context of SLA management, we will study the user's cloud needs that are causing changes in his demands. In fact, these needs emerge in a given context, which can significantly influence how a need can be met, and thus affect the actual performance of the service (e.i., choose an implementation that conforms to the current context of the user). We opt to improve the SLA by examining the cloud consumer context to proactive intervention in order to ensure a reliable QoS.

The remaining of this paper is organized as follows: In the next section, a brief introduction to the necessary concepts related to the paper will be given. In the third section, we will be describing the motivation scenario, where the importance of cloud consumer context information and ontology in SLA are shown. Next, we will present the related work. Then, in section 5, we intend to provide an architecture of our approach Ontology-Based Context-Aware SLA Management for Cloud Computing. After that, in section 6, we will present a part of our prototype Cloud SLA contextual Ontology (CSLAC'Onto) and some inference rules in order to validate our approach. In section 7, we will argue the effectiveness of our approach by feasibility and scalability tests. Finally, section 8 will be devoted to the conclusion.

2   Backgrounds

In this section, concepts related to our approach, that is, Service Level Agreement, Context-Awareness and Ontology, are described.

2.1   Service Level Agreement

There are many definitions for SLA, according to TM Forum [3]: "A Service Level Agreement (SLA) is a formal negotiated agreement between two parties. It is a contract that exists between the Service Provider (SP) and the Customer. It is designed to create a common understanding about Quality of Service (QoS), priorities, responsibilities, etc. SLAs can cover many aspects of the relationship between the Customer and the SP, such as performance of services, customer care, billing, service provisioning, etc. However, although a SLA can cover such aspects, agreement on the level of service is the primary purpose of a SLA".

SLA consists in governing the relationship between suppliers and customers by defining their terms of engagement and expectations. It is composed of a set of elements necessary for its definition. Among these elements we cited, for example, parties that describe the organizations or individuals involved in SLA and their roles (e.g., suppliers, and consumers). The Service Level Objectives (SLO) describe the level of services that both parties agree on. It usually includes a set of indicators such as the level of service availability, performance and reliability. The penalties include all penalties that occur when the service is not able to achieve the objectives of SLA, etc [4].

2.2   Context-Awareness

In the recent years, a growing body of research has been focusing on the use of context-awareness as a technique for developing computing applications that are flexible, adaptable, and capable of acting autonomously on behalf of the users without any explicit user interaction. According to [5], "A system is context-aware if it uses a context to provide relevant information and/or services to the user, where relevancy depends on the user's task". However, the context is considered as "any information that can be used to characterize the situation of an entity". One goal of context-aware systems is to use information on the context in order to provide services that are appropriate to the people. Thus, context awareness is the ability to sense and react to situation variations towards better operations.

2.3   Ontology

Several definitions of ontology are provided in the literature. The best known and the most appropriate is written by [6]: "An ontology is an explicit specification of a conceptualization." However, ontologies are used in many domains as web semantics, artificial intelligence, systems engineering, biomedical informatics, etc. They are also used for many purposes; such as enabling modeling, sharing concepts and reasoning to infer new knowledge. In this paper, we used ontology because it preserves the semantic relationships between SLA concepts and better knowledge representation. Indeed, the benefits of inference in ontology are very important. Thus, using inference rules and reasoning techniques, we can deduce new information that can help us in our work.

3   Motivation

In this section, we present our motivating scenario and our requirements for context awareness and ontology in cloud computing SLA.

3.1   Motivating Scenario

Due to the dynamic nature of the cloud, SLAs between consumers and providers appear as an essential aspect. Indeed, the use of resources in the cloud is affected by heavy load variations, which makes the monitoring of QoS attributes difficult [7]. In order to avoid costly SLA violations and react in time to environmental changes, causes and factors that provoke SLA violations must be investigated. To better specify these causes, we present an example of using cloud resources.

Example: Assume that the company x uses cloud resources according to the distribution shown in Table 1:

Table 1. Variation in use of cloud resources

Period (days) Resources	1-15	16-30
Use of Virtual Machines (VM)	50	500
Use of storage space	10	100

We observe that there is a sudden and significant increase in the use of cloud resources during the 16th day. However, this increase is due to a change in the work strategy of company x. Its needs have increased in a way that requires more resources to use. At this stage, we can distinguish two scenarios.

Scenario 1: the cloud provider has no information concerning company x.

Result1: At the 16th day, the resources used usually are not enough anymore. Then, a decrease in measurement of QoS is noted, which causes an SLA violation.

Scenario 2: the cloud provider has some information about company x which has increased its debit (10 times).

Result2: An increase in using resources is planned in advance and the cloud provider has arranged more resources for this company. So, the QoS measurement remains stable and SLA parameters are respected.

With this example, we note that using cloud consumer's information can help us manage sudden changes and intervene in time to maintain a reliable QoS and respect SLAs parameters. In the next section, we will explain in detail our different requirements in order to identify the methods used to adapt cloud services according to the consumers' context in SLA.

3.2 Requirements for Context-Awareness in Cloud Computing SLA

As shown in the previous example, the dynamic nature of the cloud is due, in part, to the complexity of the consumer's demands that vary according to his needs. These needs must be studied in detail. However, SLAs are actually written taking into account the interests of the providers and not according to the consumers needs. Indeed, some providers offer an SLA which can be unsuited to their clients. These SLAs do not take into account the users' needs and do not specify their requirements. We can deduce that there is an imperative need to take into account the users' requirements in SLA to suit the dynamic nature of cloud computing.

However, the user's needs emerge in a given context that can greatly influence how a need can be met, and thus influence the service execution. In order to dynamically adapt to the changes of needs and contexts of the consumer, it is necessary to study the context-awareness. Thus, context critically matters in the completion of several tasks namely reasoning and interpretation. It can be seen as the set of parameters that can influence the services behavior. As shown in the preceding example, the contextual parameter 'debit' can change the use of cloud resources by a consumer. The consideration of this parameter, and other contextual parameters considered useful, allows us to adapt cloud services depending on the context of the consumer and subsequently avoid costly SLA violations. In the next section, we will present the requirements for using an ontology in the SLAs of cloud computing.

3.3 Requirements for an Ontology in Cloud Computing SLA

Many available investigations of SLAs publicly showed that, despite their large number, there are few harmonizations between their various parameters and vocabulary. The lack of coordination between these elements is due to the inexistence of a universally accepted SLA cloud format. There is neither a clear guidance on how the different terminologies will be organized nor the necessary policies that can be assigned to an SLA [1]. In addition, several studies have shown conflicts and ambiguities in the SLAs. Like any legal document, the SLA can be complex. This complexity is increased in the cloud due to the fact that the SLA is conceived for the best interests of the provider and not for the customer's requirements [4]. Indeed, in cloud computing, the detection of service violation is done by consumers. For example, the most prominent cloud provider, Amazon EC2, puts the burden of proving SLA violations on the consumer [7], which is a major problem.

In this regard, consumers need practical techniques to develop and evaluate SLAs. Obtaining a formalized SLA helps set up an enforcement process to be automated and hence relieves consumers from that burden. Thus, the common point observed in the latest offers of SLA suggests the existence of a basis for the standardization of SLA terminology. A primary question is how to design a model that incorporates the common terms of the SLA. The specification of this model could allow SLA to be partially evaluated, thus reducing costs for cloud consumers and increasing understanding in offers of cloud services. Expressing an SLA in a machine-readable format using ontologies could be a production step to construct the SLA document and to support automated assessment of these terms and conditions.

Moreover, having spoken of context awareness in the previous section, several authors mention that data and context parameters must be formally represented in a model to allow verification of their consistency. A good context information modeling formalism reduces the complexity of context-aware applications and improves their maintainability and innovativeness. In this regard, several Context-aware information modeling techniques, such as Key-value model, Markup scheme model, Graphical model, Object oriented model, and ontology based model, were presented [8]. Ontology based model is considered the most promising approach to provide a rich formalism for structuring contextual information [9]. The validity of the coded information is ensured by the reasoning techniques which avoid the contradictory information modeling. In addition, ontologies allow deducing new information through inference. Inference rules are rules set by the developer who assist in deducing or inferring new knowledge from a set of captured raw data. They provide a formal support to express beliefs and knowledge in a domain.

With these clearly identified needs, we proceed to improve SLAs in the cloud. To do this, we prefer to use context-awareness to adapt cloud services depending on the context of the consumer in order to avoid costly SLA violations. However, the use of the ontology is essential for two reasons. On the one hand, it allows the modeling of SLA to be readable and automatically evaluated, thus reducing costs for cloud consumers and improving understanding in offers of cloud services. On the other hand, it allows the modeling of contextual information which reduces the complexity of context-aware applications and improves their feasibility and scalability. Indeed, using the benefits of inference in ontology, we can deduce, from contextual parameters, new knowledge about cloud consumers.

4   Related Works

The research on SLA and QoS metrics has been considered by many researchers in many domains, such as E-commerce and web services. In these domains, many efforts have been undertaken concerning the representation of quality of service concepts. Some of them are oriented to define specific languages (such as WSLA or WS-Agreement) to present all concepts considered useful in SLA. Other works use ontology to provide a machine understandable semantic representation of QoS information and SLA parameters.

Before the appearance of Cloud Computing, Dobson et al. [10] present an initiative to create a unified QoS/SLA ontology applicable to the main scenarios, such as Web services selection based on QoS, monitoring QoS and adaptation QoS. Fakhfakh [11] proposes an intention-based semantic approach for service level agreement modeling, negotiation and monitoring for service-oriented architectures. She processed all stages of the SLA life-cycle and defines the model 'SLAOnt' to specify the required levels of quality.

In cloud computing, Patel et al. [7] propose a mechanism for SLA management using WSLA framework. Thus, they use a third party that supports the functionality of WSLA to delegate control tasks and application to other entities in order to solve the problems of trust. However, [7], [12], [13] mention that WSLA and WS-Agreement specifications are not suitable for cloud computing as the nature and type of resources provided and delivered are different from those in service oriented architecture (SOA). For this reason, Alhamad et al. [12] present the main criteria that must be considered when designing a cloud computing SLA. Then, using these criteria, a study of negotiation strategies between the provider and the consumer cloud is proposed to maintain trust and reliability between all parties involved in the negotiation process. In addition, García García et al. [13] propose the "Cloudcompaas" platform to dynamically and completely manage the life-cycle of resources cloud PaaS satisfying the multiple requirements of the users. To do this, a new architecture headed by SLA for automatic provision, planning, allocation and dynamic resource management for Cloud is presented. This architecture is based on an extension of the specification WS-agreement. It is adapted to the specific needs of Cloud Computing and allows the definition of QoS rules and automatic actions for arbitrary and corrective preventions. Thus, in order to automate the process of managing SLAs in the cloud, Dastjerdi et al. [14] present architecture for the deployment of cloud services. This architecture is able to describe, deploy (discover, organize and coordinate) and execute monitoring services in an automatic way. For this reason, the WSMO ontology was used for the modeling and description of SLAs monitoring capabilities. This ontology built an inter-Cloud language that allows the semantic correspondence between the SLAs of different cloud layers. In addition, the effects of QoS dependencies between services that generate SLA violations were treated. To overcome these violations, the deployment of appropriate service monitoring and filtering report violation is performed using dependency knowledge. Emeakaroha et al. [15] also present a new framework (LoM2HiS) to manage correspondence between low level metric resources and high level SLAs parameters. The LoM2HiS framework facilitates the management and implementation of autonomous SLAs. Thus, it is able to detect violations and future threats in SLA and can operate to prevent these threats by exploiting and managing cloud resources. Kouki [16] proposes an SLA-driven cloud elasticity management approach. He address the trade-offs between the benefit of SaaS vendor and customer's satisfaction. Thereby, his work aims to provide a solution to implement the elasticity of cloud computing to meet this compromise. The main occupations of his work are the definition of SLA, the SLA dependencies between XaaS layers and the management of resource capacity.

However, we noted that there is a lack of representation for the SLA parameters and QoS measurements using ontologies in cloud computing. Most studies use a representation by defining specific languages while ignoring semantic aspects. In addition, because of the new features of the cloud, we need new models of SLA. These models are required to provide a flexible, scalable and dynamic approach to manage the entire life-cycle of SLAs between consumers and providers taking into account the consumers' requirements. Furthermore, we note that some of these works have focussed on changes that occur in the cloud to avoid costly SLA violations. There is no one address changes of consumers' requirements or their contextual information. Therefore taking into account the cloud consumers' context is necessary regarding its influence on the variation of using cloud services and resources, and thereafter on the QoS specified in the SLA.

5   Ontology-Based Context-Aware SLA Management for Cloud Computing

In the section below, we will present our approach for SLA management based on context-Awareness in Cloud Computing to guarantee a reliable quality of service for cloud computing consumers and providers. This approach supports the whole SLA life cycle which is based, in its turn, on the main three phases [16]. First of all, the SLA establishment phase is accomplished and it consists of the definition and followed by the negotiation steps. These steps allow the specification of an SLA. Then, the SLA validation step where the prediction of changes and the interventions due to these changes are made sequentially in order to adapt the cloud service to the consumers' needs. Finally, SLA monitoring phase is achieved by detecting violations and verifying the reliability of the QoS. This phase must be performed throughout the service execution and in an automatic way to ensure that the QoS is always reliable. However, these phases are improved and enhanced with semantic and contextual aspects, which is the originality of our work. These improvements allow getting an autonomic SLA management where appropriate actions are taken to predict and avoid future SLA violations in cloud computing.

Modeling all information contained in cloud computing SLA is performed by an ontology which considered the core of our approach. As a consequence, we take advantage of benefits in sharing knowledge and maintaining semantic information. Ontologies contain the main concepts of the SLA document, their properties, their relationships and axioms to predict changes depending on the condition and situation of concepts. Contextual information related to the consumers is also presented in this ontology. This type of information is represented as a contextual dimension containing the necessary parameters to maintain a reliable QoS in cloud SLA. Hence, we take another advantage of ontology which is the inference. Inference is considered as one of the most powerful features of the semantic web. It makes each data item more valuable, because it can have an effect on the creation of new information. Each new piece of information has the capacity to add a great deal of new information via inference [17]. Hence, semantic inferences allow us to detect indirect correspondences that are not detectable by the different SLA languages.

In addition, our approach provides both consumers and providers needs. Firstly, it helps consumers to understand the SLA and adapt dynamically cloud services to different variations of consumer's context in order to offer software, hardware and QoS requirement to the consumers in times. This avoids costly SLA violations. In addition, it facilitates the detection of service violation which is a major problem for cloud consumers. Secondly, it allows providers to finely express contracts so that services self-adaptation capabilities are improved. This minimizes service costs and penalties to the cloud provider which maximizes its revenue. Figure 1 presents our approach which will be explained in the rest of this section.

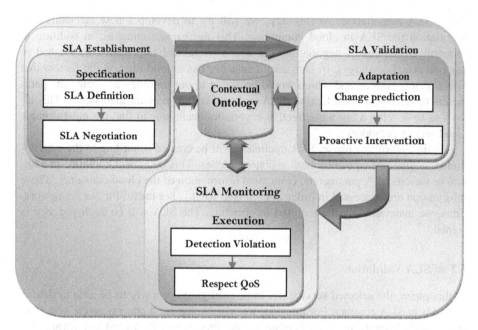

Fig. 1. Ontology-Based Context-Aware SLA Management for Cloud Computing

5.1   SLA Establishment

This phase allows the construction of SLA document for cloud computing. It is composed of two main parts: SLA definition and SLA negotiation.

(i)   SLA Definition: in order to minimize the complexity of SLA document, we opt for its modeling using ontology. This helps consumers understand the SLA and provides a semantic appearance for its different terms. Among the terms which are going to be agreed: pricing model, SLA parameters and penalties will be specified. Pricing model defines the manner of service payment used by the service provider. Pay as you go manner is considered the most used by cloud providers such as Amazon, Google App Engine and Windows Azure. More details about cloud computing pricing model are presented in [18]. However, depending in service models, SLA parameters are specified and measured. Alhamad et al. [12] present the most important parameters for consumers who are interested in using cloud as IAAS, PAAS or SAAS. In addition, penalties are calculated and performed by a party that is in charge of ensuring what is promised in this warranty. All these information are presented in our SLA with semantic meaning throughout ontology. Moreover, our SLA must take into account the different characteristics of cloud computing as self-elasticity, multi-tenancy, etc. Increasingly, it is necessary to take into account different service models (IAAS, PAAS, SAAS) and to represent both functional and non functional requirements in SLA. Despite the importance of this work, we note that there is very little research on this field. Due to the limited space, it is not possible to describe in details this step which is our ongoing work.

(ii)   SLA Negotiation: At this step, we will try to develop a new mechanism of negotiation for SLA in cloud computing. This mechanism contains, in addition to different algorithms of negotiation, the user's contextual information (contained in our contextual ontology). In fact, each consumer has a good idea on the factors that affect their workload and which would be added to our ontology as contextual parameters to achieve a more flexible SLA and to take into account their needs. This allows us to develop a fast and effective negotiation technique to find the most suitable cloud service providers.

By the end of this phase, SLA document will be created according to the negotiation strategies and signed by both signatory parties. This document contains, in addition to various SLA parameters, contextual information of the cloud consumer. These information are processed in order to eliminate what is not useful for our framework. Thus, we maintain only the required information. The SLA will be deployed as it is signed.

5.2   SLA Validation

In this phase, the selected service has to be configured properly to be able to deliver its SLOs in SLA contract. For this end, we will implement a context aware system to enable self-elasticity in cloud computing. According to NIST, elasticity means that capabilities can be rapidly and elastically provisioned, in some cases automatically, to quickly scale out and rapidly released to quickly scale in [1]. To do so, cloud service adaptation depending on the consumer's context is a very important step that must be studied. We propose two main parts:

(i)   Change prediction: The dynamic nature of cloud computing and the difficulty of predicting changes are the cause of the decreased level of QoS. Following reasoning techniques and inference rules made in our contextual ontology, change prediction in using cloud services can be deduced. The contribution of contextual information is provided in the ontology through inference of explicit and implicit consumer's information. The reaction to these changes is performed in the next step.
(ii)   Proactive intervention: To maintain QoS stable, immediate adaptation following the changes in the consumption of cloud services is required. This adaptation is dynamically performed following the study of cloud consumer context-awareness performed in our contextual ontology. The manner, the type, and the consequences of this dynamic adaptation are identified by the prototype that will be developed.

The goal of the context aware system implemented in this phase is to avoid costly SLA violations. These systems are capable of acting autonomously on behalf of the users without any explicit user interaction. In addition, these systems adapt to changing context information. Context-aware systems have to perceive the situation of the cloud consumer and his environment and consequently adapt all their behavior to that situation without an explicit demand from the consumer. This is benefic for both cloud consumer and provider. It maintains a reliable QoS which is the purpose of the consumer and respects the SLA parameters which avoid expensive penalties and therefore maximize providers' revenue. Modeling and reasoning on contextual information contained in our context-aware system are performed using ontologies. They allow deducing new knowledge from contextual parameters using the benefits of inference [19].

5.3   SLA Monitoring

Deployment of services which are capable of monitoring SLA contracts has to be completed in this phase. Then, monitoring services have to be executed to evaluate cloud services based on SLO [14]. Thereby, the measurement of QoS is calculated using an algorithm to ensure that it is maintained equivalent to what has been negotiated and deduced in the SLA. Hence,

(i)   The SLA violation has to be reported when a monitoring service detects that a service is not performing according to its SLA contract. Thus, the guarantees actions such as elasticity policies, penalties and notification of violation must be automatically and instantly triggered. For this end, in SAL document, the guarantees actions must define explicitly what should be done when a parameter value violates the agreed value. The service provider must be treated as the SLA document says.

(ii)   Reliable QoS guarantees that the SLA is respected. Therefore, cloud consumers needs and providers purposes are met.

In this phase, SLA monitoring services based on inferential reasoning allow us to detect violations and even undetectable degradations without using semantics. These SLA violations are detected and managed automatically and periodically as negotiated in SLA document. Checking type of violation differs from one SLA parameter to another depending on his influenced factors (e.i., time for availability parameter). To enable mechanisms capable of reasoning and inferring on each type of violation, semantic inferences are used in our ontology.

6   Cloud SLA Contextual Ontology (CSLAC'Onto): Parties Concepts

In order to evaluate our approach, we present, in this section, a part of CSLAC'Onto. This ontology is our ongoing work, therefore, we will limit ourselves in this paper to describe the parties which are considered by the SLA. Our aim is to guarantee the quality of service by predicting changes and quickly allocating cloud resources to cloud consumers dynamically depending on agreed SLAs. When a cloud consumer suddenly requires processing more jobs, a cloud provider has to quickly allocate more resources to cloud consumer. However, each resource has its characteristic related to QoS and executes the service taking into account the SLO to meet the agreed SLA. We use the Ontology Web Language (OWL) [20] to describe classes, constraints, and properties of the CSLAC'Onto in this paper. The OWL allows us to give semantic meaning to SLA concepts as well as combine and connect them in a manner understandable by machines.

Figure 2 presents the generic structure of the parties' concept in CSLAC'Onto. The root of this model is the SLA concept. It represents the contract class that we can instantiate from CSLAC'Onto. This class has its implicated parts in the contract which are the supporting and the signatory parties. The supporting parties provide the necessary entities for the quality of service measurement defined in the contract. The signatory parties are generally the service providers and their customers. We have introduced, for the customer, some contextual information as date and debit. These parameters are necessary to predict changes in our approach. Furthermore, the cloud consumer uses some resources to execute his applications. As the use of resources in the cloud is affected by heavy load variations, the cloud consumer can be classified into three types: Cloud consumer peak consumption, Cloud consumer drop consumption and Cloud consumer normal consumption. These variations also affect the quality of resources (VM in our example) which can be classified into three categories: sufficient-VM, insufficient-VM and very-sufficient-VM.

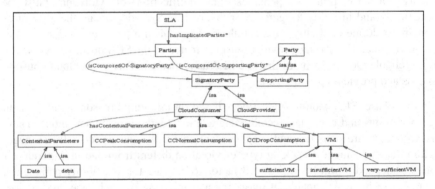

Fig. 2. Parties concepts in CSLAC'Onto

To ensure a good exploitation of this ontology, a reasoning step is essential. We have defined some inference rules using the Semantic Web Rule Language (SWRL) [21]. A rule of the SWRL has a semantic meaning by expressing the relation between an antecedent and a consequent in order to infer or deduce new knowledge from a set of implicit data. We have made some simulations in "Protégé" [22] to ensure the proper functioning of inference rules. Thus, we have populated our ontology with individuals, defined object properties and datatype properties related to those individuals and launched the inference engine.

Table 2 shows some inference rules in SWRL that are defined to predict changes which influence the QoS. Using cloud consumers' contextual information, we can deduce that there will be an increase or a decrease in cloud resource utilization. For example, we can deduce, for a company x which makes its inventory at the end of each year, there will be a peak resource consumption when the date is december 25. The second rule also deduces that there will be a peak resource consumption when the debit value suddenly increases because the higher the connection speed is, the more cloud consumer use cloud services. The opposite case can also be deduced, when the debit value decreases, we can predict a drop of consumption in cloud resource as

shown in rule 3. Rules 4 and 5 are related to VM capacity in executing the job requested from cloud consumer. If we deduce that there will be a peak consumption
from cloud consumer and the MIPS (Million of Instruction Per Second) value of the
VM is as defined when creating the VM, so we can say that this VM will not be sufficient. The opposite case can also be deduced in rule 5. In our case, we can also combine a rule with other rules to identify more information. For example, the combination of rule 1 and rule 4 allows the inference engine to be more flexible. In addition,
we can ameliorate our ontology and our inference rules in consequence by introducing other contextual parameters. Similarly, the accuracy of our contextual parameters
has a great importance. With an autonomic aspect, these parameters can even determine the number and the nature of resources to make available. This guarantee the
dynamic aspect of cloud computing. These ameliorations will be taken into account in
our future work.

Table 2. Inference rules of the CSLAC'Onto

NO	Domain rules
1	CloudConsumer(?x) ∧ Date(?y) ∧ hasContextualParameters(?x, ?y) ∧ date(?y, ?z) ∧ swrlb:equal(?z, "2014-12-25") → CCPeakConsumption(?x)
2	CloudConsumer(?x) ∧ debit(?y) ∧ hasContextualParameters(?x, ?y) ∧ Deb(?y, ?z) ∧ swrlb:greaterThanOrEqual(?z, 10) → CCPeakConsumption(?x)
3	CloudConsumer(?x) ∧ debit(?y) ∧ hasContextualParameters(?x, ?y) ∧ Deb(?y, ?z) ∧ swrlb:lessThan(?z, 10) → CCDropConsumption(?x)
4	CCPeakConsumption(?x) ∧ VM(?y) ∧ use(?x, ?y) ∧ MIPS(?y, 1000) → insufficientVM(?y)
5	CCDropConsumption(?x) ∧ VM(?y) ∧ use(?x, ?y) ∧ MIPS(?y, 10000) → very-sufficientVM(?y)

7   Evaluation

Our approach was evaluated using the simulation. The CloudSim 3.0.3 [23]
simulation framework is employed in the tests. Based on an example explained in
section 3, we present the contribution of our approach shown in the previous sections.

For our simulation, the size of virtual machines used to host applications in the experiment is 1000MB. Virtual machines have 512MB of RAM memory and 10MB of
available bandwidth. Simulated hosts have x86 architecture, virtual machine monitor
Xen and Linux operating system. Machines have 2 GB of RAM and 100GB of storage. Each machine has 4 CPUs, and each CPU has a capacity power of 1000 MIPS.
A time-shared policy is used to schedule resources to VMs.

As shown in table 1, our example is consists of two periods. In the first 15 days,
company x executes for example, 10 cloudlets (tasks) and uses only one data center
which hosts 5 virtual machines. At the 16th day, company x executes 40 cloudlets
instead of 10. As a consequence, we can distinguish two scenarios in this example.

The first one consists of modeling the case where the cloud provider has no information concerning the consumers. In this model, even on the 16th day, all requests

from the consumers are processed by a single data center which has only 5 virtual machines allocated to the application. However, this data center is insufficient because a peak traffic happens at unexpected times (the 16th day in our example). This causes an increase of execution times (from 21 to 324 seconds) as shown in figure 3 (Scenario 1). As most providers of cloud use a threshold to determine if there is a violation, we suppose that, in our SLO, the execution times does not exceeds 10 seconds per VM. Therefore, we can deduce in this scenario that the increase of execution times causes a QoS violation (execution times more than 10 seconds per VM).

In the second scenario, in which the cloud provider has some information concerning the consumers, we can predict an increase in using resources caused by an augmentation in cloudlet number. This prediction is deduced by our ontology as presented in the previous section. Hence, we can quickly react and arrange more resources for this company. As shown in figure 3 (Scenario 2), the variation of execution times is not huge (from 21 to 144 seconds). Thus, the QoS is maintained stable (execution times less than 10 seconds per VM) and there is no violation.

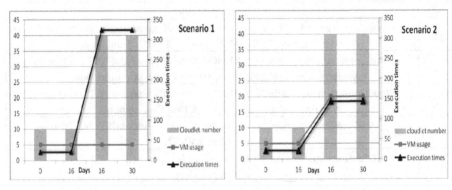

Fig. 3. Performance measures compared with existing execution scenario

For each one of these scenarios, performance is measured for the same number of cloudlets. Hence, using our contextual ontology (scenario 2), we can predict changes before the 16th day and allocate consequently more resources. The most notable comparison is that the execution times are very different in both scenarios. This fact is due to the ability of our ontology to predict an increase in the load and react quickly deploying new VMs. The first scenario was performed with the existing execution manner in CloudSim. The execution times attain 324 seconds and we can detect a QoS violation. However, in the second scenario, using the information that was inferred in our contextual ontology, execution time decreased to 144 seconds. This maintains a reliable QoS.

8   Conclusion

An effective SLA management in Cloud is the key to improve service reliability and confidence level between the provider and the consumer cloud. Due to the dynamic nature of cloud computing, the use of resources is affected by heavy variations that greatly influence the QoS. In this paper, we present an Ontology-Based Context-Aware SLA Management for Cloud Computing. Using the benefits of representation and inference of ontology, we can adapt cloud services and resources depending on the consumers' context in order to ensure reliable QoS and ameliorate SLA document. We tested our approach with an example using inference rules in ontology. In addition, the CloudSim simulation framework is employed to show the efficiency and effectiveness of the proposed work in cloud computing. The result of this work is the basic tool for reliable QoS and ameliorated SLA while satisfying cloud consumers' needs. In the ongoing work, we are modeling our Cloud SLA Contextual Ontology while taking into account the different characteristics of cloud computing. For future work, we can ameliorate our ontology and our inference rules in consequence by introducing other contextual parameters. Similarly, with an autonomic aspect, these parameters can even determine the number and the nature of resources to make available. Furthermore, we will detail each phase of our approach and propose efficient techniques to be implemented and tested on cloud management platform as OpenStack.

References

1. Badger, M.L., Grance, T., Patt-Corner, R., Voas, J.M.: Cloud Computing Synopsis and Recommendations. National Institute of Standards and Technology (NIST) (May 2012)
2. Hussain, O., Dong, H., Singh, J.: Semantic Similarity Model for Risk Assessment in Forming Cloud Computing SLAs. In: Meersman, R., Dillon, T., Herrero, P. (eds.) OTM 2010, Part II. LNCS, vol. 6427, pp. 843–860. Springer, Heidelberg (2010)
3. TM Forum, SLA Management Handbook: Volume 2 Concepts and Principles, Release 2.5, TeleManagement Forum, GB 917-2 (2005)
4. Wieder, P., Butler, J.M., Theilmann, W., Yahyapour, R.: Service Level Agreements for Cloud Computing. Springer, Heidelberg (2011), Library of Congress Control Number: 2011939783, ISBN 978-1-4614-1613-5, e-ISBN 978-1-4614-1614-2, doi:10.1007/978-1-4614-1614 -2
5. Dey, A.K., Abowd, G.D.: Towards a Better Understanding of Context and Context Awareness. In: Proceedings of the Workshop on the What, Who, Where, When and How of Context-Awareness, affiliated with the CHI 2000 Conference on Human Factors in Computer Systems, The Hague, Netherlands. ACM Press, New York (2000)
6. Gruber, T.: A Translation Approach to Portable Ontology Specifications. Knowledge Acquisition 5(2), 199–220 (1993)
7. Patel, P., Ranabahu, A., Sheth, A.: Service Level Agreement in Cloud Computing, The Ohio Center of Excellence in Knowledge-Enabled Computing (Kno.e.sis), Dayton, Ohio U.S. state (2009)
8. Changboka., Chang, H., Ahn, H., Choi, E.: Efficient context modeling using OWL in mobile cloud computing. In: International Conference on Future Energy, Environment, and Materials. Energy Procedia, vol. 16, pp. 1312–1317. Elsevier Science Publishers (2012)
9. Bettini, C., Brdiczka, O., Henricksen, K., Indulska, J., Nicklas, D., Ranganathan, A., Riboni, D.: A survey of context modelling and reasonning techniques. In: Pervasive and Mobile Computing. Elsevier Science Publishers (2010)

10. Dobson, G., Sánchez-Macián, A.: Towards unified QoS/SLA ontologies. In: Proceedings of the IEEE Services Computing Workshops, SCW 2006 (2006)
11. Fakhfakh, K.: Approche sémantique basée sur les intentions pour la modélisation, la négociation et la surveillance des contrats de qualité de service. Ph.D. thesis, research units: LAAS-CNRS and ReDCAD (2011)
12. Alhamad, M., Dillon, T., Chang, E.: Conceptual SLA Framework for Cloud Computing. In: 4th IEEE International Conference on Digital Ecosystems and Technologies, DEST (2010)
13. García García, A., Blanquer Espert, I., Hernández García, V.: SLA-driven dynamic cloud resource management. The International Journal of Grid Computing and eScience Future Generation Computer Systems (October 2013) ISSN: 0167-739X
14. Dastjerdi, A., Tabatabaei, S., Buyya, R.: A dependency-aware ontology-based approach for deploying service level agreement monitoring services in Cloud. Software: Practice and Experience (2011)
15. Emeakaroha, V.C., Brandic, I., Maurer, M., Dustdar, S.: Low Level Metrics to High Level SLAs - LoM2HiS Framework: Bridging the Gap Between Monitored Metrics and SLA Parameters in Cloud Environments. In: International Conference on High Performance Computing and Simulation (HPCS), pp. 48–54. IEEE (2010)
16. Kouki, Y.: Approche dirigée par les contrats de niveaux de service pour la gestion de l'élasticité du "nuage". Ph.D. thesis, research unit: Computer Laboratory of Nantes-Atlantique, LINA (2013)
17. Hebeler, J., Fisher, M., Blace, R., Perez-Lopez, A., Dean, M.: Semantic Web Programming. Published by Wiley Publishing, Inc. (2009) ISBN: 978-0-470-41801-7
18. Al-Roomi, M., Al-Ebrahim, S., Buqrais, S., Ahmad, I.: Cloud Computing Pricing Models: A Survey. International Journal of Grid and Distributed Computing (2013)
19. Mtibaa, A.: Ontologie de multi-représentation pour la spécification des besoins. Presses Academiques Francophones (2013) ISBN-13: 978-3841620804
20. OWL Web Ontology Language Reference, W3C Recommendation, http://www.w3.org/TR/owl-ref/
21. SWRL: A Semantic Web Rule Language Combining OWL and RuleML, W3C Recommendation, http://www.w3.org/Submission/SWRL/
22. Protégé, http://protege.stanford.edu/
23. Buyya, R., Ranjan, R., Calheiros, R.N.: Modeling and simulation of scalable cloud computing environments and the cloudsim toolkit: Challenges and opportunities. In: 7th High Performance Computing and Simulation, HPCS (2009)

Mapping XML Documents Using Complex SQL Data Types

Kai Schweinsberg and Lutz Wegner

Universität Kassel, FB 16 Elektrotechnik/Informatik,
D-34121 Kassel, Germany
{ks,wegner}@db.informatik.uni-kassel.de
http://www.db.informatik.uni-kassel.de

Abstract. This contribution looks at new ways to map XML documents to relational database systems preserving their hierarchical structure. In particular we take advantage of the advanced features available following the SQL:2003 standard, which defines complex structure and collection types. Starting out with a survey of existing methods, basic questions concerning appropriate and efficient forms of mapping XML documents to SQL-compliant data types are addressed. This leads to a reversible conversion method, which is subsequently implemented in a prototype application. The design of the mapping is geared towards existing, mature relational database management systems (DBMS). It turns out that among the products considered, IBM Informix seems to offer the best support for complex structure and collection types in the context of our application. To better assess the performance of the mapping process, the observed running time and the required in-memory and database storage of the implementation are measured and evaluated.

Keywords: XML mapping, SQL:2003 complex types, performance evaluation.

1 Introduction

1.1 Motivation and Structure

The markup language XML is used for annotating documents and has established itself as data exchange format. Consequently, there is a need to store and transfer these documents not only as pure text files, but also in a better structured way in persistent storage. This can be achieved by means of particular XML or relational database systems. Traditionally, relational databases either store the XML documents unchanged as binary or string objects, or they are broken up and stored normalized in conventional relational tables (so-called flattening or shredding of the hierarchical structure). This paper takes a new approach which kind of lies in the middle of the previous solutions. It takes advantage of the opportunities of the advanced features in the SQL standard. SQL:2003 defines complex structure and collection types (tuples, arrays, lists, sets, multisets). They allow a mapping of XML documents to a relational schema

Y. Ait Ameur et al. (Eds.): MEDI 2014, LNCS 8748, pp. 209–223, 2014.

which preserves the hierarchical structure. This offers two advantages: on one side, proven technologies, which originate from the area of relational databases, are available without any restrictions. On the other side, using SQL collection types preserves the inherent tree structure of XML documents, so in rebuilding documents, expensive joins over the tuples from normalized and distributed tables can be avoided. The paper starts with basic questions concerning appropriate and efficient forms of mapping XML documents to SQL:2003-compliant data types. Based on this, a suitable, reversible conversion method is developed which is subsequently implemented in a prototype application and then analyzed. The design of the mapping aims at a later use with an existing, mature relational database management system (DBMS). However, support of SQL:2003 in the commercial DBMS world is still incomplete. Thus we investigate to what extent the various systems are suited for the implementation of the mapping process. The paper closes with a performance evaluation of our Informix-implementation which includes a comparison with a rival method, here Oracle's object-relational storage.

1.2   XML

We assume familiarity with the *Extensible Markup Language*, short XML, as defined by the W3C (World Wide Web Consortium) in [29] and for which numerous tutorials and textbooks exist [14]. XML itself is a meta language which defines other markup languages, e.g. MathML or SVG (Scalable Vector Graphics). Languages derived from XML serve two major purposes: firstly they define well-formed – and if combined with a schema document (DTD or XML Schema) even valid – documents as containers for information. Stylesheets guide the visual representation for the most common mode of usage, namely viewing the documents in a browser. Secondly XML plays a big role in defining standards for data exchange, notably for SOAP and XBRL.

XML documents can be classified as either *document-centered* (also called *text-centered*) or *data-centered*. As an example, the ordering of elements is important for the first type, while it does not matter much for the second type, where pieces of content are often retrieved using XQuery.

All in all, XML documents are ordered tree-like structures with seven types of nodes: a root, elements, texts, attributes, namespaces, processing instructions, and comments. Whatever mappings are devised, they must take care of the specific requirements of each node type, in particular, if the mapping is to be reversible (see Subsection 4.4 below). Properties of the nodes, how to address them and the data model as a whole are defined in the XML Path Language and XPath Data Model standards [23,33].

2   Object-Relational Database Systems and SQL:2003

2.1   The SQL Standards

Most readers will be familiar with SQL (Structured Query Language) and its standardization after 1986. Table 1 lists the evolution steps of the SQL standard.

Table 1. Evolution of the SQL standards

Year	Name
1986	SQL-86 (SQL-87)
1989	SQL-89
1992	SQL-92 (SQL2)
1999	SQL:1999 (SQL3)
2003	SQL:2003
2006	SQL:2006 (only part 14: SQL/XML)
2008	SQL:2008
2011	SQL:2011

In the context of this contribution, we focus on the revisions and extensions introduced with SQL:2003 [15]. The most important innovations which the standard established in 2003 were XML-related functions, support for the programming language Java, and the introduction of sequences and columns with identities and automatically generated values. Furthermore there is now a multiset data type and there are table-valued functions, both extending object-relational concepts already introduced in SQL:1999. Worth mentioning is also a new, comfortable variant of the CREATE TABLE command which uses an SQL query as declaration base. Michels et al. [26] give a good overview of the new features.

Although over ten years old now, SQL:2003 is by no means outdated. In fact, many of the features outside of the minimal subset, called *Core SQL*, have not been (or differently) implemented by the big RDBMS vendors. This will be seen in our implementation considerations below (cf. Subsection 2.2).

Furthermore, SQL:2006 three years later added only one small part, namely SQL/XML, which also defines how XQueries can be embedded into SQL queries. We consider SQL/XML as part of the review of mapping alternatives further below (Subsection 3.4). The subsequent standard SQL:2008 defined commands already present in many implementations, like TRUNCATE TABLE, extended CASE and MERGE and introduced INSTEAD OF triggers, but did not touch the new data types from 2003. The currently last standard SQL:2011 added insert, update and delete operations inside queries and introduced temporary tables together with other minor changes. Thus, SQL:2003 (together with SQL/XML from 2006) still remains the standard which defines what an object-relational DBMS should offer for XML storage and retrieval.

2.2 The Object-Relational Type System and Its Implementations

It is impossible to describe the type system of the SQL standards from 1999 and 2003 together with the implementations of the dialects in Oracle, DB2, and Informix on less than ten pages. Not to mention the religious wars among database people surrounding the terms "object" and "object reference". We must therefore refer the reader to the literature, in particular to the excellent text

Table 2. Support for object-relational data types

Data Type	SQL:1999	SQL:2003	Oracle	DB2	Informix
ROW (unnamed)	X	X			X
ROW (named)					X
SET (unnamed)					X
MULTISET (unnamed)		X			X
TABLE (named)			X		
LIST (unnamed)					X
ARRAY (unnamed)	X	X			
ARRAY (named)			X		
OBJECT (named)	X	X	X	X	
REF (unnamed)	X	X	X	X	

book by Türker [35]. However, Table 2 summarizes the offered types sufficiently well and we comment on the deficiencies with respect to our mapping task. It is obvious from a short glance that the support of object-relational data types differs very much among the database systems. None of the SQL:2003 data types is supported by all three systems. Whatever XML mapping one may devise will be very implementation specific if one decides to use these advanced features.

Informix offers good support in the area of tuple and collection types, but misses out on object and object reference types. Many database researchers therefore prefer to call Informix an extended relational database system. Conversely, DB2 knows object and reference types but lacks built-in types for collections and tuples. Finally, Oracle is a more balanced implementation and object and reference types may be declared, although syntactically different than defined in the SQL standard. There are array types, but other than in the SQL:2003-standard, it is a named constructor. Instead of multisets, Oracle offers a type TABLE but with much of the same functionality. We return to this topic once the mapping method has been fixed.

3   Alternatives in Storing XML Documents

Apart from the classification of XML documents into data-centric vs text-centric, XML documents may come in many variations. Thus it is difficult to devise a mapping which guarantees optimal storage and retrieval (called "publishing") regardless of the document structure. It is not surprising that the research community came up with many intricate solutions after 1999, few however with the claim to be an industry strength solution. In the Ph.D. thesis which forms the base for the article here, Schweinsberg [31] classifies the approaches and gives examples of the storage result when applied to e.g. the well-known mondial-document [24]. We use this taxonomy and list the methods which go into each category, but for lack of space without examples. The main purpose is to set our method into perspective.

Three fundamental storage methods are distinguished:

- *text-based* methods which store the complete XML document as text.
- *structure-based* methods which examine the XML documents and store them in database tables whose schemas reflect the document structure.
- *model-based* methods which choose a generic model which reflects the general, tree-like structure of XML documents without regard for the particular document instance.

Some authors use different terms. Lausen [19] calls structure-based content-based, while model-based becomes structure-based.

3.1   Text-Based Methods

Storing the documents as long strings has several advantages. There is no need for schema information, in fact it is possible to store fragments only. If the documents come with a signature, the signature remains valid as the documents are retrieved with byte-for-byte fidelity. On the other hand, the granularity of access is large and fast retrieval of particular elements or attributes is not possible. In practice, full-text indexing can solve some of these problems.

The simplest way to implement text-based storage is to rely on the file system of a server. However, no transaction processing is possible and it is a step backwards into pre-database times. Consequently, a better approach is to use LOB (*Large Object*) columns in the DBMS, possibly supplemented by additional attributes. In SQL:2003, the data type is called `CLOB` (*Character Large Object*) and all commercial databases provide something similar. Oracle knows `CLOB`, `NCLOB` for the Unicode character set, and `BLOB` without string semantics. LOB-types can take data up to at least 2 GB, often more. However, unlike the `VARCHAR2`-type in Oracle, which is limited to 4000 characters, neither direct string comparisons nor using the `LIKE`-operator is possible. To offset these shortcomings, Oracle provides additional functionality in its *OracleText*-package which understands XPath-expressions.

3.2   Structure-Based Methods

When a large number of documents obey the same schema definition, structure-based methods can generate a database schema which maps the XML elements, attributes and texts of the document into appropriate entities, relations and attributes. The mapping can be done manually or by a mapping algorithm. Storage and retrieval of data is provided by a RDBMS module or through middleware. The schema can be optimized to support frequently accessed elements or attributes. However, this can turn into a disadvantage, if applications or document structures change. Overall, structure-based methods are geared towards data-centric documents with a stable structure over time.

As for the mapping, one can either dissect the documents s.t. the nodes fit into ordinary "flat" database tables or map the structure into non-normalized tables which resemble the NF^2-data model [30].

The first method is generally known as "shredding" (see [7] for an introduction into this technique). Whether to pack elements into one table or to start new tables for elements with sub-elements differs from algorithm to algorithm. Use of ordinal numbers to maintain sequence order is common but creates problems if the documents are updated later on. General difficulties arise with the mapping of XML value types to SQL types, with the XSD schema types choice and any, mixed content and recursion. Mapping algorithms and performance considerations are discussed e.g. in [1, 3, 8, 13, 17, 22] and [36, p. 486ff.]. [12] considers mapping XPath-expressions into equivalent clauses of SQL queries.

The second method makes use of the collection types of the database system as discussed for SQL:2003 above. In particular, if lists are available (as in case of the eNF^2-data model [10]), the ordering problem can be solved in an elegant way. Variant and optional parts of the XML document lead to NULL-values in the database. Mixed content and recursion, however, are still difficult to map. Oracle and other DBMS provide built-in mapping methods between XML documents and object-relational tables which resemble the NF^2-model above. They all require registering the XML schema with the DBMS. We will use the Oracle-mapping in Section 5 on performance evaluation as comparison. A disadvantage of this second method is the creation of large database schemas with corresponding sparsely filled tables. Algebraic operations for querying and transforming XML documents, which are stored in NF^2-relations, are given in [18].

3.3   Model-Based Methods

This method provides a generic mapping for XML documents without looking at schema definitions. The general task is to record an ordered tree structure in database tables. It is the most thoroughly researched concept and we can only hint at the available algorithms.

- **Edge table.** All nodes in the tree are assigned a number in some order of traversal. In addition, for each node, the ID of the predecessor node is recorded and some ordering to reconstruct the sequence of child-nodes. Finally, the type of node, its name and value must be stored. With a document-ID, one table can hold several documents. Edge tables can become very large and performance for XQuery is poor. Optimizations are possible, e.g. by splitting up the edge table as done in *XRel* [39] or storing parent-child relations in another table as in *XParent* [16].
- **Labeling schemes.** Nodes in the tree are given labels which are chosen in such a way that the node position can be reconstructed from the label [28,34]. The art is to find ordering schemes which allow insertions and deletions of nodes without extensive relabeling. Several such schemes exist. A fairly simple one relies on the rank of a node in pre- and post-order traversals. Another one is the Dewey-scheme, which records the path to a node in the label. If documents change frequently, the original Dewey-scheme requires expensive relabeling. The *Ordpath*-method, used in Microsoft's SQL Server, is based on Dewey, but avoids relabeling using some tricks in naming the nodes. Similarly, the dynamic Dewey-labeling scheme (DDE) [38] claims to solve this

problem. Next, labels can be derived from intervals. Each node records start, end, and level. Predecessor and successor, as well as parent-child relations, are easily computed. Insertions, however, destroy the scheme and leaving gaps in the numbering system is of limited use. Finally there are labeling schemes based on mathematical principles (prime labeling scheme [37]) and schemes based on coding theory (QED, Dynamic Quaternary Encoding [21]), which use some type of lexicographic ordering.

- **IBM DB2 pureXML.** Starting with Version 9, IBM DB2 offers XML support. The new functionalities are called *pureXML* and provide a column-type XML, which stores XML documents in a native format. This involves parsing the document and creating a DOM tree in which all names of elements and attributes are replaced by integers through a table SYSXMLSTRINGS. These integers are even valid across several documents with identical names. Another interesting point is how the documents are mapped to memory pages by means of a so called regional index. Details can be found in [27]. Like Oracle, DB2 offers native XQuery support.

- **eXist.** We should mention eXist, which is one of the twenty native XML databases discussed in [5]. eXist uses a labeling scheme based on publications by Lee and Shin [20,32] and models the document as a k-tree. Labels quickly become large, but with a modification of the pure k-tree definition, 8-byte integers are sufficient in eXist for almost all documents.

3.4 SQL/XML

In reviewing and classifying XML-to-RDBMS methods, SQL/XML stands out as a standardized approach [15] and detailed descriptions can be found in Melton et al. [11, 25] and in [35]. SQL/XML provides functionalities for the following tasks:

- XML output from queries over relational data
- storage and processing of XML data in relational databases
- queries over XML data and output of results either in XML or relational format
- mapping of relational data and identifiers to and from XML

The standard makes no recommendations concerning the storage formats. In practice, textual storage is widespread for its easy implementation. SQL/XML defines a data type XML which also accepts XML fragments or forests. There are publishing functions to be used inside SQL queries for converting relational data to XML elements and attributes. There are mappings for values and identifiers including handling the different data type universes. How XML Schema should be incorporated into the mapping process is not prescribed by the standard, but Melton strongly recommends to register schemas with the DBMS to avoid validation conflicts of previously stored documents resulting from subsequent schema changes (which the DBMS would prohibit for registered schemas).

4   A New Method and Its Prototype Implementation

Having reviewed storage and retrieval alternatives for XML documents in relational databases, we now propose a new bijective mapping from XML to SQL:2003-conformant data types. We start with properties and requirements, then identify which DBMS suits these goals best, and finally describe our Java application which maps into object-relational data structures and back.

4.1   Properties and Requirements

Essentially we look for a model-based mapping which mirrors the tree structure of the XML documents in a most "natural" way. To this end, SQL:2003 offers the collection types LIST, SET, MULTISET, and ROW. This will allow us to combine a set (or list) of child nodes directly with its parent node. Clearly, text-based methods, complete shredding or tricky labeling schemes do not reveal this parent-child relation in such an obvious form.

Of course, any database designer will immediately recognize, that a hierarchical relation can be mapped into a table where each child carries the identifier (or primary key) of its parent. We argue that for XML documents this would correspond to a processing from the leaves to the root, while, in fact, most elements are accessed with path expressions which start at the root element or at least process the tree top-down. For attributes it is even more preferable that an element can see directly the set of attributes which belongs to it, rather than having each attribute carry the ID of the element it belongs to.

Mixed content is another point to watch for. Intermittent text can be considered as a text-child and could go with sub-elements into a list of children. Long attribute and element names (tags), say longer than 30 characters, are rare, but to be on the safe side, allowing more characters in the database should be possible. Proprietary functionalities of any particular DBMS will not be considered, as they cause trouble with respect to portability. Stored procedures and easy access from a programming language, say in Java through the JDBC interface, would be helpful.

4.2   Selecting a Suitable Database

As indicated in Table 2 above, support for the object-relational SQL:2003 data types differs among commercial vendors. The situation with SQL Server and with open source products is rather bad. MySQL has no collection types. PostgreSQL offers an array type and a composite type which together resemble LIST and ROW, but lacks sets and multisets. In comparing the three big commercial products Oracle, IBM DB2, and Informix, DB2 dropped out of the race early on as it does not offer collection types which could be used for table definitions. ARRAY-types are supported which could represent set-valued types, but they are restricted to processing in stored procedures written in SPL, they are not first-class citizens for column definitions.

Oracle looked like a winner for a long time, in particular since we run it at our institute for teaching, content management and administrative tasks. Collection types are available, but they are not as orthogonal as in Informix. Furthermore, a first prototype in Oracle turned out to be rather cumbersome to manage. Fact is that Oracle is so powerful and has included so many new features, that even the so-called Enterprise Manager, which is an independent module with a graphical interface, often hides problems occurring deeper down instead of tracing them.

It came as somewhat a surprise, that Informix offered the best choice. Although smaller in its range of functionalities, it offered all collection types in an easy to manage environment. The only missing feature were object methods, identities, and references. For the prototype we had in mind, this constituted no drawback and everything can be done with relational functionalities and collection types. Informix SPL for stored procedures has no encapsulation for data and code, but otherwise it is on par with Oracle's PL/SQL. Experiences with early implementations both in Oracle and Informix supported our view, that for the given SQL:2003-compliant mapping, Informix Dynamic Server 11.7 was the DBMS of choice. For the downside of this comparison, it is clear that porting the implementation to another DBMS, despite trying to be SQL:2003-conformant, would require considerable rewriting.

4.3   Data Structures

The most direct way to map the hierarchical structure of elements and sub-elements is to define nested tables in the sense of the NF^2-data model. As XML documents may have an arbitrary depth of nesting, defined by a recursive DTD or XML Schema definition, we need recursive collection types[1]. A closer look at user-defined data types in SQL:2003 [15, p. 632ff.], however, reveals, that an attribute of a user-defined type may not be based on the type to be declared. Accordingly, none of the three DBMS, which we considered for the implementation, allows direct or indirect recursion.

As a way out, we can replace the sub-elements by references to sub-elements. The references could use object identifiers generated by the system or a user-generated identification system. In a structure-based model, each element definition in a DTD or XML Schema would generate a unique type for the database, which can handle text content, sub-elements, and attributes. The object references then go into a list-valued attribute.

Alternatively, a generic structure with object references can be devised to reflect one parent-child level. Mixed content is again difficult but can be accommodated with some tricks. This approach belongs to the model-based methods and no DTD or XML Schema is needed. On the other hand, it is hard to validate insertions, deletions and updates of stored documents in the database without extracting the complete document. Balmin et al. [2], however, show that incremental checking is possible using an additional data structure whose size is in the order of the size of the document.

---

[1] [9] reports that, in practice, more than half of all DTDs are recursively built.

```
CREATE ROW TYPE ATTRIBUTE(
    NAME          VARCHAR(30),
    VALUE         LVARCHAR(30000)
);

CREATE ROW TYPE ELEMENT(
    DOCID             INT,
    NODEID            INT,
    NAME              VARCHAR(30),
    ATTRIBUTES        SET(ATTRIBUTE NOT NULL),
    TEXT              VARCHAR(30000),
    SUBELEMENTREFS    LIST(INT NOT NULL)
);

CREATE TABLE ELEMENTS OF TYPE ELEMENT(
    UNIQUE (DOCID,NODEID)
);
```

Fig. 1. Type definition instructions

```
...
<city is_country_cap="yes" country="L">
  <name>Luxembourg</name>
  <longitude>6.08</longitude>
  <latitude>49.4</latitude>
  <population year="87">76600</population>
</city>
...
```

Fig. 2. A city element in the mondial-document

The implementation which we present uses this generic approach. As Informix doesn't know object tables, nor object identifiers or references, we take typed tables, based on tuple types. Each row takes one instance of this type. Object-IDs will be modeled by foreign key relations (named NODEID). An additional document-ID (DOCID) is introduced to store multiple documents in one table. Together they form the composite primary key. The following Figure 1 shows the necessary SQL commands for the type-definitions in Informix. The definitions should be self-explaining in connection with the following example (cf. Figures 2 and 3) taken from the mondial-document [24]. For the other node types in XML documents, additional tuples must be inserted.

As an example, consider text in XML documents, which can be very long. Texts longer than the 30,000 characters defined above as LVARCHAR are split up into separate sub-nodes of 30,000 characters each with node name !TEXT. Elements which contain these over-length texts receive a list of node-IDs in the SUBELEMENTREFS attribute for the fragments. This allows proper reconstruction regardless of tuple order. The limits we mention result from a length restriction of 32,767 bytes for the row-type of tables in Informix.

DID	NID	NAME	{}ATTRIBUTES		TEXT	<>SUBREFS
			NAME	VALUE		
...	...	...		...		...	...
815	32	city	is_country_cap	yes	–	<33, 34, 35, 36>
			country	L		
815	33	name		–	Luxembourg	–
815	34	longitude		–	6.08	–
815	35	latitude		–	49.4	–
815	36	population	year	87	76600	–
...	...	...		...		...	...

Fig. 3. Mapping of elements and attributes (names shortened)

4.4 XML2DB Implementation

Mixed content is handled similarly. Details for all other node types and properties – document root, XML version, standalone attribute, coding, comments, processing instructions, CDATA-sections, document type declarations, entities, and namespaces – can be found in [31]. The thesis contains also a description of the command-line tool XML2DB which handles storage and extraction of XML documents into and from the database. The insertion method works recursively in post-order, i.e. all sub-nodes are inserted as tuples first and return their node-IDs. These are collected and then stored as a list in the parent tuple.

Finally, the question of byte-fidelity arises. Because attributes are stored as *sets* of name-value tuples, the order may change in a reconstructed document. Similarly, single and double quotes around the values are converted into double quotes, entities are replaced by their texts, and ignorable whitespaces are condensed. Although a byte-by-byte identical reconstruction was not implemented, as it is prohibitively expensive both in time and added space, the mapping does produce logically identical documents as defined by the "Canonical XML" [6] standard.

5 Performance Evaluation

To evaluate the mapping, the two most relevant questions are:

– How fast is the mapping into and out of the database?
– How much space is consumed by the database in storing a document?

To answer them, a thorough performance evaluation of the Informix prototype was performed. It involved different document styles and a comparison with the Oracle implementation. Readers are again referred to [31] for detailed results.

To give a short idea, we list some figures from the previously mentioned mondial-document. With a total of 1.73 MB, it is a rather large XML file. It is data-centric with 30,822 elements, 30,015 attributes, at most 5 attributes per element, at most 1357 child elements in one parent, a nesting of elements up to 5 levels, and 330,625 ignorable whitespaces. The other documents were `bible.xml`, `purchaseOrder.xml`, and `SigmodRecord.xml`. Experiments were conducted on an isolated server to eliminate influence from traffic and repeated ten times with the identical document. With the exception of `purchaseOrder.xml`, which is a very small document, all figures were very close to each other when scaled against the number of DOM nodes.

As an example, inserting the mondial-document into the database required a total of 18.275 s, of which 0.939 s involved parsing (instantiating the Xerces DOM parser, parsing the XML document and building the DOM tree in main memory), 1.030 s for deleting the old document (with same document-ID), 0.080 s other DB-operations, and finally 16.227 s for the actual insertion into the database. This last figure can again be broken down into 14.946 s for the DB-inserts and 1.203 s for the JDBC handling. Of the 14.946 s for DB-inserts, 14.929 s concern element insertions, which includes attributes. Everything else, e.g. texts/CDATA, comments, processing instructions, DocType-declarations can be neglected.

One very important fact must be mentioned. Even though `XML2DB` is a model-based method, a DTD existed for each document and could be used to recognize ignorable whitespaces by the parser, which are then deleted. Without a DTD, they must go into the database as text nodes. If that is the case, the number of database entries in the `ELEMENTS`-table doubles both in the mondial- and in the bible-document. Accordingly, the performance suffers and the execution time climbs from 14.946 s to 23.432 s, resp. 4.884 s to 7.415 s for the bible-document.

Reconstructing a document takes more time than insertion. For the mondial-document with DTD, we need 26.686 s in total, of which 25.891 s belong to the actual retrieval. Of these, 6.513 s are attributed to the JDBC handling. Only 0.313 s – or up to 3 % of the total time – go into the serialization of the DOM tree into an output document, once the tree has been constructed from the database tuples.

To answer the second question (storage space) we looked at the required heap and non-heap space in memory for document insertion. Across all documents, the non-heap space is largely invariant at about 9 MB, while the heap space grows with the document size. For the larger documents, between 200 and 400 bytes are needed per DOM node. The situation is similar for the retrieval of documents.

Now for the database storage. The mondial-document had a file size of about 1.7 MB. When stored in the database, using a DTD for parsing, but without compression, it takes up 7.0 MB – a growth by a factor of 4! This might come as a surprise considering that XML documents are claimed to be verbose. In the database, additional overhead comes from type and length information, texts and names are just as long as in the XML documents. This changes when compression is applied for which Informix has an option. Now `mondial.xml` takes only 2.5 MB database storage, in case of the bible-document, the storage even drops below the original document size with a factor of 0.87. Insertion times also drop by about 3–4 %, extraction times remain unchanged.

Finally, to get a feeling for the quality of our mapping method, we ran the same experiments, but restricted to the mondial-document, using Oracle's built-in structured (object-relational) storage method. Oracle's mapping guarantees DOM fidelity. It requires registering the document schema, but does not accept DTDs. Thus we rewrote the DTD into an XSD document. Oracle then generates a suitable table of type XMLType and nested sub-tables to map the hierarchic structure of the document. In the case of mondial.xml, 34 sub-tables were required. Also, one attribute value had to be shortened, as it exceeded an unexpected Oracle-limit of presumably 2000 bytes.

Insertion and retrieval required 3.563 s, resp. 5.973 s. This is by a factor of 3.3, resp. 4.5, faster than what XML2DB could achieve under Informix. However, the differences are not, or at least not entirely, due to the mapping design. They lie in the database access: XML2DB runs outside the database using a JDBC connection to issue SQL statements. In contrast, Oracle's insertions and retrievals occur inside the database in a built-in module, which may profit from kernel-related optimizations.

6   Conclusion

We reviewed the XML-to-RDBMS mapping problem and offered a taxonomy. A model-based method was devised which makes use of SQL:2003-conformant collection types. A prototype was then built and implemented for Informix, which came out as winner against DB2 and Oracle as far as type-requirements were concerned. A performance evaluation revealed that the prototype is considerable slower than a comparable built-in method in Oracle, in part due to the JDBC connection. Storage requirements are acceptable when Informix compression is used. Although the storage method is generic, having a DTD when parsing the documents during insertion time is essential for dropping ignorable whitespaces. This cuts execution times in half.

Future research should go into update functionality under the given mapping. In particular, document changes should map into local, incremental database updates (cf. [2]) and their validity should also be checked locally inside the database. Index optimizations and XQuery translations are other natural themes to look into.

Acknowledgements. We like to thank the reviewers for their valuable comments which helped to improve this contribution.

References

1. Algergawy, A., Mesiti, M., Nayak, R., Saake, G.: XML data clustering: An overview. ACM Comput. Surv. 43(4), 25 (2011)
2. Balmin, A., Papakonstantinou, Y., Vianu, V.: Incremental validation of XML documents. ACM Trans. Database Syst. 29(4), 710–751 (2004)
3. Barbosa, D., Freire, J., Mendelzon, A.O.: Designing information-preserving mapping schemes for XML. In: Böhm, et al. (eds.) [4], pp. 109–120.

4. Böhm, K., Jensen, C.S., Haas, L.M., Kersten, M.L., Larson, P.Å., Ooi, B.C. (eds.): Proceedings of the 31st International Conference on Very Large Data Bases, Trondheim, Norway, August 30-September 2. ACM (2005)
5. Bourret, R.P.: XML database products (June 2010), http://www.rpbourret.com/xml/XMLDatabaseProds.htm
6. Boyer, J.: Canonical XML version 1.0. W3C recommendation, W3C (March 2001), http://www.w3.org/TR/2001/REC-xml-c14n-20010315
7. Chamberlin, D.D., Draper, D., Fernández, M.F., Kay, M., Robie, J., Rys, M., Siméon, J., Tivy, J., Wadler, P.: XQuery from the Experts: A Guide to the W3C XML Query Language. Addison Wesley (August 2003)
8. Chaudhuri, S., Chen, Z., Shim, K., Wu, Y.: Storing XML (with XSD) in SQL databases: Interplay of logical and physical designs. IEEE Trans. Knowl. Data Eng. 17(12), 1595–1609 (2005)
9. Choi, B.: What are real DTDs like? In: WebDB, pp. 43–48 (2002)
10. Dadam, P., Küspert, K., Andersen, F., Blanken, H.M., Erbe, R., Günauer, J., Lum, V.Y., Pistor, P., Walch, G.: A DBMS prototype to support extended NF2 relations: An integrated view on flat tables and hierarchies. In: Zaniolo, C. (ed.) SIGMOD Conference, pp. 356–367. ACM Press (1986)
11. Eisenberg, A., Melton, J.: Advancements in SQL/XML. SIGMOD Record 33(3), 79–86 (2004)
12. Fan, W., Yu, J.X., Li, J., Ding, B., Qin, L.: Query translation from XPath to SQL in the presence of recursive DTDs. The VLDB Journal 18(4), 857–883 (2009)
13. Genevès, P., Layaïda, N., Quint, V.: Impact of XML schema evolution. ACM Trans. Internet Techn. 11(1), 4 (2011)
14. Harold, E.R.: XML 1.1 Bible. Wiley & Sons (2004)
15. ISO: International standard: Information technology – database languages – SQL. Tech. rep., International Organization for Standardization (December 2003), ISO/IEC 9075(1-4, 9-11, 13, 14):2003
16. Jiang, H., Lu, H., Wang, W., Yu, J.X.: Path materialization revisited: An efficient storage model for XML data. In: Zhou, X. (ed.) Australasian Database Conference, vol. 5. Australian Computer Society (2002)
17. Kulic, L.: Adaptability in XML-to-relational mapping strategies. In: Shin, S.Y., Ossowski, S., Schumacher, M., Palakal, M.J., Hung, C.C. (eds.) SAC, pp. 1674–1679. ACM (2010)
18. Lau, H.L., Ng, W.: Querying XML data by the nested relational sequence database system. In: IDEAS, pp. 236–241. IEEE Computer Society (2003)
19. Lausen, G.: Datenbanken – Grundlagen und XML-Technologien. Spektrum Akademischer Verlag (2005)
20. Lee, Y.K., Yoo, S.J., Yoon, K., Berra, P.B.: Index structures for structured documents. In: Digital Libraries, pp. 91–99. ACM (1996)
21. Li, C., Ling, T.W.: QED: a novel quaternary encoding to completely avoid relabeling in XML updates. In: Herzog, O., Schek, H.J., Fuhr, N., Chowdhury, A., Teiken, W. (eds.) CIKM, pp. 501–508. ACM (2005)
22. Lu, H., Yu, J.X., Wang, G., Zheng, S., Jiang, H., Yu, G., Zhou, A.: What makes the differences: benchmarking XML database implementations. ACM Trans. Internet Techn. 5(1), 154–194 (2005)
23. Marsh, J., Fernandez, M., Walsh, N., Malhotra, A., Nagy, M., Berglund, A.: XQuery 1.0 and XPath 2.0 data model (XDM), 2nd edn. W3C recommendation, W3C (December 2010), http://www.w3.org/TR/2010/REC-xpath-datamodel-20101214/

24. May, W.: Web-page to the mondial-database maintained at the institute for informatics of the Georg-August-Universität Göttingen (2010),
http://www.dbis.informatik.uni-goettingen.de/Mondial/

25. Melton, J., Buxton, S.: Querying XML – XQuery, XPath, and SQL/XML in Context. Morgan Kaufmann (2006)

26. Michels, J.E., Kulkarni, K.G., Farrar, C.M., Eisenberg, A., Mattos, N.M., Darwen, H.: The SQL standard. IT - Information Technology 45(1), 30–38 (2003)

27. Nicola, M., der Linden, B.V.: Native XML support in DB2 universal database. In: Böhm, et al. (eds.) [4], pp. 1164–1174

28. O'Connor, M.F., Roantree, M.: Desirable properties for XML update mechanisms. In: Daniel, F., Delcambre, L.M.L., Fotouhi, F., Garrigós, I., Guerrini, G., Mazón, J.N., Mesiti, M., Müller-Feuerstein, S., Trujillo, J., Truta, T.M., Volz, B., Waller, E., Xiong, L., Zimányi, E. (eds.) EDBT/ICDT Workshops. ACM International Conference Proceeding Series. ACM (2010)

29. Paoli, J., Sperberg-McQueen, M., Yergeau, F., Cowan, J., Bray, T., Maler, E.: Extensible markup language (XML) 1.1, 2nd edn. W3C recommendation, W3C (August 2006), http://www.w3.org/TR/2006/REC-xml11-20060816

30. Schek, H.J., Scholl, M.H.: The relational model with relation-valued attributes. Inf. Syst. 11(2), 137–147 (1986)

31. Schweinsberg, K.: Abbildung von XML-Dokumenten auf SQL:2003-konforme Datentypen. Ph.D. thesis, Universität Kassel, Germany (2012)

32. Shin, D., Jang, H., Jin, H.: BUS: An effective indexing and retrieval scheme in structured documents. In: ACM DL, pp. 235–243. ACM (1998)

33. Simeon, J., Berglund, A., Boag, S., Robie, J., Chamberlin, D., Fernandez, M., Kay, M.: XML path language (XPath) 2.0, 2nd edn. W3C recommendation, W3C (December 2010), http://www.w3.org/TR/2010/REC-xpath20-20101214/

34. Tatarinov, I., Viglas, S., Beyer, K.S., Shanmugasundaram, J., Shekita, E.J., Zhang, C.: Storing and querying ordered XML using a relational database system. In: Franklin, M.J., Moon, B., Ailamaki, A. (eds.) SIGMOD Conference, pp. 204–215. ACM (2002)

35. Türker, C.: SQL:1999 & SQL:2003 - Objektrelationales SQL, SQLJ & SQL/XML. Dpunkt-Verlag (2003)

36. Türker, C., Saake, G.: Objektrelationale Datenbanken. Dpunkt-Verlag (2006)

37. Wu, X., Lee, M.L., Hsu, W.: A prime number labeling scheme for dynamic ordered XML trees. In: Özsoyoglu, Z.M., Zdonik, S.B. (eds.) ICDE, pp. 66–78. IEEE Computer Society (2004)

38. Xu, L., Ling, T.W., Wu, H., Bao, Z.: DDE: from dewey to a fully dynamic XML labeling scheme. In: Çetintemel, U., Zdonik, S.B., Kossmann, D., Tatbul, N. (eds.) SIGMOD Conference, pp. 719–730. ACM (2009)

39. Yoshikawa, M., Amagasa, T., Shimura, T., Uemura, S.: XRel: a path-based approach to storage and retrieval of XML documents using relational databases. ACM Trans. Internet Techn. 1(1), 110–141 (2001)

GBXT – A Gesture-Based Data Exploration Tool for Your Favorite Database System

Stefan Achler

Universität Kassel, FB 16 Elektrotechnik/Informatik,
D-34121 Kassel, Germany
achler@db.informatik.uni-kassel.de
http://www.db.informatik.uni-kassel.de

Abstract. This paper presents a prototype for generic, gesture-based data exploration over arbitrary relational database systems. The application aims at users who need to navigate through interconnected relational tables in search of needed information in an ad-hoc fashion using mostly visual clues. Typically, users only have a vague understanding of the underlying database schema and attribute names, preventing them from successfully formulating SQL queries. On the other hand, a pure text search would deliver too many and meaningless results. Thus the prototype combines schema visualization with instance presentation, using a form of nested relational view for foreign key expansion. As our prototype shows, this dual schema/instances approach, when combined with direct interaction through gestures on a tablet computer or smartphone, provides intuitive, mobile, responsive interaction with structured data. The argument is then that this makes it an ideal, light-weight generic tool for anybody in the field needing quick information from partially unknown relational sources, when a customized, domain-specific interface isn't available.

Keywords: Visual queries, RDBMS, schema exploration, gesture-based interaction.

1 Introduction

1.1 Application Domain

These days information is stored in a multitude of ways. Although it often seems as if it comes off a web page, it is in many cases data retrieved from some type of database system. The database system is either a classical relational or some NoSQL DBMS. The returned data, restricted according to some selection criteria, are then dynamically inserted into a presentation page. Of course, there is also the endless universe of pure document-centric data storage, say as XML documents in a file system, which does not rely on database technology. In any case, a browser is the universal front end through which the information is viewed and selected.

Y. Ait Ameur et al. (Eds.): MEDI 2014, LNCS 8748, pp. 224–237, 2014.

Users then have a choice of either retrieving the needed information through the provided interface, which usually is form-oriented and therefore restricted to pre-defined queries, or do a pure text-based search, usually relying on information retrieval systems. If the data come from relational or other structured sources (RDBMS, XML store), which is assumed here, ad-hoc queries in SQL or XQuery would be an alternative. However, this requires sufficient knowledge of the database or document schema including table and attribute names etc.

The argument here is that for many situations in the business and engineering world, a generic data exploration tool sitting on top of a RDBMS, yet light-weight enough to run its client with gesture recognition on a tablet computer, would be useful. The ad-hoc exploration should be guided by viewing both the schema (*"Where else can I look?"*) and the instances (*"Where does this data item lead to?"*) in a synchronized way. The proposed tool GBXT thus aims at a moderately experienced user, say one that could read and interpret an ER diagram, without being an expert for the particular application domain.

1.2 Visual Database Languages and Schema Exploration

Looking for alternative ways to SQL for querying data from relational databases, in particular for naive users, is a mature research field and various academic prototypes and industry products have been developed in the past. The main motivation is the difficulty in formulating correct SQL queries, resulting from SQL being a curious mix of relational calculus and algebra. As soon as SQL (then still called SEQUEL) came into wide-spread use in the mid-seventies, empirical evidence appeared which suggested that user-formulated solutions quite often failed. Reisner [20] reported that in exams taken by CS students which included "hard" queries – in particular those with GROUP BY and HAVING – more than 50 % of all queries were wrong, either for syntactic errors or for not delivering the intended result. Thus concurrent to the development of SQL, researchers investigated alternative ways for query formulation and query design right after the relational model became popular. Catarci et al. [3] reviewed *Visual Query Languages* and suggested a classification into *graphical (diagrammatic), iconic, tabular* or combinations of the three design paradigms. An orthogonal classification would distinguish by query strategy: schema navigation, connected path, subquery composition, insertion of stored queries, matching by pattern. The following list names some of the proposals, mainly as a starter for further searches, as there are far too many to be comprehensive. The list includes also schema exploration tools without query formulation capability, as the distinction is sometimes weak.

- *QBE* as the oldest and most cited proposal belonging to the tabular class [26]
- *BEx Query Designer* as part of the SAP Business Explorer Suite [22]
- *DataGuides* as query formulation tools for semi-structured databases by Goldman and Widom [11]
- *QueryViz* as a query visualization [6]
- *GUIDE* by Wong and Kuo as a graphical user interface for database exploration [25]

- *HyperFlow* as an example of a *Dataflow Language* [7]
- a way of automatically generating query forms from query logs by Jayapandian and Jagadish [15]
- a context-aware assistance for textual completion of SQL queries as suggested by Khoussainova et al. [16]
- *Prefuse* for interactive visualizations of extended schemas [13]
- *Schemaball*, a schema viewer for SQL databases[1]

Schema exploration and visualization usually comes in conjunction with design, evolution, and conceptual merges of schemas. Of course. ER diagrams are the mother of all schema visualizations. Tools for ER, EER, and UML design, normalization support, alternative schema visualizations go into the hundreds. Today, schema exploration should also cover non-relational sources, as discussed below.

Because schema exploration or design requires some knowledge regarding the role of functional dependencies, they are not intended for the naive user. This changes when the schema exploration merely supports query formulation or visual searches over the instances (*"Which tables are available? What attributes come with them? How are they related to each other?"*). Thus, a playful, speculative data exploration is the main intention behind GBXT which is presented here.

Finally, as the resolution of graphical displays increased, more sophisticated data exploration tools became available, variously labeled as *Business Intelligence, Mobile Reporting*, and – for heterogeneous sources – *Mashup Tool*. Some memorable names to list are

- *Rombi*, a reporting solution for mobile devices[2]
- *Infragistics* development tool for data analysis[3]
- *Yahoo! Pipes* as a mashup tool for web pages[4]
- *Mashroom* as a nested table mashup tool [12]
- *Polaris*, now called *Tableau*, by Stolte et al. [23] for query, analysis, and visualization of multidimensional data
- *TouchViz* for direct interaction through touch screens [8]
- *dbTouch* for touch-based data exploration with emphasis on the database kernel supporting fast data delivery [14].

and more can be readily found in the Internet using the given keywords above.

2   Generic Exploration Using a Dual Schema/Instances Approach

2.1   Application Design

GBXT is an application which, similar to a middleware, queries relational and non-relational data sources, prepares (groups) them in a consistent, tabular way, and

---

[1] http://mkweb.bcgsc.ca/schemaball/
[2] http://www.roambi.com/
[3] http://infragistics.com/
[4] http://pipes.yahoo.com/pipes/

offers this view for browsing and interaction to the user by means of a graphical client running in a conventional browser. The view is dual in that it combines schema and instances (data items) information simultaneously. Schema information is first extracted from the sources and mapped to an internal, uniform meta-schema model which is memory-resident inside GBXT. For the end user, there is no need to rely on a domain-specific back/front end and GBXT is thus generic to the extend that it will accept any source which has a JDBC or REST interface.

Currently, the import from the common RDBMS is operational and demonstrated in this paper. However, the meta-schema format has been designed to also handle other types of data stores, such as XML, graph, or key-value data stores, provided they can be addressed via REST. In the long run, the current exchange protocol could be replaced by a standard protocol like *oData*[5] from *OASIS*. The client application itself has been written in HTML5/JavaScript and will therefore run on all mobile devices which offer one of the common browsers for hand-helds, say Chrome, Firefox, or Safari.[6]

2.2 Visualization Design

As just mentioned, any particular schema from the given data source is mapped into an internal meta-schema. From this a *view* is generated which must allow the user to explore the data based on clues (hints) both from the schema and the actual data. The term *view* can be taken both in the database sense (view offered in the external model) and in the visualization (GUI) sense. In our experience, the nested relational data model, also called non-first normal form (NF^2) data model [10], is best suited for this purpose. It provides an intuitive mental

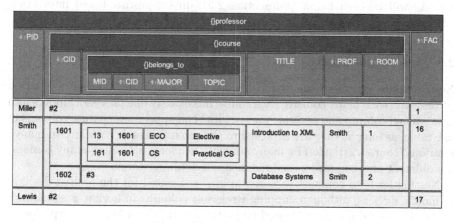

Fig. 1. Nested table in GBXT

---

[5] http://www.odata.org/

[6] The prototype presently runs on a Samsung Galaxy 10.1 and on an Apple iPad 2.

model, at least for common hierarchical structures, and an easily understood visualization resembling the common spreadsheet. Figure 1 shows a nested table, taken from the prototype, which is presented here. Details regarding the visual hints both in the schema and the data area will be explained below in Section 3. The database is taken from an academic environment with courses held by professors and attended by students, who major in certain studies.

Indeed, GBXT is not the first application which discovered these pleasant properties. The *CRIUS System* [19] allows users to manipulate NF^2-tables from a graphical interface using the "drag-and-drop" paradigm. However, the implementation requires a prior mapping of (flat) relational tables to nested tables and thus cannot be applied directly to existing relational database systems. *DataPlay* [1] also uses a form of NF^2-tables for various data sources (databases, XML, and JSON). The relations are contracted into a single, nested, universal relation and represented in this way. SQL as a query language is replaced by a graphical interface for both existential and universal quantification with emphasis on trial-and-error incremental modifications. To this end, the results include observable complements. A similar presentation of query results in some form of nested table is also a feature of *TableTalk* as part of a non-implemented design study [9].

Mashroom [12] is a mashup tool for the integration of inhomogeneous, remote data services (XML, JSON, RDBMS via REST or SOAP) geared at the end user. The internal data model also strongly resembles the NF^2-model. Data can be manipulated much like in a spreadsheet through an algebra, which is about as expressive as XQuery.

Finally, we need not hide the fact, that the author's institution has a long research history of dealing with NF^2-tables and their visualization and manipulation in an editor called *Escher* [10]. However, they stem from a time when direct interaction through devices with multi-touch properties wasn't possible yet. As will be seen below (Subsection 2.3), direct, gesture-based interaction adds substantially to an intuitive handling of data presented in nested tables.

2.3   Interaction Design

Nested tables represent hierarchical relations. The "many-side" of a relation (professors teach many courses, each course has exactly one professor) moves into a set-valued column and several "many-sides" can appear as separate columns in one table, as long as they are attached to the same "one-side". "Many-to-many" relations (courses attended by many students, students attending many courses) are different and can lead to redundancies, if actually stored.

Nesting leads to compact representations well suited for the limited displays of mobile devices, although clipping irrelevant columns in a view is sometimes useful. Relationships are expressed by juxtaposition, much like in a map. Zooming in and out of these data landscapes is possible. Alternatively, if the list of data items for the "many-side" becomes too long, techniques from windowing systems (e.g. scroll bars) can be fitted into set-valued fields within a tuple.

In contrast, a graph representation shows entities as nodes and relationships as edges (cf. the exploration and query tool described by Rontu et al. [21]). While diagrams are an intuitive way to show relations in a conceptual schema or to indicate the actual existence of a connection together with some label (*there are 30 students attending lecture X, it takes 2 hours to travel from Kassel to Frankfurt by train*), diagrams fail when they have to show instance details (*lecture X together with names of all students attending it, departure and arrival times of all trains connecting daily Kassel to Frankfurt*).

Still, nested table visualizations can be cumbersome as well. In general, GBXT splits the screen horizontally into a data area at the bottom and a schema area above, the latter also called the dashboard. When a relationship is explored, a new set-valued column is opened with a swipe gesture and automatically attached to the right of the selected column. Simultaneously, the newly added attributes are shown nested one level deeper in the dashboard (see Figures 2 below for the schema overview and Figure 1 above for a partial view in nested form). Thus the dashboard keeps track of which tables have been explored and how they have been nested so far. Circular traversals are possible and harmless. Often, some attributes of a table are of no interest when exploring a relationship (when listing the students attending a course, their matriculation numbers or study semester might not be needed). Those unwanted attributes may be projected out (clipped) by appropriate action in the dashboard. A more detailed tour of the prototype implementation follows in Section 3 below.

2.4   Gesture-Based Interface

Classical computers and laptops are gradually loosing their market share in favor of smartphones and tablets. Without a mouse and keyboard, the WIMP (windows, icons, menus, pointer) interaction and presentation paradigm has to be rethought. But even if a mouse or keyboard were available, touch panels provide the most direct way of scrolling through lists or shuffling data items around. However, starting database operations (selections, projections, joins, unions) through gestures, whether in a nested table view – as suggested here – or over flat tables as in Nandi's *Query-by-gesture* [17], is a tricky task.

As an example, consider the just mentioned prototype *Query-by-gesture*, also called *QWiK* (Querying Without Keyboards). A flipped schema representation (attributes are stacked as rows) is used to initiate joins over compatible attributes which are physically close to each other. Much thought goes into hints (feedback) regarding what to expect as result of, say a join, and how fast they can be computed to make the system feel alive. As Nandi writes [17, Subsec. 3.2]:

> Results are generated in an online fashion, allowing for time-bounded computation of feedback. The feedback loop runs incrementally, reusing computations (stored in the context) from the previous iteration.

The goal for the query formulation process has then some similarity with the trial-and-error approach from *DataPlay* [1] above.

Another project to mention in connection with gestures is *Data3* which uses Microsoft Kinect and an event processing engine *AnduIN* for the recognition of body gestures which control an OLAP application. Similarly we are experimenting with the *Leap Motion Controller*[7] for 3D hand gestures, but ignore these types of gestures and their capturing devices for the discussion here, as it concerns more HCI issues.

3   A Guided Tour of GBXT

When a user tells GBXT which database he or she wants to explore, the application collects the schema information, maps tables and relations into its own internal meta-schema and presents to the user a first overview by means of a classical ER diagram in case the source is a RDB. Rather than implementing this representation anew from scratch, GBXT relies on the *SchemaSpy* implementation[8]. Figure 2 shows the diagram for our example scenario. From the diagram, a user

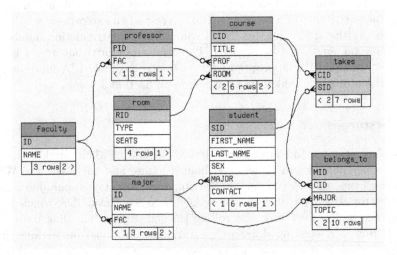

Fig. 2. ER overview

can learn which tables are available, what primary keys there are and how the tables are related to each other by means of foreign keys. Additional information can include cardinalities, min-/max-values, number of null values and other statistical data. The user then selects a table to start his or her exploration. At any stage of the navigation, the ER overview can be recalled or hidden with a three-finger-swipe.

Assume the user is a student who has picked the professor-table from our sample database. Three professors are listed in our example and attribute PID

---

[7] https://www.leapmotion.com/product
[8] http://schemaspy.sourceforge.net/

(a)

(b)

(c)

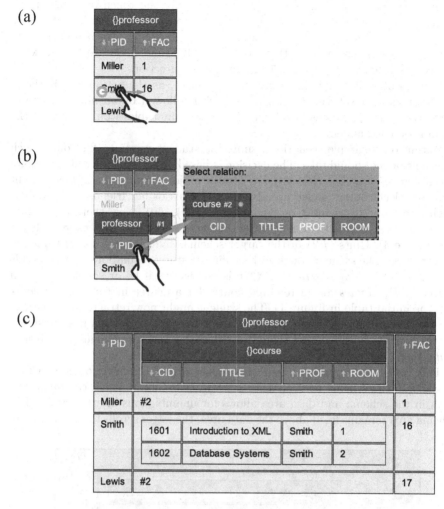

Fig. 3. Courses which Prof. Smith teaches

is the key. An orange down-arrow and numerical value 1 in the schema indicate that PID is referenced by exactly one other table. Being interested in lectures by Prof. Smith, the student swipes from left to right over Smith (cf. Figure 3a).[9] A token (select-object) appears consisting of the table name, selected attribute(s)[10] (here PID) and selected data item (here Smith). To the right of the token, possible target schemas appear (see Figure 3b). In this case the course-schema, which

---

[9] The gesture for the expansion is a swipe from left to right over the corresponding element (both in the schema or the data area). The inverse (reduction, fold-in, abort) is signaled by a right to left swipe over the element to close. Pinch gestures are reserved for zooming and rotation of views.

[10] Composite keys are possible but not yet operational.

is the only one with PID as foreign key. Dragging the token over the target expands the tuple (see Figure 3c). Our student now sees that Prof. Smith offers two courses, *Introduction to XML* and *Database Systems*. Green up-arrows in the inserted schema indicate that attributes PROF and ROOM are foreign keys. Indeed, we just traveled the PROF-link in reverse direction.

Courses of Miller and Lewis are not expanded, as the action was initiated on the instance level. However, a hash-marker followed by an integer (here in both cases #2) appears as hint indicating how many tuples would appear if the column were expanded.

Within our example scenario, assume the student wants to find out, which course he or she should take. The decision is based on restrictions which regulate which courses may be selected for a certain major. Secondly, a student might want to select courses which are also taken by his or her friends. The student might start out by swiping over course-ID (CID) 1601. Now there is a choice dragging the generated token over the belongs_to or over the takes schema (see Figure 4). Hints (#2) in the target schemas indicate how many tuples to expect there. The student starts with looking at study regulations first and finds out, that *1601 – Introduction to XML* is an elective if he or she studies for a degree in *Economics* and a required course for a degree in *Computer Science* (see the initial table in Figure 1). The student might now retract, going back to the two lectures and find out which of his or her fellow students has registered for the course, check whether there is a risk that a certain seminar (like *Achler: Data Modelling*) will not take place due to lack of audience etc.

This concludes our guided tour. The schema design is fairly obvious: Curly brackets in the schema area indicate a set-valued column, equal column width both in the schema and data area allows for unambiguous interpretation. The schema area remains fixed above the data area, the latter scrolls to accommodate

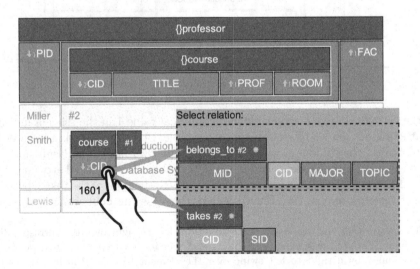

Fig. 4. Choice for following foreign key

large tables. Swipe and hold actions in the schema area lead to expansion or collapse of complete columns (in all tuples) or start filter actions. Also, apart from representations of the usual atomic types (e.g. strings, integers, floats), pixel object representations (for BLOBs) could also go into the table visualization.

4 Prototype Status and Usability Issues

Figures 1 to 4 are actual screenshots from the running prototype. Table 1 shows exploratory actions and their assigned gestures which have been implemented so far or are under construction at the time of this writing. Others will be added as required.

The tour hopefully made clear that a gesture-based exploration tool for relational data requires a new interaction concept. To cite again Nandi et al. [18]:

> Direct, ad-hoc interaction with databases has typically been performed over console-oriented conversational interfaces using query languages such as SQL. With the rise in popularity of gestural user interfaces and computing devices that use gestures as their exclusive modes of interaction, database query interfaces require a fundamental rethinking to work without keyboards.

The lack of keyboard and mouse makes traditional control structures, like menu bars or the context menu, obsolete and should not be mimicked for touch panel interaction by, say, arbitrary matching of gestures to relational operations (one tap is selection, two taps is projection, ...). At the same time, gesture control requires a data visualization with a lower bound for the size of objects to be manipulated (see the Apple, MS, Android style guides). This doesn't prevent the user from zooming out occasionally to gain an overview, followed by a dive down into details. Similar concepts are known from the OLAP cubes in the data warehousing world [4], where *roll-up* provides an overview, *drill-down* more details, and *slice and dice* (projection) reduces the data space.

While it is definitely too early to make a well substantiated statement concerning the usability of the exploration tool, it is clear that the limited real estate on a tablet screen together with a gesture-based interface is a challenge. In particular, it is not easy to separate gestures intended for the browser, say a vertical swipe in the data area to scroll a longer list, and a vertical drag in the schema to initiate a projection (drop column from view). Starting filter operations will certainly not be possible without additional pop-up dialogs. Cutting out tuples and placing them into a "shopping basket" is currently being implemented and considered useful for import/export, intersection and union operations, including subqueries. A general guideline for gesture-based interfaces can be found in e.g. the book by Wigdor and Wixon [24]. Clearly, our approach also needs a systematic empirical evaluation proving (or disproving) user acceptance and advantages over other data exploration tools, as suggested by all reviewers.

On the technical side, the client performs sufficiently fast, even for larger data collections, and the server side connects without problems to a variety

Table 1. Actions and related gestures (images courtesy *GestureWorks*)

Action	Image	Gesture	Object	Description
Expand view		One-finger-swipe right	Cell, column name	Extend cell, trigger select target schema
Reduce view, abort action		One-finger-swipe left	Cell, column name, selection token	Reduce an extended row, abort an action like select relation
Hide column		Drag down or up	Column name	Drag a column name to hide it
Hide multiple columns		Pinch in	Column names	Pinch more than one column to hide a sequence of columns
Show hidden columns		Hold	Table name	Unhide all hidden columns
Show & hide overview		Three-finger-swipe	On all objects	Swipe right shows ER overview, left hides it
Filter		Hold	Column name	Hold on a column name and a filter dialog with sliders appears
Select relation		Drag and drop	Select token	Drag select token on a target schema
Sort		Swipe vertical	Colum name	Swipe column name down (sort desc) or up (sort asc)
Zoom table		Pinch out	Table	Shows only pinched table (hide all other outer nested tables)
Select rows		Draw rectangle	Rows, cells	Draw a rectangle around rows/cells to select them

of DBMS[11]. To reduce bandwidth in mobile environments, clever caching and pre-fetching algorithms need to be investigated.

As for the look&feel, the visualization is biased towards tables and text. However, hints could have an iconic form indicating, say with a dice or a pixel cloud, how many target tuples to expect. Highlighting selections in the data area is another possibility, similar to the awareness/focus/nimbus techniques of

---

[11] We run MySQL, MS SQL Server, and Oracle at our place and have it up with all of them, as long as foreign key declarations are included in the schema.

Benford and Fahlén [2], e.g. if data exploration takes place as part of a groupware scenario. Using other input channels, say voice or a camera, is another option, but a discussion would be outside the scope of this contribution.

5   Conclusion

A prototype application was presented which allows generic data exploration over relational and other structured sources. The exploration can be started on visualizations of the data (instances) or in the schema area. Foreign key interconnections lead to full (when started in the schema) or partial (on a particular data item) extensions of the link target. The result appears as a set-valued column, thus resembling a nested table view. It is argued that this type of presentation has advantages over graph-based visualizations, at least on the instance level, and is particularly suitable for a gesture-based interface. As mentioned earlier, the tool aims at situations where pure SQL queries are difficult to formulate and a customized, domain-specific interface isn't available. This will often be the case in the intended application scenarios, namely mobile users equipped with a smartphone or tablet, doing ad-hoc trial-and-error searches in the field, say in emergency situations or for maintenance work.

As indicated in the *Introduction*, data and schema exploration by means other than SQL is an old and fruitful research area which has gained new impetus through mobile, touch-based devices. Today, data sources can be very large and if the information is retrieved through several joins, fetching them for a casual browse can be a costly thing. Furthermore, contents are sometimes delivered in a stream-like fashion (infinite scroll), creating a challenge for thin clients when the user scrolls over thousands of tuples without consideration. Quite likely, solutions from the OLAP world concerning materialized views, pre-computed aggregations and heuristics on user behavior could be applied here too.

Acknowledgements. The author would like to thank the reviewers for the valuable suggestions which helped to improve content and structure of this contribution.

References

1. Abouzied, A., Hellerstein, J.M., Silberschatz, A.: Playful query specification with DataPlay. Proc. VLDB Endow. 5(12), 1938–1941 (2012)
2. Benford, S., Fahlén, L.E.: Awareness, focus, and aura: A spatial model of interaction in virtual worlds. In: Salvendy, G., Smith, M.J. (eds.) HCI (2), pp. 693–698. Elsevier (1993)
3. Catarci, T., Costabile, M.F., Levialdi, S., Batini, C.: Visual query systems for databases: A survey. Journal of Visual Languages and Computing 8(2), 215–260 (1997)

4. Chaudhuri, S., Dayal, U.: An overview of data warehousing and OLAP technology. SIGMOD Rec. 26(1), 65–74 (1997)
5. CIDR 2013, Sixth Biennial Conference on Innovative Data Systems Research, Asilomar, CA, USA, January 6-9 (2013), Online Proceedings, http://www.cidrdb.org
6. Danaparamita, J., Gatterbauer, W.: QueryViz: Helping users understand SQL queries and their patterns. In: Ailamaki, A., Amer-Yahia, S., Patel, J.M., Risch, T., Senellart, P., Stoyanovich, J. (eds.) EDBT, pp. 558–561. ACM (2011)
7. Dotan, D., Pinter, R.Y.: HyperFlow: An integrated visual query and dataflow language for end-user information analysis. In: VL/HCC, pp. 27–34. IEEE Computer Society (2005)
8. Drucker, S.M., Fisher, D., Sadana, R., Herron, J., Schraefel, M.: TouchViz: A case study comparing two interfaces for data analytics on tablets. In: Proceedings of the SIGCHI Conference on Human Factors in Computing Systems, CHI 2013, pp. 2301–2310. ACM, New York (2013)
9. Epstein, R.G.: The TableTalk query language. Journal of Visual Languages & Computing 2(2), 115–141 (1991)
10. Fischer, B., Thamm, J., Wegner, L.M., Wilke, S., Zirkelbach, C.: ESCHER's complex objects: A demonstration of simplicity. In: Ioannidis, Y.E., Klas, W. (eds.) VDB. IFIP Conference Proceedings, vol. 126, pp. 175–178. Chapman & Hall (1998)
11. Goldman, R., Widom, J.: DataGuides: Enabling query formulation and optimization in semistructured databases. In: Jarke, M., Carey, M.J., Dittrich, K.R., Lochovsky, F.H., Loucopoulos, P., Jeusfeld, M.A. (eds.) VLDB, pp. 436–445. Morgan Kaufmann (1997)
12. Han, Y., Wang, G., Ji, G., Zhang, P.: Situational data integration with data services and nested table. Service Oriented Computing and Applications 7(2), 129–150 (2013)
13. Heer, J., Card, S.K., Landay, J.A.: prefuse: A toolkit for interactive information visualization. In: Proceedings of the SIGCHI Conference on Human Factors in Computing Systems, pp. 421–430. ACM (2005)
14. Idreos, S., Liarou, E.: dbTouch: Analytics at your fingertips. In: CIDR 2013 [5]
15. Jayapandian, M., Jagadish, H.V.: Automating the design and construction of query forms. IEEE Trans. on Knowl. and Data Eng. 21(10), 1389–1402 (2009)
16. Khoussainova, N., Kwon, Y., Balazinska, M., Suciu, D.: SnipSuggest: Context-aware autocompletion for SQL. Proc. VLDB Endow. 4(1), 22–33 (2010)
17. Nandi, A.: Querying without keyboards. In: CIDR 2013 [5]
18. Nandi, A., Jiang, L., Mandel, M.: Gestural query specification. PVLDB 7(4), 289–300 (2013)
19. Qian, L., LeFevre, K., Jagadish, H.V.: CRIUS: User-friendly database design. Proc. VLDB Endow. 4(2), 81–92 (2010)
20. Reisner, P.: Human factors studies of database query languages: A survey and assessment. ACM Comput. Surv. 13(1), 13–31 (1981)
21. Rontu, M., Korhonen, A., Malmi, L.: System for enhanced exploration and querying. In: Proceedings of the Working Conference on Advanced Visual Interfaces, AVI 2006, pp. 508–511. ACM, New York (2006)
22. SAP AG: Working with BEx Query Designer, http://help.sap.com/saphelp_nw70ehp2/helpdata/

23. Stolte, C., Tang, D., Hanrahan, P.: Polaris: A system for query, analysis, and visualization of multidimensional databases. Commun. ACM 51(11), 75–84 (2008)
24. Wigdor, D., Wixon, D.: Brave NUI World: Designing Natural User Interfaces for Touch and Gesture. Morgan Kaufmann, Burlington (2011)
25. Wong, H.K.T., Kuo, I.: GUIDE: Graphical user interface for database exploration. In: Proceedings of the 8th International Conference on Very Large Data Bases, pp. 22–32. Morgan Kaufmann Publishers Inc., San Francisco (1982)
26. Zloof, M.M.: Query-by-Example: A data base language. IBM Systems Journal 16(4), 324–343 (1977)

Replicated Convergent Data Containers

Tobias Herb and Odej Kao

Technical University Berlin, Germany
{tobias.herb,odej.kao}@tu-berlin.de

Abstract. Managing replicated data in distributed systems that is concurrently accessed by multiple sites is a complex task, because consistency must be ensured. In this paper, we present the Replicated Convergent Data Containers (RCDCs) - a set of distributed data structures that coordinate replicated data and allow for optimistic inserts, updates and deletes in a lock-free, non-blocking fashion. It is crucial that continuous data harmonization among containers takes place over time. This is achieved by a synchronization mechanism that is based on a technique called Operational Transformation (OT) which continously reconciles diverging containers. A generic architecture is placed on top of this underlying synchronization mechanism that allows to realize a multitude of different RCDCs. Two container specializations are presented: (a) the linear container that organizes data in an ordered sequence, (b) the hierarchical container that organizes the data in an n-ary tree.

1 Introduction

Managing data in distributed systems that is concurrently accessed and modified by multiple processes is a complex task, e.g. in a groupware software where multiple clients try to edit the same document. The main problem consists in maintaining the consistency and integrity of the data without loss of performance. A common solution to that challange is to serialize all concurrent write accesses, so that at any time only one process perform its modifications. In order to improve the overall throughput, there exist advanced transactional techniques that allow simultaneous access for non-conflicting modifications. The disadvantages of this approach are despite well-developed techniques the need for continuous access to the remote data storage and the resultant high access latency. We present in this paper an approach for optimistic data synchronization where we pursue the idea of embeddeding and organizing replicated data in abstractions similar to collections that are well known from programming. We call these structures Replicated Convergent Data Containers (RCDCs). The container abstractions offer a common interface where data can be inserted, retrieved, updated and deleted in a lock-free, non-blocking fashion. It is crucial that consistency among the replicas is established and a continuous harmonization takes place over time. This is achieved by a synchronization mechanism that is based on a technique called Operational Transformation (OT). This mechanism continously reconciles diverging container states in background by exchanging and transforming container modification operations. The key requirement that enforces the use of OT

Y. Ait Ameur et al. (Eds.): MEDI 2014, LNCS 8748, pp. 238–249, 2014.

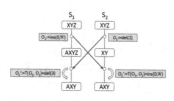

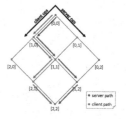

Fig. 1. simple OT scenario

Fig. 2. client/server paths in state-space

is to preserve the internal arrangement of data, which means that not only data itself but also the structure within the container is synchronized. This is relevant in cases where not only the data elements themselves but also the arrangement of the data within the container is important. A generic architecture is placed on top of this underlying synchronization mechanism that allows to realize a multitude of different RCDCs. Two container specializations are presented: (a) the linear container that organizes data in an ordered sequence, (b) the hierarchical container that organizes the data in an n-ary tree.

1.1 Contributions

The contributions of this paper are the following:

- We propose the novel concept of syncable data containers that enable lock-free, non-blocking modifications.
- We provide a simple "topological" classification of different container types. A abstract architecture is derived on the basis of this classification.
- We present the linear container type and its embedding in our overall architecture. In addition, we introduce a stable iterator allowing container traversals while updated.
- Finally we present the hierarchical container organizing items in a tree structure. We show the associated transformations are designed and how to safely delete in hierarchical structures.

2 Preliminaries

This section gives a basic introduction to the theoretical framework of operational transformation (OT) that solve the challenge of consistency maintenance of distributed replicas.

2.1 Operational Transformation

Operational Transformation (OT) is a theoretical framework for concurrency control that enables consistency maintenance of replicated data objects in a

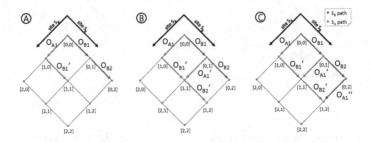

Fig. 3. multistep divergence in client/server processing

distributed environment [13]. Each site is allowed to modify any part at any time of the replica by applying operations on it. The operations are instantaneously executed without being blocked or delayed and stored in a history buffer (HB). After local execution the operation is propagated to the remote sites. Operations arriving from remote sites must be transformed along all concurrent operations that reside in the HB. Concurrent operations in the HB are determined via Lamport- or vector clocks [5,8] attached to the operations. The transformation "includes" the effects of the HB operations in the remote operation. This can be well illustrated by a simple text editing scenario (see figure 1). A character sequence XYZ is replicated on two sites. Site S_1 inserts character A at position 1 (O_1), resulting in local state $AXYZ$. Site S_2 deletes the character Y at position 2 (O_2), resulting in state XZ. The operations are locally executed, stored in the HB and then exchanged, respectively. By applying OT the position-parameter of the incoming operation is adjusted according to the (concurrent) operations in HB. On site S_1 the position of the incoming delete operation is incremented in respect to the insert operation on the lower position. On site S_2 the local delete operation has no influence on the incoming insert operation, because the deletion takes place behind the insert. The essence of keeping the distributed replicas coherent with OT is the application of the transformation function on pairs of concurrent operations that are processed in different order on different sites. This kind of transformation is called *inclusion transformation* (IT) in OT theory [13]. It owns the general signature: $T(O_x, O_y) = \{O'_x, O'_y\}$. The function produces adapted pairs of the input operations, in a sense that the resulting operations take the "effect" of each other into account. It must be noted that transformation function can only be applied on pairs of concurrent operations which originate from the same state. The general interaction between two sites can be well visualized with a so-called two-dimensional state space graph (see figure 2). As operations are processed, the two sites walk down the state space. If they process the operations in the same order, then they take the same path through the state space. If client and server process different operations, then their paths begin to diverge. In the illustrated scenario both sites move to state [1,1] together since both processes first executes the operation of site 1 and thereafter operation of site 2. At state [1,1] they execute different operations, moving to [2,1] and [1,2], respectively. To reach again a common state, both sites transform the remote operation against the buffered operation and executes it. The transformation can be applied because both originate from state [1,1]. To guarantee sound transformations, must convergence property of the function between all possible combinations of available operations must be ensured, the so called TP1-property [3]: $O_x \circ O'_y \equiv O_y \circ O'_x$. If the two sites ($S_A$ and S_B) diverge more than one step, we can not directly apply the transformation function, because these operations have no common origin. The state space diagram in figure 3 depicts such a situation: S_A and S_B begin to diverge at state [0,0], where S_A executes the local operation O_{A1} and S_B executes subsequently O_{B1} and O_{B2} (A). S_A receives the operation O_{B1} and is able to transform it against its local operation O_{A1} to obtain the adapted server operation O'_{B1}. The first transformation step works, because O_{A1} and O_{B1} were generated at same state [0,0]. When S_A receives the second server operation, the transformation of O_{B2} against O_{A1} does not work, because they were generated in different states. At this point the transformed local operation O'_{A1} of the first transformation process $T(O_{A1}, O_{B1}) = \{O'_{A1}, O'_{B1}\}$ is required, because this operation bridges the gap between client state and server state. The remote operation O_{B2} must be transformed against O'_{A1} to retrieve a correct adapted operation O'_{B2} (B). To achieve consistency between S_A and S_B, the site S_B only needs to transform successively the incoming operation O_{A1} against O_{B1}, O_{B2} (resulting O''_{A1}) and execute it (C).

2.2   Control Algorithm

We use a client/server based OT control algorithm that controls transformation (including multistep divergence). This algorithm has both client and server parts which drive the transformation of operations. The presented algorithm is derived from the Jupiter algorithm [9] and follows the descriptions of [14]. The server maintains a unique operation history for all clients. This implies the restriction on incoming client operations, which have to be parented at some point on the server path (in state space). The server only needs to transform all incoming client operations from this point against the concurrent operations lying on the server path. In return, the client needs to keep track of the server state and is responsible for the transformation of the local operations into the server space (insofar known to the client). The tracing of the servers path on the client site is called inferred server path [14]. To keep the inferred server path valid during interaction, every transmitted client operation have to be acknowledged by the server.

3   Replicated Data Containers

This work presents a new kind of data structures which automates data synchronization among multiple processes in a distributed system. We call our data structures syncable data containers. The containers are replicated on all sites in the system. Each site can (optimistically) modify any part at any time of the container. The underlying OT framework hereby ensures convergence among the container instances. In this approach the data synchronization is achieved by a two-party synchronization protocol. Each site synchronizes only with the server. The server serializes and transforms all changes and propagates them further to the other replicas (see control algorithm). The containers with their lock-free, non-blocking property allow highly interactive application scenarios. For example is it relatively easy to build realtime collaborative application on top of these data structures. A key aspect that must be observed is the convergence behavior of these containers. Due to the optimistic modifications and the continous background reconcilation, cannot be guaranteed that all container instances have a consistent view on the data at any time. Our set of data containers provide an eventual consistency model [11] and are therefore not suitable for consistency critical applications. The core abstraction of these container types is similar to the data collections in general purpose programming languages (e.g. Java Collections Framework [1]). The containers manage a group of data objects. These objects are called data items and represent the basic unit that is controlled by the container. A data item itself can be atomic (i.e. primtive type) or any arbitrary composite types. Our data containers stores the data items in an organized way that is amenable to the underlying synchronization mechanism. Two different containers types are presented in this work, the linear container that implements a finite ordered sequence of data items, similar to an abstract list data type [7]. The second type is the hierarchical container that organizes the contained data items in a hierarchical structure.

3.1   Topological Classes

Data collections in programming languages are always specialized according to the way how contained elments are organized, e.g. lists, trees and graphs. The notion of so called topological classes is introduced to make this distinction of the organizational structure more general and abstract. We define three general topological classes. The classification is based on restrictions of the linkage among data items. **(1) Unrestricted:** The unrestricted topology has no limitations on the item linkage and can represent arbitrary graphs. **(2) Hierarchical:** Every data item can have only one predecessor (or parent), but any number of successors (or childs). **(3) Linear:** Data items can have only one predecessor and one successor. The idea behind this classification scheme is to build for each topological class a basic container type that is able to embed and organize the contained data items according to the given topology.

3.2   Architecture

We derive on the basis of the topological classification an abstract architecture that defines the common implementation structure for different data container types. All types are built up of three main components:

Data Model: The data model defines the internal representation of a data container and defines how operations provided by the *Operation Model* interact with this internal representations. There are no specific assumptions or restrictions how a data model has to be designed, i.e. it can contain arbitrary complex logic and representations of the contained data items.

Operation Model: All container types have a common set of basic operations. This set defines the so called **CRUD** operations: A **C**reate operation to create (or add) new data items, a **R**etrieve operation to read/get data items, an **U**pdate operation to update existing data items and a **D**elete operation to remove data items. These basic operations, except Retrieve, are used by the underlying OT system for synchronization. Retrieve is purely local operation and does not change any state of the container or of the contained elements. That is why read operations in general must not be propagated over the network. The signatures of *create, update, delete* operations are container type independent defined as:

$$create(C) : \Gamma \times \Theta \times N \to \Gamma$$

$$update(U) : \Gamma \times \Theta \times \Delta \to \Gamma$$

$$delete(D) : \Gamma \times \Theta \to \Gamma$$

Γ is the type of the container instance on operations are applied. Θ is a container type dependent parameter that determines access to data elements. This access parameter selects the data item on which or next to it (that depends on the operation type) the operation is performed. Containers of different topological classes require therefore different representations for the access parameter type. For example elements in a linear container can be simply accessed by an positional index. For more complex topologies must the access parameter describe a path (see hierarchical container). N is the new data items that is inserted in the container. The parameter Δ occuring in update operation is a map that contains the (attributes) updates that are performed on the selected data item.

Transformation Model: The transformation model contains the set of transformation functions for all possible operations combinations in the operation model. This results in a 3×3 matrix where each element represents a transformation function of two concurrent operations:

$$\begin{bmatrix} T(C_L, C_R) & T(C_L, U_R) & T(C_L, D_R) \\ T(U_L, C_R) & T(U_L, U_R) & T(U_L, D_R) \\ T(D_L, C_R) & T(D_L, U_R) & T(D_L, D_R) \end{bmatrix}$$

L - Local, R - Remote

The transformation of operations is specific to the underlying topology, because the transformation functions adapt the access parameters Θ of the concurrent local and remote operations. The exact properties of such a transformation are discussed in the OT section.

3.3 Conflicting Operations

In some transformation cases occur conflicts, that must be explicitly resolved. A conflicting transformation is a transformation where the effect of one operation loose its original intention or the operation gets completely lost. This situation occurs either if two concurrent operations modify the same element (or rather the operations relate to the same position) or if one operation modifies an element and the other operation deletes the element. For example the concurrent insertion of two data items at the same position lead to a conflict, because it must determined if either the local or the remote insertion have precedence and takes place at the specified position. The matrix below identifies all possible conflict cases for our **CRUD** operation model:

$$
\begin{array}{c c c c}
 & \mathbf{C} & \mathbf{U} & \mathbf{D} \\
\mathbf{C} & \left(\begin{array}{c c c} X & - & - \\ \mathbf{U} & - & X & X \\ \mathbf{D} & - & X & - \end{array} \right)
\end{array}
$$

The solving of conflicts is in general application dependent [11]. In systems where such conflicts ($\Leftrightarrow$ lost updates) rarely happen or the data is not critical predefined mechanisms can be applied. In other scenarios the decision should be passed to an external decider that has more knowledge to manually resolve the conflict. As a result of these considerations the conflict-solver logic must be separated from the transformation model to preserve the freedom to hook in domain specific behavior. All conflict cases of the transformation function are delegated to an external handler where the application specific behavior can be defined. If no domain specific conflict handler is provided, then default strategies are applied. The default strategy combines two simple tactics. First, an operation precedence for the different conflict generating operations is defined. Operations with higher precedence win against operations with lower precedence in conflict situations. The conflict solver replaces the operation with lower priority with no-op (no-operation), for example delete-operations win over update-operations. If two operations of the same precedence are in conflict, a last-writer win strategy (LWW) is applied. LWW means that in the client case the local operation always wins against the incoming remote operation. For the server side in turn means that the incoming operation always wins against 'local' operation. In the case of concurrent update operations targeting the same data item does only exist a conflict if the delta sets (attribute changes) of the update operations are not disjoint: $\Delta(U_L) \cap \Delta(U_R) \neq \varnothing$.

4 Linear Container

The linear container organizes the contained data items in an ordered sequence. It can be regarded as a distributed list collection. The contained data items are managed by positional access and can be created, retrieved, updated and deleted (see **CRUD** operation model) at any time. Beyond this basic functionality a stable iterator [4] exists that allows to iterate over the content while the container is concurrently modified. These stable iterators will be discussed in detail in the next section. Due to the way the container organizes the containing data items by their numerical position, the access parameter Θ of the corresponding operation model is an simple integer index. This index determines the position in the sequence where the operation is applied. The associated linear transformations for this type are well known from collaborative text editing and can be taken for example from [9]. A common way to implement the underlying data model that supports the positional access would be to use internally a linked list or a growable array. This whole attachment of operation model, transformation model and OT algorithm can be seen as a kind of proxy on top of a normal list collection that extends the data structure to distributed, lock-free, non-blocking synchronization.

4.1   Iterators

Another important aspect is the traversal over the container content. Data items are continuously created, updated and deleted by the user or control algorithm process which usually leads to an invalidation of an concurrent iteration process. We propose the idea of so-called transformable cursors that allows iterations over the original container while being modified. A transformable cursor is pointer to a concrete data item consisting in the case of the linear container of a simple index. This index participates in the OT transformations and is transposed according to the local and remote changes. It keeps always the positional reference to the assigned data item as long as this data item is not deleted. If the referenced item is deleted, the cursor points to the up moving successor item. The cursor additionally provides an *advance* function that let the cursor manually move on to the successor item. It must be ensured that transformation call for the cursor and the *advance*-call are well synchronized to keep the cursor position consistent.

5   Hierarchical Container

This section presents the concept of an hierarchical container that organizes data items in a n-ary tree arrangement. Arbitrary many child items can be attached to each item. Items with a linked subtree are called nodes else they are called leafs. The deletion of a node thus deletes all linked sub-items, comparable to the deletion of a folder in a filesystem. The synchronization of delete operations is more complex in the case of the hierarchical topology because concurrent operations may exist that refer to items belonging to the attached subtree of the deleted node. We later introduce the exact deletion algorithm that is used to keep the containers synchronized. The container organizes the hierarchical structure by nested lists. For each item, a ordered collection is maintained that keeps references to the associated child items. Access to a data item is carried out via its root path (path from root to node). Paths are realized as so-called **access vectors**, where each element is an index in the associated child-list reffering to

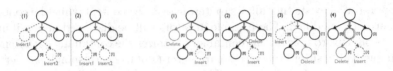

Fig. 4. create-create   **Fig. 5.** create-delete

the subjacent item. Thereby corresponds the number of elements to the tree-level of the selected item. The access parameter Θ of the operation is thus bound to an access vector of type $\mathbb{N}_0^X$ where X is the tree-level of the referenced item. The *create*-operation handles the access vector slightly differently compared to the update- and delete-operation. The elements $a_0...a_{n-1}$ of the access vector $\begin{bmatrix} a_0 & ... & a_{n-1} & a_n \end{bmatrix}^T$ are interpreted as the path from the root to the target item and the last element a_n as position in the target child-list where the new item is inserted. Update and delete interpret all elements $a_0...a_n$ as path to the target item. In the hierarchical container all concurrent operations do not necessarily have to influence each other. Operations become in general **effect-dependent** and need to be transformed, if either an operation has an impact along the access path of a concurrent operation or the operations refer to the same target node. The first case requires the adaption of the relevant index in the access vector of the affected operation. The second case equates to the linear transformation. To capture the relationship of concurrent hierarchical operations formally is the following relation introduced:

Definition 1 *Effect Dependence*
Operations O_X and O_Y are effect dependent $O_X \rightsquigarrow O_Y$ iff:
  (i) *The access path of O_X is part of the access path of O_Y or vice versa or they are equal:*
    (a) $\Theta(O_X) \subset \Theta(O_Y)$
    (b) $\Theta(O_X) \supset \Theta(O_Y)$
    (c) $\Theta(O_X) \equiv \Theta(O_Y)$

  (ii) *If (a) or (b) and the positional reference of the shallow access path is less than or equal to the corresponding component of the deeper access path of the concurrent operation.*

On basis of the effect dependence relation, the possible transformation cases of the underlying operation model are derived. For lack of space we do focus only on the transformations related to the *create*- and *delete*-operations.

The *update*-operation has no impact on access paths and for the accompanying conflict cases the presented conflict handling can be applied. The **create-create** transformation consists of two essential cases, presuming the conditions of effect dependence are fulfilled (see figure 4). *(1)* If a create-operation targets an item at deeper level in the hierarchy than another concurrent create-operation and the target index (the components of the access vector) of the second operation is less than or equal to the index of the first operation, then an index transposition

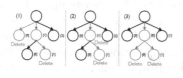

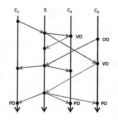

Fig. 6. delete-delete

Fig. 7. bulk-delete scenario

at the corresponding component of first operation must take place to get obtain the correct access vector. *(2)* If both operations target the same node then both indices have to be adapted. For the **create-delete** transformation four different cases are considered (see figure 5). *(1)* The delete-operation removes an item along the access path of the create-operation. *(2)* The opposite case is a create-operation that inserts a new item along the access path of a concurrent delete-operation. *(3)* If a (local) delete operation removes a node that lies on the access path of a (remote) create-operation then the create-operation has no effect and can be transformed to no-operation. *(4)* If both operations target the same node then both indices have to be adapted as in the linear transformation cases. The *delete-create* transformation is symmetric and must not considered further. The **delete-delete** transformation is the last combination that is considered here (see figure 6). *(1)* The delete-operation removes an item along the access path of the second delete-operation. *(2)* If a (local) delete operation removes a node that lies on the access path of a (remote) delete-operation then the delete-operation has no effect and can be transformed to no-operation, because the effect is already included in the upper delete-operation. *(3)* If both operations target the same node then both indices have to be adapted.

5.1   Bulk Deletes

The deletion of a data item in the hierarchical container as well leads to the deletion of all child data items that are contained in the connected subtree, we call this a *bulk delete*. This results in additional problems, because concurrent operations (generated by other processes) may still buzz around in the system that target these deleted items. The problem is solved by lifting the local deletion to a system-wide coordinated process which ensures that no more concurrent operations are in the system that operate on these deleted items. The actual removing of the data items is deffered until all concurrent operations were carried out. Our algorithm handles the *bulk delete* by dividing the process into two phases, the so-called *virtual delete phase* and *physical delete phase*. In the virtual delete phase all data items (the delete target + linked subtree) are marked as deleted and removed form the *index*-mapping, preventing the generation of new operations that target deleted items. All deleted marked items are stored under a unique deletion-key in an additional index structure. The delete-operation is propagated, together with the deletion-key, to all replicated containers. On receipt of the delete-operation are also all data items marked as deleted and removed from the *index*-mapping. Additionally is a vdel-operation (virtual-delete) containing the deletion-key appended to the local transmit buffer of that container. This vdel-operation marks the boundary between all possible concurrent operations that still may target the deleted items and the subsequent operations (following the vdel-operation) that respect the deletion. Concurrent operations that target deleted items do lead to a conflict. Conflicts can be either explicitly handled by the process according to specific application semantics or default strategies can applied (see Conflicts), e.g. operations on deleted items are transformed to *no-operation*. The OT server collects all vdel-operations and acknowledges them all at once. On receipt of the vdel-acknowledge are all as deleted marked items for that deletion-key physically deleted and removed from the delete-index.

6   Related Work

Modern web technologies for data management [2] do support automatic and manual synchronization of data on multiple clients and server-side. But these approaches do not allow optimistic insertions and deletions on ordered sequence of data items. An alternative to the OT approach is *Operation Commutativity (OC)*. In OC does all operations commute when they are concurrent. This approach does not need a explicit concurrency control compared to OT [6]. Shapiro et al. introduced the Commutative Replicated Data Types (CRDTs) [12]. They developed a shared sequential data structure, where concurrent operations can be executed in an arbitrary order on different sites. A further approach presented by Hyun-Gul Roh et al. in [10] is also based on operation commutativity. They developed the so-called Replicated Abstract Data Types (RADTs), a set of replicated linear data structures: replicated fixed-size array (RFAs), replicated hash tables (RHTs) and replicated growable array (RGAs). They exploit the commutativity of the operations with a principle called precedence transitivity (PT). PT allows to derive a unique order of concurrent operations.

7   Conclusion and Outlook

We presented an approach for distributed data containers that coordinate replicated data and allow for optimistic inserts, updates and deletes in a lock-free, non-blocking fashion. The required synchronization mechanism responsible for reconcilation of diverging containers is based on Operational Transformation. We developed a generalized architecture on top of this synchronization mechanism to support structures with different topologies like linear and hierarchical containers. In general can these sort of convergent data containers be used to efficiently build a wide range of applications with realtime collaborative features. The major advantage of our approach is the unified architecture consisting of common components which massively simplifies the development of multiple

RCDCs with different properties and behaviour. An important next step is to extend the containers for offline capability. Changes should be made locally without beeing conntected to the system, when a connection is restored are the local changes reintegrated in the global state. This enables the data to be (asynchronously) available and workable at anytime and at anyplace, which makes it especially interesting for mobile environments.

References

1. The collections framework @MISC, http://docs.oracle.com/javase/7/docs/technotes/guides/collections/
2. Granite data services @MISC, https://www.granitedataservices.com/
3. Ellis, C.A., Gibbs, S.J.: Concurrency control in groupware systems. SIGMOD Rec. 18(2), 399–407 (1989), http://doi.acm.org/10.1145/66926.66963
4. Gamma, E., Helm, R., Johnson, R., Vlissides, J.: Design Patterns: Elements of Reusable Object-oriented Software. Addison-Wesley Longman Publishing Co., Inc., Boston (1995)
5. Lamport, L.: Time, clocks, and the ordering of events in a distributed system. Commun. ACM 21(7), 558–565 (1978), http://doi.acm.org/10.1145/359545.359563
6. Letia, M., Preguiça, N., Shapiro, M.: Consistency without concurrency control in large, dynamic systems. SIGOPS Oper. Syst. Rev. 44(2), 29–34 (2010), http://doi.acm.org/10.1145/1773912.1773921
7. Liskov, B., Zilles, S.: Programming with abstract data types. In: Proceedings of the ACM SIGPLAN Symposium on Very High Level Languages, pp. 50–59. ACM, New York (1974), http://doi.acm.org/10.1145/800233.807045
8. Mattern, F.: Virtual time and global states of distributed systems. In: Parallel and Distributed Algorithms, pp. 215–226. North-Holland (1988)
9. Nichols, D.A., Curtis, P., Dixon, M., Lamping, J.: High-latency, low-bandwidth windowing in the jupiter collaboration system. In: Proceedings of the 8th Annual ACM Symposium on User Interface and Software Technology, UIST 1995, pp. 111–120. ACM, New York (1995), http://doi.acm.org/10.1145/215585.215706
10. Roh, H.G., Jeon, M., Kim, J.S., Lee, J.: Replicated abstract data types: Building blocks for collaborative applications. J. Parallel Distrib. Comput. 71(3), 354–368 (2011), http://dx.doi.org/10.1016/j.jpdc.2010.12.006
11. Saito, Y., Shapiro, M.: Optimistic replication. ACM Comput. Surv. 37(1), 42–81 (2005), http://doi.acm.org/10.1145/1057977.1057980
12. Shapiro, M., Preguiça, N., Baquero, C., Zawirski, M.: Conflict-free replicated data types. In: Défago, X., Petit, F., Villain, V. (eds.) SSS 2011. LNCS, vol. 6976, pp. 386–400. Springer, Heidelberg (2011)
13. Sun, C., Ellis, C.: Operational transformation in real-time group editors: Issues, algorithms, and achievements. In: Proceedings of the 1998 ACM Conference on Computer Supported Cooperative Work, CSCW 1998, pp. 59–68. ACM, New York (1998), http://doi.acm.org/10.1145/289444.289469
14. Wang, D., Mah, A., Lassen, S.: Google wave operational transformation type @MISC (2010), http://wave-protocol.googlecode.com/hg/whitepapers/operational-transform/operational-transform.html

A Methodology and Tool for Rapid Prototyping of Data Warehouses Using Data Mining: Application to Birds Biodiversity

Lucile Sautot[1,2], Sandro Bimonte[3], Ludovic Journaux[4], and Bruno Faivre[1]

[1] Biogéosciences UMR CNRS-uB 6282, University of Burgundy, Dijon, France
l.sautot@agrosupdijon.fr
[2] AgroParisTech, Paris, France
[3] Irstea, TSCF, 9 avenue Blaise Pascal CS20085, 63178 Aubière France
sandro.bimonte@irstea.fr
[4] LE2I, UMR CNRS 6306, University of Burgundy, Dijon, France
ludovic.journaux@agrosupdijon.fr

Abstract. Data Warehouses (DWs) are large repositories of data aimed at supporting the decision-making process by enabling flexible and interactive analyses via OLAP systems. Rapid prototyping of DWs is necessary when OLAP applications are complex. Some work about the integration of Data Mining and OLAP systems has been done to enhance OLAP operators with mined indicators, and/or to define the DW schema. However, to best of our knowledge, prototyping methods for DWs do not support this kind of integration. Then, in this paper we present a new prototyping methodology for DWs, extending [3], where DM methods are used to define the DW schema. We validate our approach on a real data set concerning bird biodiversity.

Keywords: Data Warehouse design, OLAMining, Rapid prototyping.

1 Introduction

Data Warehouses (DWs) are huge data repositories aimed at supporting the decision-making process by enabling flexible and interactive analysis on data [10].

A distinction is made on DW design methodologies depending on the role given to user requirements [10,16]: in requirement-driven approaches, a conceptual schema of the DW is designed starting from the user requirements; in source-driven approaches, a conceptual schema is (semi-automatically) derived starting from the schemata of the data sources that will be integrated in the DW; in mixed approaches, the two processes are carried out in parallel. Rapid prototyping of DW is crucial when dealing with complex application and it has been investigated in some work [3,6,9]. In [3], authors presented an agile requirement-driven design methodology and tool, called ProtOLAP. ProtOLAP is based on using DW conceptual models and automatic implementation of DW and OLAP models. Then, decision-makers must manually feed sample data into the prototype, dimension by dimension and level by level for each hierarchy to simulate an ETL process in the context of a requirement-driven

Y. Ait Ameur et al. (Eds.): MEDI 2014, LNCS 8748, pp. 250–257, 2014.

methodology. However, we have noted that feeding DW with sample data can be not a simple task. Furthermore, in some cases, the dimensional data have not a hierarchical structure that can be predefined according to user's requirements.

Some work about the integration of Data Mining (DM) and OLAP systems has been done to enhance OLAP operators with mined indicators [8], and/or to define the DW schema [17,18]. In [8] classical OLAP operators (drill-down and roll-up operations, slicing, dicing, pivoting) are completed by analysis operators based on DM algorithms. [13] presents an OLAP aggregation operator, named OpAC, performing clustering on data with an Agglomerative Hierarchical Clustering. The goal of this new operator is to group facts that are significantly similar. Thus the integration of OLAP and DM can be achieved by enhancing OLAP operators with DM algorithms (i.e. *DM over OLAP*), but DM can be also used in the DW design's physical and conceptual phases (i.e. *OLAP design by DM*). For example, [4,18] uses DM clustering algorithms to define hierarchies, and [12] to define physical models. In the context of conceptual modeling a lot of effort has been done for the DW design. Indeed, several work propose conceptual models for DW using ad-hoc formalism, ER based models or standards such as UML (see [1] for a review). Some works propose conceptual models for DM (e.g. [15]). On the other hand, only [8] presents an integrated framework, based on UML, to define conceptual models for DM algorithms on warehoused data according to the DM over OLAP approach.

Finally, rapid prototyping DW methodologies are based on interactive and iterative multidimensional schemata defined by users [3], where statistical methods [9] are only used to select a subset of data to feed fact and dimensions data. To conclude to best of our knowledge no rapid prototyping methodology for *OLAP design by DM* has been addressed yet.

Thereby, in this paper we present a new prototyping methodology for DWs, extending [3], where DM methods are used to define the DW schema. In particular, (i) we present an extension of the UML profile for spatial DW integrating the Hierarchical Agglomerative Clustering for defining dimension hierarchies [17], we (ii) extend the prototyping methodology and (iii) tool to handle with DM setting, and (iii) we validate our approach on a real data set concerning bird biodiversity.

The paper is organized in the following way. Section 2 describes the case study of the paper; the ProtOLAPMining methodology and its supporting tools are presented in Sections 3 and 4; Section 5 gives some hints to future work and concludes the paper.

2   Motivations

We present an example from an ecological study: a bird census program along the Loire River (France) [5]. This program aims to detect temporal and spatial changes of bird communities. One hundred ninety eight points were located each 5 Km along the river, and at each point birds were numbered using a point count census method: Punctual Abundance Index. Birds have been censused in four occasions during the last 20 years (1990, 1996, 2002 and 2011). Decision-makers of that project are unskilled OLAP users, and then they need DW prototypes to validate their analysis needs in terms of dimensions and facts. However, they identify a numerical value as analysis subject representing the abundance and three dimensions that characterize it: time, space and the species. The dimensions that describe species and time are easy to design. However, the design of the spatial dimension is more complex. Environment has been described around each point in the years chosen for bird census. To explain bird abundances and their variations, abundances were correlated with environmental variables (such as altitude, etc.).

However, environmental variables belong to different categories: continuous, discrete, ordinal and qualitative variables. In this context, the design of a spatial hierarchy is not obvious, because the description of each point along the river consists of a mixed data set, with no evident hierarchical structure (the French administrative division does not make sense). In other terms, this dimension has not a well defined hierarchical schema, but for example a hierarchical clustering algorithm can be used to derive groups.

In this kind of context, the design methodology of such DW should be based on a particular methodology that allows:

1. Include data mining at conceptual level to create the hierarchy schema and instance. Indeed has been widely recognized that conceptual models are useful in complex application to provide a ridge between users and information technology experts [1].
2. The data mining algorithm should:
    1. Generate a strict, onto and covering hierarchy [14] since they are easily handled by all existing OLAP server.
    2. Generate a hierarchy with several levels.
    3. Generate labels for each level and each member of each level, since hierarchical levels represent a semantic concept.
    4. Control the number of levels of the calculated hierarchy since too much levels are not useful in a classical OLAP exploration.
3. Adopt an agile prototyping paradigm [3]: our design tool must offer the possibility to go back to some of the key steps of the design in order to revise the choices made and refine the DW modeling and DM setting.
4. Being a mixed methodology [16]: our methodology should allow decision-makers to define their functional requirements and at the same time analyze existing data sources to be mined during the hierarchy creation process.

3   ProtOLAPMining

In this section we present our methodology (Sec 3.1), the DM algorithm used (Sec 3.2) and the extension of the ICSOLAP profile [2] (Sec 3.3).

3.1   The Methodology

The classical DW development has been extended with agile steps (from 3 to 8), and integrates DM functional requirements in steps 1 and 2, as described in the following (Figure 1):

1. Decision-makers informally define the functional multidimensional needs (i.e. analysis axes and subjects). In our case study, the decision-makers want to analyze the bird abundance according to three analysis axes: time, space and species.
2. Decision-makers informally define the functional data mining needs (i.e. data mining parameters). In particular, the decision-makers choose a variable set for each automatically hierarchical dimension, specify the variable type (qualitative or quantitative) and choose metric and linkage. In our case study, a decision-maker can choose the spatial dimension and three variables: altitude, stream and geology. The altitude is a quantitative variable while the stream and the geology are qualitative variables. The selected variables are qualitative and quantitative, so the metric and the linkage must be adapted. The only metric that we propose for the mixed data set, is the Gower index that is detailed in section 3.2. Several linkage methods are available for mixed data set, so the decision-maker can choose one of them such as the Unweighted Pair Group Method with Arithmetic mean (UPGMA) (c.f. Sec 3.2)
3. Designers create a *conceptual multidimensional-DM schema*, meaning starting from the users' analysis needs defined in step 2. We note *conceptual multidimensional-DM schema* a classical conceptual multidimensional schema enriched with DM methods for hierarchy creation. In our case study, the designers create two classical dimensions (the time and the species dimensions) and a dimension with an automatically generated hierarchy (the spatial dimension) (c.f. Sec 3.3).
4. Decision-makers set a data sample for the DM algorithm.
5. The system automatically creates the DW hierarchy using the DM algorithm with data of step 4 and parameters of step 3.
6. The system automatically create the DBMS and the OLAP server models
7. Decision-makers feed classical dimensions with sample data.
8. Decision-makers explore the DW with an OLAP client. If hierarchy created using the DM algorithm is not suitable go to Step 2. If multidimensional structures (dimensions and facts) are not adapted go to Step 1.
9. Implementing the prototype (ETL and DM running) on all the data set.

Our methodology satisfies the requirements 1, 3 and 4 described in Section 2. Indeed, it allows decision-makers and DW experts to easily define and validate their DW prototypes enriched with DM algorithms for hierarchical design in an incremental way. Let us now describe what DM algorithm we use that satisfies requirement 2 of Section 2.

3.2   The DM Algorithm: Agglomerative Hierarchical Clustering

In the implementation of our methodology we have chosen as DM algorithm the Agglomerative Hierarchical Clustering (AHC). Main steps of this algorithm are: (1) Calculation of distances between individuals; (2) Choice of the two nearest individuals. (3) Aggregation of the two nearest individuals in a cluster. The cluster is considered an individual. (4) Go back to the step 1 and loop while there is more than one individual.

For steps 1 and 3, we need to define a metric in order to measure the distance between individuals (distance) and a method to aggregate individuals in different clusters (linkage). Our data set contains qualitative and quantitative variables (mixed data set). With qualitative variables we cannot define a cluster as the centroïd of these members. In this context, several linkage methods can be used. As it shown in [11], we choose the unweighted average distance (UPGMA), because, without knowledge on the data structure, this linkage appears to be the best summary of the distance between two clusters. The distance between two individuals must mix quantitative and qualitative variables. We suggest measuring the distances between individuals with an index that comes from biology: the Gower similarity index [7].

The calculated hierarchy contains numerous levels with numerous clusters. But the users of AHC do not traditionally use the complete hierarchy. In an OLAP context, we cut the calculated hierarchy according to a desired number of levels.

However, our algorithm is based on an unsupervised clustering algorithm. Thereby this algorithm cannot generate labels for levels or clusters.

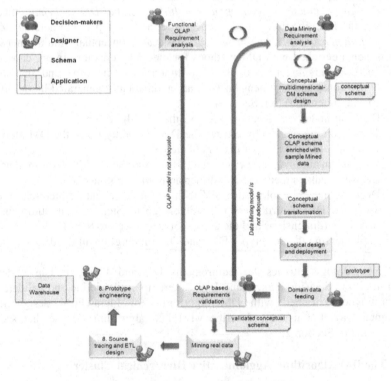

Fig. 1. OLAPMining protyping methodology

3.3   DMICSOLAP UML Profile

As previously described our methodology is based on the formalization of data mining and multidimensional requirements using a conceptual multidimensional-DM model. Then, we extend the ICSOLAP UML profile [3] to include DM parameters (DMICSOLAP UML Profile). Our approach is based on the ProtOLAP methodology where the conceptual multidimensional schema is defined using the UML Profile for spatial data warehouses ICSOLAP. In ICSOLAP model, for each multidimensional element, a stereotype or a tagged value is defined. In particular dimensions represented as packages are composed of hierarchies that hierarchically organize levels. In particular, a level ("AggLevel" stereotype) is a class composed of a set of descriptive attributes ("DescriptiveAttribute" stereotype) and an identifying attribute. "SpatialAggLevel" designs spatial dimension levels whose geometries are represented with geometric attributes stereotyped "LevelGeometry". A fact is represented using the stereotype "Fact", which is a class with attributes that are measures ("NumericalMeasure").

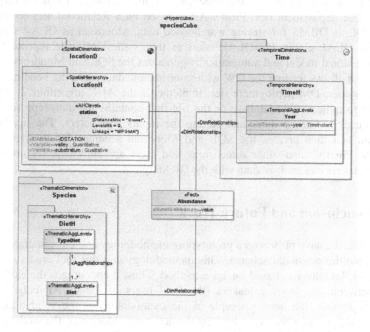

Fig. 2. Conceptual multidimensional-DM schema

Our extension of ICSOLAP defines a new stereotype <<AHClevel>> that extends a level with set of attributes with the <<variable>> stereotype. The <<variable>> stereotype represents the variables used by the AHC algorithm, for example the substratum. A <<Variable>> can be Quantitative or Qualitative. Moreover, we define a tagged value Linkage representing the linkage parameter of the algorithm such as UPGMA as in our case study. In the same way we have defined three tagged values representing the distance used when only quantitative variables are used (DistanceQuantitatve), only qualitative variables (DistanceQualitatve), and DistanceMix when qualitative and quantitative variables are used. In our case study DistanceMix has the value Gower. Finally, the number of levels needed by decision-makers is represented with the LevelsNb tagged value.Figure 2 is shown the conceptual multidimensional-DM model of our case study. We can note three dimensions, where two dimensions are classical dimensions (temporal and thematic) and one dimension is composed of hierarchy LocationH with a <<AHClevel>> level Station. This hierarchy has a most detailed spatial level representing the stations, which are grouped in at most 9 coarser levels. The hierarchical relationships are created using the AHC algorithm using Gower index and WPGMA on data representing the stations, which are clustered using the substratum and the valley variables. The fact represents the abundance.

4   ProtOLAPMining Tool

ProtOLAPMining is the system implementing our methodology. It extends ProtOLAP with the DM deployment tier. ProtOLAP is based on a Relational architecture with PostgreSQL as DBMS for storing warehoused data, Mondrian as OLAP server and JRubik as OLAP client. ProtOLAP takes as inputs the UML file representing the multidimensional model and automatically generates the SQL and Mondrian schemas. Moreover, it allows feeding the DW with same sample data using the Feeding tier.

The new tier, DM deployment tier, implements the AHC algorithm. It allows in particular to indicate the database or the file that contains the data representing the <<AHCLevel>> (mined data) and setting the inputs parameters. The tier runs the algorithm, and then creates the SQL and Mondrian schemes for the new created hierarchy. Finally, also other dimensions and facts are automatically created and decision-makers can analyze data with the OLAP client.

5   Conclusion and Future Work

In this work, we have presented a prototyping methodology and the associated tool, to design a multidimensional schema. This methodology and this tool are extensions of [3]. The methodology is based on agile method. Thus, it encourages the exchange of views between the decision-makers (the final users of the OLAP cube) and the designers. In fact, the main principle of the methodology is the validation, by the decisions-makers, of a prototype built by the designers. Moreover, the methodology is augmented with a DM algorithm. Our tool uses a clustering algorithm to create automatically a hierarchy in a dimension of the prototype of OLAP cube. This algorithm is based on AHC and is able to build hierarchy with mixed data, that contain quantitative and qualitative variables.

As future work, we expect to complete our methodology and our tool with other data mining methods. The integration of other data mining methods, as classification algorithm, can offer to the decision-makers and to the designers new strategies to build the most suitable OLAP cube. Moreover, the integration of other algorithms can permit the automation of a greater part of the tool and offer a more efficient tool. In addition, we will evaluate the methodology on a panel of users.

References

1. Abelló, A., Samos, J., Saltor, F.: YAM2: a multidimensional conceptual model extending UML. Information Systems 31(6), 541–567 (2006)
2. Bimonte, S., Boulil, K., Pinet, F., Kang, M.-A.: Design of Complex Spatio-multidimensional Models with the ICSOLAP UML Profile – An Implementation in MagicDraw. In: Proceedings of the 15th International Conference on Enterprise Information Systems (ICEIS), vol. 1, pp. 310–315 (2013)
3. Bimonte, S., Edoh-Alove, E., Nazih, H., Kang, M.-A., Rizzi, S.: ProtOLAP: rapid OLAP prototyping with on-demand data supply. In: Proceedings of the ACM Sixteenth International Workshop on Data Warehousing and OLAP (DOLAP), pp. 61–66 (2013)
4. Favre, C., Bentayeb, F., Boussaid, O.: A knowledge-driven data warehouse model for analysis evolution. Frontiers in Artificial Intelligence and Applications 143, 271–278 (2006)
5. Frochot, B., Eybert, M.C., Journaux, L., Roché, J., Faivre, B.: Nesting birds assemblages along the river Loire: result from a 12 years-study. Alauda 71(2), 179–190 (2003)
6. Golfarelli, M., Rizzi, S.: Data warehouse testing: A prototype-based methodology. Information and Software Technology 53, 1183–1198 (2011)
7. Gower, J.C.: A general coefficient of similarity and some of its properties. Biometrics 27(4), 857–871 (1971)
8. Han, J.: Olap mining: An integration of OLAP with data mining. In: Proceedings of the 7th IFIP, vol. 2, pp. 1–9 (1997)
9. Huynh, T.N., Schiefer, J.: Prototyping Data Warehouse Systems. In: Kambayashi, Y., Winiwarter, W., Arikawa, M. (eds.) DaWaK 2001. LNCS, vol. 2114, pp. 195–207. Springer, Heidelberg (2001)
10. Kimball, R.: The Data Warehouse Toolkit: Practical Techniques for Building Dimensional Data Warehouses. John Wiley (1996) ISBN 0-471-15337-0
11. Kojadinovic, I.: Agglomerative hierarchical clustering of continuous variables based on mutual information. Computational Statistics & Data Analysis 46(2), 269–294 (2004)
12. Mahboubi, H., Darmont, J.: Data mining-based fragmentation of XML data warehouses. In: Proceedings of the ACM Eleventh International Workshop on Data Warehousing and OLAP (DOLAP), pp. 9–16 (2008)
13. Messaoud, R.B., Boussaid, O., Loudcher Rabaséda, S.: A data mining-based OLAP aggregation of complex data: Application on XML documents. International Journal of Data Warehousing and Mining (IJDWM) 2(4), 1–26 (2006)
14. Pedersen, T.B., Jensen, C.S., Dyreson, C.E.: A foundation for capturing and querying complex multidimensional data. Information Systems 26(5), 383–423 (2001)
15. Rizzi, S.: UML-based conceptual modeling of pattern-bases. In: Proceedings of International Workshop on Pattern Representation and Management, PaRMa (2004)
16. Romero, O., Abelló, A.: A Survey of Multidimensional Modeling Methodologies. International Journal of Data Warehousing and Mining 5(2), 1–23 (2009)
17. Sautot, L., Faivre, B., Journaux, L., Molin, P.: The Hierarchical Agglomerative Clustering with Gower Index: a methdology for automatic design of OLAP cube in ecological data processing context. Ecological Informatics (to appear, 2014)
18. Usman, M., Pears, R.: A methodology for integrating and exploiting data mining techniques in the design of data warehouses. In: Proceedings of the 6th International Conference on Advanced Information Management and Service (IMS), pp. 361–367. IEEE (2010)

A Novel Multidimensional Model for the OLAP on Documents: Modeling, Generation and Implementation

Maha Azabou[1], Kaïs Khrouf[1], Jamel Feki[1], Chantal Soulé-Dupuy[2],
and Nathalie Vallès[2]

[1] University of Sfax, Faculty of Economics and Management, Computer Department,
MIR@CL Laboratory, University of Sfax,
Airport Road Km 4, P.O. Box. 1088, 3018 Sfax, Tunisia
`Azabou.Maha@yahoo.fr, Khrouf.Kais@isecs.rnu.tn,`
`Jamel.Feki@fsegs.rnu.tn`
[2] IRIT, University of Toulouse 1 Capitole,
2, Rue du Doyen Gabriel Marty, 31042 Toulouse Cedex 9, France
`{Chantal.Soule-Dupuy, Nathalie.Valles-Parlangeau}@ut-capitole.fr`

Abstract. As the amount of textual information grows explosively in various kinds of business systems, it becomes more and more essential to analyze both structured data and unstructured textual data simultaneously. However information contained in non structured data (documents and so on) is only partially used in business intelligence (BI). Indeed On-Line Analytical Processing (OLAP) cubes which are the main support of BI analysis in decision support systems have focused on structured data. This is the reason why OLAP is being extended to unstructured textual data. In this paper we introduce the innovative "Diamond" multidimensional model that will serve as a basis for semantic OLAP on XML documents and then we describe the meta modeling, generation and implementation of a the *Diamond* multidimensional model.

Keywords: XML Documents, OLAP, *Diamond* multidimensional model.

1 Introduction

With the boom of Internet and the ever increasing business intelligence applications, search and analysis of textual data have attracted broad attention. Several studies have proposed the reuse of On-line Analytical Processing (OLAP) technology on documentary information in order to analyze a set of textual data with their underlying semantic information. However, these studies have shown that most of standard multidimensional models (such as star and snowflake models) have not been designed to manage complex textual data (multi-structural and multi sources data requiring the resolution of semantic ambiguities). In order to overcome this lack and to satisfy the need of dealing with the semantic content of documents, we have introduced a novel multidimensional model dedicated to the OLAP on documents which we called "*diamond* model". This model is able to represent the semantic content of a collection of documents whose structures are homogeneous (same or similar XML schemas or

Y. Ait Ameur et al. (Eds.): MEDI 2014, LNCS 8748, pp. 258–272, 2014.

logical structure for example) but heterogeneous in semantics (semantic structure of each document). This innovative model will guide the design of data marts dedicated to data analysis on collections of documents according to their content and structure. In order to generate automatically this *diamond* multidimensional model, we propose a set of heuristic rules aiming at determining the various components of the model (i.e., fact and dimensions).

This paper is structured as follows. Section 2 presents the related work dealing with the multidimensional modeling of documents. Then, we present in Section 3 the conceptual modeling of *diamond* models. Section 4 describes the Meta model to keep this model in the same referential. Section 5 details the rules and process we propose to generate *diamond* multidimensional models. Section 7 concludes this paper by a review of our proposals and some future work.

2   Related Work

The conventional multidimensional modeling has been proved robust in the case of highly-structured digital data, but inappropriate for the OLAP on documents. In fact, several works have dealt with this issue in order to provide star or snowflake schemas, integrating a content description of textual fragments by term hierarchies, documents hierarchies, term clusters, AP-Dimension (AP stands for A Priori), and contextual dimension.

- Term hierarchies [9] [12] and [11]

[9] proposed a new data cube called Text cube based on the star schema in which a textual dimension is represented by terms hierarchy. This hierarchy specifies the semantic relationships between textual terms extracted from documents, which allows semantic navigation in textual data thanks to two associated operators: pull-up (which generates a term level L_0 from a lower term level L) and push-down (which generates a term level L_0 from a higher term level L). These two operators can define or change a term level, hence helping users in the multi-semantic-level analysis of textual data.

The Topic Cube proposed by [12] is a good example of Text OLAP using a topic dimension based on the star schema which extends the traditional data cube by integrating a hierarchy of topics as an analytical dimension. It is a new cube model using a topic dimension and a text content measure which carries parameters of a probabilistic model that serves to indicate how well the text content matches with the topic. Two kinds of measures are stored in a topic cube cell: word distribution of a topic $p(w_i|topic)$ and topic coverage by documents $p(topic|d_j)$. The topic coverage means the probability that document d_j covers the topic.

Based on Topic Cube and information network analysis, [11] proposed iNextCube (Information Network-Enhanced Text Cube) which integrated the capability of automatic formation of topic hierarchy through information network analysis. It is tedious and error-prone to rely on human experts to specify topic hierarchy, so it is desirable to automatically construct topic hierarchy by information network analysis.

- Term clusters

[13] have proposed a new model called MicroTextClusterCube. The main idea is to speed up on-line analysis of textual cells by doing as much preprocessing as possible. Specifically, they preprocess the documents so that to generate a good number of micro-clusters to compress similar documents. They have suggested to introduce a new analytical measure ($mean_i$, $size_i$) representing respectively the vector of weighted terms and the size of a micro-cluster.

- Document hierarchy

[7] proposed a new model called Cube Index based on a hierarchical description of each document. This hierarchy specifies relationships between words with respect to one document. It is used for the analysis of words in various levels of abstraction (L_i) in a document such as Document (L_5), Paragraph (L_4), Sentence (L_3), Word Pair (L_2) and Word (L_1). Two new operations scroll up (given a level L_i and term v belonging to L_i, the result is a higher level L_{i+1} of document hierarchy) and scroll down (inverse operator of scroll up.) are discussed exclusively for the cube index. It supports term frequency and inverted document frequency to facilitate information retrieval techniques.

- An AP-Dimension

In [3], the authors have proposed a multidimensional model that supports textual information by introducing a textual dimension (AP-dimension) obtained from a semantic structure called AP-Structure. This one is based on the frequent items named AP-sets (a priori sets) obtained by applying the a priori algorithm (a basic algorithm for frequent item set mining and Boolean association rule learning [2]) on textual attributes of a transactional database. This structure represents the hidden meaning behind the text instead of a simple word play.

- A contextual dimension

In [10], the authors have proposed a contextual text cube model called CXT-Cube, associated with contextual dimensions. The fact table includes a new measure for textual data analysis, based on an adapted vector space model to represent textual data. In order to calculate the document terms' weights, [10] have proposed a relevance propagation technique on a concept hierarchy. Also, the authors have provided a new aggregation operator denoted ORank, to aggregate the documents during the analysis process.

More recently, considerable works was directed towards online analytical processing on informational networks and mostly focusing on the Semantic Web data.

- Open Cubes

[5] introduced Open Cubes which focus on the publication of multidimensional cubes on the Semantic Web and they found the limitation of the RDF Data Cube (DC) which can only address statistical data. Their work revolves around informational OLAP aggregations. Furthermore they revisit RDF Data Cube by extending DC's capabilities to support multidimensional levels to build hierarchies and to implement other OLAP operators beside the sole Slice operator offered by DC.

- Tag cloud

In the context of Web 2.0 and OLAP applications, [1] was particularly interested in tag clouds. The principle of a tag cloud provides a visual representation of keywords on a Web site. Generally, words appear in a font size that is greater than that of the words used on the site. The keyword cloud can be viewed as a semantic abstract of the web site. Applied to OLAP, this principle can use a tag cloud to represent a cube where each keyword is a cell and where keyword size depends on the measured value of the fact (cell).This new cube representation makes it possible to use specific tag cloud operations such as sorting keywords according to their size and removing keywords with small sizes. To assist the user in his exploration of the cube, [1] built classes of similar keywords and rearranged the attributes of the dimensions.

These works have been able to manage the textual data semantics. However, after a large analysis of related work, we concluded that the structural aspect has not been taken into account in multidimensional modeling of document collections. As a result, it is impossible to achieve analyses on various structural levels.

Hence, in order to satisfy the need to represent the textual data semantics and to organize it hierarchically, we introduce a new multidimensional model dedicated to the OLAP on documents, called "diamond", allowing us to manage both document structures and the semantics of the textual content. This model includes standard dimensions with factual data (such as date, author, publisher), as well as a dimension for the semantics of the textual fragment contents (such as summary, content, paragraph). Given a set of XML text-centric documents, the main objective of this paper is the automatic generation of a *diamond* Model in order to facilitate the task of the designer. To do so, we suggest a set of heuristic rules which determine the various components of the model.

3   Diamond Multidimensional Model: Modeling

The *diamond* multidimensional model we propose is dedicated to the OLAP on documents. This new *diamond* Model consists of:

- A *fact* which corresponds to a given observation on textual documents (any kind of observation);

- A set of *dimensions* distributed as follows:

— *Standard* dimensions are the axes of analysis; these axes are constituted by the elements of the first level of the documents' structure. For each element, its descendants represent the parameters (organized into hierarchies) or the weak attributes (attached to a parameter to complement it). For example in Figure 1, Id-Movie parameter of D-Movie standard dimension completed by two weak attributes, Title and Summary;
— *Version* dimension of documents concerns the various versions of documents, as well as associated metadata, such as *Author, Date of creation,* and *Description*;
— *Semantic* dimension which is a central dimension; it consists of the following hierarchy: *Concept → Semantic resource. Concept* parameter is connected to textual elements (like *Section, Paragraph*) of documents in order to clarify the semantics of the element in an OLAP analysis. A *semantic resource* may be ontology, taxonomy, thesaurus or any other kind of resource which can be filled and validated owing to semantic web tools and sources[1].

As an example, Figure 1 presents the *Diamond* Model corresponding to the multidimensional modeling of a collection of film Festival descriptions (derived from the description of each film festival structure shown in Figure 2).

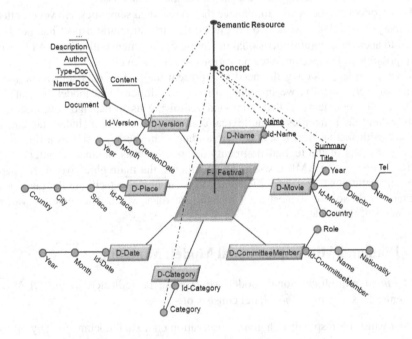

Fig. 1. Diamond multidimensional model for the Festival collection

---

[1] The study and the generation of a semantic dimension has been the subject of previous work.

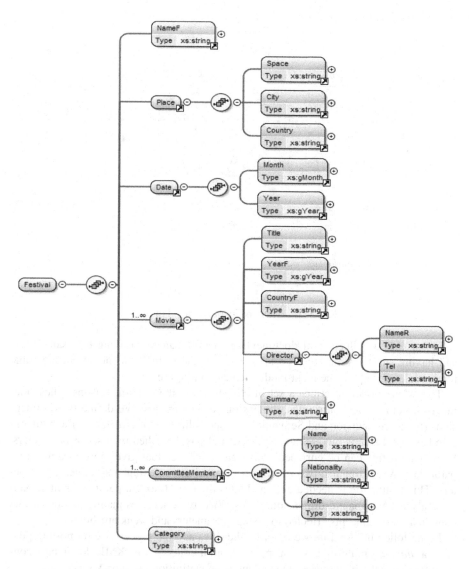

Fig. 2. Festival XSchema (generated with Oxygen tool)

4   Diamond Multidimensional Model: Meta-modeling

In our work, we propose the *Diamond* model to represent any data mart dedicated to a collection of documents.

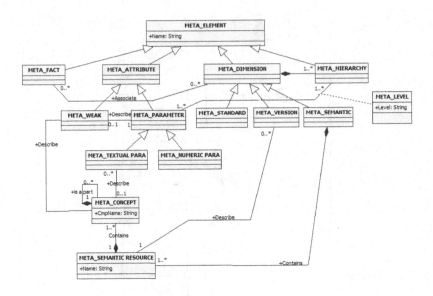

Fig. 3. The Meta model of Diamond models

In our case a collection of documents gathers documents relying to a same topic and having similar structures. To keep together these different models in the same referential, we propose the meta-model depicted in Figure 3.

This Meta model describes a set of elements and their characteristics. These elements are either facts, attributes, dimensions or hierarchies. We define three dimensions (Standard, Version and Semantic) as a specialization of dimension. Each dimension has one or many hierarchies. Each hierarchy is described by a set of parameters. Some parameters can be enriched with weak attributes that give more meaning to a parameter. We distinguish two subclasses of parameters: textual and numeric parameters. This distinction is needed and facilitates the use of textual parameters in semantic analysis. A semantic dimension is described by a set of semantic resources that contain a set of concepts affected to textual parameters and weak attributes.

In the following section, we describe the rules and the process we propose to generate a *diamond* multidimensional model from a collection of XML documents conform to a logical structure (i.e., Document Type Definition DTD or XSchema).

5   Diamond Multidimensional Model: Generation

Our objective is to generate the *diamond* multidimensional model in quasi-automatically, i.e., a way where the user's intervention is limited to the verification, rectification and approval of the generated model. Moreover, the model must include all elements of the DTD or XSchema of the considered collection of documents.

5.1   Identification of the Fact and the Dimensions

The heuristic identification rules of fact and dimensions are described in this section as follows:

Rule 1: The root A of a logical structure (DTD or XSchema) containing at least one leaf becomes a fact named $F\text{-}A$ [6].

Rule 2: Each node d immediate descendant of the root node A of the logical structure becomes a dimension named $D\text{-}d$.

Rule 3: At each dimension D will be affected an artificial identifier (surrogate key) named $Id\text{-}D$.

Example

Let us consider the *Festival XSchema* (cf. Figure 2).

According to *Rule 1*, the fact is *F-Festival*.

Rules 2 and *3*: The first descendants become the following dimensions; *D-Name, D-Place, D-Date, D-Category, D-CommitteeMember, D-Movie*, with the corresponding identifiers *Id-Name, Id-Place, Id-Date, Id-Category, Id-CommitteeMember, Id-Movie*.

Rule 4: For each node transformed into a dimension D that has no descendant, two cases may appear:

- If the D dimension contains distinct values[2] then the name of this dimension will be a weak attribute, directly connected to the identifier of D ($Id\text{-}D$).
- Otherwise, we add a parameter of rank 2 whose name is the one of the D dimension.

The intuition behind this rule is that an element having distinct values cannot be used as an aggregation criterion and, therefore could not be elected as a parameter.

Example: Let us take a part the *Festival XSchema* (cf. Figure 2). According to *Rule 4*, the *Name* element contains distinct values (two different festivals cannot have the same name); therefore the *D-Name* dimension will have *Name* as weak attribute directly connected to the *Id-Name* identifier. Conversely, the *Category* element does not contain distinct values (two different festivals may belong to the same category – long film, short film or horror film for example); then we add to the *D-Category* dimension a parameter of rank 2 named *Category*.

Rule 5: For each dimension D having descendants, the first descendant d is processed as follows:

- If d contains distinct values then d will be a weak attribute, directly connected to the identifier of D ($Id\text{-}D$) because we have already assigned an identifier to the D dimension owing to *Rule 3*.
- Otherwise, we add a parameter of rank 2 having for name d.

---

[2] Two different instances of this element cannot contain the same value.

The objective of this rule is to check if the first descendant d of a dimension D constitutes an identifier (containing only unique values).

Note: We consider that the first descendant element of the dimension D is the most appropriate one to become the identifier. However, the user can intervene to change this choice depending on his research interest.

Example: Let us take a part of the *XSchema* of Figure 2. We notice that the *Space* element in the *D-Place* dimension does not have distinct values (several different festivals may be located at the same place); hence *Space* will be a parameter of rank 2 of the *D-Place* dimension. The same logic applies for *Name* of the sub-tree *CommitteeMember*. Conversely, the *Title* element of the *Movie* sub-tree contains distinct values (we consider here that a film cannot be presented in different festivals); it will represent a weak attribute for *Id-Movie* identifier of the *D-Movie* dimension.

5.2 Identification of the Hierarchies

In order to identify hierarchies, we have to determine the Functional Dependencies (*FD*) between the elements of the document structure. In database, a *FD* from the attribute A to the attribute B, noted $A{\rightarrow}B$, expresses that each value of A is associated to one, and only one, value of B. This choice can be explained by the fact that the element A can play the role of parameter for a specific level and the element B can be a parameter of a more generic level. (Example: City$\rightarrow$ Country).

- Hierarchical organization of parameters

Let A, B and C, be the immediate descendants of a node dimension D. Our objective now is to extract the parameters of rank greater than 1.

Rule 6: Determination of FD
If there is a non-symmetrical FD $A{\rightarrow}B$ (i.e., without $B{\rightarrow}A$) then A and B constitute two consecutive parameters for D, i.e., of rank i and $i+1$ respectively.

Generally, the multidimensional acyclic constraint checks that the graph of parameters is a directed acyclic graph (DAG), i.e., with no cycles.

Rule 7: Avoiding cycles
Eliminate transitive FDs in order to respect the multidimensional cyclic constraint. Let us have the following three FDs: $A{\rightarrow}B$, $B{\rightarrow}C$ and $A{\rightarrow}C$, then the FD $A{\rightarrow}C$ is transitive and has to be eliminated. Then, we get the following hierarchy: $A{\rightarrow}B{\rightarrow}C$.

Rule 8: Determination of ith hierarchy level ($i>1$)
If there is no FD between A and all descendants of the D dimension-node, then A constitutes a parameter of rank 2 for the D dimension (i.e., A is directly connected to the identifier *Id-D* of D).

Example: Let us take the *Place* sub-tree in the *Festival XSchema* (cf. Figure 2).

Rule 6 determines the existence of three non-symmetrical FDs *Space→City*; *Space→Country* and *City→Country*. Applying *Rule 7* allows us to determine the following hierarchy: *Space→City→Country* (cf. Figure 4.a).

Now, let us continue with the *CommitteeMember* sub-tree of the *Festival XSchema* (cf. Figure 2).

Rule 6 proves the existence of a non-symmetrical FD: *Name→Nationality*.

Rule 8: No FD between *Role* and all descendants of *CommitteeMember* (*Name* and *Nationality*) because a member of a committee can be simultaneously president in a given festival and simple member in another festival, Role is then a parameter of rank 2 connected to *Id-CommitteeMember* (cf. Figure 4.b).

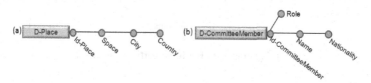

Fig. 4. Dimension D-Place (a) and D-CommitteeMember (b)

- Determination of weak attributes

Some dimension parameters can be characterized by so-called "weak attributes". A weak attribute is a descriptive attribute that gives more meaning to a parameter; it is recommended especially when the parameter values are artificial data (as a Client identifier), and facilitates the understanding of OLAP results.

Rule 9: Case of null- value
Given two attributes A and B, if there are two symmetrical FDs A→B and B→A and, if one of these two attributes can sometimes be null (has the *null* value) then we consider this eventually null attribute as a weak attribute associated to the other element (not containing null values) which becomes a parameter.

Note: This rule considers that an attribute with not null values is more important for OLAP analyses than an attribute containing null values.

Rule 10: Case of not null-valued
Given two attributes A and B, if there are two symmetrical FDs A→B and B→A and, if both attributes do not contain null values then we consider the attribute situated just to the left of the other attribute in the structure (i.e., the previous one in the structure) as the parameter and the right one becomes a weak attribute.

Arbitrary, if A and B contain both null values then the attribute situated at the left hand side of the structure is the parameter and the right one is its weak attribute.

Naturally, the designer will check in order to approve or reject this arbitrary choice with respect to the semantics of the two attributes in the application domain.

Example: Let us consider the *Movie* sub-tree in the *Festival XSchema* (cf. Figure 2).

*Rule 6 i*dentifies the existence of three non-symmetrical FDs: *Title* → *Year*, *Title* → *Country* and *Title* → *Director*.

*Rule 9 denotes the e*xistence of two symmetrical FDs *Title* → *Summary* and *Summary* → *Title*; the *Summary* attribute contains a null value and therefore it is elected as a weak attribute for the *Title* parameter.

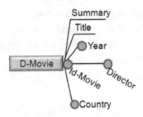

Fig. 5. Dimension D-Movie partially modeled

- **Determination of the temporal dimension**

Generally, the time dimension is included in any multidimensional model [8]. The following rule deals with this dimension.

Rule 11: *Temporal dimension*
The set of nodes of a same level that describe *temporal* components (e.g., month and day that compose a date) constitutes a temporal dimension (e.g. named *D-Date*) where each node component becomes a parameter in the hierarchy.

Example: The application of *Rule 11* on the *Date* sub-tree *Date* in the *Festival XSchema* (Figure 2) generates the following hierarchy.

Fig. 6. Dimension D-Date

Rule 12: Iterate rules from 5 to 11 for each element having descendants in order to determine its parameters and weak attributes.

Example: let us continue with the sub-tree *Movie* of the *Festival XSchema*.

According to Rule 10, there exist two symmetrical FDs *Name* → *Tel* and *Tel* → *Name. Name* and *Tel* do not contain null values; then we consider *Name* as a parameter and *Tel* is its weak attribute.

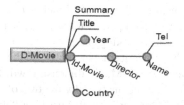

Fig. 7. Dimension D-Movie

Note that the rules we have presented here deal only with the automatic generation of the model (*standard dimensions*) from the logical structure. After that we need to add the *Version dimension* which gathers information about the different versions of each document and the *Semantic dimension* which reflects the semantics of the unstructured textual elements. Those dimensions are introduced in the next section.

5.3   Version and Semantic Dimensions

• Version dimension

Once created, documents are rarely static in time. They can be marked by an evolution in content or structure constituting several versions of the same document. These versions can be considered as different views of the same document. At this level, we add a version dimension called *D-Version,* consisting of an identifier *Id-Version*, the document Contents and two hierarchies:

i)   One temporal hierarchy related to the creation date of the document. This hierarchy is organized as follows: *CreationDate* → *Month* →*Year*;
ii)   One hierarchy describing a set of metadata (physical document *Name*, extension *Type*, *Author*, summary *Description* of the document...).

It should be noted that each version of the document will be linked with a semantic resource [4] (cf. figure 1).

• Semantic dimension

Textual data convey a fairly rich semantics. This semantics is expressed in the *Diamond* Model through the Semantic dimension, referring to a set of semantics resources and concepts describing the content of documents.

The determination of the semantic dimension for a document is evaluated according to the approach described in [4] where authors uses a taxonomy[3] as semantic resource: i) Extraction of significant terms from leaf elements of the document (leaves of the tree structure of the DTD or XSchema), ii) Choice of a taxonomy describing the semantics of a document, iii) Associate concepts of the selected taxonomy to the leaf elements of the document (concepts that best reflect the semantics of the given terms that describe leaf element), and iv) Inference of concepts for non-leaf elements.

---

[3] Taxonomy allows a hierarchical representation between its different concepts.

The Semantic dimension in the *Diamond* Model is represented and integrated as follows: i) connection of the Version parameter with the Semantic resource parameter of the semantic dimension and ii) linking the parameters of the standard dimensions, rich in semantic text, with the Concept parameter of the semantic dimension. For example, the Title attribute of the D-Movie dimension will be connected to the Concept parameter. Thus, we can do the analysis by the title of movies or by related concepts (for example, "money", "power", "Wall Street" or "New York stock exchange" concepts for "The Wolf of Wall Street" Martin Scorcese's film).

6   Contribution Review and Future Work

In this paper, we proposed a new multidimensional model, called *Diamond* Model, dedicated to the design of textual data marts and On-Line Analytical Processing (OLAP) on XML documents according to their content and structure. This model mainly consists of a *fact*, a set of *standard dimensions* (constructed from the structure of a set of documents), a *document Version* dimension and a *Semantic* dimension. The main objective of the Semantic dimension is to switch from the simple text to a semantic level.

We also proposed a specific method to semi-automatically generate a *Diamond* model starting from the XML structure (DTD or XSchema) of the collection of documents we want to analyze .We described in this paper the different steps and rules for the generation of the *Diamond* model. All the proposed rules are automated. When the generation of the *Diamond* model is achieved, the designer (assisted by the decision-maker) verifies and validates the obtained *diamond* multidimensional model. He can rename, delete the multidimensional elements and the links between dimensions, or reorganize the parameters and so on.

To illustrate our generation method, we have applied the steps and rules on a collection of Film Festival descriptions (festivals are described by the Festival Xschema of Figure 2) to obtain the *diamond* model shown in Figure 1.

Furthermore, in order to validate our proposals, we have developed a software prototype supporting our rules and allowing a 3D visualization of the generated *diamond* multidimensional model. The *diamond* model corresponding to the Festival collection is depicted in Figure 8. This prototype has been developed in Java using the Oracle RDBMS 10g extended for the management of XML.

Several perspectives for this work are possible. It would be interesting to define a process of instantiation of these diamond models from the contents of documents and visualization of analysis' results in the cubes' form or multidimensional tables. It is also important to propose new OLAP operators that take into consideration the specificities of this new multidimensional model. These operators will allow facilitating the interpretation of the results of the multidimensional analyses on the textual data, or at the level of documents or classes of documents (according to the aggregates of analysis). We also intend to exploit techniques of text mining to extract knowledge from documents so as to enhance the semantic dimension in the Diamond Model.

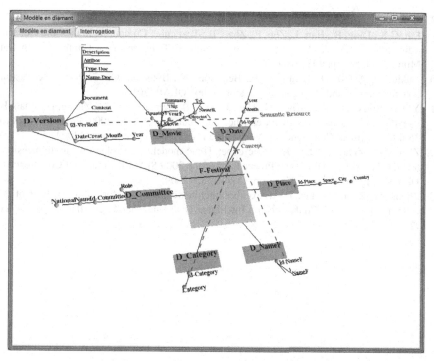

Fig. 8. A 3D visualization of the Diamond multidimensional model automatically generated for the Festival structure of Figure 2

References

1. Aouiche, K., Lemire, D., Godin, R.: Web 2.0 OLAP: From Data Cubes to Tag Clouds. In: Cordeiro, J., Hammoudi, S., Filipe, J. (eds.) WEBIST 2008. LNBIP, vol. 18, pp. 51–64. Springer, Heidelberg (2009)

2. Agrawal, R., Srikant, R.: Fast Algorithms for mining Association rules. In: Proceedings of VLDB, Santiago, Chile (September 1994)

3. Bautista, M., Molina, C., Tejeda, E., Vila, A.: A new multidimensional model with text dimensions: definition and implementation. In: International Conference, IPMU, Dortmund, Germany, pp. 158–167 (2013)

4. Ben Mefteh, S., Khrouf, K., Feki, J., Soulé-Dupuy, C.: Semantic Structure for XML Documents: Structuring and pruning. Journal of Information Organization 3(1), 36–46 (2013)

5. Etcheverry, L., Vaisman, A.A.: Enhancing OLAP Analysis with Web Cubes. In: Simperl, E., Cimiano, P., Polleres, A., Corcho, O., Presutti, V. (eds.) ESWC 2012. LNCS, vol. 7295, pp. 469–483. Springer, Heidelberg (2012)

6. Hachaichi, Y., Feki, J.: An Automatic Method for the Design of Multidimensional Schemas from Object Oriented Databases. International Journal of Information Technology and Decision Making 12(6), 1223–1260 (2013)

7. Janet, B., Reddy, A.V.: Cube Index for Unstructured Text Analysis and Mining. In: Proceedings of the 2011 International Conference on Communication, Computing & Security, ICCC 2011, pp. 397–402 (2011)

8. Kimball, R., Ross, M.: The Data Warehouse Toolkit. Wiley, New York (2003)
9. Lin, C.X., Ding, B., Han, J., Zhu, F., Zhao, B.: Text cube: Computing in measures for multidimensional text database analysis. In: Eighth IEEE International Conference on Data Mining, vol. 54, pp. 905–910 (2008)
10. Oukid, L., Asfari, O., Bentayeb, F., Benblidia, N., Boussaid, O.: CXT-cube: contextual text cube model and aggregation operator for text OLAP (2013)
11. Yu, Y., Lin, C., Sun, Y., Chen, C., Han, J., Liao, B., Wu, T., Zhai, C., Zhang, D., Zhao, B.: iNextCube: Information network-enhanced text cube. In: VLDB 2009: Proceedings of the 35th International Conference on Very Large Data Bases, Lyon, France (2009)
12. Zhang, D., Zhai, C., Han, J.: Topic cube: Topic modeling for olap on multidimensional text databases. In: SDM 2009: Proceedings of the 2009 SIAM International Conference on Data Mining, Sparks, NV, USA, pp. 1124–1135 (2009)
13. Zhang, D., Zhai, C., Han, J.: Mitexcube: microtextcluster cube for online analysis of text cells. In: The NASA Conference on Intelligent Data Understanding (CIDU), pp. 204–218 (2011)

CobWeb Multidimensional Model: From Modeling to Querying

Omar Khrouf, Kaïs Khrouf, and Jamel Feki

MIR@CL Laboratory, University of Sfax,
Airport Road Km 4, P.O. Box 1088 - 3018 Sfax, Tunisia
Omar.khrouf@yahoo.fr, Khrouf.Kais@isecs.rnu.tn,
Jamel.Feki@fsegs.rnu.tn

Abstract. Nowadays, the volume of information handled by enterprises continues to increase. This information can be derived from their operational sources (databases) or also from their manipulated and exchanged documents. The decision-makers are interested by new applications in order to extract and deduce knowledge from information of documents. In this context, we propose a new multidimensional model for the OLAP (On-Line Analytical Processing) of documents, named *CobWeb*, based on a combination of different standard facets extracted from XML documents. In this paper, we describe the conceptual, logical and physical modeling of the *CobWeb* model.

Keywords: XML documents, Facets, Multidimensional model, OR-OLAP.

1   Introduction

The optimal management of documents is an essential factor for the continuity and the success of any company. These documents constitute a knowledge capitalization of their production systems, but they are generally collected from dispersed and heterogeneous sources. For the decision-makers, analyzing the content of these documents represents a current challenge.

In this context, certain works were interested in applying OLAP (On-Line Analytical Processing) on documents; they adopt specific multidimensional models as the galaxy model [12] and diamond model [1], or by resorting the classical multidimensional model; i.e., as the star, snowflake and constellation models ([6] and [7] for data-centric documents; [12] for document-centric documents). However, these studies require the definition of parameters and hierarchies manually.

Other works such as [5], [8] and [11] were interested in the multi-representation of documents by using a set of facets for describing useful aspects of documents. These facets do not only take into consideration the semantic aspect, but also other factors related to the exploitation context of documents in order to better satisfy the user's needs. However, various facets proposed vary according to the application field. Therefore, it would be interesting to define standard facets which permit the representation of documents for any application domain.

Y. Ait Ameur et al. (Eds.): MEDI 2014, LNCS 8748, pp. 273–280, 2014.

In order to give more flexibility to the user in task of OLAP analysis, we propose a new multidimensional model called *CobWeb* model dedicated to the OLAP of documents based on standard facets. Each facet includes a set of data and is considered as a means of expression for the user's needs; that is why we transform every facet into a dimension. This model differs from classic models proposed in the literature by the following specificities: exclusion constraint between dimensions, recursive parameter, duplicated dimension, correlated dimension.

This paper is organized as follows. Section 2 describes the related work dealing with the OLAP on documents. In Section 3, we describe the *CobWeb* multidimensional model focusing on its specificities. We present in the Section 4 the logical model as well as the rules for its derivation. Finally, we describe the physical model and the phase of interrogation by using the automatic generated queries.

2   Related Work

In this section, we overview some of the pertinent works interested in the OLAP of documents. Most works have adopted the three proposed models in the literature for the factual data (star model, snowflake model and constellation model [10]) and suggested approaches or functions for the analysis of textual content.

The authors of [3] propose a modeling in snowflake of multidimensional XML data with data mining methods. However, these studies allow the analysis of complex data, but are not adapted for the analysis of textual data from XML documents. In [13], the authors use the star model for the OLAP of documents. However, it is limited to a simple count of general documents (e-mails, articles, Web pages...) with dimensions from metadata defined by the Dublin Core [4].

The authors of [12] propose a multidimensional model, named Galaxy, adapted for the analysis of XML documents. This model is based on compatible dimensions. However, this work does not take into account the heterogeneity of document structures. In [1], the authors propose a diamond model, which is the star model enriched with a central dimension that attempts to represent the semantics of the document. The parameters of this semantic dimension are linked to parameters of other dimensions. The main disadvantage of this work is the fact that it proposes a model made by a collection of documents with the same structure. [14] proposed a new model based on a star schema titled Topic Cube for widening the traditional cube of data by a hierarchy of themes Topics as a dimension of analysis. This model proposes two probabilistic measures: distribution of a word in a theme p (w_i) and the cover of a theme by documents p $(topic_j)$. However, Topic Cube supports only a predefined set of themes.

As a conclusion, works dealing with the OLAP of documents provide analyzes for documents having the same or similar structures. The purpose of this paper is to propose a multidimensional model for analyzing heterogeneous documents (structure and content). Specifically, we propose to integrate the notion of facet in the OLAP model saw its interest in representing documents from several viewpoints.

3   Conceptual Modeling

A facet describes a useful aspect to the exploitation of one or many documents according to a viewpoint, which allows the user the ability to view the same document or set of documents from multiple views (facets) and he has a more targeted access to information as needed. In our work, we define a set of five facets (*Content* Facet, *Structural* Facet, *Metadata* Facet, *Keyword* Facet and *Semantic* Facet [9]) for the two following reasons: they must be standard, i.e. independent of any specific domain of application, and the automatic extraction of these facets.

Based on these defined facets, we present a new multidimensional model dedicated to the OLAP of documents which we call *CobWeb* model in order to provide more opportunities for the expression of analytic queries and a vision more targeted of the data to decision makers compared to the classical multidimensional models. The main idea consists in transforming every facet into a dimension since those facets may represent a way of expression of user's requirements. Indeed, the different facets combine different information and metadata about the analyzed documents. Besides, we added the dimension *Document* in order to link the information from different facets (represented as dimensions) to their documents. Figure 1 represents the *CobWeb* multidimensional conceptual model.

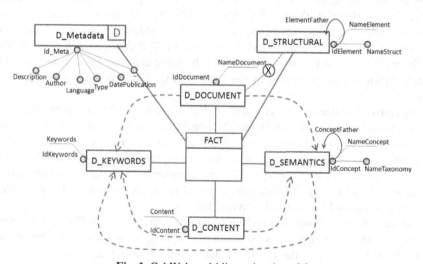

Fig. 1. CobWeb multidimensional model

The *CobWeb* multidimensional model is an extension of the star model; it differs from existing models by the following: The model is a faceless fact model; i.e., the fact of this model has no measures of analysis. Indeed, for a multidimensional query, one dimension (with the corresponding parameters) may become the subject of analysis (the fact). For example, if we want to analyze the number of documents by author, keywords and thematic (*Semantic* dimension). The system then generates the following multidimensional schema.

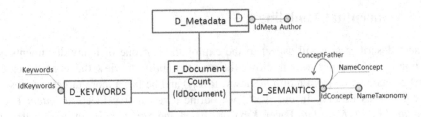

Fig. 2. Example of generated multidimensional model

In the same way, the other dimensions (*Structural, Semantics, Keywords* and *Metadata*) can be converted into facts.

For the dimensions, we propose the following constraints:

— **Exclusion Constraint between Dimensions:** The exclusion constraint requires that a couple of dimensions cannot participate simultaneously in the same OLAP query of documents. In *CobWeb*, the exclusion constraint concerns: the Content dimension and the Structural dimension. Graphically, this constraint is denoted by a circle containing the letter **X** connected to the involved dimensions (cf. Figure 1).

— **Duplicated Dimension:** The multidimensional star model does not permit the use of the same dimension twice in an analysis. Let's suppose that we want to analyze the documents by Authors and Language. This type of query is not possible because these two parameters belong to the same *Metadata* dimension. To solve this problem, we propose a new type of dimension called *duplicated dimension*. This dimension can participate many times in the same analysis. Graphically, a duplicate dimension is symbolized by the letter **D** in the concerned dimension (cf. Figure 1).

— **Recursive Parameter:** In classical multidimensional schemas, parameters and dimension hierarchies are known in advance. In our work, the hierarchical structure of documents may differ from one collection to another and the semantic structure of documents is determinate from taxonomies (semantic resources with the hierarchical representation of concepts). For the representation of these two dimensions, we will use a new type of parameters, named *recursive parameter* that is schematized graphically by a directed loop (cf Figure 1).

— **Correlated Dimension:** The multidimensional operators "Drill-Down" and "Roll-Up" conventionally applies to the parameters belong to the same hierarchy of a dimension. However, in the OLAP of documents, it would be interesting, for the same query, to move between dimensions. For this purpose, we propose the concept of correlated dimensions that are represented by dashed arrows (cf Figure 1).

4   Logical Modeling

In the literature, logical models for OLAP systems have been proposed: ROLAP (Relational OLAP), MOLAP (Multidimensional OLAP) and HOLAP (Hybrid OLAP).

We note that the ROLAP systems are the most used because they are associated to the relational model which is well known by software designers. However, ROLAP systems require that the fact contains a foreign key that references each dimension linked to the fact. Specifically, every value of a foreign key corresponds to a single row of the dimension table. In our works, a fact can concern several keywords; this is the reason why we propose the Object-Relational OLAP (OROLAP) system which allows single valued links (to reference a single row, as a foreign key) as well as multivalued links from the fact table to the dimension table for referencing multiple rows at once. In addition, single valued and multivalued links (as pointers) are more efficient when performing queries instead of foreign keys. The multidimensional conceptual model is transformed into a logical model OROLAP according to the following rules:

— Every dimension d is transformed into a relational table composed a set of columns those represent the parameters and the weak attributes of the hierarchies of d. The primary key of d is defined by the dimension identifier.
— The recursive parameters are transformed by the recursive single valued links.
— The correlation between the dimensions is transformed by the multivalued links if we reference the *keywords* dimension, and by the single valued links for the other cases.
— The fact is transformed into a relational table composed by a multivalued link for the *Keywords* dimension and by the single valued links towards the other dimensions. The primary key of the fact is obtained by the concatenation of attributes representing the single valued and the multivalued links.

The transformation of our *CobWeb* model into a logical model is depicted in Figure 3.

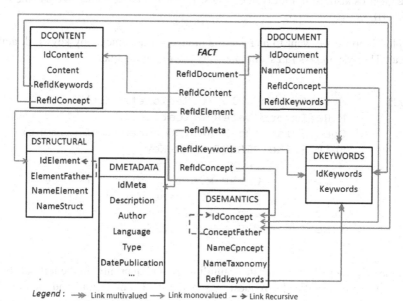

Legend : ⟶» Link multivalued ⟶ Link monovalued – ⟶ Link Recursive

Fig. 3. Logical model OROLAP

5   Physical Modeling and Querying

In order to validate the proposals presented in the two previous sections, we have implemented this logical model under Oracle 10g by using the REF attribute type for single valued links and the Nested Tables for multivalued links (Destined primarily for the *Keywords* dimension).

For the multidimensional querying, the user should specify his query by indicating the fact with its measures and the various dimensions. Thereafter, the system generates automatically the needed queries. We distinguish two types of queries:

- The Queries using only the single valued links (without the *Keywords* dimension). So, we use the implicit join.

Example: Suppose we want to analyze the new publications (i.e. last year of publications) by author, language and thematic (*Semantic* dimension). The system generates automatically the following query:

```
SELECT      F.RefIdeMeta.Author, F.RefIdMeta.Language,
            F.RefIdConcept.NameConcept,
            Max(TO_CHAR(F.RefIdMeta.DatePublication,
            'YYYY'))
FROM        Fait F,
GROUP BY    F.RefIdMeta.Author, F.RefIdMeta.Language,
            F.RefIdConcept.NameConcept
```

- The Queries also using multivalued links (*Keywords* Dimension). We use the operator THE.

Example: Suppose we want to analyze the number of documents by keyword, author and year. The system generates automatically the following query:

```
SELECT      Nt.refmct.motcle, F.RefIdMeta.Author,
            F.RefIdmeta.DatePublication,
            Count(Distinct(F.RefIdDocument.IdDocument))
FROM        Fait F,The(SELECT M.EnsKey
                        FROM FAIT M
                        WHERE M.RefIdContenu.IdContenu=
                        F.RefIdContenu.IdContenu)Nt
GROUP BY    Nt.refmct.motcle,F.RefIdmeta.Author,
            F.RefIdMetad.DatePublication
```

We have developed a GUI for the multidimensional querying. In the left part of the interface, the user specifies his request by specifying the dimensions and the fact. The right part is devoted to the results of the query as a multidimensional table. Figure 4 shows the results of the previous query in a multidimensional table with the columns and the lines represent the first two dimensions (author and date) and the plans represent the third dimension (Keyword).

The measures are placed in the intersection of a line and a column to a given plan. The symbol * indicates that there is no value for the measure.

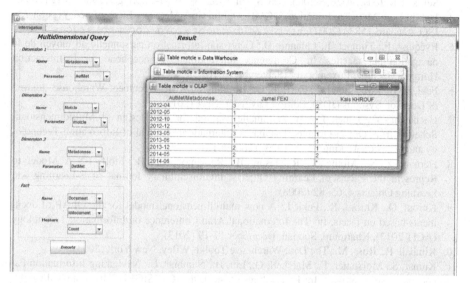

Fig. 4. Graphical multidimensional querying

6   Conclusion

In this paper, we proposed a conceptual, logical and physical modeling of a new multidimensional model dedicated to the On-Line Analytical Processing (OLAP) of XML documents, called *CobWeb* model. We have ensured that this model is generic that is to say, not limited to a predefined set of documents. This model differs from existing models by the following extensions: the flexible fact (every dimension can be transformed into a fact), the exclusion constraint, the recursive parameters, the duplicate dimension and the correlated dimensions.

Several perspectives for this work are possible. It is important to propose new OLAP operators that take into consideration the specificities of this new multidimensional model. We also intend to widen our multidimensional model by the introduction of the collaborative aspect which allows the sharing of the analyses OLAP between the users of the same organization.

References

1. Azabou, M.: Khrouf, k., Feki, J., Vallès, N., Soulé-Dupuy, C.: Modèle multidimensionnel en diamant dédié à l'OLAP sémantique de documents. In: Conférence Magrébine sur les Avancées des Systèmes Décisionnels, Marrakech, Maroc (Mai 2013)

2. Ben Mefteh, S., Khrouf, K., Feki, J., Soulé-Dupuy, C.: Semantic Structure for XML Documents: Structuring and pruning. Journal of Information Organization 3(1), 36–46 (2013)
3. Boussaid, O., Messaoud, R.B., Choquet, R., Anthoard, S.: X-Warehousing: An XML-Based Approach for Warehousing Complex Data. In: Manolopoulos, Y., Pokorný, J., Sellis, T.K. (eds.) ADBIS 2006. LNCS, vol. 4152, pp. 39–54. Springer, Heidelberg (2006)
4. Dublin Core Metadata Initiative (DCMI), Dublin Core Metadata Element Set, Version 1.1, ISO Standard 15836 (2007), http://dublincore.org/documents/dces/
5. Evéquoz, F., Thomet, J., Lalanne, D.: Gérer son information personnelle au moyen de la navigation par facettes. In: Conférence Internationale Francophone sur I 'Interaction Homme-Machine, Luxembourg (September 2010)
6. Feki, J., Ben Messaoud, I., Zurfluh, G.: Building an XML Document Warehouse. Journal of Decision Systems (JDS), Edition Lavoisier, No.1 (2013)
7. Hachaichi, Y., Jamel, F.: An Automatic Method for the Design of Multidimensional Schemas from Object Oriented Databases. International Journal of Information Technology and Decision Making 12(6), 1223–1260 (2013)
8. Hernandez, N., Mothe, J., Ralalason, B., Ramamonjisoa, B., Stolf, P.: A Model to Represent the Facets of Learning Objects. Interdisciplinary Journal of E-Learning and Learning Objects 4, 65–82 (2008)
9. Khrouf, O., Khrouf, K., Feki, J.: A new multidimensional model for the OLAP of documents based on facets. In: The International Arab Conference on Information Technology (ACIT 2013), Khartoum, Soudan, December 17-19 (2013)
10. Kimball, R., Ross, M.: The Data Warehouse Toolki. Wiley, New York (2003)
11. Kumar, S., Morstatter, F., Marshall, G., Liu, H., Nambiar, U.: Navigating Information Facets on Twitter (NIF-T). In: Proceedings of the 18th ACM SIGKDD International Conference on Knowledge Discovery and Data Mining, Beijing, China (August 2012)
12. Ravat, F., Teste, O., Tournier, R., Zurfluh, G.: Designing and Implementing OLAP Systems from XML Documents. In: Special issue New Trends in Data Warehousing and Data Analysis. Annals of Information Systems, vol. 3, pp. 295–315. Springer (November 2008)
13. Tseng, F.S.C., Chou, A.Y.: The concept of document warehousing for multidimensional modeling of textual-based business intelligence. Decision Support System (DSS) 42(2), 727–744 (2006)
14. Zhang, D., Zhai, C., Han, J.: Topic cube: Topic modeling for olap on multidimensional text databases. In: SDM 2009: Proceedings of the 2009 SIAM International Conference on Data Mining, Sparks, NV, USA, pp. 1124–1135 (2009)

Columnar NoSQL Star Schema Benchmark

Khaled Dehdouh, Omar Boussaid, and Fadila Bentayeb

ERIC Laboratory/ University of Lyon 2
5 avenue Pierre Mendes-France 69676 Bron Cedex, France
{Khaled.Dehdouh,Omar.Boussaid,Fadila.Bentayeb}@univ-lyon2.fr

Abstract. Benchmarking data warehouses is a means to evaluate the performance of systems and the impacts of different technical choices. Developed on relational models which have been for a few years the most used to support classical data warehousing applications such as Star Schema Benchmark (SSB). SSB is designed to measure performance of database products when executing star schema queries. As the volume of data keeps growing, the types of data generated by applications become richer than before. As a result, traditional relational databases are challenged to manage big data. Many IT companies attempt to manage big data challenges using a NoSQL (*Not only SQL*) database, and may use a distributed computing system. NoSQL databases are known to be non-relational, horizontally scalable, distributed. We present in this paper a new benchmark for columnar NoSQL data warehouse, namely CNSSB (Columnar NoSQL Star Schema Benchmark). CNSSB is derived from SSB and allows generating synthetic data and queries set to evaluate column-oriented NoSQL data warehouse. We have implemented CNSSB under HBase column-oriented database management system (DBMS), and apply its charge of queries to evaluate performance between two SQL skins, Phoenix and HQL (*Hive Query Language*). That allowed us to observe a better performance of Phoenix compared to HQL.

Keywords: Data warehouses, columnar databases, decisional benchmark.

1   Introduction

The benchmark databases like TPC-H, TPC-D and SSB are developed on relational model [1] which respect the ACID properties (Atomicity, Consistency, Isolation, Durability) [2] and that have been the most used in recent years to support classical data warehousing applications. Indeed, DBMS relational model are originally designed to support transactional operations then adapted to implement data warehouse [3]. However, traditional relational storage models have shown their limitations in terms of storing and managing big data [4]. The solution appears to be from NoSQL databases that are known to be non-relational, horizontally scalable, distributed and, for the most part, open source. NoSQL databases have sacrificed the ACID properties in favor of system performance and data availability to allow data warehouse architecture to be deployed in the cloud and a high scalability whilst delivering high

Y. Ait Ameur et al. (Eds.): MEDI 2014, LNCS 8748, pp. 281–288, 2014.

performance [5]. In this context, a column-oriented NoSQL database system is a storage model which is highly adapted to data warehouses and online analysis [6][7].

We present in this paper a new benchmark for columnar NoSQL data warehouse, namely CNSSB (Columnar NoSQL Star Schema Benchmark). CNSSB flattened the SSB and denormalizes the fact table to avoid using the join operation between tables, which is prohibitively slow and therefore, typically not supported by the column oriented NoSQL databases. The attributes belonging to the same dimension are grouped into a structure called the column family (CF). This helps to differentiate the attributes representing the dimensions and those representing measures. CNSSB is column-oriented NoSQL data warehouse, and allows generating synthetic data and queries set to evaluate columnar NoSQL DBMS performance. We have implemented CNSSB under HBase[1] column-oriented database management system (DBMS), and applied its charge of queries to evaluate performance between two SQL skins, Phoenix[2] and HQL[3]. That allowed us to observe a better performance of Phoenix compared to HQL. The rest of this paper is organized as follows. Section 2 gives the state of the art on decisional benchmark for evaluating the performances of data warehouses. Section 3 presents an overview of columnar NoSQL databases. Section 4 contains a detailed description of the Columnar NoSQL Star Schema Benchmark. In section 5 we implemented our CNSSB, and conducted experiments in section 6. Finally, we conclude this paper in section 7.

2   State of the Art

The benchmark edited by Transaction Processing Performance Council (TPC) is the most used to evaluate various DBMS performance, and is the efficient means for enterprise to invest in the new systems. TPC-C and TPC-D are the two main benchmarks of TPC to be published, the first is assigned to transactional system (OLTP) and the second is assigned to decisional system (OLAP). TPC-D benchmark [8] appeared in the mid-90s, and exploits a classical product-order-supplier which is relational database schema. TPC-D benchmark was replaced by TPC-H and TPC-R [9] the use of which is different. TPC-H is for ad hoc querying and queries are not known in advance, while TPC-R is for reporting and queries are known in advance. TPC-H and TPC-R are succeeded by TPC-DS, which is more normalized, and represents snowflake model of data warehouse. On the other hand, we can also cite SSB [1] which is a more denormalized model of TPC benchmarks represents a star data warehouse and manages LINEORDER (fact table) according to dimensions, PART, SUPPLIER, CUSTOMER and DATE. All these benchmarks were developed in ROLAP (Relational OLAP) environment, and cannot be implemented into NoSQL DBMS, which is based on non-relational environment.

---

[1] http://hbase.apache.org
[2] http://www.orzota.com/sql-for-hbase
[3] http://hive.apache.org/

3   Columnar NoSQL Database

Columnar databases store data column by column, and it helps in compressing the data greatly, which makes the columnar operations like aggregate functions very fast. This storage technique makes it possible to store values belonging to the same column into a single disk block, and only allows access to columns necessary for the decisional query execution [6]. This benefit can be efficiently exploited in the case of data warehouses and OLAP analysis. Columnar NoSQL database have non-relational data representation logic. The main benefits are their performance and capacity to process big data [10]. Compared to relational databases, the join operation between tables is prohibitively slow (thus, typically not supported) and referential integrity constraint does not exist, consequently column-oriented NoSQL database suggests grouping columns into one table. We can cite HBase and Cassandra[4] DBMS which are Apache project originally developed by Facebook, and BigTable[5] by Google.

However, native (*Application Programming Interface* - API) interfaces of the column-oriented NoSQL DBMS require several, often complex, lines to be written for using data. In order to simplify the handling of data by users, SQL (API) interfaces have been developed and adapted to column-oriented storage. This has led to a significant reduction in the quantity of code that needs to be written. Moreover, the SQL interface offers the option of making improvements to boost the performance of column-oriented NoSQL DBMS. CQL (*Cassandra Query Language*) and Phoenix for Cassandra and HBase respectively, are two examples. These SQL interfaces offer the best way of combining the features of data handling to express a selection of data and apply predicates.

4   Columnar NoSQL Star Schema Benchmark

Columnar NoSQL Star Schema Benchmark (CNSSB) is designed to measure performance of columnar NoSQL data warehouse, and consists of one table with several columns. Unlike the relational model, CNSSB flattened the SSB. The attributes belonging to the same dimension are grouped into a structure called the column family (CF). This helps to differentiate the attributes representing the dimensions and those representing measures. CNSSB is derived from SSB, and manages LINEORDER (fact table) according to dimensions, PART, SUPPLIER, CUSTOMER and DATE. LINEORDER is denormalized and dimension attributes are now grouped in column families. Thus every dimension is represented by column family, and encapsulated into fact table. CNSSB allows generating synthetic data and queries set to evaluate columnar NoSQL DBMS performance.

4.1   Data Model

CNSSB is derived from SSB, and manages LINEORDER (fact table) according to dimensions, PART, SUPPLIER, CUSTOMER and DATE. CNSSB is the result of a

---

[4] http://cassandra.apache.org
[5] http://fr.wikipedia.org/wiki/BigTable

denormalizing process of SSB tables into a single table. We have denormalized fact table LINEORDER, and combined dimension tables PART, SUPPLIER, CUSTOMER and DATE into a single LINEORDER table. This denormalization is standard in warehousing [3]. This simplifies the schema considerably; both for writing queries and computing queries. Thus, queries do not have to perform the join and users writing queries against the schema do not have to express the join in their queries. However, to give a better managing for CNSSB as warehouse, we grouped attribute dimensions into column families. Consequently, CNSSB comprises the following column families CF_CUSTOMER, CF_SUPPLIER, CF_PART and CF_DATE, as dimensions. The denormalization process requires some modification in particularly at key referencing (primary at level dimensions and foreign at the fact table). We merged foreign keys in the fact table Custkey, Suppkey, Partkey and Datekey which were used to ensure correspondence between the fact table and dimension, with the attributes of their dimensions. Thus, Custkey, Suppkey, Partkey and Datekey do not be considered as keys since they cannot uniquely identify all tuple values of the fact table. We decided dropping the Datekey of CF_DATE, which is a surrogate key [3], this attribute would no longer have a role in this model. The complete schema is depicted in figure 1.

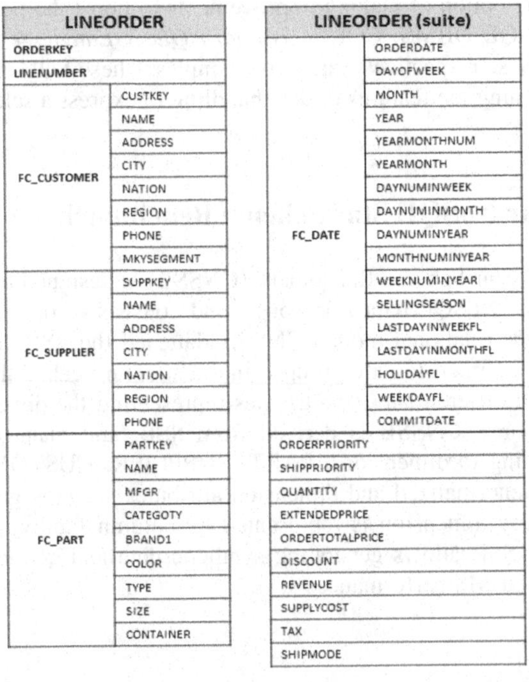

LINEORDER			LINEORDER (suite)	
ORDERKEY				ORDERDATE
LINENUMBER				DAYOFWEEK
	CUSTKEY			MONTH
	NAME			YEAR
	ADDRESS			YEARMONTHNUM
	CITY			YEARMONTH
FC_CUSTOMER	NATION			DAYNUMINWEEK
	REGION			DAYNUMINMONTH
	PHONE		FC_DATE	DAYNUMINYEAR
	MKYSEGMENT			MONTHNUMINYEAR
	SUPPKEY			WEEKNUMINYEAR
	NAME			SELLINGSEASON
	ADDRESS			LASTDAYINWEEKFL
FC_SUPPLIER	CITY			LASTDAYINMONTHFL
	NATION			HOLIDAYFL
	REGION			WEEKDAYFL
	PHONE			COMMITDATE
	PARTKEY		ORDERPRIORITY	
	NAME		SHIPPRIORITY	
	MFGR		QUANTITY	
	CATEGOTY		EXTENDEDPRICE	
FC_PART	BRAND1		ORDERTOTALPRICE	
	COLOR		DISCOUNT	
	TYPE		REVENUE	
	SIZE		SUPPLYCOST	
	CONTAINER		TAX	
			SHIPMODE	

Fig. 1. CNSSB data model

To summarize, CNSSB consists of one large fact table called LINEORDER which contains 53 columns whose primary key consists of two attributes ORDERKEY and LINENUMBER, 41 attributes grouped into four column families CF_CUSTOMER,

CF_SUPPLIER, CF_PART and CF_DATE each representing an analysis axis. As for the ten other attributes of the fact table, they represent the measurements to analyze.

4.2   Data Population

Like in SSB, data in CNSSB is uniformly distributed, and all column families have selectivity hierarchies, which allows better control and manages the row selectivity of queries. For instance, in CF_CUSTOMER, there are dependency hierarchies REGION, NATION and CITY, noted REGION → NATION → CITY and uniform data distribution, this means that, for example ten different values for CITY, twenty five different values for NATION and five different values for REGION will result in a selectivity of 1/10 for each CITY value, (1/10 * 1/25 = 1/250) for each NATION value and (1/250 * 1/5 = 1/1250) for each REGION value.

4.3   CNSSB Queries

We decided to translate SSB queries into our schema. Our motivation is that SSB and CNSSB shared practically all attributes which are differently structured. Thus, the charge of CNSSB queries consists of thirteen decisional queries divided into four flights.

Flight 1 is composed of three queries that have a restriction on one column family, CF_DATE. They aggregate the (sum (extendedprice*discount)) with selectivity on the discount and quantity attributes, for a year in the first query, month in the second query and week for the third query.

Flight 2 is composed of three queries that perform a roll-up, and have a restriction on two column families, CF_DATE and CF_PART, and aggregate the revenue (sum (revenue)). These queries use the dependency hierarchy BRAND1 → CATEGORY → MFGR of CF_PART, and order the results by YEAR and BRAND1.

Flight 3 is composed of four queries that perform a drill down and roll-up on column families CF_CUSTOMER and CF_SUPPLIER, and aggregate the revenue (sum (revenue)), and use the dependency hierarchy CITY → NATION → REGION of both CF_CUSTOMER and CF_SUPPLIER column families

Flight 4 is composed of three queries that perform a drill down and roll-up on column families CF_PART, CF_CUSTOMER and CF_SUPPLIER, and aggregate the profit (sum (revenue - supplycost)), and use the dependency hierarchies BRAND1 → CATEGORY → MFGR of CF_PART column family and CITY → NATION → REGION of both CF_CUSTOMER and CF_SUPPLIER column families.

5   Implementation

We have modified the data generator (DBGEN) of SSB to generate data according to the model CNSSB, and we have developed queries generator (QGEN) to generate the query set associated to CNSSB model. We integrated DBGEN and QGEN to an API which allows generating data and queries for Columnar NoSQL Star Schema Benchmark. DBGEN has a scale factor (SF) as parameter to define the size of the warehouse; it generates a csv file according to the CNSSB model. QGEN generates thirteen decisional queries for the data warehouse CNSSB, and generates randomly the condition values of the query (*Where Clause*) which define restrictions on column families.

6   Experiments

We conducted two experiments. The first evaluates two aspects in data generation: (1) data generated size according to the scale factor and (2) time required to generation of data. The second experiment uses the CNSSB queries to evaluate performance between two SQL skins, Phoenix and HQL (Hive Query Language) under the oriented NoSQL DBMS columns HBase. Noted that HQL is an SQL interface for Hive that is once integrated in HBase, which allows data stored in HBase to be handled using HQL [11].

6.1   Experiment 1

In this section, we evaluate the data generator of CNSSB compared to SSB, and we are interested in the size of data generated by the scale factor, and we note the different execution time for generating different sizes of data.

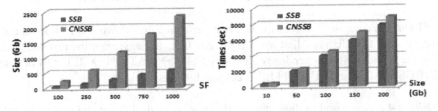

(a) Size of data generated by the scale factor   (b) Execution time for generating different sizes of data

Fig. 2. Performance study of the CNSSB compared to the SSB

We observe that the sizes of data generated by the data generator of CNSSB and SSB in the figure (a) are closely related with the scale factor. When a scale factor equals to 100, DBGEN of SSB generates 56.8 GB and for 1000, it generates 580 GB.

According to these results, the ratio between the scale factor and the size of generated data varies from 0.56 to 0.58. On the other hand, when a scale factor equals 100, the DBGEN of CNSSB generates 235 GB and for 1000, it generates 2360 GB, thus, the ratio between the scale factor and the size of generated data is 2.3 on average. Therefore, with the same scale factor, we note that data generator of CNSSB allows to have larger size compared to SSB, and makes it a good tool which can be used towards the simulation of large warehouses NoSQL category.

Moreover, in the figure (b), we observe that the time required to generate data with data generator of CNSSB is higher than SSB, but still it remains reasonable such as represented by linear function.

6.2   Experiment 2

In this experimentation, we use the CNSSB queries to evaluate performance in terms of execution time, between two SQL skins, Phoenix and HQL under the column-oriented NoSQL DBMS HBase in distributed environment. To conduct our experiment, we used a data sample of 1 TB, which is obtained by data generator of CNSSB, and installed a test environment which is a cluster made up of 15 machines (nodes). Each machine has an intel-Core TMi3-3220 CPU@3.30 GHZ processor with 4GB RAM. These machines operate with the operating system Ubuntu-12.10 and are interconnected by a switched Ethernet 100 Mbps in a local area network. One of these 15 machines is configured to perform the role of *Namenode* in the *HDFS* system, the master and the *Zookeeper* of HBase [12]. However, the other machines are configured to be *HDFS DataNodes* and the HBase *RegionServers*. The results we obtained are shown in the following figure.

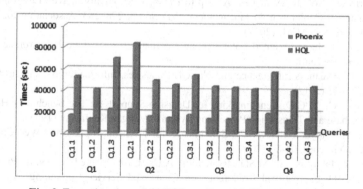

Fig. 3. Execution time of CNSSB queries with Phoenix and HQL

We showed that Phoenix allows better time of decisional queries execution compared to time HQL. Indeed, using the HQL interface requires the migration of HBase data to HIVE. This migration involves exporting data from HBase table to HIVE. This export requires the table to be scanned, which adds time and results in longer execution times. By cons, Phoenix is a skin over HBase. This does not add a new layer; rather it exposes HBase functionality through SQL using an embedded *JDBC driver* that allows clients to run at native HBase speed. The *JDBC driver* compiles SQL into native HBase calls. Therefore, Phoenix offers the opportunity to benefit from the power of HBase. Given the results, we found that querying data in HBase with phoenix is more efficient compared to HQL.

7   Conclusion

We have presented in this paper CNSSB, which is a new benchmark for columnar NoSQL data warehouse. CNSSB is derived from SSB and allows generating synthetic data and queries set to evaluate column-oriented NoSQL data warehouse. We have used CNSSB under HBase column-oriented database management system (DBMS), and applied its charge of queries to evaluate performance between two SQL skins, Phoenix and HQL. That allowed us to observe a better performance of Phoenix compared to HQL.

References

1. O'Neil, P., O'Neil, B., Chen, X.: The Star Schema Benchmark (SSB) (2009), http://www.cs.umb.edu/~poneil/StarSchemaB.PDF
2. Codd, E.: TA Relational Model of Data for Large Shared Data Banks, pp. 377–387. Association for Computing Machinery (ACM) (1970)
3. Kimball, R., Ross, M.: The Data Warehouse Toolkit, 2nd edn. Welly (2002)
4. Leavitt, N.: Will NoSQL databases live up to their promise?, pp. 12–14. IEEE Computer Society (2010)
5. Pokorny, J.: NoSQL Databases: A Step to Database Scalability in Web Environment. In: International Conference on Management of Data, pp. 278–283. Association for Computing Machinery (ACM) (2011)
6. Matei, G.: Column-Oriented Databases, an Alternative for Analytical Environment. Database Systems Journal, 3–16 (2010)
7. Jerzy, D.: Business Intelligence and NoSQL Databases. Information Systems in Management, 25–37 (2012)
8. Ballinger, C.: TPC-D: Benchmarking for Decision Support. In: The Benchmark Handbook for Database and Transaction Processing Systems. Morgan Kaufmann (1993)
9. Poess, M., Floyd, C.: New TPC Benchmarks for Decision Support and Web Commerce. SIGMOD Record, 64–71 (2000)
10. Hecht, R., Jablonski, S.: NoSQL Evaluation: A Use Case Oriented Survey. In: Proceedings of the 2011 International Conference on Cloud and Service Computing, pp. 336–341 (2011)
11. Apache Hive (2014), https://cwiki.apache.org/confluence/display/Hive/HBaseIntegration
12. Hunt, P., Konar, M., Junqueira, F.P., Reed, B.: ZooKeeper: Wait-free Coordination for Internet-scale Systems. In: Proceedings of the 2010 USENIX Conference on USENIX Annual Technical Conference, pp. 11–24 (2010)

Scalable Spectral Clustering
with Weighted PageRank

Dimitrios Rafailidis, Eleni Constantinou, and Yannis Manolopoulos

Department of Informatics, Aristotle University of Thessaloniki,
54124 Thessaloniki, Greece
{draf,econst,manolopo}csd.auth.gr

Abstract. In this paper, we propose an accelerated spectral clustering method, using a landmark selection strategy. According to the weighted PageRank algorithm, the most important nodes of the data affinity graph are selected as landmarks. The selected landmarks are provided to a landmark spectral clustering technique to achieve scalable and accurate clustering. In our experiments with two benchmark face and shape image data sets, we examine several landmark selection strategies for scalable spectral clustering that either ignore or consider the topological properties of the data in the affinity graph. Finally, we show that the proposed method outperforms baseline and accelerated spectral clustering methods, in terms of computational cost and clustering accuracy, respectively.

Keywords: Spectral clustering, sparse coding, databases.

1 Introduction

Spectral Clustering (SC) comprises several goals, by adapting to a wide range of non-Euclidean spaces and detecting non-convex patterns and linearly non-separable clusters. The key idea is to achieve graph partitioning by performing eigendecomposition of the graph Laplacian matrix. Given a set of d-dimensional data points [1] $\{\mathbf{x}_1, \mathbf{x}_2, \ldots, \mathbf{x}_N\} \in \mathbb{R}^d$, SC methods construct an undirected graph $\mathcal{G} = (\mathcal{V}, \mathcal{E})$, represented by its $W \in \mathbb{R}^{n \times n}$ affinity matrix (or the respective adjacency), where $\mathcal{V}$ and $\mathcal{E}$ are the sets of vertices and edges, respectively. The goal is to find a k-way partitioning [2] $\{V_c\}_{c=1}^k$ to minimize a particular objective. SC methods differ in how they define and construct the Laplacian matrix and thus which eigenvectors are selected to represent the graph partitioning. Ulrike von Luxburg's tutorial [15] includes examples of different Laplacians' constructions. For example, Ratio Cut [5] tries to minimize the total cost of the edges crossing the cluster boundaries, normalized by the size of the k clusters, to encourage balanced cluster sizes. Normalized Cut (NCut) [22] uses the same objective criterion as Ratio Cut, normalized by the total degree of each cluster, making thus

---

[1] Following standard notations, we use capital italic letters for matrices (e.g. A), lowercase bold letters for vectors (e.g. $\mathbf{a}$) and calligraphic fonts for sets (e.g. $\mathcal{A}$).

[2] k disjoint data subsets whose union is the whole data set.

Y. Ait Ameur et al. (Eds.): MEDI 2014, LNCS 8748, pp. 289–300, 2014.
© Springer International Publishing Switzerland 2014

the clusters to have similar degrees. The aforementioned baseline SC methods firstly calculate the degree matrix $D = \sum_j W_{ji} \in \mathbb{R}^{n \times n}$, a diagonal matrix whose entries are column (or row, since W is symmetric) sums of W. Then, SC methods use the top-k eigenvectors of the $L = D - W \in \mathbb{R}^{n \times n}$ Laplacian matrix corresponding to the k smallest eigenvalues as the low k-th dimensional representation of the data. Finally, the k-means algorithm is applied to generate the clusters.

SC methods have a number of real-world applications such as image segmentation [26], face recognition [4], feature fusion [12], speech recognition [16], 3D shape retrieval [25] and protein sequences clustering [21]. However, irrespective of the selected approach, there are two important factors for applying a SC method to a real world application: (a) the scalability of the method to large datasets; and (b) the high clustering accuracy.

With respect to the first key factor, baseline SC methods require $O(n^3)$ time to calculate the eigendecomposition of the corresponding $L \in \mathbb{R}^{n \times n}$ Laplacian matrix. The cubic complexity prohibits the direct application of SC for generating clusters in large-scale data sets. Several accelerated methods have been proposed in the literature trying to reduce the initial problem size of n data points by selecting p ($\ll n$) samples/landmarks of the data set. Accelerated methods in their approximations perform the eigendecomposition to a highly reduced $L \in \mathbb{R}^{p \times p}$ Laplacian matrix. Consequently, accelerated methods significantly decrease the high complexity $O(n^3)$ of the baseline SC methods [5,22]. Nevertheless, with respect the clustering accuracy, the accelerated SC methods depend on the sampling strategy that is used to perform the eigendecomposition of the highly reduced matrix.

In this paper, we present an accelerated SC method using a landmark selection strategy based on the weighted PageRank algorithm. In doing so, the most important nodes in the data affinity graph are selected as landmarks. With the help of the selected landmarks and a landmark spectral clustering technique we achieve scalable and accurate clustering. In particular, our contribution is summarized as follows:

- High clustering accuracy is achieved by following the proposed landmark selection strategy of weighted PageRank.
- The complexity of the proposed spectral clustering method is preserved low, by following the landmark selection strategy of weighted PageRank and a landmark-based spectral clustering technique.
- In our experiments with two benchmark face and shape image data sets, several landmark selection strategies are examined for scalable spectral clustering.
- Finally, we show that the proposed method outperforms baseline and accelerated spectral clustering methods, in terms of computational cost and clustering accuracy, respectively.

The rest of the paper is organized as follows, Section 2 summarizes related work. The proposed method is presented in Section 3 and our experimental results on two benchmark image data sets are discussed in Section 4. Finally, we draw the basic conclusions of our study in Section 5.

2 Related Work

Several accelerated SC methods have been proposed in the literature for overcoming the scalability issue. The key idea is to use sampling techniques and consequently to reduce the high complexity of SC in the L Laplacian matrix' eigendecomposition step. The k-means-based approximate SC (KASP) method [29], firstly performs k-means on the data set with a large number cluster number p and then, a baseline SC method is applied on the p cluster centers, with each data point being assigned to the cluster as its nearest center.

In [10], Fowlkes et al. applied the Nyström [20] method to accelerate the eigendecomposition step. Given a random set of p samples, a $W \in \mathbb{R}^{p \times p}$ affinity submatrix is computed and then, the calculated eigenvectors are used to estimate an approximation of the eigenvectors of the original affinity matrix.

In [14], Kulis et al. followed a kernel approach for graph clustering in a unified framework for graph/vector-based approaches, where they showed that there is a connection between weighted kernel k-means [9] and graph clustering minimization criterion objectives. Establishing the aforementioned connection led to algorithms for locally optimizing graph clustering objectives and thus, improving the clustering accuracy of SC methods. However, weighted kernel k-means is prone to problems of poor local minima and sensitive to the initial centroids selection [8].

In [7], Chen and Cai proposed an accelerated SC method with landmark-based representation (LSC). By selecting p landmarks, a $Z \in R^{n \times p}$ affinity submatrix was created, by expressing the pairwise similarities between the p landmarks and the n data points. By using a sparse coding technique, authors significantly reduced the preprocessing cost in $O(p^3 + p^2n)$ time to compute the eigenvectors. Two variations of LSC are presented: (a) the LSC-R method, based on which the selections of the p landmarks is performed randomly; and the LSC-K method, based on which a preprocessing step is added into LSC for performing k-means for the p landmarks selection. As it was experimentally shown, LSC-K outperformed LSC-R in terms of clustering accuracy. However, by performing the k-means method, LSC-K adds a significant preprocessing cost into LSC. Moreover, the topological properties of the nodes/data points in the affinity graph are ignored. In doing so, the landmark selection strategy of LSC-K has limited clustering accuracy.

3 Proposed Method

3.1 Mathematical Formulation

Given (a) a set of d-dimensional data points $\{\mathbf{x}_1, \mathbf{x}_2, \dots, \mathbf{x}_n\} \in \mathbb{R}^d$, denoted by a $X \in R^{d \times n}$ matrix, forming thus the data affinity graph $\mathcal{G}$ of nn closest neighbors; and (b) the p landmarks, the goal is to partition the n points into k discrete clusters, with the boundaries of the k clusters lying afar. According to [7] the goal is to design the $W \in \mathbb{R}^{n \times n}$ affinity matrix as $W = \widehat{Z}^T \widehat{Z}$, where $\widehat{Z} \in \mathbb{R}^{p \times n}$ is the p-th dimensional representation of the n data points, expressed as similarities/affinities of the n data points to the p landmarks. The $X \in R^{d \times n}$ matrix can be approximated as $X \approx UZ$, where the columns of matrix $U \in \mathbb{R}^{d \times p}$ are called basis vectors, i.e. the d-dimensional vectors of the p landmarks. Therefore, the goal is to minimize the approximation error $\min_{U,Z} \|X - UZ\|^2$, where $\| \cdot \|$ denotes the Frobenius norm of a matrix.

3.2   Landmark Selection Based on Weighted PageRank

In the first step of the algorithm, we used the weighted pageRank algorithm to select the p most important nodes in the affinity graph $\mathcal{G}$. According to [28], the weighted PageRank algorithm assigns rank values to nodes according to their importance. This importance is assigned in terms of weight values to incoming and outgoing links, in our case links represent the respective content-based relationships, denoted by $w^{in}_{<a,b>}$ and $w^{out}_{<a,b>}$, respectively. $w^{in}_{<a,b>}$ is the weight of link $< a, b >$. It is calculated on the basis of number of incoming links to node b and the number of incoming links to all reference nodes of node a:

$$w^{in}_{<a,b>} = \frac{i_b}{\sum_{c \in \mathcal{R}_a} i_c} \tag{1}$$

where i_b is the number of incoming links of node b, i_c the number of incoming links of node c and $\mathcal{R}_a$ is the reference node set (content-based nearest neighborhood) of node a. Accordingly, $w^{out}_{<a,b>}$ is the weight of link $< a, b >$. It is calculated on the basis of the number of outgoing links of all the reference nodes of node a:

$$w^{out}_{<a,b>} = \frac{o_b}{\sum_{c \in \mathcal{R}_a} o_c} \tag{2}$$

where o_b is the number of outgoing links of node b and o_c is the number of outgoing links of node c. Then, the weighted PageRank value $wpr(b)$ for a node $b \in \mathcal{V}$ is calculated as follows:

$$wpr(b) = (1 - damp) + damp \sum_{a \in \mathcal{R}(b)} wpr(a) w^{in}_{<a,b>} w^{out}_{<a,b>} \tag{3}$$

where $damp$ is a dampening factor that is usually set to 0.85 [13]. Finally, the p nodes with the highest wpr values are selected as landmarks.

3.3   Sparse Representation of the Affinity Submatrix

Following the sparse coding strategy of [7], based on the Nadaraya-Watson kernel regression [11], for any data point $\mathbf{x}_i$ its $\widehat{\mathbf{x}}_i$ approximation is calculated as:

$$\widehat{\mathbf{x}}_i = \sum_{j=1}^{p} z_{ji} \mathbf{u}_j \tag{4}$$

where $\mathbf{u}_j$ is the j-th column vector of U and z_{ji} is the ji-th element of Z. Then, to create the sparse representation of the Z affinity sparse matrix, the z_{ji} value is set to 0, if $\mathbf{u}_j$ is not among the $r \leq p$ nearest landmarks. Let $U_{\langle i \rangle} \in \mathbb{R}^{d \times r}$ denote a submatrix of U, composed of r nearest landmarks of $\mathbf{x}_i$. Then each element z_{ji} is computed as:

$$z_{ji} = \frac{\Phi(\mathbf{x}_i, \mathbf{u}_j)}{\sum_{j' \in U_{\langle i \rangle}} \Phi(\mathbf{x}_i, \mathbf{u}_{j'})}, \qquad i \in 1 \ldots n \text{ and } j \in U_{\langle i \rangle} \tag{5}$$

where $\Phi(\cdot)$ is a kernel function with bandwidth σ. The Gaussian kernel $\Phi(\mathbf{x}_i, \mathbf{u}_j)$ $= \exp(-\|\mathbf{x}_i - \mathbf{u}_j\|/2\sigma^2)$ is one of the most commonly used, where σ controls the local scale of each data point's neighborhood. Therefore, based on (5), the $Z \in \mathbb{R}^{p \times n}$ sparse representation is calculated. Consequently, for the W affinity matrix it holds that $W = \widehat{Z}^T \widehat{Z}$, where $\widehat{Z} = D^{-1/2} Z$ is the normalized Z by the $D = \sum_j Z_{ji}$ degree matrix.

3.4   Clusters' Generation

Let the Singular Value Decomposition (SVD) of $\widehat{Z} = A \Sigma B^T$, where $\Sigma = diag(\sigma_1, \ldots, \sigma_p)$ and $\sigma_1 \geq \sigma_2 \geq \ldots \geq \sigma_p \geq 0$ are the singular values of $\widehat{Z}$, $A = [\mathbf{a}_1, \ldots, \mathbf{a}_p] \in \mathbb{R}^{p \times p}$ and $\mathbf{a}_i$'s are called left singular vectors, $B = [\mathbf{b}_1, \ldots, \mathbf{b}_p] \in \mathbb{R}^{n \times p}$ and $\mathbf{b}_i$'s are called right singular eigenvectors. It is easy to verify that B are the eigenvectors of matrix $\widehat{Z}^T \widehat{Z}$ and A are the eigenvectors of matrix $\widehat{Z}\widehat{Z}^T$. Since the size of $\widehat{Z}\widehat{Z}^T$ is $p \times p$, we can compute A in $O(p^3)$ and then according to [7] B can be computed as $B = \Sigma^{-1} A^T \widehat{Z}$. The overall time is $O(p^3 + p^2 n)$, which is a significant reduction from $O(n^3)$ since $p \ll n$. To obtain the final k clusters the traditional k-means method is applied to the n right singular eigenvectors, $\mathbf{b}_i$'s, i.e. the rows of B.

4   Experimental Results

4.1   Data Sets

In our experiments we used two high-dimensional benchmark data sets [3], including a shape image data set of the Columbia University Image Library (COIL100

---

[3] All data sets were downloaded in the .mat format, publicly available at
http://www.cad.zju.edu.cn/home/dengcai/Data/data.html

[18]) and a face data set (CMU-PIE [23]) of Carnegie Mellon. COIL100 contains 100 objects, where the images of each object were taken five degrees apart as the object is rotated on a turnable view, generating thus for each object 72 shape images. The size of each image is 32×32 pixels, with 256 grey levels per pixel. Thus, each image is represented by a $d =1024$-dimensional vector. Therefore, COIL100 consists of $n=7,200$ vectors of $d =1,024$ dimensions with $k =100$ clusters, where each cluster represents the shape images of each object. Additionally, CMU-PIE is a database of 41,365 face images of 68 people, each person under 13 different poses, 43 different illumination conditions and with 4 different expressions. We used the face evaluation data set of [3], which consists of $n =11,554$ vectors of $d =1024$ dimensions with 68 clusters, where each cluster represents the face images of each person.

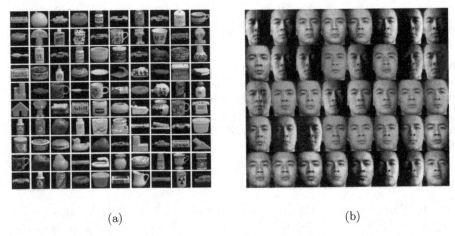

(a)   (b)

Fig. 1. (a) The 100 objects of the COIL100 data set; (b) examples of face images of the CMU-PIE data set

4.2   Evaluation Protocol

In our experiments, the performance was measured in terms of (a) clustering accuracy, (b) Normalized Mutual Information and (c) preprocessing cost.

The clustering accuracy (Acc) [2] is defined as:

$$Acc = \frac{\sum_{i=1}^{n} \delta(c_i, map(c_i'))}{n} \tag{6}$$

where c_i is the true class label and c_i' is the cluster label of $\mathbf{x}_i$ obtained from the clustering algorithm, $\delta(\cdot)$ is the delta function and $map(\cdot)$ is the best mapping function. The $map(\cdot)$ function matches the true class labels and the best mapping is solved by using the Kuhn-Munkres algorithm [17]. The Acc values range from 0 to 1, where a larger Acc indicates a better performance.

Let $\mathcal{C}_{gnd}$ denote the set of clusters obtained from the ground truth and $\mathcal{C}_{alg}$ obtained from a given clustering algorithm. Their Mutual Information $MI(\mathcal{C}_{gnd}, \mathcal{C}_{alg})$ is defined as:

$$MI(\mathcal{C}_{gnd}, \mathcal{C}_{alg}) = \sum_{c_i \in \mathcal{C}_{gnd}, c'_j \in \mathcal{C}_{alg}} p(c_i, c'_j) \log \frac{p(c_i, c'_j)}{p(c_i)p(c'_j)} \tag{7}$$

where $p(c_i)$ and $p(c'_j)$ are the respective probabilities that an arbitrary sample of the data set belongs to the clusters c_i and c_j, respectively. $p(c_i, c'_j)$ is the joint probability that the sample belongs to c_i and c'_j. Then, the Normalized Mutual Information (NMI) [24] is defined as:

$$NMI(\mathcal{C}_{gnd}, \mathcal{C}_{alg}) = \frac{MI(\mathcal{C}_{gnd}, \mathcal{C}_{alg})}{\sqrt{H(\mathcal{C}_{gnd})H(\mathcal{C}_{alg})}} \tag{8}$$

where function $H(\mathcal{X}) = - \sum_{c_i \in \mathcal{X}} p(c_i) \log pc_i$ is the entropy of the $\mathcal{X}$ clusters. It is easy to check that $NMI(\mathcal{C}_{gnd}, \mathcal{C}_{alg})$ ranges from 0 to 1, with $NMI=1$ if the two sets of clusters are identical and $NMI=0$ if the two data sets are independent. In our experimental results, Acc and NMI are expressed as a percentage.

All experiments were performed on a Windows 7 PC with Intel core i7 2700K at 3.50 GHz, 8GB Ram using Matlab 2011a.

4.3   Results

In this first set of experiments, we evaluate the following landmark selection strategies:

- **Random**: nodes are randomly selected as landmarks, irrespective of their topological features in the affinity graph.
- **k-means**: the k-means algorithm is used to determine the landmarks. For p landmarks, $k = p$ centroids of the clusters are selected as landmarks.
- **Degree centrality**: is defined as the number of links incident upon a node. Nodes with the highest degree centrality are selected as landmarks.
- **Betweenness centrality**: is a measure of a node's centrality in a graph [1]. It is equal to the number of shortest paths from all vertices to all others that pass through that node, expressing how each node controls the flow within the graph. Nodes with the highest betweenness centrality are selected as landmarks.
- **PageRank**: is the widely known Google's PageRank measure [13], which estimates the importance of a node in the graph. To consider the weights of the links we used the weighted PageRank algorithm of [28]. Nodes with the highest PageRank values are selected as landmarks, as described in Section 3.2.

With respect to the computational cost, degree centrality has the less complexity, i.e. 0.01 and 0.02 seconds for the COIL100 and CMU-PIE data sets, whereas betweenness centrality requires 52.6 and 222.47 seconds, respectively. The computational cost of betweenness centrality is high, since it requires the calculation of all-to-all paths in the graph. Weighted PageRank needs 0.83 and 1.56 seconds for the COIL100 and CMU-PIE data sets, respectively. The landmark selection strategy using the centroids of the k-means clustering depends on the number of landmarks. Therefore, for $p = 5, 10, 15, 20\%$ landmarks, expressed as a percentage of the data set size n, k-means requires 1.39, 1.61, 3.09 and 3.46 seconds for COIL100 and 3.15, 6.37, 8.78 and 12.06 seconds for the CMU-PIE data set.

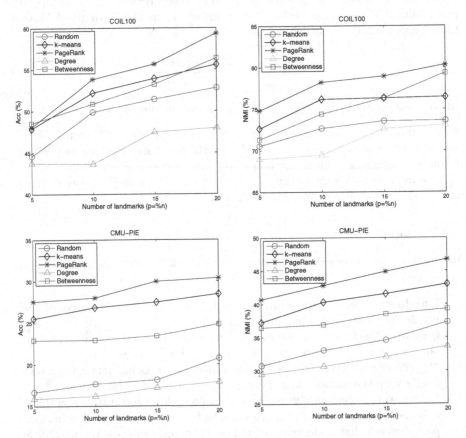

Fig. 2. Landmark selection strategies for Landmark Spectral Clustering (LSC)

In Fig. 2, we present the experimental results of the Landmark Spectral Clustering (LSC) method (Sections 3.3 and 3.4), for the different landmark selection strategies, where PageRank clearly outperforms the competitive strategies. This happens because PageRank identifies the most important nodes of the affinity graph, improving thus the clustering accuracy of LSC. The landmark selection strategy based on the Degree centrality reduces the clustering accuracy, making LSC prone to problems of poor local minima. Therefore, the proposed landmark

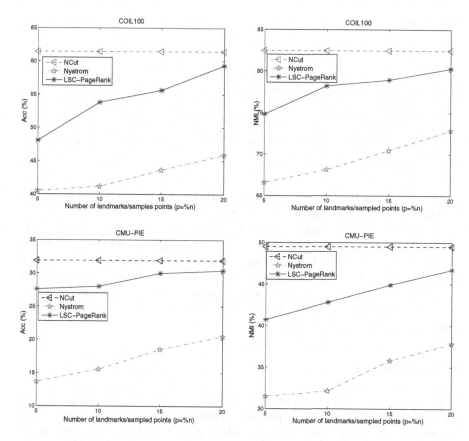

Fig. 3. Comparison of the proposed LSC-PageRank method against (a) the baseline NCut and (b) the accelerated Nyström spectral clustering methods.

selection strategy of weighted PageRank achieves high clustering accuracy, by adding a low preprocessing cost to LSC, in contrast to the rest of landmark selection strategies.

The proposed LSC-PageRank method is compared against the baseline NCut method [4] [22] and the accelerated Nyström spectral clustering method with orthogonalization [5] [10]. According to the experimental results of Fig. 3, LSC-PageRank achieves high clustering accuracy, comparable to the clustering accuracy of the baseline NCut method (in the case of p =20% landmarks), while significantly outperforming the accelerated Nyström method for all number of landmarks/sampled points variations. In Table 1, the computational cost of each examined method is presented. The baseline NCut method has high preprocessing cost $O(n^3)$, due to the eigendecomposition of the Laplacian matrix $L \in \mathbb{R}^{n \times n}$, whereas the accelerated Nyström method and the proposed

---

[4] http://vision.ucsd.edu/~sagarwal/clustering.html
[5] alumni.cs.ucsb.edu/~wychen/sc.html

Table 1. CPU-time (sec) of the baseline NCut, the proposed LSC-PageRank and the accelerated Nyström spectral clustering methods.

COIL100				CMU-PIE		
	NCut	LSC-PageRank	Nyström	NCut	LSC-PageRank	Nyström
$p = 5\%$	361.69	3.99	2.05	1,388.1	5.55	4.16
$p = 10\%$	361.69	4.99	5.38	1,388.1	6.99	17.14
$p = 15\%$	361.69	5.28	13.43	1,388.1	7.66	50.57
$p = 20\%$	361.69	6.54	28.45	1,388.1	9.08	115.27

LSC-PageRank method have a low computational overhead, by performing the eigendecomposition to a highly reduced matrix.

Summarizing, the proposed landmark selection strategy of weighted PageRank improves the clustering accuracy of LSC, by adding a low computational cost, in contrast to the rest of selection strategies that either ignore or consider the topological features of the nodes in the affinity graph. Additionally, the proposed LSC-PageRank method significantly outperforms the baseline NCut and the accelerated Nyström spectral clustering, in terms of preprocessing cost and clustering accuracy, respectively.

5   Conclusion

In this paper we presented an efficient method for accurate and scalable spectral clustering. In particular, we propose a landmark selection strategy based on the weighted PageRank algorithm for selecting the most representative nodes in the data affinity graph. As we experimentally showed, the proposed method outperforms state-of-the-art landmark selection strategies, that either ignore or consider the topological properties of the nodes in the affinity graph. Finally, by following a landmark spectral clustering method we showed that the proposed method significantly outperforms competitive methods of baseline and accelerated spectral clustering, in terms of preprocessing cost and clustering accuracy, respectively.

In real-world applications continuously and efficiently updates are required, over the data sets evolution. Recently, several incremental strategies [19] have been proposed in the literature, able to handle not only insertion/deletion of data points but also similarity changes between existing points. In our future research we plan to examine the incremental strategy of the proposed method.

Additionally, several semi-supervised spectral clustering methods [8,27] have been proposed in the literature to improve the clustering accuracy, by adding must-link and cannot link constraints to the affinity graph. Nevertheless, irrespective of the final constructed affinity graph, where the constraints have been embedded to, the eigendecomposition of the respective Laplacian matrix $L \in \mathbb{R}^{n \times n}$ is still performed, preserving thus the high complexity of the baseline spectral clustering methods. However, the influence of must-link and cannot link constraints to the affinity graph must be further examined, since the most important nodes may vary, modifying thus the proposed landmark strategy of weighted PageRank.

Finally, modern web databases require a significantly large preprocessing cost for spectral clustering in billions of data. For instance, the work of Chen et al [6] introduced a parallel spectral clustering in distributed systems. Towards this aim, in our future work we plan to design the proposed method for distributed databases.

References

1. Brandes, U.: A faster algorithm for betweenness centrality. Journal of Mathematical Sociology 25(2), 163–177 (2001)
2. Cai, D., He, X., Han, J.: Document clustering using locality preserving indexing. IEEE Transactions on Knowledge and Data 17(12), 1624–1637 (2005)
3. Cai, D., He, X., Han, J.: Efficient kernel discriminant analysis via spectral regression. In: Proceedings of the 7th IEEE International Conference on Data Mining (ICDM), Omaha, NE, pp. 427–432 (2007)
4. Cevikalp, H., Triggs, B.: Face recognition based on image sets. In: Proceedings of the 23rd IEEE Conference on Computer Vision and Pattern Recognition (CVPR), San Francisco, CA (2010)
5. Chan, P., Schlag, M., Zien, J.: Spectral k-way ratio cut partitioning. IEEE Transactions on CAD-Integrated Circuit and Systems 13, 1088–1096 (1994)
6. Chen, W.Y., Song, Y., Bai, H., Lin, C.J., Chang, E.Y.: Parallel spectral clustering in distributed systems. IEEE Transactions on Pattern Analysis and Machine Intelligence 33(3), 568–586 (2011)
7. Chen, X., Chai, D.: Large-Scale spectral clustering with landmark-based representation. In: Proceedings of the 25th AAAI Conference on Artificial Intelligence (AAAI), San Francisco, CA, pp. 313–318 (2011)
8. Chen, W., Feng, G.: Spectral clustering: a semi-supervised approach. Neurocomputing 77, 229–242 (2012)
9. Dhillon, I., Guan, Y., Kulis, B.: Kernel k-means, spectral clustering and normalized cuts. In: Proceedings of the 10th ACM SIGKDD International Conference on Knowledge Discovery and Data Mining (KDD), Seattle, WA, pp. 551–556 (2004)
10. Fowlkes, C., Belongie, S., Chung, F., Malik, J.: Spectral grouping using the nyström method. IEEE Transactions on Pattern Analysis and Machine Intelligence 26 (2004)
11. Härdle, W.: Applied non-parametric regression. Cambridge University Press (1992)
12. Huang, H.-C., Chuang, Y.-Y., Chen, C.S.: Affinity aggregation for spectral clustering. In: Proceedings of the IEEE Conference on Computer Vision and Pattern Recognition (CVPR), Providence, RI, pp. 773–780 (2012)
13. Kleinberg, J.: Authoritative sources in a hyper-linked environment. Journal of the ACM 46(5), 604–632 (1999)
14. Kulis, B., Basu, S., Dhillon, I., Mooney, R.: Semi-supervised graph clustering: a kernel approach. Journal of Machine Learning 74, 1–22 (2009)
15. Luxburg, U.: A tutorial on spectral clustering. Statistics and Computing 17(4), 395–416 (2007)

16. Iso, K.: Speaker clustering using vector quantization and spectral clustering. In: Proceedings of the IEEE International Conference on Acoustics, Speech, and Signal Processing (ICASSP), Dallas, TX, pp. 4986–4989 (2010)
17. Munkres, J.: Algorithms for the assignment and transportation problems. Journal of the Society for Industrial and Applied Mathematics 5(1), 32–38 (1957)
18. Nene, S.A., Nayar, S.K., Murase, H.: Columbia object image library. Department of Computer Science, Columbia University, New York, Technical Report CUCS-005-96 (1996)
19. Ning, H., Xu, W., Chi, Y., Gong, Y., Huang, T.S.: Incremental spectral clustering by efficiently updating the eigen-system. Pattern Recognition 43(1), 113–127 (2010)
20. Nyström, E.J.: Über die praktische Auflösung von Integralgleichungen mit Anwendungen auf Randwertaufgaben. Acta Mathematica 54, 185–204 (1930)
21. Paccanaro, A., Chennubhotla, C., Casbon, J.A., Saqi, M.A.S.: Spectral clustering of protein sequences. In: Proceedings of the International Joint Conference on Neural Networks (IJCNN), Portland, OR, pp. 3083–3088 (2003)
22. Shi, J., Makil, J.: Normalized cuts and image segmentation. IEEE Transactions on Pattern Analysis and Machine Intelligence 22(8), 888–905 (2000)
23. Shim, T., Baker, S.: The CMU pose, illumination and expression database. IEEE Transactions on Pattern Analysis and Machine Intelligence 25(12), 1615–1617 (2003)
24. Strehl, A., Gosh, J.: Cluster ensembles: a knowledge reuse framework for combining multiple partitions. Journal of Machine Learning 3, 583–617 (2002)
25. Tatsuma, A., Aono, M.: Multi-Fourier spectra descriptor and augmentation with spectral clustering for 3D shape retrieval. Visual Computer 25(8), 785–804 (2009)
26. Tung, F., Wong, A., Clausi, D.A.: Enabling scalable spectral clustering for image segmentation. Pattern Recognition 43(12), 4069–4076 (2010)
27. Wagstaff, K., Cardie, C., Rogers, S., Schroedl, S.: Constrained k-means clustering with background knowledge. In: Proceedings of the 18th International Conference on Machine Learning (ICML), Williamstown, MA (2001)
28. Xing, W., Ghorbani, A.: Weighted PageRank algorithm. In: Proceedings of the 2nd Annual Conference on Communication Networks and Services Research (CNSR), Fredericton, Canada, pp. 305–314 (2004)
29. Yan, D., Huang, L., Jordan, M.I.: Fast approximate spectral clustering. In: Proceedings of the 15th ACM SIGKDD International Conference on Knowledge Discovery and Data Mining (KDD), Paris, France (2009)

Efficient Algorithm to Approximate Values with Non-uniform Spreads Inside a Histogram Bucket

Wissem Labbadi and Jalel Akaichi

BESTMOD Lab, ISG of Tunis, Computer Science Department, Bouchoucha,
20 Rue de la Liberté, 2000 Bardo, Tunisia
{wissem.Labbadi,jalel.akaichi}@isg.rnu.tn

Abstract. Most of the histograms, maintained by the actual DBMSs, make the *uniform frequency* assumption and most commonly approximate all frequencies in a bucket by their average. Thus, these histograms require storing the average frequency for each bucket. Hence, the accuracy of any estimation performed using the histogram depends highly on the technique used for approximating values into each bucket. Several approaches for approximating the set of attribute values with in a bucket have been studied in the literature. Some of histograms record every distinct value that appears in each bucket and other ones make crude assumptions about it. The most significant are the *continuous values* assumption, the *uniform spread* assumption and finally, the *point value* assumption. Other existing approaches are based on sampling techniques to approximate values inside a histogram bucket. The problem here is that all the proposed techniques assume that attribute values have equal spreads. Motivated by the inaccuracy of previous approaches in approximating value sets with non uniform spreads and by the significant estimation error that can be reached with the various assumptions, we need to compute d distinct values $v_1, v_2, \ldots, v_d$ that lie between the lowest and highest values in the range of each bucket without making any assumption about the values spreadsheet. For this reason, we propose an efficient algorithm for calculating these d values dynamically as new values are inserted into the attribute. The problem can be returned to calculate values of $(d\text{-}2)$ quantiles; namely, the $1/d\text{-}$, $2/d\text{-}$, ..., $(d\text{-}2)/d$-quantiles, along with the lowest and highest values in the bucket. For each quantile to be estimated, we maintain a set of five markers that are updated after every new value inserted in the attribute. The results of a set of experiments comparing the accuracy of the proposed algorithm to the *uniform spread* assumption using various sets of values, over different types of histograms, show the effectiveness of our technique especially when values have non-equal spreads.

Keywords: quantile, values approximation, bucket, estimation error, algorithm.

1   Introduction

A histogram is maintained to approximate the frequencies of values in the attributes of relations. First, a histogram begins by partitioning the corresponding frequencies into β (≥ 1) buckets in some technique. Then, it approximates the frequencies and

Y. Ait Ameur et al. (Eds.): MEDI 2014, LNCS 8748, pp. 301–312, 2014.
© Springer International Publishing Switzerland 2014

values in each bucket in some succinct fashion. So, the accuracy of the approximations done by a given histogram inside a bucket depends highly on the assumptions employed to determine the approximate values and their corresponding approximate frequencies within this bucket. Several types of histograms have been proposed and evaluated experimentally in terms of their accuracy, including *Equi Width* [1], *Equi Height* [2], *Serial* [3, 4], *Maxdiff* [6], *V-Optimal* [7, 8] and recently *Compressed-V2* [9] which is an improved version of *Compressed* histograms [6]. All these histograms make the *uniform frequency* assumption and approximate all frequencies in each bucket by their average. The basic idea was to represent each bucket by a single summary frequency used to return for each value in the bucket an estimate of its actual frequency. The simplest and most widely used summary technique is the average of bucket frequencies [11]. This assumption requires storage of the number of distinct attribute values in each bucket.

Concerning the approximation of the set of attribute values within a bucket, it exist four different approaches. The most significant are the *continuous values* assumption, where all possible values that lie in the range of the bucket are assumed to be present [5] and the *uniform spread* assumption, under which distinct values are assumed to be placed at equal distances between the lowest and highest values in the bucket range [6]. Another approach is the *point value* assumption which assumes that only one attribute value is present in each bucket. Finally, the technique considered in [7] that record every distinct attribute value that appears in each bucket. Other existing approaches are based on sampling techniques to approximate values inside a histogram bucket.

The problem handled in this paper is the inaccuracy of previous approaches in approximating value sets with non-uniform spreads. That's the uniform spread, continuous values and point value assumptions assume that attribute values have equal spreads. The experimental results shown in [6] indicate that the techniques used in previous histograms can lead to significant estimation errors.

In this paper, motivated by the above issues, we introduce a novel technique for computing approximate values, under which each value of interest is approximated by a specific marker among a list of maintained ones for each value. Finally, we compare empirically the accuracy of our technique and previous ones using a large set of data distributions and range queries. The results of these experiments prove that the proposed technique produces estimates almost as precise as those obtained by the straightforward methods.

2   Approaches to Approximate Values within a Bucket

Four different approaches have been proposed in the literature to approximate values within a bucket of a histogram [5, 2, 7, and 6]. This section discusses the different assumptions that have been considered in these approaches.

2.1   Continuous Values Assumption

The continuous values assumption was proposed in [5] in the context of choosing access paths for queries in a relational database management system. Under this assumption, the value domain is approximated by a continuous distribution in the bucket range [1]. That's all possible values in domain D that lie in the range of the bucket are assumed to be present. When D is an unaccountably infinite set, (e.g., an interval of real numbers), the contribution of a bucket to a range query result size is estimated by linear interpolation. This assumption requires storage of the lowest and highest value in each bucket. Note that, for singleton bucket, this requires storing only one attribute value.

2.2   Point Value Assumption

The point value assumption was proposed for the first time in [2] in the context of proposing the equal-depth histogram. That's information about attribute values is stored as a list of distribution steps. Each step represents the unique value assumed to be present in a given bucket e.g., usually the lowest among those actually in the bucket, such that the fraction of values less than a step i is less than or equal to i divided by the number of total steps. For example, suppose we have 10 steps, step 4 is a value such that about 40% of all values are less than step 4. This assumption requires storage of this single attribute value.

Example 1 Consider a histogram for a non-negative integer-valued attribute. Assume that the range of a given bucket is equal to [1..100], the actual number of distinct values in it is equal to 10, and the sum of frequencies of values in it is 200. Under the continuous values assumption, the values in the bucket are 1, 2, ..., 100, each value has a frequency of 2 and under the point value assumption, only one value in the bucket is 1 with a frequency of 200.

We see clearly from the previous example, that both assumptions assume that attribute values have equal spreads. That's under the continuous values, respectively the point value assumption, each value within a bucket is assumed to have a spread equal to 1, respectively to the bucket range. But, the inconvenient is that both assumptions don't use the actual number of distinct value when approximating values within a bucket. To overcome this problem, the uniform spread assumption was introduced in [6], which also assumes that attribute values have equal spreads. But, instead of making crude assumptions about the number of distinct values in each bucket, it stores the actual one.

2.3   Uniform Spread Assumption

The experiment results presented in [6] shows that the continuous values and point value assumptions can lead to significant estimation errors. To overcome this problem, authors in [6] introduced the uniform spread assumption which consists at uniformly placing m values in the bucket range, where m is the total number of distinct values of V grouped into that bucket. That's non null values are located at equal distance, between the lowest and highest values in the bucket, from each other which is equal to the bucket average. This assumption requires storage of the lowest and highest value in each bucket together with the number of distinct attribute values in the bucket.

Example 2 Continuing with the histogram from Example 1 where the number of distinct values in the bucket is 10, under the uniform spread assumption, the 10 values in the bucket are 1, 12, 23, ..., 89, 100, each having a frequency of 20. The use of this approach requires techniques for computation of the number of distinct values that lie between the lowest and highest value in the bucket range, which incurs an additional CPU time and intermediate storage.

One of the most serious drawbacks of the continuous values, the point value and the uniform spread assumptions is their inaccuracy in approximating value sets with non-uniform spreads. That is in most cases, attribute value distributions don't have any closed functional description where the only description is the distribution itself. As indicated by the experimental results in section 4.2, estimations based on histograms using one of these approaches can have significant errors. To overcome this problem, some of histograms propose to record every distinct value that appears in each bucket.

2.4   Record Every Distinct Value

This straightforward technique proposed in [1] includes the histograms that record every distinct attribute value that appears in each bucket, (i.e., no assumptions are made). Such histograms require an auxiliary index for efficient access when estimating the result size of a query. Although this approach is simple and exact, it is too expensive to exactly compute distinct values for the large relations typically encountered in practice. That is this approach requires too much CPU time and intermediate storage, due to the extensive hashing and/or sorting required. We therefore focus on algorithms that compute approximate distinct values within a bucket.

3   Approximation of Values using Equidistant Quantiles

In this section, we propose an approach approximate simultaneously and in a dynamic way the set of an attribute values within a histogram bucket. This approach is proposed to overcome the drawback of previous approaches which is their inaccuracy in approximating value sets with non uniform spreads.

Although, the *uniform spread assumption* is distinguished among the other previous approaches by using the actual number of distinct values in each bucket, its serious drawback remains its inaccuracy in choosing the right values. That is assuming that each distinct value within a bucket has a spread equal to the bucket average may not really matching the real distinct values within this bucket. To circumvent the limit of the *uniform spread assumption*, we propose to, dynamically, approximate the set of distinct values within a bucket as new values are inserted into the attribute. The proposed method is based on the *uniform frequency assumption* inside each bucket.

All histograms make the *uniform frequency assumption* and approximate all frequencies in a bucket by their average. That is the approximated values of an attribute X occur equally within a bucket, which mean that the percentage of the distribution that lie below each of the approximated value is the same.

Formally: Let $v_1, v_2, v_3, \ldots, v_d$ be the distinct values of X to approximate, within a bucket, between the lowest and highest values in the bucket range. We have:

$$P(X \leq v_1) = P(X \leq v_2) = P(X \leq v_3) = \ldots = P(X \leq v_d). \tag{1}$$

In the context of simulation modeling, the value below which 100p percent of the distribution lies is known by the p-quantile [10]. Then, the problem of approximating the set of d values within a bucket can be returned to calculate values of $(d-2)$ equidistant quantiles; namely, the $1/d$-, $2/d$-, $\ldots$, $(d-2)/d$-quantiles, along with the lowest and highest values in the bucket. So, to plot within a histogram bucket d distinct values having probably the same percentage of distribution that lie below each one, all we need is to calculate the values of d equidistant quantiles with the minimum and the maximum correspond to the extreme values in the bucket range.

The straightforward method to estimate the values of quantiles requires a prior knowledge of the whole distribution and a large space to store all the observations. To solve these problems, we propose, instead of storing all the attribute values, to maintain for each quantile a marker where its value corresponds to the current estimated quantile value. The first d attribute values are sorted to initialize the d markers with values equal to the current estimates of the lowest value, $1/d$-quantile, $2/d$-quantile, $\ldots$, $(d-2)/d$-quantile, and the highest value in the histogram bucket. Then, the markers values are updated as more values are generated.

The updating of given marker consists in keeping, after each new value added to the attribute, its actual position usually close to its desired position on the curve of the distribution function. The desired position of a quantile is calculated and is current position is adjusted as follows. For each marker, whose value is greater than the new added value, its actual position is incremented by one. In addition, after n inserted values into the attribute, the positions of some markers whose values are less than the n values may deviate by more than one position from their desired positions. In this case, the actual position of each marker is adjusted using a parabola passing through the two adjacent markers and this marker.

An algorithmic description of the method proposed to approximate the set of d distinct values within a bucket, based on the estimated values of d equidistant quantiles which are produced dynamically as new values are inserted into the attribute, is proposed below. The initialization of the algorithm requires d values sorted and used as the initial values of the markers. The actual positions are initialized respectively from 1 to d. First some useful notation:

ev_i estimated value of the i-th quantile, $1 \leq i \leq d$

n_i actual position of the i-th marker, $1 \leq i \leq d$

n'_i desired position of the i-th marker, $2 \leq i \leq d-1$

Algorithm
Phase I: INITIALIZATION
Sort the first d attribute values to initialize values
and actual positions of the d markers

$$ev_i \longleftarrow v_i$$
$$n_i \longleftarrow i \qquad i = 1, \ldots, d$$

Phase II: UPDATING OF MARKERS
For each new value v_j, $\{j \geq d+1\}$, inserted into the
attribute **DO**
Begin

1. Adjust, if necessary, the lowest and highest value in
   the bucket (ev_1, ev_d)
   IF ($v_j < ev_1$) **THEN**
   $ev_1 \longleftarrow v_j$
   ELSE IF ($v_j > ev_d$) then $ev_d \longleftarrow v_j$;

2. Increment by 1, if necessary, the actual positions of
   markers 2 until $d-1$
   FOR $i := 2$ to $d-1$ **DO**
   IF ($ev_i > v_j$) **THEN**
   $n_i \longleftarrow n_i + 1$;

3. Adjust, if necessary, values and actual positions of
   markers 2 until $d-1$
   FOR $i := 2$ to $d-1$ **DO**
   Begin
   - calculate desired marker position
   $n'_i \longleftarrow 1 + (i - 1)(n_i - 1)/d$;
   IF $((((n'_i - n_i) \geq 1$ and $(n_{i+1} \geq n_i + 2))$ OR
   $((n'_i - n_i) \leq -1$ and $(n_{i-1} \leq n_i - 2)))$[1] **THEN**
   Begin
   $n_i \longleftarrow n'_i$
   - Adjusting ev_i
   $ev'_i \longleftarrow ev_i$: from parabolic formula
   IF ($ev_{i-1} < ev_i < ev_{i+1}$) **THEN**
   $ev_i \longleftarrow ev'_i$
   ELSE $ev_i \longleftarrow ev_i$: from linear formula[2];
   END IF
   END FOR
End.

Output:
  ev_1, ev_2, ev_3, ..., ev_d: are the approximated values that lie between the lowest (ev_1)
and the highest (ev_d) values in the histogram bucket.

---

[1] The movement of the marker's actual position to the left or to the right is always one position.
[2] The linear formula is used only when the adjusted value of a marker using the parabolic
formula would cause decreasing order of the marker values.

This algorithm doesn't require prior knowledge of all the attribute values nor a large amount of memory since the estimated values of quantiles are produced dynamically as new values are inserted into the attribute. These estimated values correspond almost to the real values having each one a frequency equal to the bucket average frequency. This precision proves the efficiency of this algorithm in obtaining good estimates of different quantiles.

4   Experimental Results

In this section, we investigated the effectiveness of our approach for approximating values with in a histogram bucket. The average error due to our approach was compared with others common approaches over a large set of queries and non-uniform data distributions. The histogram types, data distributions and queries considered in our experiments are described in section **4.1**.

4.1   Effect of Non-uniform Spreads

To study the effect of non-uniform spreads of attribute values on the accuracy of frequencies approximations made by the histograms that assume that attribute values are uniformly distributed inside a bucket, we present the typical behavior of the errors resulting from the approximations of four Compressed-v2 histograms (Compressed-v2(D1), Compressed-v2(D2), compressed-v2(D3), and Compressed-v2(D4)) constructed respectively based on four data distributions (D1, D2, D3, and D4) with varying the spreads of values from a distribution to another. The bucket boundaries in the four histograms were computed exactly by sorting all of the values in each set. All values are non negative integers and spreads are generated according to one of four alternative distributions: zipf_inc (increasing spreads following a Zipf distribution), zipf_dec (decreasing spreads following a Zipf distribution), cusp_min (zipf_inc for the first D/2 elements followed by zipf_dec), and cusp_max (zipf_dec for the first D/2 elements followed by zipf_inc). The approximated frequencies based on the different histograms in a given bucket are calculated as the average of frequencies in this bucket. The histograms errors in approximating the selectivity of the different queries conditions are plotted in Fig 1 with the parameter z for the Zipf distributions was 2. The queries used in the experiments are of the form (x = **a**) where **a** is an integer lying between the minimum and maximum values in the bucket range.

As indicated by Fig1, we see clearly that the uniform spread assumption, adopted by the four Compressed-v2 histograms and by most of the popular histograms to approximate the value set within buckets, was failed to accurately approximate the set of values of four non-uniformly distributed data sets such as zipf_inc, zipf_dec, cusp_min and cusp_max distributions. In spite of its efficiency and wide use in approximating frequencies, the uniform spread assumption usually returns a non null frequency when the requested value belongs to a bucket range even if this value doesn't really occur in the attribute.

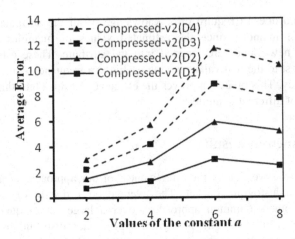

Fig. 1. Effect of non-uniform spreads on frequency approximation

4.2   Error of Value Approximation within a Bucket

All histograms make the uniform frequency assumption and approximate all frequencies in a bucket by their average. This estimation remains the best average frequency estimation for the approaches that use the actual number of distinct attribute values when creating their approximate frequencies [6, 7]. That's for each distinct value d in the actual distribution there is exactly a unique approximate value d' in the approximate value distribution over all the attribute values (i.e., no extra distinct values or minus in the attribute). This symmetric relation makes from the approximation on average the simplest and most widely used technique. So, the accuracy depends only on how much the approximate frequencies, obtained from a histogram, can be close to the actual ones and this accuracy has been higher with the new partition constraints that aim to group only contiguous values into buckets [3, 6, 7, and 8]. However, under the approaches that make crude assumptions about the number of distinct values, the accuracy of the frequency approximations depends not only on the degree of deviation between the actual and approximate distributions but also on how accurate the actual number of distinct values is estimated. For this purpose, we define the error incurred in using an approximate data distribution.

Definition 1 *Let H be a histogram approximating the set of values of an attribute X without storing the actual number of distinct values in each bucket, the error of H in approximating the value distribution of X is defined as the difference between E(X), respectively E'(X) the errors incurred in using an approximate frequency distribution of length equal to, respectively different than (longer or shorter than), the length of the actual frequency distribution, i.e.,*

$$EVA(X) = Abs\ (E\ (X) - E'\ (X)).\qquad\qquad(2)$$

E(X) is defined in [8] as the squared deviation of the actual and approximate distributions over the entire attribute values in the domain of X, i.e.,

$$E(X) = \sum_{d \in D} (f_X(d) - f'_X(d))^2 . \qquad (3)$$

Where, $f_X(d)$ is the approximate frequency of d in the attribute X, obtained from a histogram.

In the following table, we present using the formula (1) the errors incurred in using approximate value distributions obtained from the four histograms cited in Figure 1. The corresponding actual values distributions are those used in section 4.1.

Table 1. Error of value approximation

Histogram	EVA
Compressed-v2 (D1)	2
Compressed-v2 (D2)	3
Compressed-v2 (D3)	2.5
Compressed-v2 (D4)	4

4.3 Accuracy of Quantile-Based Approach

A histogram maintained on a data distribution permits to provide an approximate frequency distribution that can be used in place of the actual frequencies in many estimation tasks. The accuracy of the approximated frequencies depends on the technique used to approximate distinct values within each bucket of the histogram. For example, under the uniform spread assumption, the approximated frequency of a value belonging to a given bucket is usually not null even if this value doesn't really occur in the attribute.

Let $D = \{v_i \mid 1 \leq i \leq d\}$ be the set of actual distinct values present in a histogram bucket b maintained on an attribute X. We estimate the distinct values of D from a histogram H as:

$$D'_H = \{v'_i \mid 1 \leq i \leq d\} . \qquad (4)$$

where, v' is the approximate value of v obtained from a histogram.

In order to investigate the efficiency of the different techniques, an important issue to be addressed is how close the set D'_H matches the set D for each bucket in H. For this purpose, we define the error incurred in using an approximate values distribution.

Definition 2 *The error of a histogram H in approximating the set of d distinct values of an attribute X that lie between the lowest and highest value of a bucket b is defined as the squared deviation of the actual and approximate set of distinct values within b, i.e,*

$$E_H(b) = \sum_{i=1..d}(v_i - v'_i)^2. \tag{5}$$

We define then, based on this definition, the error of a histogram in approximating the set of distinct values of an attribute X over β buckets as follows:

Definition 3 *The error of a histogram H in approximating the set of distinct values of an attribute X is defined as the squared deviation of the actual and approximate set of distinct values over all the histogram buckets, i.e,*

$$E_H = \sum_{i=1}^{\beta} E_H(b_i). \tag{6}$$

In the following, we compare the accuracy of the approximations of values obtained from two histograms H1 and H2 using respectively the proposed technique based on quantiles and the uniform spread assumption. The experiments were conducted based on the distributions D1, D2, D3 and D4 cited before. So, to do that, let us first define the histogram optimality.

Definition 4 *The optimal histogram for approximating the set of attribute values within buckets is the histogram with the least estimation error among all the histograms using the actual number of distinct values within each bucket.*

The errors of H1 and H2 in approximating values in the four data sets D1, D2, D3 and D4 are respectively presented in Fig 3.a, 3.b, 3.c and 3.d. Looking at the different figures, it can be seen clearly that the error of H1 resulting from the approximation of one value is, most of the time, less than the error obtained with H2 when approximating the same value. We observe also that as skew increases, the uniform spread assumption fails to approximate the set of values because as the skew increases, the deviation between the actual and the uniform distributions increases too. However, the proposed method based on equidistant quantiles achieves good accuracy on both uniform and irregular distributed data. In conclusion, the comparison between the two techniques shows that the accuracy of the approximation of values, using histograms, can be reached more with the proposed technique, rather than the uniform spread assumption especially when the data is not uniformly distributed. However, when the actual distribution is not required, the uniform spread assumption remains so useful since it only stores two values per bucket, minimum and the number of distinct values where the quantile approach requires storing d values.

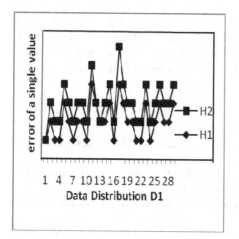

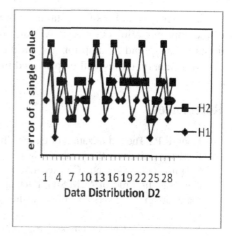

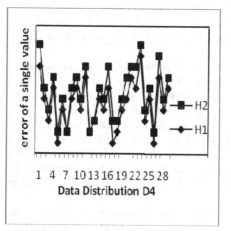

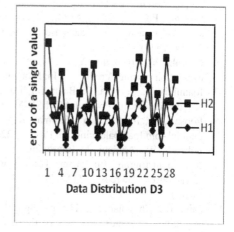

Fig. 2. Error of H1and H2 in approximating the set of distinct values in the distribution a) D1, b) D2, c) D3, and d) D4

5   Conclusions

All histograms make the uniform frequency assumption and approximate all frequencies in a bucket by their average. The estimation on average has been shown to be very efficient especially with the new partition constraints that make the approximate frequencies very close to the actual ones. However, one of the most serious drawbacks of the uniform frequency assumption is it inaccuracy in approximating   even if the requested value doesn't occur in the attribute, a non null approximate of its frequency is obtained from a histogram. To overcome this problem, we introduced an algorithm based on quantiles for dynamic calculation of distinct approximate values within a histogram bucket.

The experimental results obtained from the empirical comparison of the accuracy of the approximations of values within a bucket obtained, on the one hand, based on the uniform spread assumption and on the other hand, based on the estimated values of equidistant quantiles will be provided in an extended version of this paper.

References

1. Kooi, R.P.: The optimization of queries in relational databases. PhD thesis, Case Western Reserver University (September 1980)
2. Shapiro, G.P., Connell, C.: Accurate estimation of the number of tuples satisfying a condition. In: Proc. of ACM SIGMOD, pp. 256–276 (1984)
3. Ioannidis, Y.: Universality of serial histograms. In: Proc. of 19th VLDB, pp. 256–267 (1993)
4. Ioannidis, Y., Christodoulakis, S.: Optimal histograms for limiting worst-case error propagation in the size of join results. In: Proc. of ACM TODS (1993)
5. Selinger, P.G., Astrahan, M.M., Chamberlin, D.D., Lorie, R.A., Price, T.T.: Access path selection in a relational database management system. In: Proc. of ACM SIGMOD, pp. 23–34 (1979)
6. Poosala, V., Ioannidis, Y., Haas, P., Shekita, E.: Improved histograms for selectivity estimation of range predicates. In: Proc. of ACM SIGMOD, pp. 294–305 (1996)
7. Ioannidis, Y., Poosala, V.: Balancing histogram optimality and practicality for query result size estimation. In: Proc. of ACM SIGMOD, pp. 233–244 (1995)
8. Poosala, V., Ioannidis, Y.: Estimation of query-result distribution and its application in parallel-join load balancing. In: Proc. of 22nd VLDB, pp. 448–459 (1996)
9. Labbadi, W., Akaichi, J.: Improving range query result size estimation based on a new optimal histogram. In: Larsen, H.L., Martin-Bautista, M.J., Vila, M.A., Andreasen, T., Christiansen, H. (eds.) FQAS 2013. LNCS, vol. 8132, pp. 40–56. Springer, Heidelberg (2013)
10. Jain, R., Chlamtac, I.: The p^2 algorithm for dynamic calculation of quantiles and histograms without storing observations. Communications oh the ACM, 1076–1085 (1985)
11. Jagadish, H.V., Koudas, N., Muthukrishnan, S., Poosala, V., Sevcik, K., Suel, T.: Optimal histograms with quality guarantees. In: Proc. of 24th VLDB, pp. 275–286 (1998)

Modeling a Smart Home for Elderly

Kissoum Yacine[1], Maamri Ramdane[2], and Sahnoun Zaidi[2]

[1] Faculty of Sciences, Computer Science Department, Université 20 Août 1955, Skikda. Algeria
[2] Lire Laboratory, Université Constantine 2, Constantine, Algeria
{kissoumyacine,rmaamri,sahnounz}@yahoo.fr

Abstract. In the near future, our homes will be equipped with many sensors, actuators and devices able to smartly interact in order to offer complex services providing even richer functionalities. Among the general population, those most likely to benefit from the development of these systems are the elderly and dependent people who wish to continue living independently in their home as opposed to being forced to live in a hospital. However, today's systems are mainly based on ad hoc and proprietary solutions. To cope with the ad-hoc nature of smart home systems design process while taking into account both dimensions of time and space, it is required to use a suitable formal model that is able to handle smart home domain specific nature. This paper proposes an approach that uses reference nets to model a smart home which is sensitive, adaptive and responsive to elderly's presence, needs and preferences.

Keywords: Ambient intelligence, Agents, Elderly, Reference net, Timed net, Smart home.

1 Introduction

In recent years, there has been an important growth in the field of Ambient Intelligence (AmI) [2] [10] such that the results promise to revolutionize daily human life by making people's surroundings flexible and adaptive. The vision of Ambient Intelligence implies a seamless environment of computing and advanced networking technology that is aware of human presence, personalities, needs and which is capable of responding intelligently to spoken or gestured indications of desire, and even in engaging in intelligent dialogue.

Moreover, the percentage of elderly in today's societies keeps on growing. With the current trends in population demographics, it is becoming increasingly difficult for governments worldwide to fully support the health and social care systems [1]. The use of smart technologies, including smart homes could arguably relieve the pressure on aged care health and social support services [8]. The challenge with smart home technologies dedicated to elderly is to create a home environment that is safe and secure to reduce falls, disability, stress, fear or social isolation [3].

Like any other system, smart home development starts with a high level model and proceeds through a process of refinement, simulation, verification, implementation and test. Much of processes used for smart home design are ad-hoc [6],. By time,

Y. Ait Ameur et al. (Eds.): MEDI 2014, LNCS 8748, pp. 313–320, 2014.

all the gritty details of implementation are taken care with the original system description has pretty much been lost, causing a lack of design oversight and a surplus of one-time-only design artifacts [9]. Besides, very little can be done within a smart home system without an explicit or implicit reference to where and when the meaningful events occurred. For a system to make sensible decisions it has to be aware of where the inhabitants are and have been during some period of time.

To cope with the ad-hoc nature of smart home systems design process and to take into account both dimensions, space and time, to understand key elements of a situation under development, it's required to use a suitable formal model that is able to handle smart home domain specific nature. The proposed approach for modeling smart home for elderly proposed so far is based on such a model called Reference net. Reference nets are based on the nets within nets paradigm that generalizes token to data types and even nets.

The rest of this paper is organized as follow: In section 2 we give a short introduction on the timed net. After the description of the smart home for elderly case study in section 3, we present how the basic components of such a case study are modeled using the reference net paradigm. Finally, the section 5 concludes with discussion about issues and future work.

2   Timed Nets

The paradigm of nets within nets formalizes the aspect that tokens of a Petri net can also be data types and even nets. Taking this in consideration it is possible to model hierarchical structures in an elegant way. Before discussing timed nets, a short introduction of the implementation of certain aspects of nets within nets called Reference net will be given. Reference nets are a graphical notation that are especially well suited for the description and execution of complex, concurrent processes. As for other net formalisms, there exist tools for the simulation of reference nets called Renew (for Reference Net workshop). Reference nets extend black and colored Petri nets by means of net instances, nets as token objects, communication via synchronous channels, and different arc types. Definitions of these extensions are given in [7].

While pure Petri nets capture the causality and conflict situations of a system nicely, there are reasons to add a notion of time to the formalism in order to model additional dependencies. In timed nets, a time stamp is attached to each token. It denotes the time when the token becomes available. Delays may be used with arcs in order to control the time stamps of token and the firing times of transitions. A delay is added to an arc by adding to the arc inscription the symbol @ and an expression that evaluates to the number of time units. For example, x@t indicates that the token value x has to be move after t time units.

3   Smart Home for Elderly Case Study

Let us imagine a house with several rooms: living room, kitchen, bed room, next room, bath room and the front yard. To be smart, such a house should contain a large set of services that cooperate to simplify the life of the owner, to make energy saving, and to provide comfort and security solutions. Fig. 1 show an example of a smart home where various home devices are scattered over rooms to constitute a cooperating environment that provide smart services to the owner.

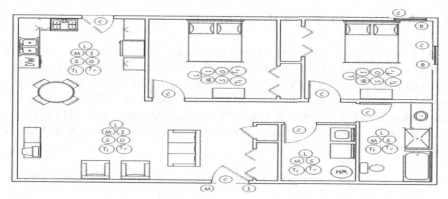

Fig. 1. The smart home case study

Our overall system will be designed according to MULAN [4] architecture. MULAN is implemented in RENEW[1] and defines four levels of abstraction in terms of system net. The first level is the agent system, which places contain agent platforms as tokens. The transitions describe communication or mobility channels, which build up the infrastructure. By zooming into an arbitrary place, its structure becomes visible, shown in Fig. 2. The central place agents host all agents, which are currently on this platform. Each platform offers services to the agents. Agents can be created (transition *new*) or destroyed (transition *destroy*). Agents can communicate by message exchange (*internal communication and External communication*). Also mobility facilities are provided on a platform: agents can leave the platform via the transition *send agent* or enter the platform via the transition *receive agent*.

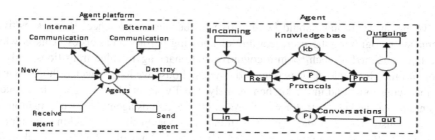

Fig. 2. The structure of the platform and the agent system net (adapted from [7])

Agents are also modeled in terms of nets. Agents can be intelligent, since they have access to a knowledge base. The behavior of the agent is described in terms of protocols,

---

[1] Available at www.renew.de

which are again nets. Protocols are located as templates on the place protocols. Protocol templates can be instantiated, which happens for example if a message arrives. An instantiated protocol is part of a conversation and lies in the place conversations.

4   Modeling the Smart Home Agents

Using nets within nets as a modeling paradigm allows for the direct use of system models at execution time. This can be exploited as follows: The overall system will be designed as a system net with places defining locations (rooms). Transitions model possible movements between these rooms (green transitions), Fig. 3. Due to the paper size limitation, only a subset of services will be presented here to highlight the modeling concept. The idea can be further extended to any smart home room and to any additional services.

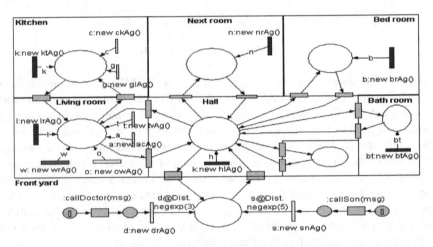

Fig. 3. The smart home system net

To be smart, rooms should be sensitive to the human presence. Being sensitive demands recognizing the user, learning or knowing her/his preferences. This is why we have attached to each room a cognitive stationary agent (blue transitions). Also, from all the electronic devices scattered over the house we have selected those laying in the living room and in the kitchen, namely: the TV agent, the AC agent, the cooker agent and gas leakage detector which are modeled again as agents (brown transitions). There is also one particular agent (red transition) responsible of checking the blood pressure and/or glucose rate of the elderly at random times of a day. It may take the form of a bracelet hanging on the wrist of the elderly. Finally, this model of house is filled with life by implementing human house inhabitants (yellow transitions). These ones are the owner (the elderly); his doctor and his son (the creation and arc inscriptions of these two agents will be detailed so far). All these agents share the same structure depicted in right side of Fig. 2.

Human preferences and moods are part of these agent's knowledge bases. In simple cases the knowledge base place can be implemented for example as subnets. This is true in the case of sensors (modeled as reactive agents). Unfortunately, using such implementation for cognitive agents leads to a closed model that is often needed to rethink completely before introducing any modification. For this kind of agents advanced implementations of the knowledge place as the connection to Java Expert System Shell (JESS) [5] will be used. As for other expert systems, JESS is composed from a rule base, the fact base and its inference engine is composed from the pattern matcher which decides what rules to fire and when and the agenda which schedules the order in which activated rules will fire.

At home, the behavior of the owner is highly dependent on the timeframe in which he is located. Thus, different scenarios related to such parts of the day can be imagined. The *"wakeup mode"*, the *"leave home mode"* and the *"return home mode"* are examples of these scenarios. Before discussing one of them, we start by defining the working memory and the rule bases of each of our agents. A particular attention will be given to the living room and the kitchen agents. These ones store information about the elderly, its environment as well as other agents. Also, they must exchange their respective information to ensure the welfare of the elderly. For that, each JESS rule engine holds a collection of knowledge nuggets called facts. Every fact has a template. The template has a name and a set of slots. Let us start by defining the ACL message template as following:

```
(deftemplate ACLMessage (slot communicative-act) (slot
sender) (slot receiver) (slot conversation-id) (slot pro-
tocol) (slot language) (slot ontology) (slot content))
```

It is important to note that elderly preferences, described in each agent's working memory, depend on the room in which he is. It will be favorite program TV or multimedia playlist for the living room agent and light dimming and air conditioner levels for the bed room agent. The following templates define the owner of the house (the elderly) and people close to him.

```
(deftemplate elderly (slot name) (slot sex) (slot age)
(multislot disease) (multislot TVprefer) (multislot Food-
prefer))
(deftemplate related (slot name) (slot sex) (slot age)
(slot type) (slot telephone))
```

Other facts are necessary to our room's agents to create the desired ambiance once the owner enters the living room or the kitchen. The elderly suffering from one or more diseases (usually chronic), agents should be able to analyze the significant factors related to these diseases. Therefore, our agents will use the following templates:

```
(deftemplate bloodpressure (slot maxVal) (slot minVal))
```

Assigning values to these slots allows room's agents to identify persons having access to the house. An example of authorized persons is as follows:

```
(assert (elderly (name Ben) (sex male) (age 69) (disease
Diabetes Hypertension) (TVprefer News Docs Entertainment)
(foodprefer tea fish salad)))
```

```
(assert (related (name Tim) (sex male) (age 45) (type
doctor) (telephone 077777777))
```

Now we can define some JESS rules. Examples of such rules are the following. In the first one, as soon as the owner enters the living room, the agent will check the current time (morning in this case) then turn on the TV and the AC on owner's desired channel and temperature. In the second, the kitchen agent will ask the coffee machine to prepare a tea without sugar.

```
(defrule rule1 (enter {name == Ben && room == living room
&& time >= 8 && time <= 10})(elderly {Tvpref == news}) =>
(assert (television (state ON) (channel NSN)))
(assert (airCond (state ON) (temperature 25)))
(defrule rule2 (enter {name == Ben && room == kitchen &&
time > 10 && time <= 12}) (elderly {foodpref == Tea}) =>
(assert (coffeeMaker (drink Tea) (sugar No)))
```

In addition, the following rule allows the bracelet agent to decide on the health of the elderly based on his blood glucose.

```
(defrule rule3 (glucose {rate < 0.60 }) => (assert (ACL-
Message (communicative-act INFORM) (sender wrAg) (receiv-
er lrAg) (content "hypoglycemia ") (conversation-id "call
son"))
```

Let us focus on the elderly agent. Suppose that we are in the "*wakeup mode*", the execution of its JESS program concludes with a valid fact "*take breakfast*". Driven by this fact, the elderly agent selects a plan to execute: "*enter kitchen*". Actually the plan execution corresponds to the selection, the instantiation and the commencement of the conversation. Fig. 4 shows such a protocol.

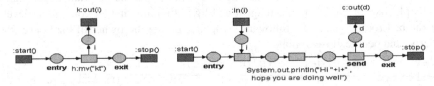

Fig. 4. The enter kitchen and the welcome protocol

After its instantiation, the transition *mv("kt")* produces a performative *i* that define the entering agent's identity, and which is directed to kitchen agent main interface over the *k:out(i)* channel; subsequently the agent terminates (by enabling the *:stop()* transition). The *k:out(i)* is met by synchronizing with the same transition in the kitchen agent net (*:in(i)*) which induce the enabling of transition *rea* on agent main net. Influenced by the identity of the person entering the kitchen and the inference results provided by the JESS program of the kitchen agent, this one will instantiate the "*welcome*" protocol. This protocol welcomes the entering person, produces a performative *d* defining the kind of the drink to prepare and over the channel *c:out(d)*, it will send it the "*request drink*" protocol (Fig. 5). Forthwith, on such protocol, the transition *compose* produces a performative containing a string that is directed over the channel *c:out(s)* to the coffee maker agent; subsequently the protocol is blocked waiting for an answer message. An arriving answer enables the transition *answer*. After its occurrence the protocol is not blocked any further, and the receiver will process the answer, Fig. 5.

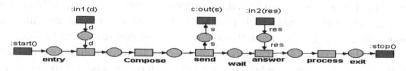

Fig. 5. The request drink protocol

Fig. 6 shows the prepare drink protocol. The transition *:in(dr)* is responsible of passing the kind of drink (tea, coffee, or milk). Then the protocol starts by verifying randomly if the required quantity for the drink preparation is less to the available quantity. If yes, the *prepare* transition is enabled (drink preparation may take five minutes on average). Otherwise, the transition *supply* is executed and the transition *:out(res)* will inform the sender (the kitchen agent) that his request is fulfilled or not.

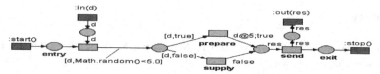

Fig. 6. The prepare drink protocol

The above protocols describe how agents collaborate to assist elderly in the *wake up* scenario. Let us see how these agents take care of elderly health. Remember the bracelet agent that checks the glucose rate of the elderly at random time of a day. It is modeled as a mobile agent that is transported by the elderly agent. Using the set of JESS rules defined in its knowledge base, this agent can decide whether the situation is an emergency or not. If so (a hyperglycemia for example), a message is addressed to the room agent which execute the adequate protocol, depicted in Fig. 7.

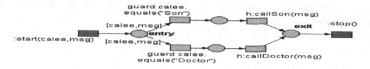

Fig. 7. The emergency protocol

The *callSon* or the *callDoctor* transitions are modeled to meet by synchronization the same transitions in the house net (see Fig. 3). Doctor, for example, takes three hours on average with a negative-exponential distribution to reach the front yard place.

5   Conclusion

In this paper we have presented an approach for modeling of cooperating ambient agent cohabiting an elderly's home. An important argument for using the reference nets paradigm is its strong expressiveness, openness and versatility without losing formal accuracy. Indeed, using such a paradigm, the modeling process concludes with a running system model. We think that such robust and easy-to-use tool reduces considerably the large initial effort in term of man-hours required mainly in constructing and validating smart home models. In fact, using reference nets as a modeling paradigm makes easy to see the state of the overall system by looking at the system net. Thus, it is possible to take control of the whole agent system by just double clicking on one of the tokens. Renew will then display the corresponding net allowing for a complete inspection of the running system without interrupting it.

Additional services such as fire system, curtain control, climate control system, multimedia control system and so on, will be directly integrated in the design of the reference net based multi agent system architecture MULAN.

References

1. Agoulmine, N., Deen, M.J., Jeong-Soo, L., Meyyappan, M.: U-health smart home: Innovative solutions for the management of the elderly and chronic diseases. IEEE Nanotechnology Magazine 5, 6–11 (2011)
2. Anastasopoulos, M., Bartelt, C., Koch, J., Rausch, A.: Towards a Reference Middleware Architecture for Ambient Intelligence Systems. In: ACM Conference on Object-Oriented Programming, Systems, Languages, and Applications (2005)
3. Barlow, J., Venables, T.: Will technological innovation create the true lifetime home? Housing Studies 19, 795–810 (2004)
4. Duvigneau, M., Moldt, D., Rölke, H.: Concurrent architecture for a multi-agent platform. In: Giunchiglia, F., Odell, J.J., Weiss, G. (eds.) AOSE 2002. LNCS, vol. 2585, pp. 59–72. Springer, Heidelberg (2003)
5. JESS (Java Expert System Shell), http://herzberg.ca.sandia.gov
6. Kissoum, Y., Maamri, R., Sahnoun, Z.: Modeling smart home using the paradigm of nets within nets. In: Ramsay, A., Agre, G. (eds.) AIMSA 2012. LNCS, vol. 7557, pp. 286–295. Springer, Heidelberg (2012)
7. Köhler, M., Moldt, D., Rölke, H.: Modelling mobility and mobile agents using nets within nets. In: van der Aalst, W.M.P., Best, E. (eds.) ICATPN 2003. LNCS, vol. 2679, pp. 121–139. Springer, Heidelberg (2003)
8. Morris, M., Ozanne, E., Miller, K., Santamaria, N., Pearce, A.: Smart technologies for older people: A systematic literature review of smart technologies that promote health and wellbeing of older people living at home. IBES, The University of Melbourne, Australia (2012)
9. Nabih, A.K., Gomaa, M.M., Osman, H.S., Aly, G.M.: Modeling, Simulation and control of smart home Using Petri Nets. International Journal of Smart Home 5(3) (July 2011)
10. Pan, J.I., Yung, C.Y., Liang, C.C., Lai, L.F.: An intelligent homecare emergency service system for elder falling. In: World Congress on Medical Physics and Biomedical Engineering, pp. 424–428. Springer, Heidelberg (2006)

Theme Identification in RDF Graphs

Hanane Ouksili, Zoubida Kedad, and Stéphane Lopes

PRiSM, Univ. Versailles St Quentin, UMR CNRS 8144, Versailles, France
firstname.lastname@prism.uvsq.fr

Abstract. An increasing number of RDF datasets is published on the Web. A user willing to use these datasets will first have to explore them in order to determine which information is relevant for his specific needs. To facilitate this exploration, we present an approach allowing to provide a thematic view of a given RDF dataset, making it easier to target the relevant resources and properties. The main contribution of this work is to combine existing clustering techniques with some semantic preferences set by the user to identify the themes. The proposed approach comprises three steps: (i) capturing users preferences, (ii) applying a clustering algorithm to identify the themes and (iii) extracting labels describing each of them. In this paper, we describe the main features of our approach.

Keywords: Theme idendification, RDF(S) data, Clustering.

1 Introduction

An increasing number of RDF datasets is published on the Web, making a huge amount of data available for users and applications. In this context, a key issue for the users is to locate the relevant information for their specific needs. A typical way of exploring RDF datasets is the following: the users first select a URI (seed of interest), then they explore all the URIs reachable from this seed by submitting queries to obtain information about the existing properties.

To facilitate this interaction, we propose to provide the users with a thematic view of an RDF dataset in order to guide the exploration process. We argue that once the data is presented as a set of themes, it is easier to target the relevant resources and properties by exploring the relevant topics only. In this paper, we present our approach for theme identification.

The main contribution of this work is to combine existing clustering techniques with a set of preferences stated by the user to express his point of view regarding the semantics of the resulting themes. We consider that the more a set of resources is connected, the more likely it is that they belong to the same cluster, and we have therefore used a density based graph clustering algorithm [1] to identify clusters, each one corresponding to a theme. Also, we will consider two kinds of user preferences. The first one expresses that two resources belong to the same cluster if they are related by a given property, the second one states that two resources belong to the same cluster if they have the same value for a given property.

Y. Ait Ameur et al. (Eds.): MEDI 2014, LNCS 8748, pp. 321–329, 2014.

The paper is organized as follows. Section 2 gives an overview of our proposal. Section 3 details the preprocessing step and section 4 presents the clustering algorithm. Label extraction for describing the resulting themes is discussed in section 5. Related works are provided in section 6, and finally, section 7 concludes the paper.

2   General Principle of Theme Identification

Given an RDF dataset, our goal is to identify a set of themes and to extract the labels or tags which best capture their semantics. Providing this thematic view raises several questions: Which information could be used to define a theme? As different users may not have the same perception of the data, how to capture their preferences and use them for building the themes? Finally, once the themes have been identified, how to label them so as to make their semantic as clear as possible to the user?

The problem of theme identification can be defined as partitioning an RDF graph into k possibly overlapping subgraphs, each one representing a coherent set of semantically related resources defining a theme. k is obviously not known in advance. Our approach relies on the idea that a theme corresponds to a highly connected area on the RDF graph. We will therefore use the structure of the RDF graph by applying a graph clustering algorithm which identifies highly connected areas and their neighborhood in order to form clusters, each one corresponding to a theme.

The structure of the graph alone is not sufficient to provide meaningful themes. Indeed, different users may have distinct perceptions of what a theme is. This difference is expressed as preferences that will be used for identifying the themes, in addition to the structure of the graph. User preferences are captured by specifying the characteristics of resources which should be assigned to the same cluster (for example, resources having the same value for a property or linked by a given property). Each preference will be mapped into one or several transformations applied to the graph.

Our approach comprises three main steps, (i) preprocessing, where transformations are applied on the RDF graph, (ii) graph clustering, where themes are identified, and (iii) label extraction which provides a summary of the content of each cluster (see Figure 1).

3   Preprocessing

The initial RDF graph is transformed prior to the execution of the clustering algorithm. Some transformations are systematic regardless of the context, others consist in integrating user preferences in the graph. This section describes both of them.

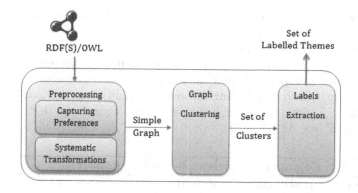

RDF(S)/OWL

Set of
Labelled Themes

Preprocessing
Capturing
Preferences
Systematic
Transformations

Simple
Graph

Graph
Clustering

Set of
Clusters

Labels
Extraction

Fig. 1. Overview of our Approach

3.1 Capturing User Preferences

As stated earlier, the structure of the graph alone is not sufficient for the identification of meaningful clusters. Sometimes the density of the graph doesn't fully
capture semantic closeness: for example, two resources might not be located in
a very connected area of the graph, but if there is an edge in the graph relating them, and if this edge expresses a strong semantic link (e.g. *owl:sameAs*),
the two resources should be assigned to the same cluster. Furthermore, for the
same dataset, different users might have different points of view and be interested in distinct properties. To capture this need, the clustering should take into
account these properties as semantic criteria. In our approach, user preferences
are captured by mapping each of them into one or several graph transformation
primitives. We consider that there are mainly two kinds of preferences a user
might want to express. The first one is that two resources related by a given
property should belong to the same theme. The second one is that a set of resources having the same value for a given property should belong to the same
theme.

Grouping Two Resources Related by a Property. Some properties express a
strong semantic link that should be used as a clustering criteria. For example, resources linked by the *owl:sameAs* property should obviously be assigned
to the same cluster, and this is true for any user in any context. Besides, some
users may wish to give a property more importance than other users. For example, if we consider a dataset containing information about scientists in different
research domains, a given user might consider that the resources *Student* and
Scientist related by the *dbo:doctoralAdvisor* property should be grouped in the
same cluster. This kind of preference is taken into account by merging the two
resources.

An RDF graph is a set of triples. Each triple (s, p, o) is represented by an
edge that connects the two nodes representing the *subject* (the resource being
described) and the *object* (the value of the property). The edge is labeled by the
name of the *predicate* (the property). If we consider the three disjoint sets U, B

and L representing respectively URI nodes, blank nodes and litteral nodes, then the triple $(s, p, o) \in (U \cup B) \times U \times (U \cup B \cup L)$.

Consider a graph $G = (V, E)$, and assume the user wants to group resources related by the property p_g. the graph will be modified by introducing for each edge (s, p_g, o) a new node $s.o$ in V and removing the two nodes s and o from V. Consequently, each edge having s or o as its origin (resp. destination) will be removed from E and a new edge having $s.o$ as its origin (resp. destination) will be added in E (see Algorithm 1).

Algorithm 1. Capturing Preferences: Related by Property

Require: $G(V, E)$: RDF graph, p_g: Property
Ensure: $G'(V', E')$: modified RDF graph

1. $G_{p_g} \leftarrow \{(s, p_g, o) \in E\}$ /*Set of triples containing the property p_g*/
2. $G_{in} \leftarrow \{(s, p, o) \mid (s, p, o) \in E \setminus G_{p_g} \wedge [\exists\, x \in V \mid (o, p_g, x) \in G_{p_g} \vee (x, p_g, o) \in G_{p_g}]\}$
   /*Set of triples such that the object is a resource appearing in G_{p_g}*/
3. $G_{out} \leftarrow \{(s, p, o) \mid (s, p, o) \in E \setminus G_{p_g} \wedge [\exists\, x \in V \mid (s, p_g, x) \in G_{p_g} \vee (x, p_g, s) \in G_{p_g}]\}$
   /*Set of triples such that the subject is a resource appearing in G_{p_g}*/
4. $E' \leftarrow E \setminus \{G_{p_g} \cup G_{in} \cup G_{out}\}, V' \leftarrow V$
5. **for all** $(s, p_g, o) \in G_{p_g}$ **do**
6. $V' \leftarrow V' \setminus \{s, o\}$
7. $V' \leftarrow V' \cup \{s.o\}$
8.   **for all** $(s, p, o') \in G_{out}$ **do**
9. $E' \leftarrow E' \cup \{(s.o, p, o')\}$ /*Adding outgoing edges from the subject*/
10.   **for all** $(o, p, o') \in G_{out}$ **do**
11. $E' \leftarrow E' \cup \{(s.o, p, o')\}$ /*Adding outgoing edges from the object*/
12.   **for all** $(s', p, s) \in G_{in}$ **do**
13. $E' \leftarrow E' \cup \{(s', p, s.o)\}$ /*Adding edges coming into the subject*/
14.   **for all** $(s', p, o) \in G_{in}$ **do**
15. $E' \leftarrow E' \cup \{(s', p, s.o)\}$ /*Adding edges coming into the object*/

Grouping Resources According to Values of a Property. Resources that should be assigned to the same theme are not always linked by a property; the semantic closeness between them can be expressed by the values of some shared property. In other words, a set of resources having the same value for a property p should be assigned to the same cluster. For instance, the user could state that scientists having the same value for the *dbo:field* property should be in the same cluster, thus ensuring that scientists of the same research domain are grouped together. This kind of preference is taken into account by creating in the graph a highly connected area containing the specified resources.

More formally, let $G(V, E)$ be an RDF graph and p_g a property, and suppose that the user wishes to group in the same cluster resources having the same value for this property. Consider the set of nodes in G representing resources for which the value of the property p_g is α, defined as $S_{p_g, \alpha} = \{s \mid (s, p_g, \alpha) \in G\}$. The graph is modified by adding for each pair of resources s_i and s_j in $S_{p_g, \alpha}$ a new edge $(s_i, sameValue, s_j)$ in E. (see Algorithm 2).

Algorithm 2. Capturing Preference: Same Property Value

Require: $G(V, E)$: RDF graph, p_g: property
Ensure: $G'(V', E')$: modified RDF graph

1. $V' \leftarrow V, E' \leftarrow E$
2. $V_{p_g} \leftarrow \{o \mid (s, p_g, o) \in E\}$ /*set of values of the property p_g*/
3. **for all** $\alpha \in V_{p_g}$ **do**
4. $S_{p_g, \alpha} = \{s \mid (s, p_g, \alpha) \in E\}$
5.   **for all** $s_i \in S_{p_g, \alpha}$ **do**
6.   **for all** $s_j \in S_{p_g, \alpha}, i \neq j$ **do**
7.   **if** $(s_i, p, s_j) \notin E \wedge (s_j, p, s_i) \notin E$ **then**
8. $E' \leftarrow E' \cup \{(s_i, sameValue, s_j)\}$

3.2 Systematic Transformations

Once users preferences have been taken into account, the initial graph will be transformed prior to clustering by removing the information that will not be used by the clustering algorithm. In the initial RDF graph, edges are directed and labeled with the name of a property. The clustering algorithm used in our approach will try to identify highly connected areas, regardless of the direction of the edges; what we are interested in is that some semantic relation exists between the resources. For example, if the *dbo:influenced* property, which is asymmetric in nature, holds between two resources r_i and r_j representing researchers, the direction of the edge is not important for grouping purposes, the most important is that there is a semantic relationship between the two. We can therefore simplify the graph by removing the direction of the edges. Similarly, the clustering algorithm will not use the labels of the edges, and they are also removed from the graph.

An RDF graph contains several types of nodes which can be either resources or literals. A literal is related to one resource and is a characteristic of this resource. Obviously, a resource and the related literals should be grouped into the same cluster. We could therefore apply the clustering algorithm on a simplified version of the graph which doesn't contain the literals.

The output of this transformation step is a graph where the labels, direction of the edges and literal nodes have been removed.

4 Clustering Algorithm

The clustering algorithm at the core of our approach has to fulfill a set of requirements, first of which is exploiting the density of the graph to enable the identification of clusters corresponding to highly connected areas of the graph. The second requirement is that the algorithm should not require the number of clusters as a parameter, as this information cannot be known prior to clustering in our context. Finally, resulting clusters provided by the algorithm should not necessarily be disjoint, as it is possible that two distinct resources in our initial graph belong to two different themes. The most popular algorithms that comply with these requirements are MCODE proposed by [1] and initially used in the domain of bioinformatics and CPM by [7] that is used for highly connected graph. A survey on graph clustering algorithms can be found in [5].

For our implementation, we use MCODE algorithm which operates in three steps. First, it computes the weights of each node in the graph using the concept of k-core. A k-core is a graph in which the minimal node degree is k. The weight of a node S_i is computed based on the highest possible k-core value in its neighborhood; the second step of the algorithm consists in exploring the nodes in a descending order of their weights; each node S_i will initiate a cluster, and for each adjacent node S_j such that the difference between the weights of S_i and S_j is below a threshold t, S_j is assigned to the same cluster as S_i. Threshold parameter t defines the density of the resulting clusters. The third step of the algorithm consists in enriching the clustering by checking adjacent nodes for a given cluster; if for a node S_i in a cluster C_i, if the neighborhood of a node S_i in a cluster C_i is highly connected, then all the adjacent nodes of S_i will also be added to C_i. This postprocessing step enables nodes to be part of more than one clusters.

5   Labels Extraction

The goal of this step is to provide the semantics of each cluster by extracting a set of relevant labels that describe the theme. The set of labels, extracted from the names of RDF resources, is composed of the keywords having the highest weight in the cluster C_i. The weight of a keyword in the cluster C_i is computed according to the degree of the corresponding node.

This approach can be extended to use more characteristics to calculate the weight of keywords. For instance by combining the degree of the node with the frequency of the keyword in the cluster. Castano et al. [2] use the most frequent keywords combined with the most frequent types of resources in the cluster. Another alternative would be to use an adaptation of tf-idf. In this case, the relevance of a keyword is proportional to its frequency in the cluster and its scarcity in other clusters.

We have implemented a tool to support our approach [9]. Figure 2 shows the user interface of the system. The list of themes is displayed on the left side and the initial RDF graph on the right side. The dataset is extracted from DBPedia and contains resources describing scientists working in different domains with their organizations and their countries. The cluster selected in the list can be highlighted on the graph (green nodes) or opened as a new RDF graph. The selected theme represents a set of researchers working in the field of physics. The label extracted using our approach is "Physics" as we can see in the name of the window at the bottom of the figure.

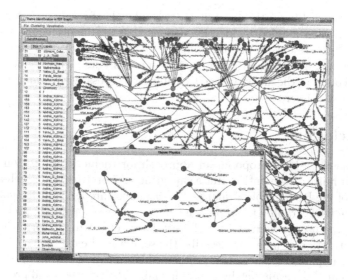

Fig. 2. Discovering Themes from the Graph

6   Related Works

Theme identification on large datasets is of interest in several contexts. Existing approaches have considered text documents [11], social networks [3], youtube documents [6]. The goal of these approaches is to facilitate the search process and the navigation. In the case of RDF(S)/OWL datasets, approaches are focused either on improving the visualization [12], RDF summarization [13,10] or ontology modularization [8,4].

In [12], a tool is proposed to enable the browsing of huge RDF(S)/OWL datasets. It provides an intuitive and visual understanding of the RDF graph. However, the proposed view can not be assimilated to a theme.

Works on RDF summarization [13,10] have adapted methods for generating summaries of text documents to RDF(S)/OWL graphs. Using PageRank, HITS and some other metrics, the centrality of nodes is calculated. The most central nodes become the summary. These works do not identify themes but only reduce the graph.

Works on ontology modularization transform an ontology into a weighted graph based on some types of properties, then use clustering algorithms to identify the modules. In [8], the subgraphs are constructed by identifying independent hierarchies using some properties like *rdfs:subClassOf*. [4] proposes an ontology modularization method which provides overlapping modules by taking into account symmetry and transitivity of properties for setting weights. These works take into account a limited number of properties to determine the hierarchies of classes.

The closest work to ours is an approach for topic identification presented in [2]. It exploits a graph generated from an RDF graph, by adding new edges between similar resources (linguistic similarity between labels of resources). A clustering algorithm is then applied to identify regions that are highly connected in the graph, which represent the topics. Similarly to our approach, this work is based on a clustering algorithm, but focuses only on identifying highly connected areas while we combine the density-based clustering process with semantic criteria capturing user preferences.

7   Conclusions

In this paper, we have proposed an approach for theme identification in RDF datasets. It relies on semantic criteria capturing user preferences as well as on the structure of the RDF graph. Semantic is considered through transformations applied to the RDF graph. Our approach comprises three stages: (1) preprocessing and capturing user preferences, (2) density-based clustering to form the themes and (3) extraction of labels to describe the semantic of each theme.

We have implemented a system for theme identification. Future works include the extension of the approach by improving label identification and providing the user with a summary of the clusters' content to describe its semantics. We are currently experimenting the use of our system and applying this approach to real world RDF datasets. Our goal is to evaluate the precision of theme identification and the performances of the system.

Acknowledgments. This work was supported by Electricity of France (EDF R&D). We would like to thank Sylvaine Nugier and Geoffrey Aldebert for their feedback and advice.

References

1. Bader, G.D., Hogue, C.W.V.: An automated method for finding molecular complexes in large protein interaction networks. BMC Bioinformatics 4 (2003)
2. Castano, S., Ferrara, A., Montanelli, S.: Thematic clustering and exploration of linked data. In: SeCO Book, pp. 157–175. Springer, Heidelberg (2012)
3. Castano, S., Ferrara, A., Montanelli, S.: Mining topic clouds from social data. In: Proc. MEDES, pp. 108–112 (2013)
4. Etminani, K., Naghibzadeh, M.: Overlapped ontology partitioning based on semantic similarity measures. In: Fifth International Symposium on Telecommunicatioin (2010)
5. Fortunato, S.: Community detection in graphs. CoRR, abs/0906.0612 (2009)
6. Gargi, U., Lu, W., Mirrokni, V., Yoon, S.: Large-Scale Community Detection on YouTube for Topic Discovery and Exploration. In: ICWSM, pp. 486–489 (2011)
7. Gergely, P., Imre, D., Illés, F., Tamás, V.: Uncovering the overlapping community structure of complex networks in nature and society. Nature 435, 814–818 (2005)
8. Hu, W., Qu, Y., Cheng, G.: Matching large ontologies: A divide-and-conquer approach. Data & Knowledge Engineering 67, 140–160 (2008)
9. Ouksili, H., Kedad, Z., Lopes, S.: A tool for theme identification in RDF graphs. In: Métais, E., Roche, M., Teisseire, M. (eds.) NLDB 2014. LNCS, vol. 8455, pp. 262–265. Springer, Heidelberg (2014)

10. Pires, C., Sousa, P., Kedad, Z., Salgado, A.: Summarizing ontology-based schemas in pdms. In: ICDEW, pp. 239–244 (2010)
11. Shahsavand Baghdadi, H., Ranaivo-Malançon, B.: An Automatic Topic Identification Algorithm. Journal of Computer Science 7(9), 1363–1367 (2011)
12. Voigt, M., Tietz, V., Piccolotto, N., Meißner, K.: Attract me!: How could end-users identify interesting resources? In: Proc. WIMS, vol. 36, pp. 1–12 (2013)
13. Zhang, X., Cheng, G., Qu, Y.: Ontology summarization based on rdf sentence graph. In: Proc. WWW, pp. 707–716. ACM (2007)

An XQuery-Based Model Transformation Language[*]

Jesús M. Almendros-Jimenez[1], Luis Iribarne[1],
Jesús J. López-Fernández[2], and Ángel Mora-Segura[2]

[1] University of Almeria, SPAIN
{jalmen,luis.iribarne}@ual.es
[2] Autonomous University of Madrid, SPAIN
{jesusj.lopez,angel.moras}@uam.es

Abstract. In this paper we propose a framework for model transformation in XQuery. With this aim, our framework provides a mechanism for automatically obtaining an XQuery library from a given meta-model. Meta-models are defined as XML schemas, and the XQuery library serves to query and create elements of an XML Schema. Transformations are XQuery programs that use the library to map source models to target models. The framework has been tested with a case study of transformation in UML, where XMI is used to represent models.

1 Introduction

XQuery [1,4] is a programming language proposed by the W3C as standard for the handling of XML documents. In spite of the main aim of XQuery is querying XML documents, XQuery can be also used as *XML transformation language*. *XSLT* [11], which was designed for XML transformations, can be encoded in XQuery [2], however XSLT code is very verbose and hard to maintain.

Model Driven Engineering (MDE) is an emerging approach for software development. MDE emphasizes the construction of models from which the implementation is derived by applying model transformations [6,10,14,18], and provides a framework to developers for transforming their models. Most of languages for describing models (*UML, BPMN, Petri Nets, WebML*, etc) have an XML-based representation (*XMI* [15], *XPDL* [17], *PNML* [9], *IFML* [5], etc). Thus, XML provides a framework for handling many modeling languages, and XQuery can be used for describing transformations in such languages. Usually, the XML-based representation of models is used for exchanging models between applications. One can argue that XML is a machine readable format, and transforming models via XQuery could be a too low-level task. However, XQuery is equipped with high-level mechanisms (i.e., modules, higher-order functions) that could make that transformations abstract from the XML representation.

[*] This work was funded by the EU ERDF and the Spanish Ministry of Economy and Competitiveness (MINECO) under Projects TIN2013-41576-R and TIN2013-44742-C4-4-R, and the Andalusian Regional Government (Spain) under Project P10-TIC-6114.

Y. Ait Ameur et al. (Eds.): MEDI 2014, LNCS 8748, pp. 330–338, 2014.

In this paper we propose a framework for model transformation in XQuery. In order to use XQuery as transformation language, the developer should be equipped with mechanisms allowing the handling of different meta-models. Models in transformations (source and target models) can conform to different meta-models. With this aim, our framework provides a mechanism for automatically obtaining an XQuery library of functions for each meta-model. This library allows to query the given meta-model and to create elements of the meta-model. Meta-models are defined as XML schemas, and the XQuery library is designed for handling an XML schema. Transformations abstract from XML representation since elements from meta-models are encapsulated by XQuery functions. Querying and creating elements from meta-models are achieved by calling suitable XQuery functions. Transformation code uses XQuery constructions, that is, *for* and *let* to traverse source models and *return* to generate target models, and *where* to express applicability conditions of the transformation. In addition, *union* operator is used to decompose a transformation into several transformation cases. In addition, the transformation can make use of *modules* and *auxiliary functions* for particular subtasks.

In order to describe a model transformation in our framework, we have to follow the next steps: **(a) Definition of XML Schemas of Source and Target Models**: we have to define the meta-models of the source and target models. Meta-models have to be described by XML Schemas; **(b) Generation of the XQuery Library**: from XML schemas of source and target meta-models, an XQuery library is automatically generated; **(c) Definition of the Transformation**: the XQuery library of the source and target meta-models can be used to define the transformations. An XQuery interpreter is used for this step; and **(d) Execution of the Transformation**: the transformations are executed obtaining target models. An XQuery interpreter is also used for this step.

The advantages of the approach are the following. Firstly, we can handle any meta-model having an XML representation. In order to handle a given meta-model it is only required to have the corresponding XML Schema. Secondly, we use a well-known programming language (XQuery) to write transformations. There are many implementations of XQuery ranging from academic to commercial ones (see http://www.w3.org/XML/Query/). Thirdly, the XQuery language provides a type system, compilation and run-time errors, a module system, higher order programming, among others. XQuery can handle in most implementations large XML documents, and therefore in our proposal large models. Finally, it is worth observing that n-m transformations can be defined making use of natural join operations in database query languages.

The framework has been tested with a case study of transformation in UML, where the XML-based representation of models is achieved by the standardized language XMI. Nevertheless, our framework is not specifically designed for UML. We have to provide the XML schema of XMI in order to transform UML models. The well-known Entity-relationship model to Relational model is used as case study, in which source and target models are class diagrams. Thus, we have to provide specifically the XMI Schema of class diagrams.

332   J.M. Almendros-Jimenez et al.

The implementation of the approach has been carried out by using the *BaseX* interpreter [8] of XQuery. We have developed a library generator from XML Schemas. The library generator has been implemented in XQuery. It takes an XML Schema as input (the XML Schema is an XML document) and generates XQuery code in plain text (as output document). BaseX is also used to edit and execute transformations. BaseX also provides XML Schema validation of source and target models. BaseX also helps in the development of code of transformations, by providing compilation error messages due to syntactic bugs and run-time error messages when the execution is accomplished. For designing XML Schemas we have used the UML Visual Paradigm tool. The use of UML VP and BaseX is not actually required in our framework. The implementation can be downloaded from `http://indalog.ual.es/mdd` together with the case study (models and meta-models).

The structure of the paper is as follows. Section 2 will describe the use of XQuery as transformation language. Section 3 will summarize related work. Finally, Section 4 will present future work.

2   Model Transformation with XQuery

Now, we describe the steps to be followed in our framework with a case study.

2.1   Case Study

The case study is a well-known transformation from an entity-relationship to relational model.

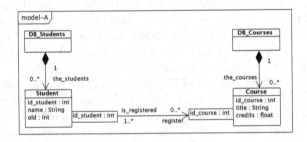

Fig. 1. Entity-relationship modeling of the Case Study

In model A of Figure 1, *Data* (i.e. entities) are represented by classes (i.e., *Student* and *Course*), including attributes. *Stores* are defined for each data (i.e., *DB_ Students* and *DB_ Courses*). *Relations* are represented by associations. Besides, *roles* are defined (i.e., *the_ students, the_ courses, is_ registered* and *register*) for each relation end. *Data attributes* are class attributes. Relations can be adorned with *role qualifiers* and navigability. In model B of Figure 2, *Tables* are composed of *rows*, and rows are composed of *columns*.

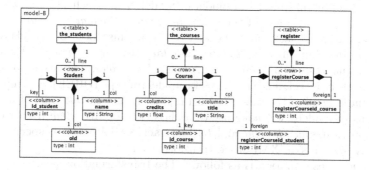

Fig. 2. Relational modeling of the Case Study

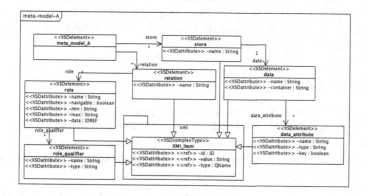

Fig. 3. Meta-model of the Source Model

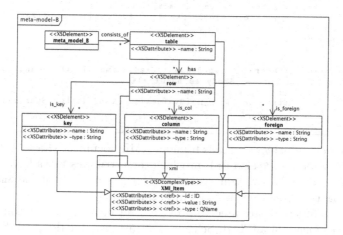

Fig. 4. Meta-model of the Target Model

Figure 3 represents the meta-model of model A in which *DB_Students* and *DB_Courses* are instances of the class *store*, while *Student* and *Course* are instances of the class *data*, and the attributes are instances of the class *data-_attribute*. In addition, *the_students* and *the_courses* are values of attribute *container*, and *register* as well as *is_registered* are *roles*. The attribute *data* of *role* is used as cross reference in the meta-model (of type IDREF), and represents the association end of the role. Figure 4 represents the meta-model of model B. In both meta-models, we make use of a class called *XMI_Item* from the XMI Schema providing an *id*, *value* and *type* for each XMI Item. It is specific to the case study, which is an XMI based transformation.

Now, the transformation is as follows. The transformation generates two tables called *the_students* and *the_courses*. In addition, given that the role *register* is navigable from *Student* to *Course*, a table called *register* of pairs is generated to represent the assignments of students to courses. The columns *registerCourseid_student* and *registerCourseid_course*, of the row *registerCourse*, taken from role qualifiers, play the role of *foreign* keys.

2.2   XQuery Library

Our framework is based on the automatic generation of an XQuery library for any XML Schema. Basically, the XQuery library consists of a set of functions that query and create items of an XML Schema (items `xsd:element` and `xsd:complextype`). With this aim, we have defined two abstract XQuery functions `readsubitem` and `createitem` as follows:

```
declare function rlib:readsubitem($model as node()*,$nameitem as xsd:QName,
        $atts as xsd:string*,$values as xsd:string*){
    for $elements in $model/* where node-name($elements)=$nameitem and
            (every $att in $atts satisfies
                        rlib:cond($elements,$att,$values[index-of($atts, $att)
                        ]))
return $elements
};

declare function clib:createitem($name as xsd:QName, $atts as xsd:string*,
        $values as xsd:string*,$body as node()*){
    element {$name}{(for $par_n in $atts return
                (attribute {$par_n}{$values[index-of($atts, $par_n)]})),
                    $body}
};
```

The function `readsubitem`, reads from an XML document ($model), the items of a certain name tag ($nameitem), in which the attributes $atts have the value given in $values. The function `createitem` creates a tag of name $name with attributes $atts whose value is given in $values.

Now, these functions are used to provide a set of XQuery function to query and create elements of an XML Schema. For instance, for the XML-Schema of Figure 3, the XQuery library contains the functions `read_store_of_meta_model_A`, `read_data_of_store`, etc., to query the elements of the XML document, as well as functions `create_store`, `create_data`, etc., to create the elements of the XML document. For instance, `read_store_of_meta_model_A` and `create_store` are defined as follows:

```
declare function mmA1:read_store_of_meta_model_A($model as node()*,
    $atts as xsd:string*, $values as xsd:string*){
  rlib:readsubitem($model,QName('http://xtl/mmA','mmA:store'),$atts,$values
      )
};
declare function mmA1:create_store($xmi_id as xsd:string, $xmi_value as xsd
    :string, $xmi_type as xsd:string, $name as xsd:string, $body as node()
    *){
  clib:createitem(
      QName('http://xtl/mmA','mmA:store'),(QName('http://xtl/xmi','xmi:id
          '),
      QName('http://xtl/xmi','xmi:value'),QName('http://xtl/xmi','xmi:
          type'),
      QName('','name')),($xmi_id,$xmi_value,$xmi_type,$name), $body)
};
```

2.3   Transformation

Now, the code of the transformation is as follows.

```
<meta_model_B xmlns="http://xtl/mmB" xmlns:xmi="http://xtl/xmi" xmlns:mmB="
    http://xtl/mmB">
{
let $model :=  doc($file)/mmA:meta_model_A
let $body := ((
for $s in mmA1:read_store_of_meta_model_A($model,(),()),
  $p in mmA1:read_data_of_store($s,(),())
  return (
    let $attrs := mmA1:read_data_attribute_of_data($p,(),())
    let $columns := er:columns($attrs)
    let $id_has := clib:create_id(($s/@xmi:id,$p/@xmi:id, "has"))
    let $id_table := clib:create_id(($s/@xmi:id,$p/@xmi:id, "table"))
    let $r:= mmB1:create_row($id_has,"","mmB:has",$p/@name,$columns)
    let $t:= mmB1:create_table($id_table,"","mmB:table",$p/@container, $r)
      return $t
  )
)
union
(
for $s in mmA1:read_relation_of_meta_model_A($model,(),()),
  $p in mmA1:read_role_of_relation($s,(),()) where (($p/@navigable = "true
      ") and ($p/@max = "*"))
    return (
    let $data := mmA1:read_data_of_role($model,$p)
    let $columns := er:foreign_keys($model,$s,$p)
    let $id_has := clib:create_id(($s/@xmi:id,$p/@xmi:id, "has"))
    let $id_table := clib:create_id(($s/@xmi:id,$p/@xmi:id, "table"))
    let $r:= mmB1:create_row($id_has,"","mmB:has",
                concat($p/@name,$data/@name), $columns)
    let $t:= mmB1:create_table($id_table,"","mmB:table",$p/@name,$r)
      return $t
)))
return $body
}
</meta_model_B >
```

Basically, the XQuery code of the transformation generates an XML document conforming to the XML Schema of model B. Therefore the result is an XML document whose root tag is `meta_model_B` and contains a `$body` including two kinds of tables: those representing `the_students` and `the_courses`, and the table representing `register`. In other words, the code represents two cases and they are joined by the *union* operator of XQuery.

The case study of transformation involves two additional transformations, that is, from the UML meta-meta-model to meta-model A, and from meta-model B to the UML meta-meta-model. Due to the lack of space these transformations are here omitted. Details can be found in `http://indalog.ual.es/mdd`.

3   Related Work

The use of XML and transformation languages for XML in the context of model transformation have been proposed in some works. All of them, as far as we know, fall on the use of XSLT. In an early work [16], the authors propose a language that uses XSLT for transforming models. The language can be seen as a first attempt to represent models and transformations in XSLT. In [12] the authors propose the use of the transformation language QVT, but they map QVT transformations into XSLT. XSLT programs are automatically obtained from QVT transformations. Therefore QVT is encoded by an XSLT transformation. They also create XML schemas for source and target meta-models using syntactic validation of source and target models. This work is the closest to our proposal. Although they use a standardized language (i.e., QVT) for describing transformations, they adopt as transformation engine an XML-based transformation language. Since XSLT can be encoded in XQuery, the proposal of these authors could be handled by XQuery instead of XSLT. The UMT (UML Model Transformation) Tool [7] also is based on XSLT (and Java). In this tool a simplified version of XMI (called XMI light) is used as representation of UML models. They directly use XSLT to write transformations. In [3], M2T transformations are also proposed in XSLT using a simplified version of XMI. We believe that simplifying XMI makes easier the definition of transformations. The drawback is that tools (especially UML VP) usually generate and require fully fledged XMI files, and it limits import and export of models. UMLX [19] uses a graphical notation that is again translated into XSLT transformations. User interface model transformation has been studied in [13], where a graphical notation is translated into XSLT (and QVT). The main aim of the transformations is to obtain a prototype of the user interface (using the XML based user interface language OpenLaszlo). In conclusion, XSLT has been the basis of works dealing with model transformations and XML. We can see our work similar to them since the proposed XQuery library of functions provides a high-level language for describing transformations, and at a low-level XQuery handles models in XML format. Obviously, our proposal could be adapted to XSLT.

4   Future Work

As future work we would like to extend our work as follows. Firstly, the XML type system is not yet used in our proposal. In other words, types in the XML Schema are not used in the generation of the XQuery library. We believe that introducing types we could improve compilation (error detection) of XQuery programs for transformation. Secondly, we are also interested to apply our framework to other modeling languages: BPM, Ontologies, etc. Finally, we are interested in test case generation for transformations in order to detect programming errors and to help transformation debugging.

References

1. Bamford, R., Borkar, V., Brantner, M., Fischer, P.M., Florescu, D., Graf, D., Kossmann, D., Kraska, T., Muresan, D., Nasoi, S., et al.: XQuery reloaded. Proceedings of the VLDB Endowment 2(2), 1342–1353 (2009)
2. Bézivin, J., Dupé, G., Jouault, F., Pitette, G., Rougui, J.E.: First experiments with the ATL model transformation language: Transforming XSLT into XQuery. In: 2nd OOPSLA Workshop on Generative Techniques in the context of Model Driven Architecture (2003)
3. Bichler, L.: A flexible code generator for MOF-based modeling languages. In: 2nd OOPSLA Workshop on Generative Techniques in the Context of Model Driven Architecture (2003)
4. Boag, S., Chamberlin, D., Fernández, M.F., Florescu, D., Robie, J., Siméon, J., Stefanescu, M.: XQuery 1.0: An XML query language. W3C Recommendation (December 14, 2010)
5. Brambilla, M., Fraternali, P.: Large-scale Model-Driven Engineering of Web User Interaction: The WebML and WebRatio experience. Science of Computer Programming (2013)
6. Czarnecki, K., Helsen, S.: Classification of Model Transformation Approaches. In: 2nd OOPSLA Workshop on Generative Techniques in the Context of Model-Driven Architecture (2003)
7. Grønmo, R., Oldevik, J.: An empirical study of the UML model transformation tool (UMT). In: Proc. First Interoperability of Enterprise Software and Applications, Geneva, Switzerland (2005)
8. Grün, C.: BaseX. The XML Database (2014), http://basex.org
9. Hillah, L.M., Kordon, F., Petrucci, L., Trèves, N.: PNML Framework: An Extendable Reference Implementation of the Petri Net Markup Language. In: Lilius, J., Penczek, W. (eds.) PETRI NETS 2010. LNCS, vol. 6128, pp. 318–327. Springer, Heidelberg (2010)
10. Jouault, F., Kurtev, I.: On the interoperability of model-to-model transformation languages. Sci. Comput. Program. 68(3), 114–137 (2007)
11. Kay, M., et al.: XSL transformations (XSLT) version 2.0. W3C Recommendation 23 (2007)
12. Li, D., Li, X., Stolz, V.: QVT-based model transformation using XSLT. ACM SIGSOFT Software Engineering Notes 36(1), 1–8 (2011)
13. López-Jaquero, V., Montero, F., González, P.: T:XML: A Tool Supporting User Interface Model Transformation. In: Hussmann, H., Meixner, G., Zuehlke, D. (eds.) Model-Driven Development of Advanced User Interfaces. SCI, vol. 340, pp. 241–256. Springer, Heidelberg (2011)
14. Mens, T., Van Gorp, P.: A Taxonomy of Model Transformation. Electr. Notes Theor. Comput. Sci. 152, 125–142 (2006)

15. OMG: XML Metadata Interchange (XMI), Tech. rep. (April 2014),
    http://www.omg.org/spec/XMI/2.4.2/
16. Peltier, M., Bézivin, J., Guillaume, G.: MTRANS: A general framework, based
    on XSLT, for model transformations. In: Workshop on Transformations in UML
    (WTUML), Genova, Italy (2001)
17. Shapiro, R.M.: XPDL 2.0: Integrating process interchange and BPMN. In: Work-
    flow Handbook, pp. 183–194 (2006)
18. Tratt, L.: Model transformations and tool integration. Software and System Mod-
    eling 4(2), 112–122 (2005)
19. Willink, E.: UMLX: A graphical transformation language for MDA. In: Model
    Driven Architecture: Foundations and Applications, pp. 3–27 (2003)

Author Index